SPEECH: content
and
communication

Science Research Associates, Inc.
259 East Erie Street, Chicago, Illinois 60611

A Subsidiary of IBM   Distributors

SECOND EDITION

SPEECH: content and communication

CHARLES S. MUDD
MALCOLM O. SILLARS
San Fernando Valley State College

Chandler Publishing Company
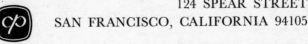
124 SPEAR STREET
SAN FRANCISCO, CALIFORNIA 94105

CONTENTS

ILLUSTRATIONS

MATERIALS

PREFACE

For the majority of college students, a one-semester or a one-quarter course in speech is their only formal training in oral communication. The greatest number of such courses take either a public speaking or a "fundamentals of speech" approach. This book is designed for use in the former: it is a text for a beginning course in public speaking.

The materials covered in this book and the principles discussed are recognizably traditional. We have given greater emphasis, however, to certain aspects of public address which are, it seems to us, often slighted in texts intended for use in a beginning course. The chapter on audience analysis (especially the section on how to use audience analysis) and the chapter on finding issues contain, we think, important principles not usually given sufficient emphasis in the beginning course. The chapters on argument stress the rhetorical aspects of persuasion and build on the concept of probability. Our approach to public speaking, then, can be seen to be audience oriented.

We have based the book on the assumption that the significant difference between beginning and advanced courses should lie not in the principles and skills developed but in the degree to which they are developed. Consequently, this text may be used not only in a one-semester or a one-quarter course, but in the traditional full-year course as well.

Users may and will cover the material in any order they see fit. In our courses, we find, the following chapter sequence in reading assignments fits nicely into a usable pattern. Such an order suggests a certain sequence in speaking assignments as well.

Chapters I, II, and III are introductory. They help to get the class under way.

Chapters VI, VII, IX, and XVII may be grouped for a unit in informative speaking.

Chapter XIX and assignments in group discussion fit in well

after informative speaking and re-emphasize material covered in that unit.

Chapters XII, XIII, XIV, and XV discuss principles important throughout but may be covered in a unit with Chapter XVI and assignments for speeches to entertain.

Chapters IV, V, X, XI, and XVIII form a block of materials most relevant to persuasive speaking. We think speaking to persuade should be the culmination of the course.

Chapter XX helps the student evaluate the messages he receives.

The writers are grateful for the comments and criticisms of colleagues who read portions of the manuscript. Arthur Hastings of Stanford University and Harold Peth of Mount San Antonio Junior College gave us their thoughtful and helpful criticisms of the first edition. James Egbert, Mary McEdwards, Fred McMahon, and Robert Rainey of San Fernando Valley State College gave valuable advice on individual chapters. Charlotte Oyer and the late Robert Canny of the San Fernando Valley State College Library gave generously of their time. We owe a special debt of gratitude to Lloyd W. Welden, Jr., of San Fernando Valley State College for his painstaking review of the original edition. His influence on our thinking is reflected in almost every chapter of the present edition.

These friends and others have contributed significantly to whatever merit the book has; they have no share in any shortcomings or errors.

Permission to reprint certain copyrighted material was kindly given. Acknowledgment is made at appropriate places in the text.

C.S.M.
M.O.S.

I

INTRODUCTION

In 1900, the editor of an anthology of famous American speeches expressed the opinion that there had been no great public speaking during the thirty-six years since the Civil War. He reasoned that because America had solved her significant problems with the formation and preservation of the Union, there had been and would be no crises to inspire great speaking. And yet, he had lived through the period of America's greatest industrial expansion, labor strife, agricultural discontent, scientific advancement, and religious upheaval; he had watched the political battle of imperialism, and he had heard such men as William Jennings Bryan, Robert G. Ingersoll, and Henry Ward Beecher speak out on topics of massive importance.

Not only did this critic grossly err in judging the past but his view of the future was also naive. The first six decades of this century have seen issues raised on a scale never before imagined. War has destroyed many millions of people. Great economic problems have cast shadows over large areas of the world. Minority groups have successfully pressed for more rights than they ever before enjoyed. The powerful irrationality of fascism and the persuasive conspiracy of international communism threaten the world.

All who live in the middle years of the twentieth century are aware that this is an age of danger. But what is surprising in that fact? To be alive is to be in danger—of death, if of nothing else. Every period in the history of civilization has been faced with problems. The significant point, then, is not whether there will be problems, nor what forms they will take. The important question is, how are they solved? Inherent in the creed of western democracy is the notion that people can best solve their problems through the medium of popular rule, the rule of an enlightened and sensible majority. As historian Carl Becker has put it, "Democratic government rests upon the principle that it is better to count heads than it is to crack them."

For this reason, western democracy has always put a high value on freedom of speech. It has assumed that all ideas must be displayed

1

and examined so that the people can make a decision. The nation, therefore, needs wise men and great speakers in every age to educate against ignorance, to analyze problems, to provide workable solutions, and to mobilize majority opinion. These difficult tasks are not the province of statesmen, scholars, and the clergy alone. If democracy is to function well, the responsibility for it falls upon all citizens and particularly upon those who would claim the right to lead.

In a 1952 presidential campaign address, Adlai E. Stevenson said to a television audience:

Struggle is the primary law of life. You struggle and you survive. You fail to struggle and you perish. . . . Your salvation is in your own hands, in the stubbornness of your mind, in the tenacity of your hearts, and such blessings as God, thoroughly tried by His children, shall give us. . . . The task is yours. Yours is a democracy. Its Government cannot be stronger or more tough-minded than its people. It cannot be more inflexibly committed to the task than they. It cannot be wiser than the people. As citizens of this democracy you are the rulers and the ruled, the law givers and the law abiding, the beginning and the end. Democracy is a high privilege, but it is also a heavy responsibility whose shadow stalks, although you may never walk in the sun.

As well as any piece of spoken rhetoric we know, this expresses a realistic basis for understanding why men must speak to the public.

Public life (and not only public life) is lived in an atmosphere of solving problems: social, economic, political, moral, and many others. Solving them calls for using the human ability to reason, an ability that is a priceless property of man. In reasoning to solve their public problems, people must communicate with one another, must speak to the public. Speech supports reasoning citizenship.

But the imperative to speak, which society imposes upon its members, in its turn imposes responsibilities on those who speak. To recognize, to accept, and to carry out these responsibilities is important enough for speakers individually and for society in general to warrant some discussion of them. What is it that a speaker should do in order to fulfill his responsibilities to himself and to his audiences?

The notion of obligation implies that some aspect of ethics or morality is relevant to rhetoric. And this is precisely the case. But rhetoric itself is amoral. Whatever power it has is indeterminate either toward good or toward ill. In this sense rhetoric is precisely like any of the other objects and abilities men use, such as materials, implements, and food. Metal may be formed into plows or swords. Swords may certainly be used for good or ill. Plows help to produce food. Food is necessary to sustain the individual; it may be subverted to the ends of gluttony. The people who use it are good or bad, and the ends to which they apply it are helpful or harmful to society.

Rhetoric has won its share of enemies through the years, principally among philosophers. Plato has given the traditional quarrel between rhetoric and philosophy its most effective, persuasive, and long-lasting expression in his dialogues. The contest as he viewed it was one of Truth versus Expediency. In Plato's view, rhetoricians were culpable because they did not seek truth or virtue or justice. It is true that many of the rhetorical sophists, the wealthy, powerful teachers of speech in Plato's time, did promise to teach their students to speak effectively on either side of any question. But Plato, as much as anyone else, argued that because an instrument can be misused it should not therefore be abandoned or destroyed. Indeed, he went to some lengths to show how the philosopher and the rhetorician might again join hands in friendship.

In much the same sense that the term sophist, with its roots in wisdom, has become an abusive epithet, so have words like rhetoric and rhetorician come to be used by many to symbolize precisely that kind of speaking and speaker that pervert the art rather than practice it honestly. The more unhappy designations of rhetoric are among those recalled for us by Donald C. Bryant: ". . . bombast; high-sounding words without content; oratorical falsification to hide meaning; sophistry; ornamentation and the study of figures of speech. . . ." (*Quarterly Journal of Speech*, December 1953, p. 402). Grouped together, these labels and others of the same sort clearly suggest a kind of speaking that warrants the opproprium heaped upon it by any Plato. But again we say, rhetoric is a human instrument and the morality of its use is a problem that must be resolved by each man every time he raises his voice to influence the thoughts and deeds of his fellows.

Very little profit can be derived from a lengthy discussion of the improper uses of rhetoric. To recognize that rhetoric may be ill-used, however, is important in at least one significant respect—it points to the pragmatic value of studying the subject. There is considerable truth in the notion that the significance of rhetoric to the well being of society, to the very existence of society, imposes the burden of speaking well. Rhetoric seems, therefore, in some sense even more crucially interwoven with the fabric of ethics and morality than are the physical, material objects of human action. To speak well must mean, in this context, not only to speak effectively but also to speak with care and honesty. What we are saying amounts to this: Be honest with yourself, with your audience, with your subject.

Many people feel powerless to take part in the operations of a free society. Perhaps this is as serious a fault as the failure to see the problems of society. You have heard these men talk. The ones who say: "What can you do about it? All the decisions are made by a few men at the top." "All that most people want in America today is to conform to the mass." "You can't do anything to change conditions." "We're all controlled by professional manipulators who take our pulse, read our minds, chart our subconscious, and then condition our responses to their will." In a very real sense, these are all variations on the old theme, "You can't fight City Hall." Certainly no man should ignore the fact that there are people who want to control him. There are great pressures on every American to act as the television advertiser, the so-called social leader, and the superpatriot think he should act.

Many are easily discouraged and confused. The many have always been easy to discourage and confuse; this weakness is what dictators and demagogues count on. But for those who take the opportunity to say something worthwhile in even a small voice to a little group to lift spirits and to clarify thought, an age of danger is an age of excitement. Surely a democracy is dependent upon having a substantial segment of the society who see its problems and offer means for resolving them. Liberal education, we are told, is primarily an education in citizenship in the finest and deepest sense of that word. Whenever an educated person is found—in business, in education, in government, in the professions, or in the home—he must have the ability to perceive and to speak. This ability is one unit in the major objective of education: to add to the community another person with insight into its problems and with ability to help solve them. Regardless of what career you may pursue, your first obligation is to develop to the fullest your own ability to recognize the human and social problems of the times and to offer constructive solutions for them.

Society takes its measure of a man from the way he communicates his convictions. Can you say from your own experience that you respect a man or distrust him without thinking of what he says or how he says it? Of course not. Most of the evaluations you make of people are actually based on what they say.

(The truly educated man is one who communicates.) He is not content to harbor his understanding; he demands the right to share his thoughts and feelings with others. (But knowledge alone does not make an able speaker.) The enormous amount of ineffective speaking one hears makes clear the fact that effective speaking requires more than having something to say. Columnist Art Seidenbaum points up this difficulty. In the Los Angeles *Times* for May 2, 1965, he points out the interesting (even frightening) anomaly that in our attempts to reach our fellow men, some of the most desperate failures occur when we are talking our hardest. "The frustration of modern man," he says, "is in not reaching the next modern man, even when both are at the top of their lungs. . . . It is not sound that is missing in this world, but meaning. . . ." Successful speaking is an art; it is learned through study, practice, criticism, and experience.

(It may seem reasonable to think that a person should learn to speak well just from speaking often.) After all, he normally begins to talk between the ages of one and two and spends the rest of his life practicing. Unfortunately, however, long practice in conversational speaking somehow fails to prepare one for more public communication. (It fails to do so in spite of the fact that there is no essential difference between a private speech situation and one that is public.) Both speech situations require the use of skills common to both. But informal speaking often lacks merit and, even when it does not, the easy mode of address that should characterize private speech does not carry over into a public situation. All speaking demands skill, and skill usually requires training of one kind or another. For all save a tiny few, training is needed to develop the skills required for effective and successful public speaking.

Perhaps the need to communicate does not seem so immediate. Your relationship to great issues and to audiences may seem remote, rather like a World Series game: viewed at first hand by some, read about by more, seen by millions on television, but played by relatively few. (Not so—public and world affairs do affect you, and in a democracy you act in the drama, in part at least, in relation to how much you want to act.)

Your conversations, your speeches, your criticisms of the speaking of others all have a part in determining the intellectual and political climate of the nation and, eventually, the actions of its leaders. Even the speeches you give in class have an effect. The presence of any audience, large or small, formal or informal, provides an opportunity and a responsibility for a speaker. Your class should be viewed as more than a training situation; it is also an opportunity for you to fulfill your obligations as a communicator.

Learning from classroom speaking experiences will be improved if you realize that each such speaking assignment is also a real-life one. It does not occur to many beginning speakers that the class they address is an audience, subject to the same kind of ideas and feelings as any other audience. In a speech class you speak to a group of real human beings. Don't ever forget that. Think of your class as you would any other audience you are called upon to address. You may feel that your classroom listeners are different because they will criticize you. But _all_ audiences criticize speakers. Therefore, search out criticism. Make this situation work to your advantage. Keep a careful record of the criticisms you get from your instructor and your classmates. Then use this information to improve your later assignments. You will never get such useful help from any other audience.

QUESTIONS

1. What function does a speaker on public issues have in a democracy?

2. What is "a priceless property of man?" For what purpose is it used?

3. What part does speech play in one of the major objectives of education?

4. Comment on the idea that good speakers are born, not made.

5. Is your speech class more than a training situation? Why?

THE BEGINNING SPEECHES

I. Selecting a subject and a purpose for the speech
II. Organizing the speech
   A. Organizing the body of the speech
      1. Chronological order
      2. Geographical or spatial order
      3. Topical order
   B. Organizing the conclusion
   C. Organizing the introduction
III. Supporting the ideas in the speech
IV. Delivering the speech
   A. Characteristics of good delivery
      1. Directness
      2. Spontaneity
      3. Involvement
      4. Vitality
      5. Intelligibility
   B. Practice
   C. Modes of delivery
      1. Speaking from manuscript
      2. Speaking from memory
      3. Speaking impromptu
      4. Speaking extemporaneously
V. Summary, questions, and exercises

II

THE BEGINNING SPEECHES

(Proficiency in the art of speech grows out of the combination of understanding and experience, of theory and practice.) Which should be taught and studied first? If a student waits until he has a good background of theory before he begins to make speeches, his speaking suffers from lack of practice; if he makes speeches from the beginning, he lacks the guidance of theoretical knowledge.

To begin speaking at the outset seems the better choice. The theoretical basis of your speaking will admittedly need development, but the value of practice is great, and your knowledge of theory will grow as you examine the principles of speaking in greater detail. It will be helpful and necessary to learn enough of the theory to do a satisfactory job early in the course.

(An effective speaker may be considered as one whom an audience thinks is worth listening to.) Audiences tend to respond in this fashion to a speaker who has something significant to say; who gives his ideas order, coherence, and form; who provides adequate grounds for his credibility; and who presents his materials well. This chapter examines briefly these four elements of any effective speech: subject, organization, supporting material, and delivery.

SELECTING A SUBJECT AND A PURPOSE FOR THE SPEECH

On any speaking occasion, two restrictions will limit your choice of a subject. You will be limited by the need for finding a subject that will be of interest to both you and your audience, and you will be limited in the amount of time you will have to speak.

Because of the restriction in time, the general subject you choose must be narrowed in scope so that it can be adequately discussed in the length of time allowed. The narrowed subject is then further specified by phrasing it as a *statement of specific purpose* which indicates what you intend to convey to your listeners about the subject.

General subject: Transistors
Specific subject: How a transistor works
Specific purpose: To inform the listeners about the way in which the phenomenon of electron borrowing makes transistor radios possible

General subject: Skin diving
Specific subject: Skin-diving equipment
Specific purpose: To inform the audience about the minimum equipment necessary for the beginning skin diver

General subject: Capital punishment
Specific subject: The effect of capital punishment on crime
Specific purpose: To persuade the audience that capital punishment is not a deterrent to crime

Notice how concrete these statements of specific purpose are. Each points to one clear-cut effort and excludes any others. Compare them with the following statements of purpose which are alleged to be specific but are multiple, diffuse, and therefore badly drawn:

Specific purpose: To inform the audience of the popularity of the transistor radio and how it works, especially how it uses electron borrowing

Specific purpose: To inform the audience of the equipment necessary for skin diving and how skin diving is not only safe but fun

Specific purpose: To persuade the audience that capital punishment does not deter crime and, as a matter of fact, that no severe punishment is effective, even with children in the home

All three of these statements of purpose are poor. They show that the speaker does not have a clear, single purpose in mind. Instead, he has some vague notions about what his subject will be. The specific purpose, once it has been carefully drawn, becomes a guide to test the organization and materials of the speech. Every statement in the speech, every piece of evidence or supporting material used, will relate directly to the accomplishment of that purpose. If it does not help to achieve the speaker's purpose, no piece of material can be justified and should be excluded from the speech.

ORGANIZING THE SPEECH

Your speech will be organized into three parts: an *introduction*, the *body*, and a *conclusion*. The body is organized first, because it bears the primary responsibility for accomplishing the purpose of the speech. The introduction and the conclusion are developed after the body of the speech has been prepared.

Organizing the Body of the Speech

If human beings were able to use some method of direct psychic communication such as that commonly called telepathy, it would perhaps be possible for your listeners to receive a whole complex of ideas in a single perceptive flash. Since audiences do not have this ability, however, you must build understanding in your listeners piece by piece. Think of the subject of your speech as a jigsaw puzzle you have made. If you give it to someone else as a jumble of pieces, he will have to work it out for himself to make an intelligible picture of it if, indeed, he bothers to do so at all. Should you, instead, hand him the pieces one at a time and in such an orderly fashion that he can easily fit them together, the picture you have made grows readily before his eyes. (Organizing a speech is very much like these two processes: first, putting together the parts of the puzzle so that you can see the picture yourself, and second, handing the pieces in proper order to someone else.)

To make sure that all the parts of your speech fit together in their proper places in the minds of your audience, that is, to make sure that it sees the same picture you do, you will need to divide the subject of your speech into a series of main points and then to arrange these in an organizational pattern that brings order to the materials and clarity to the ideas. (Together with their supporting material, these main points constitute the body of your speech.) We mention three organizational patterns here. These, and others, will be discussed further in Chapter XVII, Speaking to Inform.

CHRONOLOGICAL ORDER.   The sequence of main points in the body of the speech may be arranged in the order of their occurrence in time.

> *Specific purpose:* To inform the audience about Germany's submarine-warfare policy in World War I
>
>   I. February 1915, the British Isles were declared a war zone.

     II. May 1916, Germany pledged not to sink ships without warning.

   III. January 1917, Germany commenced unrestricted submarine warfare.

GEOGRAPHICAL OR SPATIAL ORDER. The sequence of main points in the body of the speech may follow the order of their arrangement in space. The points occur in the speech in the same order in which the listener might visualize himself moving physically from one to another.

> *Specific purpose:* To inform the audience about the major dialects of English spoken in the British Isles

     I. Ireland
    II. Scotland
  III. Northern England
  IV. Southern England
   V. Wales

TOPICAL ORDER. The main points in the body of the speech may be a list of the important parts of the idea discussed by the speaker. Added together, these parts or "topics" make up the whole idea.

> *Specific purpose:* To inform the audience about the operation of the speech mechanism

     I. Respiration
    II. Phonation
  III. Resonation
  IV. Articulation

In speeches to persuade, the body is organized in what may be thought of as a form of topical arrangement. The main points in the body of the speech to persuade are arguments, reasons for believing the truth of what the speaker is trying to prove.

> *Specific purpose:* To persuade the audience that prices at the college book store are too high

     I. The book store has increased its prices every year for the past three years.
    II. The book store made an excessive profit last year.
  III. The same books cost less at neighboring colleges.

Organizing the Conclusion

After you have organized the body of the speech, you will want to plan a *conclusion* to pull together the main ideas in the speech. One customary and effective way to end a speech is with a brief summary (which recalls for the audience the specific purpose of the speech and the main points that develop it.) A summary conclusion is particularly valuable in speaking because a listener cannot go back and rehear as a reader can go back and reread. Not all conclusions take the form of a summary, but you will find it useful in your beginning speeches. More sophisticated kinds of conclusions will be discussed later. Use these when experience has developed your skill.

Organizing the Introduction

The last section to be developed is the introduction, even though it is to be spoken first. In preparing a speech, the introduction is left until last because once the body of the speech and the conclusion are prepared, you know what you want to say to the audience. You will then be able to prepare an introduction that is more directly related to the ideas contained in the speech.

The introduction has two essential parts. First, there is some interest factor: a story, incident, description, startling statement, or quotation which will catch the attention of the audience. This interest factor should be immediately pertinent to the subject of the speech because its primary function is to arouse interest in what you are going to say and to direct that interest toward the purpose of the speech.

The second major part of the introduction is the subject sentence. In informative speeches, this is a statement which expresses the specific purpose of the speech in an informal oral style.

> *Specific purpose:* To inform the audience about the way in which the phenomenon of electron borrowing makes transistor radios possible
>
> *Subject sentence:* Transistor radios are made possible by the phenomenon of electron borrowing

(The subject sentence of a persuasive speech is very often much less direct than it might be in an informative speech.) If the audience has no strongly negative attitudes toward the proposition the speaker advocates, he will do his cause no harm by telling them openly what he wants them to accept. On other occasions, however, a specific statement of what the speaker advocates might solidify any negative attitudes the audience may have toward what he wants to say and cut off communication before the speech gets under way. (In addition, suspense and movement toward a climax have interest value.) These two factors may cause a speaker to avoid committing himself to a specific position before he has a chance to build a case for it. In any event, however, he must give the audience a clear notion of the subject area of his speech.

SUPPORTING THE IDEAS IN THE SPEECH

The statement of specific purpose and its development in the body of the speech constitute the definite idea you want the audience to have. But the idea you have in mind may not be the idea the audience understands from what you say. The task of every speaker is to improve the fidelity of his communication. (This he may do, at least in part, by proper use of supporting materials to maintain the *interest* of the audience and to lend *clarity* to what he says.) Examples, statistics, quotations, and arguments) all help to make your ideas more clear, interesting, and believable. Always use *at least* one item of such specific material in support of each important point in the body of the speech. (Usually, two or more pieces of supporting material are necessary and desirable.) This specific material will help you to make the ideas you have developed more precise and vivid and thus serve to clarify the subject, add interest, and establish belief.

(When you have determined the content and organization of the speech, you may want to prepare some notes to help you in delivery.) Whatever notes you use should be in outline form. Here is an example of standard outline form suitable for organizing either an informative or a persuasive speech early in the course. As your experience grows and you develop skill, your outlines will increase in complexity to meet the demands of more sophisticated materials and ideas.

INTRODUCTION
I. Interest factor
II. Subject sentence

BODY
I. First main point of the speech
    A. Supporting material
    B. Supporting material
II. Second main point of the speech
    A. Supporting material
    B. Supporting material
    [And so on]

CONCLUSION
I. Summary statement noting the purpose
   A. First main point
   B. Second main point
   [And so on]

DELIVERING THE SPEECH

The ideas, organization, and supporting details in any given instance of communication can be the same whether the communication is written or spoken. Except for some few differences in style (the way language is used), what most distinguishes writing from speaking is that a speech must be delivered. Indeed it doesn't become a speech until the moment of delivery. Consequently, good delivery makes a significant contribution to effectiveness in speaking. It is the vital, physical means by which ideas are transmitted to a listener.

Characteristics of Good Delivery

A highly communicative pattern of language and delivery appears in the everyday conversational speech of a large number of persons who do not carry over this quality into public speaking experiences. This fact is unfortunate, for good delivery, even in formal situations, needs all the best qualities of good conversational speech.

DIRECTNESS. Good conversational delivery is *direct*. A speaker talks to his audience. He chooses words which listeners will understand. He looks directly at them. He does not look over their heads, nor out the window, nor through them as if they were not there. He recognizes that they *are* there and he talks to them with much the same delivery and language he would use if they were guests in his home.

SPONTANEITY. Good conversational delivery appears to be *spontaneous*. This does not mean that the speaker sounds as if he were fumbling through the ideas of the speech for the first time. It contributes much more to his credibility to give the impression that he is delivering a well-thought-out, clearly developed, and carefully built speech. Spontaneity in speaking gives the delivery freshness and immediacy. It puts the speaker *in the presence of the audience*. Lacking spontaneity, delivery is dull and rotelike, much as if someone had turned on a tape recorder and left it unattended.

INVOLVEMENT. Good conversational delivery clearly manifests the speaker's personal involvement in what he is saying. His own in-

tellectual and emotional interest in his subject are vivid cues to the
audience about the significance of what he has to say and his desire to
say it to *this* audience. If the audience judges him to be uninterested
in his subject, there is certainly no reason they should be interested.

VITALITY.   Good conversational delivery has *vitality*. It usually involves variety in voice and bodily action which provide cues to the
audience about the relative importance of the materials in a speech.
Vitality in delivery demands the kind of gesture and movement which
the speaker would naturally use to emphasize a point in ordinary conversation. Some people, it is true, do not gesture very much. But nearly
everyone gestures more than he realizes. As an experiment, pay some
attention to what you and others do in everyday speaking situations.
You may be surprised to see how much gesturing is done.

INTELLIGIBILITY.   Good conversational delivery is readily *intelligible*. Nothing a speaker says will make much sense if it is difficult
for his audience to hear. But to make the members of an audience
"hear," the speaker must make them *listen*. Doing so requires that his
voice must be more than merely audible. A speaker's voice should be
loud enough not only to be heard, but also to command attention in
spite of the many normal distractions he may expect. To hold the
attention of his audience, he must be able to contend with such competitors as a noisy air conditioner in the rear of the room or with a
group of small boys playing ball outside an open window.

Besides *audibility*, a good speech has other qualities that contribute
to the intelligibility of delivery: *Articulation* (the formulation of individual sounds) should be clear and precise without being stilted.
Pronunciation should be acceptable; it should follow the standard
usage of the educated members of the speaker's community.

Practice

An audience will judge your speech as it is delivered, so you need to
prepare it in terms of that delivery. Practice the speech aloud and
listen to it as it might be heard by the audience.

When you have what you think is the final draft of your outline,
practice speaking from it several times to set the ideas in your mind.
If you can find an audience to practice on, so much the better. Don't
write the speech out or try to memorize it. Use the words that come
to you at the time of each practice delivery. The oftener you practice
during the preparation period, the better you will be able to find the
words to get the reaction you want from the audience.

Modes of Delivery

Four different methods of delivering a speech are commonly recognized. These four modes of delivery differ from each other according to the kind of preparation the speaker makes for the delivery. If the language of the speech is thoroughly prepared in advance, the speech can be delivered either from a *manuscript* or from *memory*. On the other hand, when the specific language which will be used in the speech is not chosen before the moment of delivery, the speech will be either *impromptu* or *extemporaneous*.

SPEAKING FROM MANUSCRIPT. There are three kinds of speaking occasions that may legitimately call for a speech to be read from manuscript.

The first of these is the making, by a person in a position of responsibility, of a statement so important that mistakes must not be permitted to occur. When the President of the United States speaks for this country to the world, even a simple slip of the tongue or a momentary lapse of control over his own emotions might have far-reaching and serious consequences. Similarly, an ambassador to the United Nations will almost always deliver a prepared statement from manuscript.

An occasion of great formality may demand a polish in the speech that cannot be expected except through complete preparation of language beforehand.

The third kind of occasion that may make use of a manuscript desirable occurs whenever there are strict time limits put upon a speaker. The length of time a speech will last is much more easily determined when the speech is in manuscript, and the time can much more easily be adhered to when the speech is delivered from manuscript. The most common instances of this sort can be observed in broadcasts over radio and television. The very strict time schedules of these broadcast media require a speaker to meet a specific time limit.

Apart from these kinds of occasions, however, a manuscript ought not to be used. It is totally unlikely that such demands for precision in wording will arise in a public speaking class or, for that matter, in any of the speaking that all but a few will be called upon to do in the future.

Besides being on most occasions unnecessary, manuscript speaking has certain quite definite disadvantages. William Jennings Bryan, commented on these in connection with his Madison Square Garden speech in 1896, accepting the nomination as Democratic presidential candidate:

I was compelled to choose between an extemporaneous speech, which would be less concise and comprehensive, and a speech which, because read from manuscript, would disappoint the audience. I knew, too, that in order to secure an accurate report of the speech in the daily papers it would be necessary to furnish a copy in advance of delivery, and I knew that if delivered from memory it would be taken down in shorthand and compared with the copy furnished to the press. After weighing the relative advantages of, and objections to, the two modes of delivery, I concluded that it was the part of wisdom to disappoint the few thousands who would be in the hall in order to reach the hundreds of thousands who would read it in print. Having decided to use my manuscript it was necessary to make the speech as brief as possible because the crime of reading a speech increases in heinousness in proportion to its length.

Judgments about what is required for an effective speech are a function of the audience. It is extremely difficult, therefore, for a speaker to determine in advance of the speaking situation itself precisely how his message ought to be structured. He has a much better chance of accomplishing his purpose when he speaks in simple, direct, straightforward language to an audience with whom he is making close visual and psychological contact. With this kind of delivery, it is much easier for him to make the necessary adaptations to the occasion and the idiosyncrasies of the audience. The speaker who uses a manuscript ties himself to a set pattern of words and denies himself any opportunity for adapting to his audience during the course of a speech. For these reasons, unless it is absolutely necessary to do so, a speech should not be delivered from a manuscript.

Should the occasion make it necessary to use a manuscript, the speaker's delivery should have the qualities that characterize any good delivery. These characteristics have been described above, pages 15–16. Suggestions for achieving them are discussed in Chapters XIV and XV. Note particularly pages 260–263.

SPEAKING FROM MEMORY.   In preparing a speech to be delivered from memory, a speaker will ordinarily write out a manuscript, practice from it until he knows it by heart, and then will deliver the speech from memory. This kind of speaking has few of the advantages but carries with it all of the disadvantages of the manuscript mode of delivery. Unless he is a reasonably accomplished actor, the speaker delivering a talk from memory will find it difficult to maintain close contact with the audience. Even if he is a good actor, or recites well, he will be burdened with the same lack of flexibility from which a manuscript speaker suffers. There is, moreover, another disadvantage to speaking from memory. If the speaker forgets, he is lost. We say, categorically, *never* memorize a speech. If the occasion demands that kind of preparation, prepare a manuscript and use it instead.

SPEAKING IMPROMPTU. An impromptu speech may be defined as one for which a speaker has made no immediate preparation. He is called upon to speak unexpectedly and the things he says are said on the spur of the moment. Probably nearly everyone has at one time or another imagined himself in a speaking situation wherein he is required to "think on his feet," and (since everyone sees himself as the hero of his own daydreams) has come through admirably, swaying masses of people, crushing opposition, the epitome of impromptu eloquence. The picture is unrealistic.

We are not saying that such skill is undesirable or impossible to attain. It is, however, hard to come by. Henry Ward Beecher, after delivering a splendid talk which seemed to be completely impromptu, was asked how long he had prepared for it. The answer: he had been preparing for the talk for forty years.

Except when the speaker is given no warning, no speech should be delivered impromptu. A speaker should take every opportunity to prepare as thoroughly as time will allow. If he is called upon to speak with no preparation, he should remember that the same principles of organization and support apply to all speaking. If at all possible, he should take a few moments to think through what he will say and perhaps to jot down a few notes. Even if he must react at once, he should remember that the major function of a speech is to introduce an idea, develop it, and finish discussing it—conclude. In this way, even the most hastily prepared talk can be given the quality of order.

SPEAKING EXTEMPORANEOUSLY. Under ideal circumstances, all public address would be extemporaneous. In this mode of delivery, the ideas, organization, and supporting material of a speech are thoroughly prepared in advance. Moreover, the delivery of the speech is practiced as well. The only part of such a speech that is *ex tempore* (that is, grows "out of the time" or comes at the actual moment of delivery) is the *language*. This is chosen in much the same manner as the language of an impromptu speech. The difference between impromptu speaking and extemporaneous delivery, other than the thorough preparation of the content of the latter, is in the fact that the extemporaneous speech has been "talked through" several times. The speaker does not write the speech in full, (although he may, and usually will, use an outline as speaking notes), nor does he make any effort to memorize the language he will use in delivery. Indeed, each time he practices the speech, he will use different language and work toward a more precise and clear statement of his ideas. When finally he delivers the speech, the speaker is so thoroughly familiar with what he intends to say that he can in a very real sense "ad lib" the language that will be more effective for his audience, his subject, and the occasion of his speech.

It is apparent that extemporaneous delivery has the greatest number of advantages and the fewest disadvantages of all the four modes of delivery. It lends itself to direct visual and psychological contact with the audience. It can have all the spontaneity and immediacy of casual conversation without the disorganization that often characterizes conversation. It affords the speaker great flexibility in meeting the specific and yet shifting demands of his audience. Extemporaneous speaking is the principal concern of this book and all of what is said in it is most directly applicable to this mode of delivery.

SUMMARY

Develop your beginning speeches through attention to these four basic steps: subject, organization, supporting material, and delivery. Formulate a specific purpose. Study the possible ways to divide the speech into its main points. Search for the right supporting materials to make the ideas clear, interesting, and acceptable to your audience. Practice while you are preparing the final outline and after it has been established.

QUESTIONS

1. From the general subject "Education," select a specific subject suitable for a short informative speech. Prepare a statement of specific purpose and a subject sentence.

2. Give an example of each of three types of order for the body of a speech.

3. What is the twofold purpose of an introduction?

4. Why should a speech have a conclusion?

5. What are the supporting materials mentioned in the text which make ideas most precise and vivid for an audience?

6. What mode of delivery is preferable and why?

7. What are the four characteristics of good delivery?

EXERCISES

1. From an issue of *Vital Speeches* magazine or a volume of speeches such as *Representative American Speeches*, select a speech and briefly outline it showing the division of the speech into introduction, body, and conclusion, and the main points in the body. Then write a few paragraphs analyzing the speech, noting the following:

(a) Would the beginning of the speech arouse interest?

(b) Is the subject sentence clearly stated?

(c) Does the speaker have enough or too many main points in the body?

(d) How does he conclude his speech?

2. Organize and deliver a three-minute informative speech explaining to your classmates some historic or scenic location within one hundred miles of the college.

3. From one of the general subjects mentioned below or from others assigned by your instructor, select three specific subjects and phrase them into statements of specific purpose.

(a) Automobiles

(b) Dating practices of college students

(c) Juvenile delinquency

(d) United States foreign policy

(e) Psychology

(f) Athletics

4. Listen carefully to the delivery of an instructor's lectures in another class. Compile a list of the things about his delivery which aided your understanding and a list of the things which detracted from it. How many of the detracting factors do you suppose you would have noticed if you hadn't especially looked for them? How important do you think delivery is to a speaker?

THE SUBJECT AND PURPOSE OF THE SPEECH

III

THE SUBJECT
AND PURPOSE
OF THE SPEECH

The subject of a speech is the matter a speaker considers. It is the topic under discussion. It encompasses the attitudes, opinions, and beliefs the speaker wants to convey. The purpose of a speech is the objective or goal of the speaker. It is the specific influence he wants to exert on the attitudes, opinions, beliefs, and actions of his audience. *But it is the audience and not the speaker who determines both the subject and the purpose of a speech.* Or, according to Aristotle, it is the hearer who determines the speaker's end and object. In view of this perhaps surprising fact, it would be well to see how speech subjects come about.

HOW SPEECH SUBJECTS COME ABOUT

Any message whatsoever affects the behavior of the one who receives it. Look at these examples.

When you tell a joke, you expect a laugh or at least some response appropriate to the humor in what you say. Even if the joke fails to amuse a hearer, his judgment that it is not funny is a response and, as such, is a change in behavior.

When you ask a question, you expect an answer. Even if you don't get one, you have modified the behavior of your hearer to the extent that he says he doesn't know the answer, or makes the decision not to give an answer, or makes some kind of overt or covert response to the question. Whatever reponse he makes is a change in behavior.

Instead of asking a question, suppose you make a statement. No matter what the statement, it will elicit some response. No matter what the response (and it may or may not be the one you want), it constitutes a change in behavior. These and other instances we might adduce all lead to the conclusion that no one can avoid being affected by every message he receives, even by those that elicit a response other

23

than the one the sender wants. In the light of this conclusion we might ask whether anyone speaks for reasons other than to influence the attitudes, opinions, beliefs, and actions of his listeners, that is, their general response to the world. The answer is no. What a speaker does, in effect, is to say to his listeners, "I'm talking to you because I want you to do something. I want you to modify your behavior in some way." But it is the particular change in behavior, the specific response of the listener, that is of primary importance to the speaker. Thus, the specific response he wants from his audience determines the specific purpose of a speaker on any particular occasion. To what extent does this desire to modify listener behavior justify the earlier contention that the audience, rather than the speaker, determines the subject and purpose of a speech?

Everyone sees the world in his own way. Each individual has his own attitudes, opinions, and beliefs about politics, about religion and morality, about aesthetics, and about other subjects. The familiar notion that beauty is in the eye of the beholder is an obvious instance of what we are saying. But because of different levels of intelligence and education, varied cultural backgrounds, dissimilar experiences, and unlike biological and physiological influences, no two persons share identical attitudes, opinions, and beliefs. Any speaking occasion, then, may be thought of as one person's attempt to get others to think and act as he wants them to. He does this by trying to influence one or another of an almost unlimited number of overt listener behaviors, such as buying a product, voting a certain way, waging war, or making peace; or else he tries to bring about specific, predetermined changes in one or another of an almost unlimited number of covert behaviors involving the listeners' attitudes, opinions, and beliefs. No matter whether he exhorts, advises, commands, informs, persuades, amuses, speculates, or questions, the speaker's choice of subject and purpose is a function of the audience's position in relation to the speaker's view of the world as it is or ought to be. Thus we may say that the audience determines the subject and purpose of a speech.

The subjects of speeches you make in class would ideally come about in the manner we have been discussing. It must be admitted that such considerations as grades and course requirements may very well motivate you to speak when you otherwise might not. Moreover, your speeches will be influenced by the necessity to fulfill a specific assignment. Within the framework of these limitations, however, you will be able to identify speech subjects and purposes that will meet the demands of your audience. These choices can be developd into interesting and useful instances of communication.

SPEECH PURPOSES

It is generally conceded that whenever one speaks, what he says will be interpreted by his listeners *in some sense*. (Hopefully, in the sense that the speaker intends.) (In any case, what the speaker says will cause the audience to shift along the continuum of its attitudes, opinions, and beliefs.) Viewed in this light, all speeches can be called persuasive because they attempt to influence behavior toward a predetermined goal.

Despite the fact that contemporary theory considers all speaking to be persuasive, the two-hundred-year-old practice of classifying the specific purposes of speeches into broad categories is still useful. Instead of considering these categories as identifying quite different kinds of speeches or speech goals, they are better viewed as arbitrary divisions of forms of public address based on such differences as the kind of response the speaker seeks; the amount of shift he must achieve in attitude, opinion, belief, or action to reach his goal; the level of sophistication he exhibits in using certain rhetorical techniques; the degree of audience hostility toward him, his subject, or his purpose, and other criteria.

Based on these considerations, we will establish a group of three broad speech purposes or general ends. In each case, one will be distinguished from the others on the grounds of the primary, or at least most obvious, response the speaker wants:

$$\text{General ends} \begin{cases} \text{To entertain—\textit{Amusement}} \\ \text{To inform—\textit{Understanding}} \\ \text{To persuade—\textit{Agreement}} \end{cases} \textit{Primary response}$$

Speaking to Entertain—to Give Amusement

On many occasions, both formal and informal, a speaker will have the primary purpose of entertaining his audience. Ordinarily, he will use humor as the means. When the president of the freshman class, for example, gives an after-dinner speech at the annual class banquet, he may decide to entertain his audience by building an amusing speech around the freshman's first experience with the college registration procedure. A speech to entertain should not be confused with an informative or persuasive speech which uses humor as a device for arousing interest. The use of humor as a means of arousing and retaining interest in a speech will be discussed at some length in Chapter XVI, Speaking to Entertain.

Speaking to Inform—to Bring About Understanding

When a speaker's purpose is to make something known to an audience, to clarify ideas for them, to give them facts or information, his general end is to inform. The primary response he wants from his audience is understanding: of an object, an operation, a condition, or the like. To fulfill a requirement in a course on international relations, you might give a report on the organization and function of the Presidium of the Supreme Soviet of the USSR. In a report of this kind, you have no immediate concern for the attitude the audience might take toward the Presidium or toward the Soviet Union; nor are you directly concerned with what your listeners might do with the information they get from you. Your immediate goal is that they understand and remember what you say. *Understanding* and *retention* are the criteria of a successful speech to inform. The rhetorical techniques relevant to speeches to inform are discussed in Chapter XVII.

Speaking to Persuade—to Influence Belief or Action

In a speech to persuade, the speaker gives his audience reasons for adopting his own point of view on a subject wherein the two are at odds. But for a speaker and his audience to be at odds, the difference between their attitudes need not be one of open hostility. Indeed, speaker and audience may even agree. To make persuasion necessary, it is enough for a speaker to feel that the attitudes of his audience need reinforcement. Look at the following instance: Irritated by the fact that you cannot find a clean table in the cafeteria because students frequently fail to bus their dishes, you decide to embark upon a clean-up campaign of the campus. You would need to persuade your friends to give active support to your campaign. Even though your friends agree that the cafeteria should be clean, the need for persuasion is apparent, for otherwise the conditions of which you disapprove would not exist.

The need for giving reasons (using arguments) to support a point of view is the primary basis for making a distinction between informative and persuasive discourse. An example will point up the difference between the two: suppose one were to propose an informative speech on the operation of the Security Council of the United Nations, but were to close that speech with an appeal for support of the United Nations. Such an appeal would be an indication that your primary purpose was persuasive and not informative at all. It would further indicate that you had not clearly identified the primary purpose of your own speech: to appeal for support of the United Nations. Such an appeal would require persuasive support. But the goal of informative speaking is understanding; it does not purport to give proof. The subject of a persuasive speech, however, is a matter in debate and demands proof if the speech is to change belief. Certainly, persuasion is not likely to take place in an uninformed audience, but in almost every case, more than infomation is needed to persuade. Since you considered your speech informative, you would not supply the necessary proof. Your audience, interpreting your primary purpose to be to urge the support of the United Nations, but failing to get from you the proof necessary to support that appeal, might well reject it. When a speaker accurately defines his purpose for himself, he considerably betters his odds of achieving that purpose. When he fails to do so, he can usually hope to achieve his goal only by accident.

SPEECH PROPOSITIONS

Before his position on a subject is presented to an audience, a speaker should already have formulated a precise expression of it for himself. That position is worded as a statement which expresses the attitude, opinion, or belief he wants to convey to his hearers or it specifies the action he wants them to perform. These statements are called *propositions*.

Kinds of Propositions

Propositions identify the subject matter of a speech. They appear in three forms: propositions of *policy*, propositions of *fact*, and propositions of *value*. Let us look briefly at these three forms.

PROPOSITIONS OF POLICY.   A proposition of policy is the statement which specifies a course of action (policy) and calls for its adoption. Here are two examples:

> The student council should establish a system of fines for students who neglect to bus their dishes in the cafeteria.
> The several states should adopt uniform divorce laws.

PROPOSITIONS OF FACT.   A proposition of fact is a statement which asserts that specified conditions or circumstances exist.

> There is a wide variation among the divorce laws of the several states.
> The Soviet Union will not permit open inspection of facilities for testing nuclear weapons.

PROPOSITIONS OF VALUE.   A proposition of value is a special form of the proposition of fact. The difference between the two is that the proposition of value expresses a judgment concerning the goodness, rightness, quality, merit, *value* of an object or act, whereas the proposition of fact does not.

> Professional boxing is a brutal sport.
> The American educational system is superior to the educational system of Europe.

The major distinction between propositions of fact and value on the one hand, and propositions of policy on the other, lies in the difference between what *is* and what *ought to be.* Propositions of fact and value assert that certain specified conditions or qualities *exist;* propositions of policy allege that certain specified modes of conduct *ought* to exist.

Propositions in Relation to Purposes

Speech propositions identify the subject matter of a speech much more precisely than they do the purpose of the speech. Consider these two propositions of policy:

> Congress should impose a 10 percent surtax on personal incomes.
> Congress should give Manhattan Island back to the Indians.

There is little reason to wonder which of the two examples is more likely to be the proposition of a speech to entertain and which to be the proposition of a speech to persuade. The number of times that your response to similar serious comments has been "You're kidding!" makes it clear that either statement could conceivably be the proposition of a speech to persuade. Furthermore, probably no statement can be made that cannot be used as the proposition of a speech to entertain. But there is no reason to think that an audience would interpret either of these subjects as the proposition of a speech to inform.

Consider next the following proposition of value:

> Women are better cooks than men.

Is this statement the proposition of a speech to entertain or to persuade? Without saying anything about the merits of *any* speech on this subject, we can see clearly that a speaker could have either purpose. We can also see that it is highly unlikely that an audience will consider this statement to be the proposition of a speech to inform. What about propositions of fact?

> Golf is for little old ladies.
> An earthquake is the result of complicated causes.
> Man will reach the moon within ten years.

It is reasonable to suppose that the first of these sentences expresses the proposition of a speech to entertain, the second a speech to inform, and the third a speech to persuade. In each instance, the speaker's goal will influence his development of the topic. In each instance also, however (and the point is worth repeating), it will be the audience who determines whether it is the speaker's purpose to entertain, inform, or persuade. The point to be made here is that only the proposition of fact clearly and easily lends itself to all three kinds of speaking we have been discussing.

To summarize briefly the relationships between speech purposes and speech propositions:

1. A proposition of policy or a proposition of value will be interpreted by an audience as voicing the purpose to entertain or to persuade. In making its interpretation, the audience will be guided in part by the subject matter, in part by the subject as developed, and in part by the condition of its own attitudes, opinions, and beliefs.

2. A proposition of fact can be used to express any one of the three purposes. The audience's interpretation will be based on the same factors that determine its reaction to propositions of policy and value.

We have developed the notion that of all the propositions a speaker might adduce to identify the subject and purpose of any particular speaking situation, the one he does select is determined by the audience. Perhaps a better way of stating what happens is to say that a speaking situation will not usually come about until someone recognizes that the attitudes, opinions, beliefs, and actions of someone else constitute an obstacle to some goal of his own. He then adduces a proposition which he presents and develops with an eye to changing the thinking or actions which are inimical to his goal. Such terms as "obstacle," "goal," and "inimical" suggest too strongly that all speakers must overcome active opposition. Not so.

Suppose a speaker's goal (the response he wants from the audience) to be amusement. The obstacle: "These people don't see the laughable in such-and-such a concept." That concept is then identified in a proposition of policy, value, or fact, and the speaker tries to influence the audience's meaning for that concept to include "laughable." What happens may be called a speech to entertain.

In another instance, the goal may be: "I want people to know how earthquakes happen." The obstacle: "They don't understand how complicated the process is." Thus the proposition of the speech is indicated. The speaker's purpose would be to inform.

Again, assume the goal to be: "Elect Harrison to the State Assembly." The obstacle: "This somewhat conservative audience thinks Harrison is too liberal." The proposition: "In matters most important to you, Harrison is a moderate." The purpose of this speech is clearly persuasive.

(In this manner, then, speakers identify the subjects, purposes, and propositions which particular audience conditions require them to choose on particular speaking occasions.)

All that has been said thus far in this chapter has been directed toward your better understanding the part played by the audience in the formulation of the speaker's proposition. Perhaps you have said to yourself, "All right, I've never thought of it that way before and it sounds a little odd to say that an audience determines what a speaker's proposition will be. Even so, the speaker has to *find* the proposition, he doesn't directly ask the audience to give it to him. You've been saying that of all the propositions in the world, the speaker chooses the one that is right for a particular audience at a particular time. But what I want to know is, where do all these propositions come from?"

You have asked a good question, one worth thinking about for a while.

Sources of Propositions

Suppose you and a group of friends wanted to run a candidate for Student Body President. Several questions would arise: Who should your candidate be? How should you conduct his campaign? And so on. You and your friends would explore the subject to understand better the problems involved and to make decisions about them. As a result of this exploration, you achieve understandings and beliefs you did not have before your inquiry began. In talking about the campus election, you might come to conclusions like the following: "The candidate who can get the Interfraternity Council behind him will swing the election." "Fred Byron is the best man to unite the Council behind him." "Fred Byron should be selected as our candidate for the office of Student Body President." "Fred's campaign should be built around the idea of getting for the students a more decisive voice in appropriating money from the student-activities fee." This example makes evident that the general source of propositions is questions. You will recognize that each of the conclusions you draw as a result of exploring the questions arising in connection with the student-body election is a proposition: The first is a proposition of fact, the second is a proposition of value, and the last two are propositions of policy.

These questions are given the general name of *problems*. The conclusions you reach in your attempts to solve whatever problems you meet become the propositions that you may, in speaking to others, choose to explain or to prove.

The need to solve problems of one kind or another is something that none of us escapes. The foregoing example of some of the problems that might need to be explored in a student-body election assumes that problems might be attacked by a group. This is clearly not a necessary condition. Many problems are by their nature the sort of things which, for political, social, or other reasons, one prefers to explore alone. Nonetheless, there are problems whose scope and import make appropriate a cooperative attack. Their number is great enough that group discussion (the name widely used to refer to cooperative problem-solving) has attracted the detailed interest of industrialists, politicians, and investigators in such fields as psychology, sociology and, of course, rhetoric.

The usefulness of group discussions for exploring problems has warranted a chapter in this book devoted to that kind of speaking situation. Note, however, that it is not considered to be a fourth "kind" or "general end" of speeches coordinate with speaking to entertain, to inform, and to persuade. We take group discussion to be not a *purpose* but rather an *occasion*. It equates, therefore, with such other forms of address as public speaking or debate. The goals of the participants in group discussion, the responses they seek, you have met in our earlier consideration of speeches to inform and to persuade. The members of a group intend to give and get information for *understanding* the problem (and this is the purpose of speaking to inform). Moreover, they seek *agreement* on a solution (and this is the purpose of speaking to persuade). The rhetorical techniques appropriate in group discussions are the same as those used in speaking situations of other sorts: identification of the subject (in group discussion the subject is a *problem* rather than a *proposition*), specification of the purpose (*understanding* the problem, *agreement* on a solution), collection and organization of evidence and ideas, selection of meaningful language, and effective communication through appropriate delivery.

The outcome of successful exploration of a problem is the formulation of a proposition which is presumably an acceptable solution to the problem being explored. Thus, the source of any proposition is a problem to which the proposition is at least a relevant answer. This definition implies that problems are of three kinds: *policy, fact,* and *value.*

PROBLEMS OF POLICY. A problem of policy is a question which asks for a formulation of policy. It asks what procedure, what method of operation, or what mode of conduct ought to be adopted. It says, in effect, "What should be done in order to improve such-and-such a problem situation?"

The question that phrases a problem of policy should be stated in such a way that it calls for a choice among several possible alternative courses of action. It does not ask for acceptance or rejection of any one proposal. This point can be clarified by an example. Suppose we were to ask, "Should the United States recognize Communist China?" The question is obviously concerned with a matter of policy. Is it not, then, a satisfactory question of policy? It is not, and for this reason: A policy that the United States might adopt toward Communist China is suggested in the very phrasing of the question. Instead of asking which one of *all* possible courses of action ought to be adopted, the question as stated demands a Yes or No answer with regard to *one* alternative proposal. As such, it is an invitation not to *explore*, but to *persuade.* A properly phrased problem of policy would read, "What should be the policy of the United States toward Communist China?"

PROBLEMS OF FACT.   A problem of fact is a question which asks what the conditions in a given situation are. We may ask, "What procedure does the Federal Reserve Bank employ in controlling credit spending?" Other examples range from such questions as "What were the causes of the Viet-Nam War?" and "What principles govern the operation of the neutron bomb?" to such simple matters as "What time is it?" and "What's for supper?"

PROBLEMS OF VALUE. A problem of value is a question which asks about the merit or lack of merit in a person, an item, or an idea. A value judgment must be made before an answer can be given to such questions as, "What is the greatest play in the English language?" or "When did the most significant advances in science take place?"

A problem of value is to all intents and purposes a special kind of problem of fact. That is to say, a problem of value and a problem of fact both ask that a judgment be made. There is, however, a difference between the kinds of judgments that these two problems require. As the name implies, the problem of value asks for a value judgment; the problem of fact does not. An example will make the distinction clear:

> *Problem of fact:* In how many schools is art a required part of the curriculum?
> *Problem of value:* How important is art in the college curriculum?

To insure that problems of fact and value will be explored rather than debated, avoid phrasing them as questions that can be answered Yes or No. Instead of asking "Is the defendant guilty?" ask "Who committed the crime?" Instead of asking "Is Babe Ruth the greatest baseball player in the history of the game? ask "Who is the greatest baseball player in the history of the game?"

SELECTING THE RIGHT SUBJECT

An audience will probably not listen to a speaker if he fails to give it grounds for judging him to be competent. The speaker's competence is a matter constantly at issue and an audience judges it from moment to moment during a speech. The first opportunity the speaker has to make a step toward earning an audience judgment that he is competent comes when he chooses the right subject. We say the *right* subject, rather than a "good" subject. There is, in fact, no such thing as an inherently good subject, nor is there any such thing as a bad one.

Rather than good or bad subjects, there are only good or bad speeches on any subject whatsoever. A subject is right when it is one upon which the speaker is *competent* to express his attitudes, opinions, and beliefs; when the audience will judge it to be *significant;* and, most important, when it is *appropriate* to whatever changes in thinking and action the speaker wants as an audience response. A subject with these qualities is the one a speaker wants to select if he expects to achieve his goals.

Speaker Competence

The assumption that a good speaker can talk well on any subject is an erroneous one. Winston Churchill, one of the great speakers of the modern world, spoke on propositions growing out of the political, economic, and social problems to which he devoted his public life. He would not try to tell engineers how to build a bridge or biochemists how to design a laboratory for manufacturing antibiotics. A good speaker is an avid reader and investigator. He pursues all kinds of knowledge, but he cannot be an expert on everything. He must, therefore, speak on subjects chosen from areas of his own greatest competence.

But the subject a speaker chooses need not be in an area of his competence *before* he chooses it. If this were the case, the number of his topics would be so limited that he would be reduced to virtual impotence in his own society. In fact, when a subject is chosen, the speaker may know very little about it; he may be incompetent in the sense of not having detailed knowledge. If he adds to his knowledge through study, then his initial knowledge and his research can combine to make him competent. The important thing is that he be competent *before* he makes a speech.

Significance

For a home-economics major, the fact that the spool of thread for which she used to pay a nickel now costs fifteen cents is likely to be of considerably greater interest than it is to an art major whose creativity takes forms other than sewing. An anthropology major might go out of his way to hear a lecture on the Hopi Indian. A student of political science might gladly spend time tabulating returns of a campus election in which the anthropology major had perhaps not taken time to vote. All four students would respond sharply to news that tuition at their college was to be increased 25 percent. In each of these instances, each student would be giving attention to some event which has significance for him.

The same condition applies to a speech subject. It will be of interest to an audience if it involves matters that are of significance to the audience. The greater the significance, the greater the interest. The listeners may not be aware of the extent to which the topic does concern them. Indeed, they may not have any feeling in the matter. This indifference does not mean the subject is necessarily a poor one. Instead, it means that the speaker must stimulate interest in his subject. He stimulates it by helping his listeners perceive the significance his topic has for them. Unless he makes clear why his listeners should be interested, unless he shows how and why the subject is of significance for them, they will pay him little heed. Then it will not matter that the subject offers information the audience has not had before or new insights into familiar ideas, or that the material of the speech is organized with great clarity, eminently well supported, and delivered with superior skill.

Appropriateness

The subject of a speech is appropriate only if the speaker can hope to gain the response he seeks: enjoyment, enlightenment, action, or belief. There is not much point in trying to get an audience to do something it cannot do: normally high-school students cannot vote for a sheriff. Nor is there much use in asking the audience to accept an attitude the speaker knows it is highly probable they will reject: liquor dealers will scarcely endorse prohibition.

Examples of these exercises in futility can be heard in any college speech class: "I know most of you can't vote, but if you could vote you ought to vote for. . . ." or, "Here's how I think you ought to raise your children." or, "You can have a full life after retirement." This is not to say that students who are too young to vote are not interested in who is President, nor that college students will not some day have children nor retire. It is to say, however, that speeches on subjects of this sort are not directly and immediately salient to the audience.

Consider a speech advocating that Russia should attack Red China. An American college audience might very well be interested in this event. They might even realize their existence could well depend on the outcome. However, there is not very much they can do about it.

In another kind of speech, the speaker explicates his own personal value system without any real hope of getting any audience other than a friendly (already convinced) one to enter into the affair at all. "Dancing is immoral." "*Playboy* is pornographic." "Eisenhower was a conscious tool of the communists." Such a speech is a cathartic experience for the speaker and is delivered because he has an audience. The speech can, in all probability, be delivered with as much effect in the shower.

(Usually it is a specific occasion which draws men and women together to form an audience. In choosing a subject a speaker must, therefore, consider the occasion.) A thoughtful speaker would not deliver a partisan political talk at a church meeting any more than he would tell jokes at a funeral. An address delivered on Lincoln's birthday should indicate at least an awareness of the great President's philosophy and deeds, and on the Fourth of July some phase of patriotism is traditionally in order.

Some speakers, on the other hand, use the limitations of the occasion as an excuse for not taking a responsible part in the affairs of the community. Franklin D. Roosevelt's speech on the threat of aggression prior to World War II was delivered at the dedication of a Chicago bridge. It might seem better to have delivered this "Quarantine of Aggressors" speech at a foreign-policy meeting, and to have made his appearance in Chicago the occasion for a speech on public works. The demands of the times, however (it might be called the "larger occasion"), *made* this a right occasion. Certainly the people of Chicago are interested in the question of war and peace. It might have been easy for the President to delay until Hitler marched into Poland two years later, excusing himself by saying that the right occasion for stating his views had never come along.

Similarly, you will be given many opportunities to voice your opinion on questions that concern you. Do not hesitate to let others know what you think because "the occasion is not right." This is an excuse rather than a reason. (If you are to take your place as a responsible citizen, you must be willing to state your views on the pressing problems of the times. The world is full of people who are eager to shirk this responsibility.)

SUMMARY

(All good speaking is aimed at influencing the attitudes, opinions, beliefs, and actions of an audience.) The condition of an audience (the way it thinks and acts) is, therefore, the determining factor in the selection of a speech subject and purpose. Speech subjects are expressed as propositions of policy, value, or fact.

The primary responses a speaker seeks are amusement (in speeches to entertain), understanding (in speeches to inform), and agreement (in speeches to persuade).

The sources of propositions are problems. These appear as problems of policy, value, or fact and are frequently explored in group discussions.

The right subject for a speaker to choose is one within his own competence, one that is significant for his audience, and one which is appropriate to the audience and the occasion.

QUESTIONS

1. What responses might a speaker seek?
2. How does the audience determine the subject of a speech?
3. What are the differences among problems of fact, value, and policy?
4. Discuss the qualities of the right speech subject.

EXERCISES

1. Select some campus problem and, using the examples in this chapter as models, state it as a problem of policy. Rephrase it into a proposition of policy indicating what you believe should be done.

2. Phrase a proposition of fact and a proposition of value from the same general subject. Explain, by using these examples, the difference between fact and value.

3. Select one of the audiences below or one assigned by your instructor and make a list of five speech subjects which you believe would interest them. Write a brief note after each one indicating why you think this audience would be interested.

    (a) A church club you belong to.
    (b) An assembly of the high school from which you graduated.
    (c) The freshman class at your college.
    (d) An organization to which your parents belong.

4. Make a list of five general subjects on which you believe you are qualified to speak and explain why you feel each would or would not be right for your classmates.

5. Examine the following list of expressions and determine whether each is (1) a problem or a proposition; (2) concerned with policy, fact, or value; (3) properly phrased—and if not properly phrased, why not.

(a) Girls aren't very reasonable.
(b) Should we go to the movie?
(c) What day does school open?
(d) Who is the most valuable member of the football team?
(e) What nation produced the most steel last year?
(f) The United States should give economic assistance to Poland.
(g) War is caused by greed.
(h) What should our city do about the increase in crime?
(i) Hasn't Senator Morgan lost the confidence of the people?
(j) Which automobile is best for students?
(k) What should be the college policy toward smoking on campus, or should there be one?
(l) Wouldn't Doris make a beautiful Homecoming Queen?

A LIST OF SUBJECT AREAS

The following list is intended to help you think of a speech subject. These subjects will need to be narrowed. Each of these could be a subject for entertaining, informing, persuading, or discussion. Taking the first subject on education, for instance, you might choose one of these specific purposes:

Entertain: To indicate what a large university looks like to a very small freshman.

Inform: To inform the audience about the academic organization of Columbia University.

Persuade: To persuade the audience that students get a better education at a large university.

Education

Large universities
Private vs. public education

Progressive education
College students today

Teaching a child to read
Federal aid to education
The place of athletics in education
The teaching of reading
Foreign and American colleges
Grading systems
Vocational aptitude
Junior colleges
Campus political parties
Small colleges

Revisions in the high schools
Foreign languages
Student government
Changes in education
Honors programs
Junior high schools
Counseling
Drop-outs
Academic cheating
Honor system

World Politics

Disarmament
United Nations
Israel and the Arabs
Japan's economy
Dictators
Alaska and Russia
The Middle East
International spies
Underdeveloped countries
Russia's leaders
American tourists
Yugoslavia
Berlin

Africa
China
Cuba
Canada and the United States
India
Russia's army
Past wars
Propaganda
Ambassadors
Franco's Spain
Satellite nations
Southeast Asia
Viet Nam

National Politics

Military men in public office
Revision of the Supreme Court
Constitutional amendments
Antitrust laws
The Electoral College
Straight party voting
Lobbying
Social welfare
Wiretapping
Pump-priming
Should Congress be televised?

Presidential elections
How different are the parties?
Labor disputes
Ex-Presidents
Filibuster
State offices
Public power
Withholding tax
Closed shop
Civil disobedience

Science

Great scientists
Ants
Microscopes
Photosynthesis
Growth
Man in space
Psychiatry and psychology
Radiation

Should nonscientists study science?
Solid state physics
Butterflies
Cell division
Perception
Dentistry
Fission
Disease

Atoms	Computers

Humanities

The value of the study of history	Liberal vs. technical education
Great writers	Recent novels
How to understand poetry	Modern art
"Time spent in reading is time lost from living"	Sculpture
	Does history repeat?
Civil war	Rationalism
Transcendentalism	Bertrand Russell
Semantics	Modern music
Representational vs. abstract art	Popular fiction
Huck Finn revisited	Morality in art
Should a novel have a happy ending?	Sigmund Freud
The Trent affair	Movies made from novels

Society

The Hopi Indians	Child-beating syndrome
The ideas of an ethnic group	Censorship
"All men are created equal"	Poverty
The police force	New roles for women
Subliminal advertising	A double standard?
Personal liberty	Are Americans disliked?
Distinctive features of American society	High salaries for entertainers
	Polish wedding
Television give-away programs	Racial barriers
"A woman's place is in the home"	Science in advertising
Human beings are unalike	Traffic accidents
Social Security	Capital punishment
Marriage laws	Juvenile criminals
Population explosion	Divorce
Birth control	Retail price control

Religion

The sermon in Protestantism	The election of the Pope
What is a saint?	Puritanism in New England
Varieties in Judaism	Religious wars
"The Great Awakening"	Zoroastrianism
Mohammedanism	Confucianism
Hinduism	Science and religion
Psychology and religion	Buddhism
The education of the clergy	Evolution vs. Divine creation
The symbolism of the Mass	

Definitions

Rumor	Communism
Gossip	Socialism

Capitalism
The Great Plains
Liberal education
Morality
Ethics

New Yorker
Loyalty
American
Individualism
Success

ANALYZING THE PROPOSITION

IV

ANALYZING
THE PROPOSITION

Ministers and salesmen, governors and fraternity presidents, lawyers and housewives all have ideas they want others to accept. You are barraged with efforts to persuade you; appeals and arguments of enormous variety. You try to persuade others, both individuals and groups, to accept the truth of something you believe, to value something you like, to do something you want done.

Suppose you and your friend Bob would like to take the same elective course so you can study together. You favor cultural anthropology. You might say:

"A half dozen of the fellows in the fraternity are going to take Larssill's course in anthropology next semester. Hal says Larssill's an easy grader; he doesn't even check on whether you do the reading. Last semester, he didn't call the roll half the time."

But Bob is a good student. He is not looking for a snap course; he wants one which will be worthwhile and interesting. He isn't worried about whether the professor is an easy grader. He likes to do the reading for the courses he takes. Although he recognizes that there are valuable insights to be gained from a study of anthropology, he has heard reports that the instructor is dull and fears that the course may be a bore. Therefore, while the arguments you have used seem plausible to you, they probably won't be convincing to Bob; they fail to deal with the specific questions that concern him.

ISSUES DEFINED

Before you can expect to persuade Bob, you will need to find arguments that deal with his negative reactions to your proposal. Before you can find these arguments you will need to see where your attitudes and motives are likely to conflict with his. These points of disagreement are called "issues."

43

In the question of whether Bob should take the course in anthropology, his position is somewhat like the following:

"I hear that Larssill is a very dull lecturer. He just stands up in front of the room and reads from those yellow pages he hasn't revised in twenty years; he doesn't even look at the class. I don't think it would be an interesting course."

The position you should take if you are to argue effectively must be somewhat along these lines:

"Anthropology is an interesting subject. The course has field trips to Indian burial grounds and to museums. You're already interested in sociology, and Larssill's course covers the cultural background of this very area."

The *issue* Bob raises lies in the question: "Is anthropology an interesting course?" If you argue on any grounds other than this issue that concerns Bob, your efforts more than likely will fail. Your only alternative to identifying your proposal with his interests is to change his interests. This is generally more difficult to do, although in some cases it is the only obvious alternative. But whether you argue the issue, "Is cultural anthropology an interesting course?" or "Is the ease of a course more important than its interest value?" notice that both you and Bob express your attitudes about the anthropology course in the form of *argument*. Both of you give *reasons* for the attitude. Moreover, when you carefully express the arguments, they directly oppose one another. In this relation you find the issue, that is, *the question over which the opposing arguments clash*. So, in your discussion with Bob, you attempt to enlighten him on the nature of the course in cultural anthropology:

"Cultural anthropology is a study of primitive peoples, their social structures, living conditions, and mores. The course consists of lectures and discussions over reading assignments. There is a midterm and a final examination, both of which are to be answered in essay form, and each student writes a term paper on some particular phase of a primitive society."

You have probably given the necessary information for your friend Bob to understand what the course in cultural anthropology is. You have covered what are, for him, the salient points—the issues. It might be fun to go back and ask whether these are the same kinds of evidence which would interest your friend Hal, who was quoted on page 43.

ANALYSIS—THE METHOD FOR FINDING ISSUES

The process of finding issues is called analysis. Through analysis, a speaker discovers the points of controversy which he must resolve if a speech is to be effectively persuasive.

Analyzing Propositions of Policy

When he sets out to prove that Communist China should be admitted to the United Nations, a speaker may find it necessary to prove that Nationalist China is not a symbol of democracy in Asia. By what process does he discover that he must prove the latter proposition? It seems remote from the speaker's basic purpose, but it can be an essential point in his proof. The speaker knows that his audience opposes the admission of Communist China to the United Nations on grounds like the following:

The nations of southeast Asia consider Nationalist China to be a symbol of democracy. Admitting Communist China to the United Nations would humiliate Nationalist China, discredit the symbol of democracy, and thereby weaken the confidence of southeast Asians in democracy.

To change the attitude of his listeners, the speaker must discover and remove the basic area of disagreement between his position and theirs. In the present instance, there are three points at which an issue may arise:

1. Is Nationalist China a symbol of democracy for southeast Asians?
2. Will the admission of Communist China to the United Nations discredit that symbol?
3. Will discrediting the symbol weaken democracy in Asia?

Suppose that in examining these areas of potential difference, the speaker finds himself in agreement with the audience's belief that admission of Communist China to the United Nations will discredit Nationalist China. He recognizes further his agreement with the audience on the importance of symbols. Consequently, neither of these two potential issues is a real issue. On the remaining point, however, speaker and audience do not agree. The *real issue* lies in the question whether Nationalist China *is* or *is not* a symbol of democracy among the nations of southeast Asia.

FINDING THE ISSUES IN PROPOSITIONS OF POLICY.   An example will most easily explain the method of analyzing a proposition of policy. College fraternities have been a source of controversy on American college campuses for a very long time. From time to time, the proposal to abolish fraternities has been seriously advanced. When such a proposal is made, its discussion comprises both vigorous attack and ardent defense. If you become involved in the controversy, you will need to defend your point of view. No matter which of the opposing positions you take, here is how you can make an analysis of the proposition of policy, "College fraternities should be abolished."

First draw a line down the middle of a sheet of paper. On the left side of the sheet, list all the arguments you can find which support the proposal. On the right side, list the arguments that oppose the proposition. Match the opposing arguments by pairing them against each other:

College Fraternities Should Be Abolished	College Fraternities Should Not Be Abolished
Standards for selecting members are poor. They are based on money, surface personality, and narrow identity of interests.	Standards for selecting members are high. Members are selected for their qualities of social adaptability, their character, scholarship, and leadership potential.

An identical statement sometimes supports opposing views:

College Fraternities Should Be Abolished	College Fraternities Should Not Be Abolished
Men who associate together as fraternity brothers are expected to give and receive mutual support.	Men who associate together as fraternity brothers are expected to give and receive mutual support.

On the surface, there would appear to be no disagreement and thus no issue. In circumstances of this sort, wherein statements are agreed to by both opposing parties to a conflict, the propositions accepted without objection constitute what is called waived matter. Such claims as, "Fraternities exist at the University of Illinois," "Sigma Chi is a national fraternity," or "The majority of male students at California State College at Los Angeles do not belong to a fraternity," would be accepted as waived matter by knowledgeable persons debating the proposition we are presently analyzing. Waived matter is not a part of the basis statement of issues, though it may be used as evidence to help support a speaker's position on an issue.

But the fact that both parties to a conflict make the same statement does not necessarily identify waived matter. In the case at hand, the statement that men who associate together as fraternity brothers are expected to give and receive mutual support only appears to be waived matter. The statements do clash when pertinent sentences are added, according to viewpoint: "This expectation builds cliques and factions" or "This expectation leads to life-long close friendships."

An argument in one column or the other may appear to admit of no opposition:

College Fraternities Should Be Abolished	College Fraternities Should Not Be Abolished
No apparent argument.	Members get jobs and make friends in strange towns through fraternity associations.

It is unwise to assume that such unopposed arguments constitute waived matter. The offering of the argument suggests that an issue exists. To make the analysis complete, find an argument to answer the one that seems unopposed. In your reading or thinking about the controversy, you will usually find a suitable argument to clarify the issue. For example:

College Fraternities Should Be Abolished	College Fraternities Should Not Be Abolished
This claim is a statement that fraternity members cannot verify. *Or* Fraternity membership is a false basis for selecting employees and friends.	Members get jobs and make friends in strange towns through fraternity associations.

College Fraternities Should Be Abolished	College Fraternities Should Not Be Abolished
Or While true, this claim is a trivial advantage which is outweighed by many stronger disadvantages.	Members get jobs and make friends in strange towns through fraternity associations.

When you have eliminated waived matter and found opposing points of view on all the arguments, your analysis sheets will look somewhat like this:

College Fraternities Should Be Abolished	College Fraternities Should Not Be Abolished
Fraternities discriminate against minority groups. Even where regulations no longer exist in constitutions, discrimination is practiced by "gentlemen's agreements."	Very few fraternities still have religious and racial restrictions in their constitutions.
Discrimination has no place on a college campus.	A man has a right to choose his friends.
Men who associate together as fraternity brothers are expected to give and receive mutual support. This builds cliques and factions.	Men who associate together as fraternity brothers are expected to give and receive mutual support. This leads to life-long close friendships.
The standards of selection are poor. They are based on money, surface personality, and sameness.	Fraternity members are selected for their personality, character, scholarship, and leadership.
Fraternity activities interfere with the study programs of the members.	Fraternities provide tutoring, require study hours, and in general watch the grades of their members.
Fraternities try to control the college activities for their own purposes. The member's	Fraternity members are the strongest supporters of college activities. If they control,

College Fraternities Should Be Abolished	College Fraternities Should Not Be Abolished
first loyalty is to the fraternity, not the college.	it is because they are more active than other students.
This claim is minor compared to all the damages they do the college by the actions noted above.	Fraternities do service projects for the college and the community.
This claim is a statement that fraternity members can not verify. *Or* Fraternity membership is a false basis for selecting employees and friends. *Or* While true, this claim is a trivial advantage which is outweighed by many stronger advantages.	Members get jobs and make friends in strange towns through fraternity associations.

PHRASING THE ISSUES. After the analysis sheet is prepared, the points at which the two opposing sides clash are more easily seen. The next step is to phrase as a question the clash implied in each of the sets of opposing arguments. This is done in the same manner that the clash was phrased in the example of the anthropology class on page 44. The questions that result are the issues. For example:

Fraternity activities interfere with the study programs of the members.	Fraternities provide tutoring, require study hours, and in general watch the grades of their members.

The issue that separates the opposing positions is the question: "Do fraternities hinder the scholastic achievement of their members?"

Examine each of the issues to see that all are *clearly stated*. The following issue is badly drawn:

> *Issue:* "How serious is the discrimination against minority groups?"

As it is phrased, the question presents no issue between clearly opposed points of view. Moreover, it assumes that there is discrimination when the very existence of discrimination is itself an issue that must be resolved.

REDUCING THE NUMBER OF ISSUES. Not all of the issues that are discovered by your analysis of the proposition will need to be argued. The issues in any proposition should be reduced to the smallest number which will accurately identify the important elements of the clash.

Wherever possible, combine issues that seem to overlap. The following issues involve only one point of conflict:

> *Issue:* Do fraternities develop a social life restricted to their own members?
>
> *Issue:* Do fraternities isolate their members from the normal life of the campus?

Eliminate issues which seem trivial. The following clash is not central to the disagreement:

Fraternities promote sentimentality.	No, they don't, but why waste time arguing about that?

Eliminate issues which seem to be irrelevant:

Local chapters couldn't exist without help from the national fraternity.	Many local chapters and all unaffiliated fraternities operate without financial help from a national office.

The issue exists: "Are college fraternities financially independent?" But it has no relevance to the proposition at hand.

When the job of analyzing the proposition is done, you will have a list of issues like the following:

> *Issue 1.* Do fraternities discriminate against people because of race, color, or creed? If it is admitted that discrimination is practiced, substitute the issue: Is discrimination desirable on a college campus?
>
> *Issue 2.* Do fraternity associations build detrimental cliques among students?

Issue 3. (Apart from questions of race, color, or creed) do fraternities select members for the right reasons?

Issue 4. Do fraternities hinder the scholastic achievements of their members?

Issue 5. Is a fraternity member's first loyalty to this organization or to the college?

Issue 6. Are fraternity service projects significant compared with other strengths and weaknesses?

Issue 7. Does membership in a fraternity help a student after he leaves college? If it is admitted that membership is helpful, substitute the issue: Is fraternity membership a satisfactory basis for selecting employees and friends? Or the issue: Is the help a fraternity member receives after leaving college a trivial advantage?

CLASSIFYING THE ISSUES (STOCK ISSUES). It has been traditionally assumed that to prove a proposition of policy a speaker must demonstrate the probable truth of three stock contentions: that the problem is severe enough to warrant a change, that the proposed change is more desirable than the policy currently in operation, and that the proposed policy is workable. These are frequently called, in brief, the issues over need, desirability, and practicability.

Although the concept of stock-issue analysis is useful, it can be misused when real issues are forcibly grouped under these three general heads. Not all propositions respond to such classification. Issues are created, as we have seen, not from arbitrary formulas, but from the clash of reasoning in the minds of people holding two opposing positions.

One can imagine situations wherein stock-issue analysis would serve well: Is local law enforcement unable to cope with crime? (need) Would a national police force responsible to the federal government do a better job of controlling crime? (desirability) Would such a federal police force be a workable solution? (practicability)

However, if you will look back over the seven issues we have defined in the college-fraternity proposition, you will see that in each issue need and desirability are combined and that the practicability of abolition is not even a question. The decision on that proposition will be based not on resolving stock issues but on the relative advantages and disadvantages of two opposing alternatives.

Stock issues are useful in two ways:

1. They help you to identify and interpret the specific issues you have discovered in your analysis.
2. They sometimes offer a means of grouping the specific issues by putting each one into a recognizable, workable class.

In an argument over the abolition of capital punishment, for example, some would contend that to abolish capital punishment would be desirable because innocent men are sometimes put to death (that is, the problem is severe). On the other side, you hear it argued that to abolish capital punishment would lead to an increase in crime (that is, the proposed policy is less desirable than the present one).

These two arguments and their answers constitute issues which relate to the stock issues of need and desirability. Assuming, for the moment, that no other issues were troublesome to a listener, the speaker need not concern himself with, or even mention, workability. The speaker is interested in finding *issues that divide opinion.* However, it is valuable to the speaker to know when a broad question identified by a stock issue is not at issue, or is relatively less important, in the proposition he argues. He can use this knowledge to put proper emphasis on the more important factors.

Analyzing Propositions of Value and Fact

If you look back at the issues we have identified on various propositions of policy in this chapter, you will recognize in them a common characteristic: In every instance, the question that states the issue must be answered with a proposition of value or fact. Then in order to resolve the issue, a speaker must be able to prove the proposition which states his position on the issue. Issues, in other words, are resolved and policy decisions are made on the basis of judgments of value and fact.

Proving a proposition of fact or value requires giving arguments to support it, arguments that will eliminate ground the audience may have for rejecting it. Any issues that stand between speaker and audience must be resolved. Propositions of fact and value, whether they be argued for their own sakes or in order to prove a proposition of policy, have issues of their own and these issues must be discovered. At first glance, propositions of fact and propositions of value would appear to be very much the same thing. Syntactically, they are quite alike. Every proposition of value or fact has two elements: first a subject term which refers to some idea, thing, or event; second, a judgment term which in a word, phrase, or clause says something about the subject term. But sentences of this sort can be used to express two very different kinds of judgments. The difference between these two kinds of judgments is what distinguishes propositions of fact and value from each other. Simply put, the difference lies in whether a *value* judgment is made. In 1491, Spaniards debated whether the world was flat, whether by sailing west Christopher Columbus would sail off the edge of the world. These arguments were over matters of *fact*. The judgments expressed were not the same as the value judgment no doubt widely current at the time: Christopher Columbus is a fool! But whether a proposition is one of fact or of value, the same method of analysis is applied.

The first step in finding the issues in propositions of fact and value is to formulate a successful definition of the judgment term. This definition will serve as a set of criteria for evaluating the subject term. Analyze, for example, the proposition: "Communist China is warlike." Here "Communist China" is the subject term. The judgment term is the word "warlike." A warlike nation might be defined as one which:

(1) takes direct aggresive actions against others,
(2) incites others to take aggressive actions against third parties, and
(3) operates presently in preparation for the time when it will commit one or both of the first two acts.

If these criteria satisfy a speaker as a definition of a warlike power, and if he is convinced that they will be acceptable to his listeners, the next step is to give evidence to prove Communist China has these characteristics (meets the criteria). If the speaker can convince his audience that the majority of Chinese actions fits the definition, his listeners will agree with the proposition.

THE FIVE LOCI OF POTENTIAL ISSUES

When there is disagreement on any proposition, each issue will arise at one or another of five points. These are the *loci* of the issues, the points where they are located. In analyzing a proposition he intends to prove, a speaker may expect to find in these five regions of potential issues the conflicting attitudes that identify a division of opinion. The first region applies only to propositions of policy. The last four are the sources of issues that arise from propositions of value and fact.

Issues Located in the Stated Advantages and Disadvantages

The broadest basis of potential issues is the relative value of comparative advantages and disadvantages. One can see how this issue arises when advantages of the existing system are judged against the advantages of the new proposal. Debaters using stock-issue analysis usually phrase this point of issue: Does the need justify the plan? One might argue that a massive federal program of public works is an essential part of the solution to the problem of poverty in America. Another might argue in reply that such a program would be too expensive for the country. Although these seem to constitute separate issues, they may constitute a single issue: Would a program of massive public works do enough good for the society to be worth the cost?

Issues Located in the Criteria

There may be disagreement over the validity of the criteria. That is, an issue may arise over whether the predicate term of the proposition (of fact or value) has been defined. Many speakers whose use of logic and evidence is good base their conclusions on standards that appear to be false. There is grave danger that issues will arise over definition unless such abstract terms as "good," "truth," "peace," and "prosperity" are defined with great care.

Imagine an argument that Abraham Lincoln was a great president because he was (1) more than six feet three inches tall, (2) bearded, and (3) governed in wartime. Certainly the evidence is available to show that Abraham Lincoln meets these criteria. The issue is with the criteria, which constitute a nonsense definition of a great president.

Even when the criteria have been acceptably defined they may generate issues. Cost, for example, is usually a factor in any decision. But some will argue that in some situations money should be no criterion. "Nothing's too expensive for my Annie." "When it comes to national defense, cost is no object." Thus, issues are defined which have their *locus* in disagreement over whether a particular criterion should be applied at all.

Issues Located in the Relative Importance of the Criteria

Even when there is general agreement on the criteria that should be used in making a judgment, and even when the criteria are acceptably defined, an issue may arise over the relative importance (a proposition of value) the criteria should have in influencing a judgment. Suppose you were to evaluate a baseball player's ability using as criteria (a) hitting, (b) fielding, (c) running bases, (d) team spirit. You might, when comparing two men, find that one was a better hitter and base runner but the other was a better fielder and had more spirit. The problem of deciding who is the better ball player can be solved only by deciding the issue of which of these characteristics (criteria) is most important.

Issues Located in the Application of the Criteria to Evidence

A fourth area of potential issue is in the application of the criteria to evidence. Assuming that there was complete agreement at all three of the preceding points, there might very well be an issue at the point where the actual judgment of fact or value is made. The United Nations is much concerned of late with aggression. Any delegate to the United Nations will acknowledge that the elimination of aggression is a universally accepted criterion which guides that body in many of its deliberations. No issue there. You might even get markedly similar definitions of the term "aggression" from members of widely disparate political points of view. But ask several of these same members whether Israel committed aggression against the Arabs in June of 1967. This is an issue! Were the Israeli soldiers aggressors, or were they fighting to defend their homeland?

Issues Located in the Evidence

At the base of all controversy is the possibility of disagreement over evidence (a proposition of fact). Such issues arise with great frequency between the Eastern and the Western powers in the conflict known as the cold war. Was the *Pueblo* sailing in North Korean territorial waters or was it not? Was the American ship on an assigned espionage mission or was it not? Neither faction will agree that the other side's evidence is true.

Analyzing propositions in terms of the five points at which conflicts of opinion will arise helps you to formulate the issues. This formulation helps you to identify and deal with the doubts and contrary opinions of the audience that constitute the barriers to persuasion. These barriers can be pierced—persuasion can take place—when the doubts are resolved and the opinions changed.

It is one thing to talk about persuading but it is another thing to do the job. How many speakers can resolve the doubts and meet the arguments of the audiences they face? The answer to this question is at the core of what makes public speaking a fascinating study.

HOW ISSUES ARE USED

To Indicate the Lines of Argument

Analyzing the proposition lays out the groundwork for a speech. Finding the issues points the direction the line of argument must follow. If you are to resolve the doubt and opposition in an audience, the central arguments in your speech, those which are best developed and best supported, should be the arguments which deal with the issues. A candidate for Student Council Treasurer may be an honest, intelligent, and trusted member of the college community. But if his fellow students doubt his ability to keep a good set of records, that doubt is the issue his supporters need to attack.

This emphasis on issues raises a question: Does a speaker always talk about issues? Does he ever use generally accepted ideas? In one sense you do always talk about issues, but in doing so you will use noncontroversial ideas in a very helpful way:

When you analyze a proposition, you discover points of agreement as well as areas of dispute and doubt. These points of agreement are the *waived matter* described on page 46. They serve as a common ground between you and your audience; they are the base upon which you support your position on the matters at issue.

During the campaign for Student Council Treasurer, the candidate's fellow students recognize him as a trusted person, an honest person, and a person with good ideas about student government. These acknowledgments are waived matter. His supporters can use them as arguments to help minimize the fact that he has not had the training in accounting which many of the students believe a treasurer needs. Waived matter should not be used to hide or avoid an issue. The issue is there: "Does the Student Council Treasurer need to be trained in accounting?" And the issue must be resolved. But by giving a more complete picture of the contest, arguments built on waived matter help to establish the probability that as treasurer a man might do a better job than his opponent *even though the opponent is an accounting major*. In this sense, even noncontroversial waived matter should be emphasized *in relation to the issues*.

To Group the Arguments

The practice of grouping the specific issues in a proposition of policy under stock issues is used successfully by many speakers. It is a good practice because it accomplishes several things:

1. It avoids giving the audience the impression that you have a loose collection of scattered arguments.
2. It creates the idea that you have blocks of arguments and evidence, first in one area and then in another.
3. It makes transitions easier because similar issues are annexed to one another.
4. It gives your speaking a sense of thoroughness and adds to your credibility as a person with knowledge on the proposition.

To Determine Emphasis

Since a speaker's time is limited, he must know what to emphasize for the greatest effect. The proposition that capital punishment should be abolished has been a recurring controversy in our history. We have all heard arguments for and against it but we have probably not analyzed these arguments to identify the issues. Suppose you did so, with this result:

1. Does capital punishment deter crime?
2. Is retribution (an eye for an eye) a proper standard for our society?
3. Does capital punishment save the taxpayer money?
4. Would the abolition of capital punishment return to society men who would kill again?
5. Is capital punishment discriminatory against minority groups and poor?
6. Do innocent men die through capital punishment?

You can recognize some of these issues are more important than others to an audience such as a group of college students. They are unlikely to be as concerned as some over cost, or to think in terms of "an eye for an eye." There is one great sticking point for such a group where defenders of capital punishment get their support. If you wished to persuade students that capital punishment should be abolished, you would need to show that it does not deter crime. All other points are less important to the average middle-class college student.

The final determination of emphasis requires audience analysis, which is discussed in Chapter V. However, adequate use of audience analysis is possible only if the issues have been clearly identified and related one to another.

To Determine the Nature of the Argument

Chapter X will look in more detail at the rational functions of argument. As a prelude to determining what kinds of argument we will use, it is essential that we know what kind of issue demands our attention. An issue over the nature of criteria is obviously an argument over definition and must be answered by the development of reasonable definitions. Issues over evidence can only be answered by a careful look at the sources of evidence. Issues of advantage or disadvantage lead us deep into the value systems of an audience. (See Chapter V.) Knowing the *locus* of an issue, then, is an important prelude to effective argument.

SUMMARY

In order to prove a proposition, a speaker must analyze it to find the points at which his audience is likely to be influenced by arguments against his proposal. These points of conflict are called issues.

To find the issues in propositions of policy, the propositions are analyzed by drawing out of directly opposed arguments the essential elements of clash and phrasing them as clearly stated questions. The number of these questions is reduced by combining issues that overlap, by eliminating waived matter, and by eliminating issues which seem to be trivial or irrelevant. The issues that make up the resulting list are sometimes grouped according to the stock issues that embrace them. The stock issues are three questions which apply to all propositions of policy and which the audience must be able to answer affirmatively before a proposition can be accepted as proved.

To find the issues in propositions of fact or value, define the judgment term in the proposition. This definition is used as a criterion for determining whether available evidence warrants the judgment one makes about the subject term.

Issues will arise at one or more of five *loci :*

1. Questions of the relative advantages and disadvantages of the proposed policy.
2. The acceptability of the criteria used to evaluate judgments of value and fact.
3. The relative importance of the criteria.

4. The judgment that is made when the criteria are applied to the available evidence.
5. The accuracy of the evidence itself.

The issues a speaker finds when he analyzes a proposition are used to help him find the lines of argument he should use in proving his proposition, as a means of grouping his arguments for greater strength in either attack or defense, as a basis for the application of audience analysis to determine emphasis, and as a help to selecting proper forms of argument.

QUESTIONS

1. What is an issue?
2. When does an argument not identify an issue?
3. What are stock issues?
4. What is the use and limitation of stock issues?
5. How are propositions of fact and value analyzed?
6. What must be done first to resolve disagreements where abstract terms such as "good," "truth," or "peace" are used?
7. How are noncontroversial ideas used to argue issues?
8. For what four purposes are issues used?

EXERCISES

1. What are the issues in the following controversy? On November 3, 1964, the voters of the State of California voted on a highly controversial proposal. Proposition 14 would have amended the Constitution of the State of California to prohibit any agency of state or local government from "denying, limiting, or abridging the right of any person" from selling, leasing, or renting "residential real property to any person he chooses." The measure passed but was subsequently declared unconstitutional by the State Supreme Court.

The immediate cause for this Constitutional amendment was the Rumford Act, which had been passed by the State Legislature and signed into law by the Governor. This act made it illegal to discriminate in renting, leasing, or selling property on the basis of race, color, creed, or national origin.

Although a number of years has passed since the election of 1964, the issue of open-housing laws is still with us and probably will continue to be debated for some time.

The following statements are taken from the pamphlet distributed to all California voters by the election authorities, *Proposed Amendments to the Constitution, Propositions and Proposed Laws, Together with Arguments, General Election, Tuesday, November 3, 1964*, pp. 18–20.

PROPOSITION 14

SALES AND RENTALS OF RESIDENTIAL REAL PROPERTY. Initiative Constitutional Amendment. Prohibits State, subdivision, or agency thereof from denying, limiting, or abridging right of any person to decline to sell, lease, or rent residential real property to any person as he chooses. Prohibition not applicable to property owned by State or its subdivisions; property acquired by eminent domain; or transient lodging accommodations by hotels, motels, and similar public places.	**YES**
	NO

Analysis by the Legislative Counsel

This measure would add Section 26 to Article I of the California Constitution. It would prohibit the State and its subdivisions and agencies from directly or indirectly denying, limiting, or abridging the right of any "person" to decline to sell, lease, or rent residential "real property" to such person or persons as he, in his absolute discretion, chooses.

By definitions contained in the measure, "person" would include individuals, partnerships, corporations and other legal entities, and their agents or representatives, but would not include the State or any of its subdivisions with respect to the sale, lease, or rental of property owned by it. "Real property" would mean any residential realty, regardless of how obtained or financed and regardless of whether such realty consists of a single family dwelling or as a dwelling for two or more persons or families living together or independently of each other.

The measure would not apply to the obtaining of property by eminent domain, nor to the renting or providing of any transient lodging accommodations by a hotel, motel, or other similar public place engaged in furnishing lodging to transient guests.

Argument in Favor of Proposition No. 14

Your "Yes" vote on this constitutional amendment will guarantee the right of all home and apartment owners to choose buyers and renters of their property as they wish, without interference by State or local government.

Most owners of such property in California lost this right through the Rumford Act of 1963. It says they may not refuse to sell or rent their property to anyone for reasons of race, color, religion, national origin, or ancestry.

The Rumford Act establishes a new principle in our law—that State appointed bureaucrats may force you, over your objections, to deal concerning your own property with the person they choose. This amounts to seizure of private property.

Your "Yes" vote will require the State to remain neutral: Neither to forbid nor to force a home or apartment owner to sell or rent to one particular person over another.

Under the Rumford Act, a person refused by a property owner may charge discrimination. The owner must defend himself, not because he refused, but for his reasons for refusing. He must defend himself for alleged unlawful thoughts.

A politically appointed commission (Fair Employment Practices Commision) becomes investigator, prosecutor, jury and judge. It may "obtain . . . and utilize the services of all governmental departments and agencies" against you. It allows hearsay and opinion evidence.

If you cannot prove yourself innocent, you can be forced to accept your accuser as buyer or tenant or pay him up to $500 "damages."

You may appeal to a court, but the judge only reviews the FEPC record. If you don't abide by the decision, you may be jailed for contempt. You are never allowed a jury trial.

If such legislation is proper, what is to prevent the legislature from passing laws prohibiting property owners from declining to rent or sell for reasons of sex, age, marital status, or lack of financial responsibility?

Your "Yes" vote will prevent such tyranny. It will restore to the home or apartment owner, whatever his skin color, religion, origin, or other characteristic, the right to sell or rent his property as he chooses. It will put this right into the California constitution, where it can be taken away only by consent of the people at the polls.

The amendment does not affect the enforceability of contracts voluntarily entered into. A voluntary agreement not to discriminate will be as enforceable as any other. Contrary to what some say, the amendment does not interfere with the right of the State or Federal government to enforce contracts made with private parties. This would include Federal Urban Renewal projects, College Housing programs, and property owned by the State or acquired by condemnation.

Opponents of this amendment show a complete lack of confidence in the fairness of Californians in dealing with members of minority groups. They believe, therefore, the people must not be allowed to make their own decisions.

Your "Yes" vote will end such interference. It will be a vote for freedom.

Submitted by:

L. H. Wilson, Fresno, California, Chairman, Committee for Home Protection

Jack Schrade, State Senator, San Diego County

Robert L. Snell, Oakland, California, President, California Apartment Owners Association

Argument against Proposition No. 14

Leaders of every religious faith urge a "NO" vote on Proposition 14.

Leaders of both the Republican and Democratic parties urge a "NO" vote on Proposition 14.

Business, labor, and civic leaders urge a "NO" vote on Proposition 14.

Why such overwhelming opposition? Because Proposition 14 would write hate and bigotry into the Constitution. It could take away your right to buy or rent the home of your choice.

The evidence is clear:

1. Proposition 14 is a deception. It does not give you a chance to vote for or against California's Fair Housing Law. Instead, it would radically change our Constitution by destroying all existing fair housing laws. But more than that, it would forever forbid your elected officials of the state, cities and counties from any future action in this field. It would also threaten all other laws protecting the value of our properties.

2. Proposition 14 says one thing but means another. Its real purpose—to deny millions of Californians the right to buy a home—is deliberately hidden in its tricky language. Its wording is so sweeping it could result in persons of any group being denied the right to own property which they could afford.

3. Proposition 14 is not legally sound. California's Supreme Court already has said there are "grave" doubts as to its constitutionality. It destroys basic rights of individuals and thus is in violation of the U.S. Constitution.

4. Proposition 14 is misleading. California already has a fair and moderate housing law similar to those in effect in 10 other states. In five years the Fair Employment Practice Commission, which administers this law, has dealt with over 3,500 cases in both employment and hous-

ing. <u>All but four cases were either dismissed or settled in the calm give-and-take of conciliation.</u>

5. <u>Proposition 14 is a threat.</u> It would strike a damaging blow to California's economy through loss of $276,000,000 in federal redevelopment and other construction funds. Thousands of Californians could be thrown out of work.

6. <u>Proposition 14 is immoral.</u> It would legalize and incite bigotry. At a time when our nation is moving ahead on civil rights, it proposes to convert California into another Mississippi or Alabama and to create an atmosphere for violence and hate.

For generations Californians have fought <u>for a</u> tolerant society and <u>against</u> the extremist forces of the ultra-right who actively are behind Proposition 14.

Now a selfish, mistaken group would restrict free trade in real estate in California—a powerful lobby seeking special immunity from the law for its own private purposes is asking you to vote hatred and bigotry into our State Constitution.

Do not be deceived. Join the leaders of our churches, our political parties and business and labor in voting "NO" on Proposition 14. Before you vote study! Learn why you should join us!

> Reverend Dr. Myron C. Cole, President, Council of Churches in Southern California
>
> Most Reverend Hugh A. Donohoe, Bishop, Catholic Diocese of Stockton
>
> Stanley Mosk, Attorney General of California

ANALYZING THE AUDIENCE

I. The nature of audiences
II. General attitudes of audiences
    A. Attitudes toward the speaker
    B. Attitudes toward the subject
    C. Attitudes toward the occasion
    D. Attitudes toward itself
III. Factors influencing audience attitudes
    A. Attitudes associated with sex
    B. Attitudes associated with age
    C. Attitudes associated with economic position
    D. Attitudes associated with social background
    E. Attitudes associated with group membership
IV. Speech development determined by audience analysis
    A. The amount of material
    B. The kind of material
    C. The central tendency of the audience
    D. Cross pressures in the audience
    E. Premises for argument
    F. Language fitted to the audience
    G. Organization
    H. Motivation
V. Summary, questions, and exercises

V

ANALYZING THE AUDIENCE

In every speaking situation there are three essential factors: the speaker, the message (speech), and the listener. No one of these factors is constant because every speaking situation is unique. The speaker has an image of the listener to whom he directs the message and the listener has an image of the speaker and what the speaker will do. The meaning of the message will be determined by what these respective images are.

Let us consider a simple social situation. An elderly man and a teen-age boy are seated in a living room talking. Perhaps it is a man and his grandson, who is in high school. The boy has recently been awakened to a whole new world of football, girls, automobiles, and jobs. For him his studies have a remoteness about them though he knows they are, in some vague way, a part of his future and he has learned to enjoy some of them.

The older man wants the best for his grandson. He "knows" that, by the standards of the adult society the boy must soon join, success will be measured in terms of a good job, a home, a family, and enough money to enjoy life and provide for his family. The boy also "knows" this situation, not as he "knows" an MG or the Saturday night dance, but because he has been told about it by adults.

"What kind of work do you think you will be going into, Frank?" asks the man.

"Well," says Frank, "I thought I would study engineering. I got a B in algebra last semester and I am pretty good at math and science."

"Oh, is that so?" continues the man. "Well, it is good to study hard so that you can get into a profession and it is also important to find something you enjoy doing. What college do you plan to attend?"

"I thought I would go to Harvard, if I can get the money. Otherwise, I will go to State U."

"Don't you need better grades to get into Harvard?"

"Yes. I plan to study harder next semester."

Even though he is asking questions, the man is trying to tell Frank that he should study harder and be a success. His statements clearly indicate that Frank needs guidance and he sees himself as a source of that guidance. Nothing the man says is "untrue" but it is clearly not central to the boy's thoughts. Engineering is a vague but respectable profession about which he knows little and Harvard is a university he has accepted as a symbol of the best in higher education. Frank has an image of his grandfather—"nice enough for an adult"— who is always concerned about vague things in the future. Frank's response is predictable. He has played the role he was cast into by the older man: a student preparing for a profession. But he fills such other roles as second-string linebacker, lunch-time comic, Volkswagen driver, and good dancer.

Chances are that both man and boy know the communication situation is not right. Each has cast the other in a role and the verbal currency transacted between them has produced little new meaning beyond reinforcing the other's predetermined roles.

The factors in this speaking situation, then, are the speaker with his image of himself and his predictions about the listener, the listener with his image of himself and his predictions about the speaker, and the message which changes in meaning for each of them as image and prediction change.

Messages are used to bring these two sets of images and predictions together. Too often we think of a message, a speech, as being a thing with which a speaker does something to a listener. The action, instead, is reciprocal. A listener with his images and predictions does something to a speaker. Problems in communication, represented by such statements as "He didn't understand what I said," or "he deliberately misinterpreted me," indicate how a listener can affect a speaker.

Since this is a text in public speaking we look at communication from the viewpoint of the speaker. Paradoxically, the result is that we must be most concerned with how listeners perceive messages.

To talk as nearly as possible in the same language as his listeners, a speaker must make accurate predictions about what their different responses may be. Gaining such insight requires the speaker to be conscious of the people he addresses and to be keenly aware of the things that have meaning and value for them. To understand people, he must study people, their psychology and their social behavior. Effective speakers are masters of this kind of audience analysis. They study men and social institutions to learn how people in general react to ideas and to language. They are students of art, history, literature, and, above all, of men.

THE NATURE OF AUDIENCES

We have said that every speaking situation is unique, that listeners have a variety of roles. Such statements would seem to be an invitation to chaos. But speaking situations do have similarities and, depending on how they see themselves, listeners do have images and expectations which are similar to other listeners in similar circumstances. Look back for a moment at the conversation between Frank and his grandfather. With minor variations, could this conversation have taken place with Frank's friends Randy or Van or Bruce? Would there be greater variation in the conversation, however, if it were held with his granddaughter Sally? Why? Because the aspirations which a grandfather in our society has for Sally are quite different from those he has for Frank. In this situation, the grandfather's aspirations for Bruce are little different from those he has for Frank.

Note the grandfather's words which tell us something about what is important to him: "work," "study hard," "something you enjoy doing," "better grades". And Frank responds with words which will have the greatest meaning for the other (remember, Frank plays his role well): "study engineering," "B in algebra," "good at math and science," "Harvard," "if I can get the money," "study harder". Taken as a whole, these words imply a value system which emphasizes hard work for tangible results in a socially approved way. A clearly secondary value is that one should enjoy what he does. The conversation reveals through its language a facet of what is known as the Puritan value system, a major one in our society. Adequate space is not available here to explore the various systems that flourish in American society but we can suggest several sources where one can learn more about them.

Merle Curti, *The Growth of American Thought,* third edition (New York, 1964).

Ralph Gabriel, *The Course of American Democratic Thought,* second edition (New York, 1956).

Rod W. Horton and Herbert W. Edwards, *Backgrounds of American Literary Thought,* second edition (New York, 1967).

Vernon L. Parrington, *Main Currents in American Thought* (New York, 1930).

Stow Persons, *American Minds* (New York, 1958).

For the most part, one must learn of these value systems through his education in literature, history, philosophy, and the arts, and through continued observation of how people respond to each other. Despite the uniqueness of each speaking situation, a unity in values makes it possible for a speaker who observes human reactions to analyze an audience successfully.

GENERAL ATTITUDES OF AUDIENCES

Attitudes toward the Speaker

Perhaps the most difficult attitude for a speaker to attain is an objective understanding of the audience's predictions about himself. It is natural to think that others see him as he sees himself. He may be competent, honest, and intelligent; but what he thinks he is or what he actually is is not as important as what others consider him to be. He must examine his audience carefully to gain some empathy into what they will think of him. In most cases the effectiveness of a speech will be increased by the realization of the audience that the speaker is an expert. If you are a football player, a musician, or a campus leader, an audience may be likely to accept your information on sports, music, or student government. However, in some instances this expertness can stimulate audience resistance. Thus, if a football player asks for more aid to athletics, or if a musician wants a required course in music, or if a student leader calls for more participation in student-body activities, each of these views is to be expected and the speaker may be suspected of bias. In such instances, the speaker must be aware of possible negative reactions and develop his speech accordingly.

The football player might argue that if it were not for athletic scholarships many students would not be able to attend college. An audience made up of students seeking or holding athletic scholarships would find this argument valid. But a cross section of the student body might have an entirely different reaction. Their response would be: "Of course, he favors athletic scholarships because he gets one. But what about people like me? I'd like to have a scholarship too." The speaker would do much better if he were to recognize the possibility of such a response. He would not then argue that without scholarships many athletes would not be able to go to school, nor that scholarships are the only way to build a football team. Instead, he would choose arguments that reduce the implications of his own self-interest. He might begin by noting that he already has a scholarship, and therefore is not arguing for personal gain, and then build his arguments on the benefit to the college.

This example can serve as a useful basis for noting how audiences respond to speakers. Listeners make predictions and final judgments about speakers and their messages on the basis of three or four characteristics: trustworthiness, competence, good will, dynamism. Applying this analysis to the football player mentioned above, we might see a particular listener making a prediction about the speech. "Alan is a nice guy (trustworthy) who knows what he is talking about (competent), and he is a good talker (dynamic). He will probably give a good speech but it may be a snow job because he will advocate more athletic scholarships because he is an athlete (does not have good will). Or imagine these predictions: "Janet? What does she know about football?" Or, "Scott? He is so stuck-up I just don't like him." Or, "Sure he knows a lot, but is he a dull speaker!"

Obviously, listeners don't always consciously frame their thoughts but there is no doubt that they make predictions. The speaker must consciously plan his message to reinforce favorable predictions of the audience and diminish unfavorable ones.

Attitudes toward the Subject

Audiences have general reactions to the subject of a speech. After a political campaign, listeners are frequently "tired of hearing about politics." Church groups may prefer not to be exposed to additional missionary drives, and in your speech class, a fourth talk on racial prejudice may be overworking a theme that was interesting in the first three. Each set of listeners must be analyzed to determine what their reactions are likely to be.

But what does the speaker do when what he wants his listeners to know or believe seems to conflict with what they want to hear? Change his subject and tell them what they want to hear? Certainly not. Too much of the platitudinous "God, Flag, and Mother" kind of speaking is already with us. And too many speakers fail to realize that listeners don't really want to hear this innocuous talk any more than they want to be told that they are ignorant or wrong.

When the speaker feels that his listeners are not interested in his subject but he thinks they ought to be, he bridges the gap by building interest in his subject from the interests his listeners already have. Through his analysis of the audience, he discovers what their interests are and relates his ideas to these interests. Thus, the speaker must know not only the audience's attitude toward his subject but also its attitude toward many subjects. A group of businessmen may not be interested in religion, but they could be interested in a subject which related business law to the moral systems which religions teach. Are young people interested in the problems of the aged? Perhaps not, but they could be interested in the subject if it was related to their own problems in understanding their grandparents in the difficult adjustments of old age. A good speaker can make any subject interesting if he analyzes his audience carefully.

Attitudes toward the Occasion

Although the occasion of a speech is a part of the role of the listener, we must isolate it here to call attention to some of the special problems which occasion creates in defining an audience.

The occasion upon which a speech is given can either help or hinder the response a speaker wants to win. When a geology class is assembled to learn about earthquakes and fault lines, it is not prepared to hear an appeal to support the Campus Fund. The members of a sociology class may be interested in hearing about the recently inaugurated and highly publicized charity drive; but they may not be, and the speaker should be prepared for negative reactions.

If there is audience hostility, it does the speaker little good to ignore it. Faced with negative reactions, he should treat them honestly. He can acknowledge that his listeners are met for a purpose other than to hear him speak. To overcome his disadvantage, he needs to build a speech associated with interests his audience has.

The attitude an audience has toward an occasion frequently can be used to strengthen the speech. If the occasion has some special meaning to the listeners, a speaker can associate his subject with the occasion to build interest. Holiday speeches invariably do this. The speaker at a Labor Day meeting may want to speak on world affairs but he will link his subject to the aspirations of the working man.

One of the most significant things a specific occasion does is to limit the scope of the audience's conception of itself. Two men sit side by side at a lodge meeting. Although one is a Democrat and the other is a

Republican, they think of themselves, on this occasion, as lodge members. For a time they forget or at least submerge their political preferences. They see themselves as "brothers," and in this sense they think alike. The audience's narrowed conception of itself in terms of the role it is then taking helps to polarize the group and makes it easier for the speaker. The religious convictions, political loyalties, and economic stations of the members, however, are still present although they may be latent. What a speaker says can awaken these latent associations in the audience to his own advantage or disadvantage.

Attitudes toward Itself

The attitudes which a listener has toward himself is a vital determinant of how he will respond to the speaker's message. Frequently, this attitude will be directly related to his attitude toward the speaker. If a man plays golf with his boss he may be less inclined to see himself as the good golfer he is because more central to his thinking is his relation to the other man as "Boss." When a political science professor stops to chat with one of his students who is lead cellist with the University orchestra, they discuss music. The student's attitude toward himself (the role he takes) is considerably different from his attitude toward himself inside the classroom where comparative government is being discussed.

If a listener is to receive a message with reasonable fidelity, the speaker must take into account what his listeners think of themselves.

Fred is excitedly telling his Aunt Alice about the play he saw. "Several of us went together to see *Hamlet*. It was the best play I have seen in a long time. After we left the theatre we all went over to the Hoosier Tavern and sat discussing it for hours. The thing that was so great about it was . . . ."

Aunt Alice is thinking to herself, "Fred always did have confidence in me. This is his way of telling me that he drinks. Of course, I wouldn't tell his mother. She would have a fit."

Aunt Alice's perception of herself as confidante to Fred clearly influenced the meaning received from his message.

Attitudes which listeners have toward themselves may also be unrelated to the speaker. The President of the Bellflower Kiwanis Club has a role as leader of that group which he takes regardless of the particular speaker at any particular Thursday noon luncheon. The speaker must be careful that what he says will not seem to be an insult or an affront to the role such a person takes and to the members who have their roles also. The officers and members of any organization have attitudes toward themselves which the speaker must consider.

FACTORS INFLUENCING AUDIENCE ATTITUDES

We have noted a listener's attitude toward the speaker, the subject, the occasion, and himself will affect the kinds of predictions he makes about a speaking situation and the kind of response he will give to it. Although the list is by no means exhaustive, we will isolate five factors which will tend to influence listeners' attitudes as being his sex, age, economic position, social background, and group membership. Differences in these areas will reveal differences in value systems and, therefore, differences in audience attitude.

Attitudes Associated with Sex

We would expect women to be moved by ideas that do not appeal to men, and vice versa. An audience made up primarily of mature women will ordinarily be concerned with the home and children. Women will tend to be receptive to subjects they can associate with domestic problems. Men tend to be concerned about matters of job security and working conditions.

Further evidence seems to indicate that men are more concerned about politics than women are. The differences are products of the roles which women and men have adopted for their own lives by observing their parents and peers. Better educated women tend to have interests that are more like men than do less educated women.

Naturally, every classification has its modifiers. An audience of women workers in a factory would very likely be much concerned about job security and working conditions. Clearly the role a person is called upon to take will modify the stereotype of him. As women in our society take more and more active roles in business and the professions, we will find it more and more difficult to differentiate attitudes on the basis of sex alone. Nonetheless, the role of the woman, actual or potential, as wife and mother will still make her views of the world quite different from those of a man.

Attitudes Associated with Age

Young people, it is said, tend to be flexible in their political and religious affiliations and are, perhaps, more idealistic. As they grow older, they tend to become concerned about the practical operation of ideas and to develop somewhat fixed attitudes toward religious and political affiliations. While these generalizations do not apply to all, they do provide a starting point for more specific analysis.

The age group of an audience may help a speaker anticipate reactions to specific subjects. A group of college freshmen and sophomores will usually be more skeptical of plans to increase the number of men drafted into military service than will an older group. Why? Because such a proposal affects them directly and inconveniently. Older people may be concerned if they have sons of draft age.

Attitudes Associated with Economic Position

Many problems have implications for the listener's pocketbook. Proposals that involve an increase in taxes are usually less acceptable to those who must pay the taxes than they are to those who may avoid them. Also, proposals which will benefit specific groups economically, such as support for farm income, airline subsidies, tax preference for the oil and gas companies, will find acceptance among these groups more readily than among groups which do not benefit. In your local community or college, some of the same reactions can be seen. Athletes and students interested in athletics may strongly support an increase in the student-activities fees by which athletic programs are financed. Other students who have no lively interest in athletics may object to an increase in their student fees.

It is easy to put more emphasis on economic position than is justified. Many people have come to consider all reactions as economic. These "economic determinists" ignore the many other factors which determine attitudes. Because of a strong belief in education, an upper-income person without school-age children will frequently favor aid to education despite increased taxes. And so, while their economic position can tell you much about your listeners, it must be viewed as one of the many factors that influence their reactions.

Attitudes Associated with Social Background

The past conditions of their lives, the way they grew up, and the kinds of attitudes and values their parents had make up the social background of audiences and have a significant effect on how they react to ideas. You can easily imagine that the views of one group might differ from the views of any other. Does an audience meet as a group of Polish-Americans? Of Nisei? Of Negroes? Of Southerners? Of Roman Catholics? Of Sons or Daughters of the American Revolution?

Most people find it impossible to escape their background completely. Even though a man may leave behind certain ties, such as the "old-fashioned" ideas of his parents, these ties still have the power to color his thoughts and to affect his responses. His own ideas have changed, but he still lives in the atmosphere of his background. The old values must at least be tolerated and the people who still hold them expect him to act in accordance with the value systems of the old background.

Not only does the immediate social pressure of parents and community influence people to maintain old ways and attitudes, but these values are built into the individual. He has been conditioned to them for years and when his new associations produce attitudes which are antagonistic to older attitudes, they produce cross pressures which he must resolve.

Under such cross pressures he is more susceptible to persuasion than the person who is free of them. When one has been raised with the religious conviction that abortion is immoral and then in college associates with people who believe otherwise, he is more likely to shift his position than is one who has not grown up in such a background or one who associates in college with people who also consider abortion immoral.

Many authorities believe that social background is perhaps the strongest factor in determining attitudes. Thus it may be more important that the listener you address is a Negro, a WASP, a Jew, or a Catholic, than that he is a man or that he is twenty years old.

Attitudes Associated with Group Membership

While the analysis of sex, age, and economic-social backgrounds tells much about audiences, a knowledge of their affiliations will help to pinpoint analysis much more sharply. Knowing that an audience has a substantial percentage of American Legionnaires, Protestants, or Democrats can help a speaker judge its probable attitudes toward a subject. These specific affiliations do not tell all that one needs to know about a group, but as a part of total audience analysis, they give helpful clues. Organizations such as the American Legion have specific statements of principle which will help to guide a speaker in developing a topic. Chambers of Commerce, farm groups, and labor unions usually represent recognizable social and economic attitudes. Service clubs, such as Rotary, Kiwanis, and Lions, all have projects which are important to them. Specific religious organizations—the Knights of Columbus, B'nai B'rith, the Men's Club of the First Baptist Church—have distinctive approaches to questions of faith and morals. Political clubs have their obvious partisan positions. Knowledge of the aims of these specific groups will help a speaker do a better job of persuading their members.

Group membership is an easier factor to learn than are some others; easier, for instance, than ethnic background and it is a fairly good measure of attitudes. Studies seem to show that people join groups with ideas and goals similar to their own. The group further reinforces these ideas and goals.

In groups which are brought together because of some firmly held opinion or position—as differentiated from groups such as the Kiwanis Club or the Lions Club, whose members share general goals without an issue—important factors must be considered. Such issue-oriented groups attain greater solidarity in their opinions and attitudes the more controversial their opinions are and the more they are in the minority. The American Nazi Party might well be an example of such a group. The Rotary Club will be less solid in its attitudes than is a Young Republicans Club, for instance.

Individuals who claim great independence and who join together to claim it are really not independent and they merely exchange one influence (perhaps parental) for another. Although quite different from the general society, the hippies or beatniks conform quite closely to the attitudes of their own group.

The speaker who can identify the group memberships of his audience can tell much about the attitudes of his listeners and, therefore, their predictions and reactions.

SPEECH DEVELOPMENT DETERMINED BY AUDIENCE ANALYSIS

It is impossible for a speaker to give an audience all the evidence and reasoning that support his position. He must find some basis on which to select the material. That basis is the audience. Audience analysis helps to determine eight elements of the content and development of a speech: (1) the amount of material to use; (2) the kind of material; (3) the central tendency of the audience; (4) cross pressures in the audience; (5) premises from which to reason; (6) language; (7) organization; and (8) motivation.

The Amount of Material

The amount of material needed to clarify or to prove a specific point within a speech is determined by the need of the audience. In a speech to inform, for example, you will need few specific details if you know that the audience can easily understand a given point. In persuasion, the keynote speaker at a political convention judges the amount of evidence he will need to support his arguments from knowing that the members of the convention will already agree with the position he upholds. When student-body funds are allocated to various campus activities, a lack of student interest in music may motivate the members of the student council to cut the budget for the opera program. A speaker who is aware of the student council's attitude will give a great deal of evidence when he goes before that group to ask more money for the opera program.

The Kind of Material

As you prepare a speech, you will gather more information than you can use in one speech. The process of selecting the items that are best for your purpose will be based on the nature of your audience. You will choose quotations not only because they say exactly what you want them to say but also because the authorities you quote are respected by your audience. You will draw illustrations from experiences which are understandable to the group to which you speak. If you are speaking to freshmen students who have never had a chemistry course, you will need to adjust your talk on atomic energy to take account of this fact.

The Central Tendency of the Audience

From your knowledge of the composition of the audience look for some central tendency around which your listeners' attitudes can be grouped. Will they tend to be liberal or conservative on economic and social problems? Do they have strong religious convictions? Does the age of the group affect the kinds and amount of experience they have had? What is the proportion of men and women in the audience and what effect is this likely to have on the way they view the subject of your speech?

Naturally, this central tendency provides only a general picture of what an audience is like. You cannot, in one speech, take into consideration all the possible attitudes an audience may have. Prepare your speech to appeal to the bulk of the·audience. *You cannot please everyone.*

Cross Pressures in the Audience

Although many audiences will have strong central tendencies on which a speaker can build an appeal, others will be under cross pressures. Whenever two or more central tendencies conflict in an audience at any one time, cross pressures exist.

Investigations of the American electorate in the 1952 presidential campaign revealed this example of cross pressures: While a majority of the American people had a strong emotional attachment to the Democratic party, there was present also strong dissatisfaction with conditions in the country. The Republican party resolved this cross pressure by nominating for the presidency a man who could convincingly argue that he could improve conditions in America but who was at the same time sufficiently nonpolitical to neutralize the strong emotional attachment of many people for the Democratic party. Many Democrats in 1952 were able to say, "Eisenhower is almost a Democrat. He really isn't a Republican at all." Twelve years later, in 1964, many Republicans were able to dissociate themselves from Barry Goldwater by convincing themselves that he wasn't really a Republican but was instead associated with some undefined "far right." Thus they could justify voting for President Johnson without betraying their Republican loyalties.

A common example of cross pressure is furnished by the teen-ager whose parents have always emphasized the need to do well in school. The young man agrees with his parents, but he also needs the companionship of his own friends. When his friends want him to "go with the gang to the movies" on the night before a chemistry test, he is under cross pressure. If he can find a way to go to the movie and still get his studying done, the cross pressure will be resolved and he will go to the movie after all.

It is an important part of audience analysis to discover whatever cross pressures are in the audience. A speaker must then find evidence, argument, and motivation which will resolve them. The examples given above of the elections of 1952 and 1964 show how these cross pressures are resolved. The speaker does not simply argue his case. He provides a rationale in terms of the opinions, attitudes, and beliefs which already exist within the listeners. People put labels on things in order to capsulize their attitudes in language. These attitudes may differ from one person to another. Some college students may be opposed to having a fraternity man as Student Body President because to them a fraternity man is rich or snobbish or a playboy. To argue that Gordon Silver should be Student Body President because he is the best qualified and most dedicated is not enough. Nor is there time enough to change the listener's assumptions about fraternity men. The speaker must show that Gordon "is not a fraternity man," that is, he does not have the characteristics of a fraternity man which the listener predicts he will have. The listener's cross pressure is that he must choose between the most qualified candidate who is a snob and the less qualified candidate who is not. The attitudes which form the basis of cross pressures are not formed by any significantly systematic examination of evidence. Although Gordon Silver is best qualified because he was last year's vice president, he is a fraternity man (snob). The speaker resolves the cross pressure by showing that he is not a stereotypic fraternity man.

While audiences under cross pressure are more complex and, therefore, require greater skill in understanding, they also provide the greatest possibility for change. In general, the greater the cross pressure the greater the challenge and the opportunity for persuasion.

Premises for Argument

Frequently, reasoning is based upon starting points or premises that speakers do not need to prove. Such unproved and sometimes even unmentioned premises are called assumptions. It is not necessary for a speaker to prove certain assumed premises because they are already accepted by his audience. A minister begins a sermon on the assumption that there is a God and that his congregation believes it. Frequently he assumes other theological principles which are accepted by his congregation. In most Christian churches, for example, he assumes that God is triune, but he cannot do so in the Unitarian church.

It is virtually impossible to argue without assumptions. If a speaker felt compelled to go back to first principles on every argument, he would both bore his listeners and waste valuable speaking time.

Look at such traditional documents as the Declaration of Independence and the Constitution. Observe the excellent examples of premises stated without proof.

We the People of the United States, in Order to form a more perfect Union, establish Justice, insure domestic Tranquility, provide for the common defence, promote the general Welfare, and secure the Blessings of Liberty to ourselves and our Posterity, do ordain and establish this Constitution for the United States of America.

The writers of this document assume without submitting any proof that union is desirable, that justice ought to be established, that domestic tranquillity should be insured, that the general welfare is worth promoting, and that liberty is a blessing. What proof is necessary? Would *you* reject any one of these assumptions?

A speaker should know enough about the groups he addresses to be able to use arguments based on premises which his audience already believes. To know what premises will be acceptable to a given group, the speaker must determine what assumptions his audience holds and use them as premises for his arguments.

Language Fitted to the Audience

Language is affected, even determined, by such factors as time, place, sex, and circumstances. At a Presbyterian convention, a man does not use the same language he might at a convention of Lion's club members. In many significant ways, there are differences between the language of men and the language of women. Certainly the language of the educated person is different from the language of the uneducated. Adlai Stevenson was criticized in 1952 because he "talked over the heads of the American people." But Stevenson was not being criticized for not knowing the language. Most people lauded his language. The real criticism was of his audience analysis. The Democratic party countered with the charge that Mr. Stevenson's critics were underrating the American public. In this instance, analysis of the contemporary American political audience became an actual issue in the campaign.

Organization

Chapter XVIII (Speaking to Persuade) discusses the way in which the organization of the speech is determined by the nature of the audience you address. You will want to use different methods of organization depending on the extent to which the audience agrees or disagrees with what you say.

Motivation

The motivation you select should be one that is not only related to the needs of your audience but is also acceptable to its values. The experience of the supervisor of a group of electricians working on high-tension lines illustrates this point. The accident rate among the workmen was quite high and all attempts to frighten the men by telling them of the physical dangers of not grounding the line and of not wearing safety helmets failed. Even such crudely direct approaches as showing them the dead body of a friend who failed to heed the warnings were not successful.

The supervisor was completely frustrated until he realized that self-preservation was not an acceptable motivation for the men. To them, not wearing a safety helmet and not grounding the wire were signs of manliness. They were, in their own minds, strong and able people; others had made errors because of their weakness. The emotional motivation was changed. The ego of the men was utilized as a basis of persuasion. They were told that no one cared if they wanted to kill themselves but that only fools did what they were doing. The workman who violated the safety rules was ridiculed as silly or even worse. When the men identified themselves with this concept, the number of accidents decreased. The success of this second motivation was the result of a more realistic analysis of the audience.

SUMMARY

To be effective, a speaker must adapt his speech to his listeners. He must know their ideas before he prepares his speech. The process of audience analysis, through which the speaker gains his knowledge of his listeners, is one which demands continued study and observation of people. There are no infallible rules for knowing how audiences will respond. However, some clues to the nature of the audience can be found.

A speaker must determine the kinds of attitudes an audience has toward him, toward his subject, and toward the occasion of his speech. There are, moreover, specific factors which the speaker can use to gain insight into the ideas and attitudes of his listeners. He needs to know the make-up of the audience in terms of its sex, age, economic position, social background, and affiliations.

Once the speaker has made his analysis of the audience, he can use it in a number of ways to strengthen his speech. His analysis will help him choose the amount and kind of material he should use. He can estimate what the central tendency of audience attitude is, or, in cases where there are conflicting central tendencies, he can determine what cross pressures are operating. The speaker uses the information he gains from analyzing the audience to determine what premises he can assume without the need for proof. His language and the organization of his speech will be influenced by what he knows about the audience. He uses his analysis of the audience to help him select the best motivation for the speech.

QUESTIONS

1. What general attitude of an audience is the most difficult for a speaker to assess?

2. Your class being your audience, which of the five factors of audience analysis do you consider most important? Least?

3. How do cross pressures affect audience response?

4. How is argument affected by the assumptions of an audience?

5. If you say that someone "talks over the heads of his listeners," do you mean his language is poor? If you do, then in what way?

6. How might the motivation of a teen-ager for safe driving be different from those of his parents?

EXERCISES

1. Write a brief paper (no more than three double-spaced type-written pages) in which you explain what you need to know about one of your parents or a brother or sister before you ask a favor. You will probably find it easier to write this paper if you select a specific favor to ask. Your purpose in this paper is to make an "audience" analysis of that one person, so do not write about the techniques you would use to get the favor. For instance, what do you need to know about your father's ideas and attitudes in order to successfully ask him to let you use the car for a Saturday night date?

2. Select any one of the five factors which determine the specific attitudes of an audience. Also select for consideration some specific

question of current news interest. How do you think the attitudes of any two groups of people within the classification (for example: men and women, teen-agers and middle-aged people, well-to-do people and poor people, Negroes and Caucasians) would differ *generally* on the question? What limitations do you see in this generalization? If you believe that on the question you have chosen there are no differences, explain why you believe so.

3. Make a careful and honest assessment of yourself as an "audience" for a speaker. What do people who have known you think about your knowledge and beliefs?

SUPPORTING MATERIAL:
TYPES AND USES

I. Clarity and interest
II. Types of supporting material
    A. Definition
        1. Logical definition
        2. Operational definition
        3. Definition by description
        4. Definition by comparison and contrast
        5. Definition by example
        6. Definition by figure of speech
        7. Definition by usage, etymology, or history
    B. Statements about facts: examples
        1. Real examples
        2. Hypothetical examples
        3. Extended examples
        4. Using examples for clarity and interest
        5. Using examples to prove
    C. Statements about facts: statistics
        1. Using statistics for clarity and interest
        2. Using statistics to prove
    D. Opinions about facts: testimony
        1. Using testimony
        2. Evaluating testimony
    E. Comparison and contrast
III. Summary, exercises, and questions

VI

SUPPORTING MATERIAL: TYPES AND USES

The ideas in a speech are reflections of the experiences of the speaker, and they include his research and his knowledge. An audience understands the ideas in terms of its own experience, however. A hearer interprets language based on his experience with the concepts and objects to which the language refers. An effective speaker uses language that makes it easy for an audience to visualize the concepts and objects that he is discussing. Abstractions must be made concrete, generalities must be made specific, obscurities must be made clear. The speaker uses concrete, specific, vivid details to help his listeners visualize his ideas in terms of their own experiences. These details are called supporting materials.

In any serious effort to communicate, a speaker must select the materials best calculated to make his meaning clear to his listener. In a very real sense, for every set of verbal symbols he uses, a speaker has a meaning and his listener has a meaning, but they will never be precisely the same. Unless the speaker selects materials carefully, he will be less likely to modify the listener's meaning so that it shifts toward his own.

In every kind of speaking—to entertain, to inform, to persuade— the kinds of materials used are of the same sort. As the purpose in speaking differs, however, and speakers work toward different general ends, they make different uses of the material. No matter what the speaker's goal, his materials should provide the listener with a balance of clarity and interest.

CLARITY AND INTEREST

In a sense the qualities of clarity and interest are antagonistic. Clarity increases for the listener as he is able to predict the speaker's meaning with greater certainty. Interest increases with novelty and change, when the situation is less predictable.

Clarity without interest will produce a speech that is dull and therefore difficult to listen to. Actuarial tables, for example, can be eminently clear, but they do not make good listening. On the other hand, there is harm in using materials which may be interesting in themselves, but which add nothing necessary to the clarification of the ideas. A major artistic factor in public speaking is striking a careful balance between the dull and the exciting, of finding the point where the speaker's meaning is both interesting and clear.

All supporting materials are designed to provide meaning but these materials are not things; they are statements about things. They have meaning for the listener because they refer to something in the listener's experience: things, people, thoughts, attitudes, feelings. We speak of giving evidence to support a point. Sergeant Joe Friday of *Dragnet* asks the witness to "Give us the facts, just the facts." But no one gives "facts"; he makes statements about facts. The law of gravity is a statement about a fact. A definition of communism is a statement about communism. A college president's opinion on the pass-fail system of grading is a statement about that system.

The speaker's purpose in using such statements is to make the listener believe that through these supporting materials he is learning about reality.

TYPES OF SUPPORTING MATERIAL

Supporting materials may be classified in four categories: *Definitions* are used to clarify a speaker's meaning for words or concepts which may be unfamiliar, obscure, or different from the listener's. *Statements about facts* are details found in the forms of examples and statistics. *Opinions about facts* occur in the form of the testimony of others. *Comparison and contrast* establish a relationship for the listener between the known and the unknown.

Definition

When a druggist fills a prescription, he labels his bottle of medicine so that there may be no confusion about the contents or the dosage. In a similar sense, language provides labels for ideas. The labels put on ideas, like the labels of bottles of medicine, should be recognizable, clear, and precise. But language is not always easy to use in speaking about complex or abstract ideas. "Democracy," "communism," "union shop" are not "seen" in the same sense as "aspirin" or "Vitamin C." When a speaker uses words like "aspirin" or "Vitamin C," a listener recognizes the simple denotative meaning of the speaker, even though he may not have full insight into the chemical components of the concrete things named. "Democracy," "communism," and "union shop," however, are abstract terms. These labels are used with a greater variety of meanings than are those of more concrete objects. Speakers often use language as if the labels for such abstractions were understood as easily and universally as the labels put on concrete things. Too often listeners are confused because they do not understand the labels in the sense the speaker uses them. They will, therefore, project their own meanings into what the speakers says rather than shifting their meanings toward his own. Consequently, an abstract, unfamiliar, or obscure term will need to be defined.

No amount of effort at clear definition will make certain that doubtful words have precisely the same meaning for every listener. Universal understanding is impossible, but fortunately it is also unnecessary. Ideas can be communicated adequately in spite of the inherent ambiguity of language. The closer a speaker and his audience come to a mutual understanding of language, the better the communication will be.

The basic requirements of a good definition are (1) to indicate the sense in which the speaker uses the term and, (2) to bring the speaker's meaning within the scope of the listeners' experiences.

LOGICAL DEFINITION. There are many different methods of definition, but the one that traditionally has been considered to fulfill these two requirements best is definition by classification, so-called *logical* definition. Logical definition puts the thing defined into a class with which the listener is already familiar. Then, to restrict the meaning and eliminate ambiguity, the definition distinguishes the thing defined from all other members of that class. To the baseball player, a "Texas Leaguer" is a safe hit on a short fly ball which falls to the ground between the infielders and the outfielders. It belongs to the class of safe hits, but is differentiated from other safe hits by the facts that (a) it is a short fly ball, and (2) it hits the ground between the infielders and outfielders.

OPERATIONAL DEFINITION. When someone tells you what you

must do to discover what something is, he is giving you an operational definition. He is telling you the operation you must go through to experience the meaning of the term.

"Maybe you have been somewhere for the first time, and you know that it is the first time you have ever been there, yet you have the feeling that you had been there before, even to the extent that you could predict things about the place that you couldn't possibly have known. Last summer I was driving through a town I had never been in before on a road I had never travelled before, and suddenly I felt that I had been there before. I even knew that around a corner up ahead would be a large stone church, although I couldn't see around the corner, and I knew that I had never been around that corner. I got to the corner, and there was the church, just as I knew it would be, and just where I knew it was. The feeling that I had, which you may have had at some time in your life, is called *déjà vu. . . .*"

DEFINITION BY DESCRIPTION. To describe a gambrel roof by telling what it looks like may help to clarify a hearer's understanding.
DEFINITION BY COMPARISON AND CONTRAST. In defining by comparison and contrast, a speaker tries to show his meaning for a term either by likening it to something (comparison) or by differentiating it from something (contrast) with which his listeners are already familiar:

Writing is like speaking in that its major purpose is to communicate an idea.

The union shop is not exactly like the closed shop. A man can get a job at a union shop before he joins the union, but he must already belong to a union before he can be employed in a closed shop.

Comparison and contrast may be used together for clarification. The government of the state of Nebraska is much like that of the federal government. It has three branches—Executive, Legislative, and Judicial—which carry on the usual functions of those branches. But Nebraska has only one house in the legislature.
DEFINITION BY EXAMPLE. Speakers may explain their meaning for a term by citing examples. In 1877 George William Curtis, self-educated man of letters, reformer, and popular speaker of the period, delivered the commencement address at Union College. In his speech, "The Public Duty of Educated Men," he defines public duty.

By the words *public duty* I do not necessarily mean official duty, although it may include that. I mean simply that constant and active practical participation in the details of politics without which, upon the part of the most intelligent citizens, the conduct of public affairs falls under the control of selfish and ignorant, or crafty and venal men. I mean that personal attention—which as it must be incessant, is often wearisome and even repulsive—to the details of politics, attendance at meetings, service upon committees, care and trouble and expense of many kinds, patient endurance of rebuffs, chagrins, ridicules, disappointments, defeats—in a word, all those duties and services which, when selfishly and meanly performed, stigmatize a man as a mere politician; but whose constant, honorable, intelligent, and vigilant performance is the gradual building, stone by stone and layer by layer, of that great temple of self-restrained liberty which all generous souls mean that our government shall be.

DEFINITION BY FIGURE OF SPEECH. Not all definitions purpose a specific denotative meaning for a word. In the above illustration of definition by example, the user clearly has a connotative meaning for the term. Even more connotative is definition by *figure of speech*. To say "the world is a stage" or "the Devil is a roaring lion" helps the listener to visualize, but he does so in a connotative way. In most speaking situations we will be more interested in clarity of definition, but sometimes we will want definitions which convey attitudes. In such cases more connotative forms of definition will be useful.

DEFINITION BY USAGE, ETYMOLOGY, OR HISTORY. A dictionary always reports the usage of a term:

SHOWDOWN, *n.* 1. In poker, the play in which the hands are laid on the table face up. 2. Any action or disclosure that brings an issue to a head.

The dictionary may also report the *etymology* of a word or the *history* of its development. The meaning of the word "persuasion" may be clarified by showing that it comes from the Latin phrase *per suasionem*, which means "through sweetness." To the *etymology* of the word may be added something of its *history:* The tribes of Europe, who found the declensions of the Latin language difficult and awkward, dropped off endings and used words in their root forms. Thus the phrase *per suasionem* lost its *em* ending and became the single word "persuasion." The concept of sweetness is still an important connotation of the term. The dictionary's report of usage makes no precise definition of a term; neither does the etymology of a word or the history of its development. By telling these, though, a speaker can convey enough of his meaning to make it understood.

One brief word of caution is necessary about the use of definitions. While audience analysis may reveal that many of your listeners do not understand what a speaker means by a word, there may be in the audience many who already have a meaning for the term. So, avoid comments such as, "I know that you don't undertstand what this term means so let me define it for you." If your listeners do not understand the term, you scarcely need to tell them that they don't. It is far better to put the responsibility on yourself: "To make myself clear, let me point out that by ——, I mean ——."

Statements about Facts: Examples

Examples are the product of experience and observation, either the speaker's or someone else's. Grand Teton National Park is in Wyoming. The United States was attacked at Pearl Harbor on December 7, 1941. The British burned Washington, D.C. during the War of 1812. Richard Nixon was elected President of the United States in November 1968. All of these are statements about facts which may be used as examples to illustrate some point.

If you want to become a truly effective speaker, learn to use examples well. Think of the interesting speakers you have heard, whether on a public platform or in your own living room. Remember the many examples they used to illustrate the subjects they discussed.

Examples may be either real or hypothetical, brief or extended in length.

REAL EXAMPLES. An example is an account of an incident or occurrence that a speaker relates to illustrate a point, or an object or condition that he cites. A real example refers to an incident that has actually occurred or an object that actually exists. "A good example of a great T-formation team was the old Chicago Bears." "St. Stephen's Church down on Orange Avenue is a good example of what I mean by modern church architecture." While both the examples cited above are real examples, there is a significant difference between them. It is quite clear that the listener may have actually experienced St. Stephen's Church. The speaker is asking him to remember the building as the listener probably saw it on Orange

Avenue. On the other hand, it is quite likely that the average listener never experienced the "old Chicago Bears." If he did so, it was probably so long ago that he is unable to recall the specifics of the offensive formation they used. This point is made to call your attention to the fact that some examples are more immediate in the listener's experience than others and, therefore, presumably require less detail for his understanding.

HYPOTHETICAL EXAMPLES. If an example describes an incident that did not actually occur, but might, the example is hypothetical. A speaker wanted to illustrate the idea that optimism can sometimes be foolish. He told the story of a man who was gaily whistling as he drove down a country road one day and met a neighbor.

"Bill," said the neighbor, "what makes you so happy today?"

"I'm just coming back from town where I sold a hog for $100."

"That's wonderful, Bill, that's wonderful. What did the hog cost you?"

"Just $50.00."

"And how long did you keep him?"

"Just a year."

"And how much corn did you feed him?"

"Just $50.00 worth."

"Well, Bill," continued the neighbor, "you didn't make much money on the hog, did you?"

"No," said Bill, still smiling. "I didn't make much money but I had the use of the hog for a year."

EXTENDED EXAMPLES. On occasion, a speaker will want to develop an example at somewhat greater length and in more detail than is possible in the brief form the example ordinarily takes. Such illustrations are called extended examples and may be either hypothetical or real.

On March 15, 1965, President Lyndon B. Johnson delivered what is probably his most well-received speech. That speech on the right to vote was delivered to a joint session of the Congress. In it he developed an extended personal example to illustrate the idea that "you never forget what poverty and hatred can do when you see its scars on the hopeful face of a young child."

My first job after college was as a teacher in Cotulla, Texas, in a small Mexican-American school. Few of them could speak English and I couldn't speak much Spanish.

My students were poor and they often came to class without break-fast and hungry. And they knew even in their youth the pain of prejudice. They never seemed to know why people disliked them, but they knew it was so because I saw it in their eyes. I often walked home late in the afternoon after the classes were finished wishing there was more that I could do. But all I knew was to teach them the little that I knew, hoping that it might help them against the hardships that lay ahead.

And somehow you never forget what poverty and hatred can do when you see its scars on the hopeful face of a young child.

USING EXAMPLES FOR CLARITY AND INTEREST.   There are some rules for using examples which can well be remembered by a speaker:

(1) Use extended examples only when the point to be described is an essential one. For minor points, brief examples are sufficient.

(2) Use the best example you can find for the particular idea you are discussing. Unless examples are carefully chosen, there is a danger that they will not clearly exemplify the point a speaker is making. The offering of an example which fails to illustrate his point precisely forces a speaker to say, "This isn't exactly what I mean, but . . ." The listener is thrown off the track and, after a few such instances, he may well give up listening.

(3) Be sure that the necessary value characterizations are given with the example: The Chicago Bears are not just *any* T-formation team; they are a "great" one, while the Reseda High School Regents are a "typical high-school" T-formation team.

(4) If necessary, use more than one short example for a specific point. A single example might enlighten part of the audience and not the rest, or may only partly enlighten the audience as a whole. A greater number and variety of examples will often clarify or prove when one example might fail.

(5) Use real examples whenever it is possible and give them the kind of detail which will make them seem more directly related to the listener's experience. Be specific as to time, place, and circum-stance. If possible, set them within the experience of the listener. If no real example of how to use your brakes on a slippery pavement is available you can say, "Suppose you were coming down Ventura Boulevard at about twenty-five miles an hour in a heavy rain when a truck pulled out of Balboa Boulevard. Here's what might hap-pen. . . ." Though your hearer never experienced this event, he can

visualize it and can profit by the description. This hypothetical example has the characteristics of the real example: the experience on Ventura Boulevard is not real but hearers recognize the event and have had similar experiences or heard of similar experiences which are enough to make it seem real.

USING EXAMPLES TO PROVE. When a speaker uses examples to prove a point in a speech, he must not only choose illustrations for their value in achieving clarity and interest, but he must also select instances that meet three further criteria. If the answer to all three of the following questions is Yes, the examples may be considered acceptable:

Are the examples representative? Examples must be typical, not exceptions to the rule. A father may be generous with his son to the point of indulgence. He may give the boy everything he needs or wants. But let Dad say No when Bob wants the car some night in the middle of the week and what does he hear? "Aw, Dad, you never let me have any fun." The boy singles out what is perhaps the only atypical example in an otherwise clear pattern of behavior as the basis for a unfounded generalization. A specific instance must give a true picture of the situation it illustrates if it is to be effective as a means of proof.

Are the examples sufficient in number to give clear support to the point the speaker is making? The number of instances that will be necessary is not the same in every case. One may be enough: the first sunburn you get on a cloudy day will be quite enough to establish for you the generalization that exposure to the sun is dangerous even on a cloudy day. On the other hand, it takes quite a number of baseball games to demonstrate which is the best team in the National League.

Are negative instances accounted for? It is not reasonable to expect to establish belief in an idea if there is substantial evidence to the contrary. A wealthy man may on many occasions show civic pride and social responsibility, and a speaker might try to characterize him as a good and philanthropic citizen. The speaker would not be notably successful if his audience knew the man's fortune was made in legal but morally doubtful operations in slum-area real estate.

Statements about Facts: Statistics

Statistics are figures a speaker uses to clarify an idea or to prove a proposition. The speech which brought Governor Ronald Reagan of California into the political spotlight was one he delivered over television in support of Senator Barry Goldwater's candidacy for the Presidency in 1964. In the speech the future Governor of California used statistics frequently. The following is an example from early in the speech:

No nation in history has ever survived a tax burden that reached a third of its national income. Today 35 cents out of every dollar earned in this country is the tax collector's share, and yet our government continues to spend $17 million a day more than the government takes in.

We haven't balanced our budget twenty-eight out of the last thirty-four years. We have raised our debt limit three times in the last twelve months, and now our national debt is one and a half times bigger than all the combined debts of all the nations in the world.

USING STATISTICS FOR CLARITY AND INTEREST.   When statistics employ large numbers (roughly four or more digits), it is wise to round them off. For intance, the 1960 population of Chicago, Illinois, was 3,550,404 but if you wanted to use this in a speech you would probably say, "In 1960 the population of Chicago was a little over three and one-half million." Even though 50,404 is a substantial number of people, "three and one-half million" is accurate enough for most purposes and much easier for the listener to remember.

After statistics have been rounded off, they can be made still more meaningful by comparison. The round figure of three and one-half million is easier to comprehend if it is compared: "That's approximately five times the size of our own city of San Francisco." Percentages, fractions, and proportions all help to put the compacted examples we call statistics into a clear relationship with other facts. Statistics, then, can add clarity and interest if you round them off and, by using comparison, show their relationship to other ideas.

USING STATISTICS TO PROVE.   When statistical data are used as illustrations to clarify an idea, it is important, of course, that they be accurate and meaningful as well as interesting and clear. When figures of this kind are used as evidence to support a proposition, however, it is even more important that they be examined carefully.

1. *Check the currency of the data.* The date of compilation is one of the first things to ask about statistical information. Recency is of little concern, of course, in matters that change slowly or slightly if at all. A statement of the number of times a human heart beats per minute need not be doubted today just because the subject was studied years

ago. The infant-mortality rate in American hospitals does not change rapidly enough to demand new study every day. If, however, you see a report on the number of jet fighter planes Russia is supposed to have, you would want to know when the count was made. Soviet air power is not static.

2. *Check the reliability of the source of the statistical data.* Completely apart from any interpretation put upon figures—the validity of any comparison between, let us say, the air powers of the United States and Russia—accurate reporting depends upon the reliability of sources. You must ask: Who made the statistical study? Did the information come from Soviet sources which may be intentionally misleading?

Certain governmental agencies such as the Bureau of Labor Statistics are generally accepted as a source of honest reports. The Brookings Institute is a private research group which has earned general acceptance. But, as any television viewer can tell you, many so-called independent agencies are nothing more than sources of advertising copy.

3. *Be sure the statistics measure what they appear to measure.* It would be doubtful to conclude that one-fourth of the student body of an entire college is Italian because two of the eight students in an advanced class in the Modern Language department happen to have been born in Rome. This is an insufficient sampling.

Suppose, moreover, that the average age of the same eight students is thirty years. This measure of the sample is probably a poor measure of the age of the students in the whole college, and it can be misleading in reference to the class itself. The two Italian students may be a man and his wife who came to this country after the man had retired from business and both may be sixty-five years old. If four of the other students in the class are eighteen and two are nineteen, this distribution makes the *average* age of the class thirty, but no one in the class comes within ten years of the average.

Finally, it would be wise to ask how the word "average" is used: Does it refer to the mean, the median, or the mode? The *mean* is a simple arithmetical average. To find it, add together the quantity of each item in a series and divide by the number of items. The *mode* is the figure which appears most frequently in a series. The *median* is the point above and below which half of the items fall. In the example cited above, the mean age of the students is thirty, the mode is eighteen, and the median is between eighteen and nineteen. In other words, statistical data are subject to scrutiny and interpretation. The old saying that "figures don't lie" is itself a generalization that bears investigation; although the remainder of the saying, "but liars figure," is above reproach.

Opinions about Facts: Testimony

Often the material a speaker has gathered reflects some judgment on the part of its source and comes to him as an interpretation of the data involved. These interpretations are called *testimony* and are *opinions* about facts.

USING TESTIMONY.   Using testimony in a speech makes it possible for you to tap the resources of generations of thought and expression. All that mankind has written and said becomes a vast reservoir from which you can draw the authoritative testimony of expert witnesses. You add clarity and interest to your ideas and strength to your propositions when you associate your attitudes and opinions with the thoughts and feelings of men your audiences know, respect, and admire.

The privilege of using testimony in a speech is one that brings certain obligations. Honesty demands that you identify ideas and language that you have taken from someone else. This is not merely a moral injunction against plagiarism; two other considerations are involved. First, by failing to identify your source you pass up the opportunity to add his credibility to your own and, second, if a listener recognizes that the statement is not your own, it will tend to diminish his trust in you.

Putting directly quoted testimony into a speech may bring some awkward moments. To avoid these, it is generally wise not to use the words "quote" and "unquote" to identify the beginning and end of a direct quotation. Instead, identify the source of your material as thoroughly as honesty demands, then let your voice (through pause, change in tempo, or other means) indicate which words are yours and which belong to your source.

Your use of testimony need not be in the form of a direct quotation, that is, word for word. It can be presented in your words with an indication that the explanation or comparison has some respected person as its source. If the explanation of an authority is particularly clear, you may want to quote it *verbatim*, but, in general, putting the idea into your own words will keep it on the level of language used in your speech.

Regardless of the form, testimony is always opinion *about* facts, not fact itself. Consequently, the best use of testimony will reveal how the authority cited arrived at his conclusion. Testimony which merely states an opinion asks a listener to accept the conclusion simply because he trusts the authority. It is far stronger to support this trust with the facts and reasons behind the judgment.

EVALUATING TESTIMONY. Before you decide to use a piece of testimony, you should ask yourself two questions about it:

Is the authority competent? The background, training, and experience of the person whose opinions you use as supporting material should put him in a position to know what he is talking about. To be qualified he should be speaking in his area of competence. A theologian is not usually an authority on biology. A former heavyweight champion who happens to be a Negro is not necessarily any greater authority on race relations than any other Negro. Look for sources whose competence will be clear to the listener. Sometimes, with a less well-known authority, it is necessary to give the audience evidence of his competence.

One would like to believe that competence can be objectively measured. Like all factors in rhetoric, however, it is a judgment in the minds of the audience. A speaker may be tempted to think, "Well, if you don't know who Charles Percy is, you are pretty dumb." But, objectively, if the listeners don't recognize the name of the Senator from Illinois, it is the speaker's problem to see they are informed.

Is the authority trustworthy? Even when an authority is accepted as competent he may not be considered thoroughly trustworthy on a subject. Senator J. William Fulbright of Arkansas is one of the most knowledgeable men in this country in the area of American foreign policy, but many people think him to be biased on the subject. For them, his credibility is less than it is for others. A frequent mistake of beginning speakers is to assume that any senator, historian, physicist, or economist is a source of useful testimony. His biases, whether real or only imagined by the audience, will decrease his credibility.

Comparison and Contrast

While they can be treated separately, *comparison* and *contrast* are in essence the same process. Comparisons show how things are *like* other things; contrasts show how things are *unlike*.

In comparison, the speaker chooses something familiar to the audience and likens it to the unknown factor he wishes to explain.

One student speaker, in explaining the principle of radar, compared it to bouncing a ball off a garage door in that the farther away from the garage the player gets, the longer it takes the ball to bounce and return. If he could measure the amount of time and the speed of the ball, he could determine the distance to the door. He then went on to say that ball-bouncing is roughly comparable to the way radar works. Radio waves, whose speed is known, are thrown against an object and the length of time the reflected wave takes to return indicates the distance of the object from the sender.

Contrast is used to show differences. An audience may not be clear on the difference between radar and sonar. After explaining the basic nature of radar by comparing a radio wave with the ball bounced off the garage door, a speaker can explain sonar by noting that, while radar employs radio waves, sonar employs sound waves.

SUMMARY

Effective speaking is interesting and clear. The supporting materials a speaker uses supply clarity and interest by helping an audience visualize ideas concretely and specifically. In all speaking (to entertain, to inform, or to persuade), the supporting materials are of four types: (1) definition, (2) statements about facts—examples and statistics, (3) opinion about facts—testimony, and (4) comparison and contrast.

The materials selected for a speech should be suited to the speaker's general end; they should be accurate; they should be of such quality and quantity that they satisfy the expectations of the audience.

QUESTIONS

1. What are the two major requirements which speech materials must meet?
2. Why do some words require definition while others do not?
3. What are the two basic requirements of a good definition?
4. What is a logical definition?
5. Explain three other kinds of definitions.
6. Differentiate between real and hypothetical examples.
7. What three questions are asked as tests of examples which are used to prove?
8. Explain how statistics can be made clear and interesting.

9. How should a speaker test the statistics he uses?
10. What value does testimony have in a speech?
11. What two questions should be asked in evaluating testimony?
12. Explain comparison and contrast.

EXERCISES

1. Develop a one-point speech in which you support that one point with at least one instance each of three of the four different types of supporting material.

2. From one of the other classes you are enrolled in, select a term you had never heard before. Define that term in a brief logical definition and by three other methods of definition. Decide which of the four methods has given the clearest explanation of the term. Decide which method was the least clear. Why do you think the one method is better than the other for defining this term?

3. Make a survey of opinion among some group of students on campus. For instance, what do the men at the Phi Kappa Tau fraternity house think about rock and roll? What generalization can you make from the statistics?

4. Develop three hypothetical examples, each of which has "the characteristics of a real example." Indicate the point they would be used to support.

5. In *Vital Speeches of the Day* or in *Representative American Speeches* find speeches that illustrate the use of:

operational definition statistics
extended example   comparison and contrast
   testimony (direct and indirect quotations)

SUPPORTING MATERIAL: SOURCES

  I. Personal experience
 II. Secondary experience
    A. Conversations and interviews
    B. Radio, television, lectures
    C. The library
III. Using the library
    A. The card catalog
    B. Special reference tools
      1. For basic facts and statistics
      2. For brief authoritative articles
      3. For more extensively developed articles
      4. For biography
      5. For dates
      6. For quotations
 IV. Methods of recording material
  V. Summary, questions, and exercises

VII

SUPPORTING
MATERIAL:
SOURCES

One of the nearly infallible ways a speaker can destroy his effectiveness is to be inadequately informed about the subject of a speech. No matter what the speaker's purpose is—to entertain, to inform, or to persuade—if he is to achieve that purpose, his audience must judge him to be competent, to be worth listening to. Ignorance of his subject is one of the really great offenses a speaker can commit against his audience. No matter what the subject, audience, or occasion, by appearing before a group, a speaker professes to have something to say. Unless he knows what he is talking about, he can hardly expect the audience to pay much attention to him. To have his audience believe him worth listening to, he must supply himself with supporting materials of a kind and to a degree adequate to the demands of the audience and the subject.

Making an audience identify its thoughts, feelings, attitudes, and beliefs with the purpose of a speech is rarely a simple task. A mature, resourceful speaker and a person of good judgment will not, therefore, leave any avenue untraveled in his search for clear and interesting material. The preceding chapter considered the kinds of material that are useful to a speaker and discussed the way in which they are used. This chapter examines some of the more useful sources of this material and the tools for discovering it.

PERSONAL EXPERIENCE

No other person can look back to precisely the same set of experiences you have had. Your life, the things you have done, and the things that have happened to you are unique when they are viewed as a whole. This uniqueness in your own personal experience has important implications for your speaking. First, there are some things that you know more about than anyone else. This special knowledge alone qualifies you to speak authoritatively about some subjects. A second consideration, however, qualifies the usefulness of your unique knowledge: not merely have no two persons had identical experiences; indeed, very few of your experiences have been shared by everyone. Consequently, that which is most valuable in your experience, its uniqueness, is also the most difficult to communicate. Successful communication demands a common ground of shared experience in order to bring about identification between speaker and audience. Though you may, for example, know more about automobiles, teen-age language habits, or ice hockey than any member of your audience, you can use your own personal experiences in communicating this knowledge to others only if you help your audience to interpret these experiences in the light of their own personal and unique backgrounds.

A good speaker is one who senses readily which of his own experiences are common to other people. When he draws on these common experiences and interprets them intelligently, he achieves clarity and creates interest through this common bond. The speaker who recognizes both the advantages and the limitations of personal experience as a source of supporting material can use this kind of material to bring clarity and interest to what he says. The speaker can go back into his own past and select material that makes it possible for him to explain his ideas with the accuracy and precision of immediate knowledge. A speaker who draws on his own experience can select material that helps an audience to perceive his ideas in concrete form. The man who has worked on an assembly line has absorbed countless minute details that could never come to him secondhand. Out of the vividness of his own recollection he can draw material that would not be available to him from the most meticulous research.

SECONDARY EXPERIENCE

The knowledge gained from examining what others have thought and done can be called secondary experience. Such information is necessary because frequently people must speak on subjects with which they do not have direct personal experience. Many have not been and can not be Negroes, Jews, Catholics, forest rangers, United States senators, or social workers. Consequently, personal experience must be supplemented by examining the experience of others.

When a speaker does not find in his own background some personal experience to lend vividness to his ideas, he draws from what someone else has written or said an experience that *could* have happened to anyone, including every member of his audience. This kind of supporting material brings clarity to the speaker's ideas because it brings them within the comprehension of the listener. It adds interest to the speech because it has the immediacy of direct, personal experience.

Being dependent upon others for information, however, is always a potential danger. Some of the difficulties of audience acceptance that arise in using secondary experience as speech material have been discussed in the preceding chapter. The further point is to be made here that even when a speaker chooses his speech materials carefully, the definitions, examples, statistics, and testimony he gathers from sources outside his own experience are always subject to bias. No matter how meticulous the speaker himself may be in trying to maintain an objective attitude toward his subject (and this he will seldom be able to do), the external sources he consults are as susceptible as he is to personal bias.

It is extremely doubtful that all bias can be removed from any extended discourse. The very fact that a speaker *selects* the material he uses, elects to use one datum and to dispense with another, automatically builds into a speech an inescapable bias. Even reports appearing in the news magazines and newspapers, theoretically intended to present an objective statement of newsworthy events, often demonstrate the editorial bias of the publication in which they appear. The evil in bias lies not in its being present but in its not being recognized. In order to detect the bias that will almost necessarily be present in the writing and speaking of one who is concerned with what he says, a thoughtful person will study many sources of information.

Beyond the need to be on the lookout for the bias of any source of information a speaker consults, using the experiences and ideas of others for speech material requires the speaker to evaluate what he hears and reads. He must learn to listen and read with maturity and judgment. To be ill-informed may be even worse than to be uninformed.

When they are thoughtfully evaluated and properly used, secondary materials will form a good basis for helping a listener to identify himself with the ideas of a speaker. Remembering that secondary experience must have the vividness and the immediacy of

direct personal experience, here are some of the ways in which this
kind of supporting material can be found.

Conversations and Interviews

The conversations you have with friends will frequently provide
material for a speech. Even the ideas with which you disagree can be
useful; they may be examples of concepts prevalent in our society.

Frequently you will know of some expert, perhaps a faculty member
or someone in the business community, who can help you to understand a more complex subject. You may be surprised to discover how
willing people are to help you. Remember, their fields of specializa-
tion are important to them and they are usually pleased to know
that they are of interest to others. Faculty members, for instance,
feel a bit flattered when students ask for help in finding materials.

When you solicit information from others, however, it is wise to be
sure you know what you want to ask. Begin thinking seriously about
your subject some time in advance. Do some reading before you approach the person you want to interview. Arrange for an appoint-
ment convenient to him. Tell him what you will need to know, and
the limits of the subject you intend to speak about. Give him time to
think about your questions. Then, when you have the interview, be
prepared to ask specific questions. These will form the framework
of the interview. You can expect to be disappointed with an interview
which begins like this: "What can you tell me about electronics?
I gotta give a speech tomorrow."

Radio, Television, Lectures

Radio and television programs can be valuable sources of speech
material. You will find, however, that gathering useful data from
broadcasts is more difficult than gathering them from an interview.
The major problem, of course, is that you can't ask questions. Accordingly you must be more careful in listening and in taking any
notes you may want to keep for future reference.

In many instances, radio and television programs offer data that
would otherwise be unavailable. It is not likely that a college student
could approach the President, for instance, and ask him for his views
on the relations of this country with the Soviet Union, or federal aid
to education, or government support of a program of medical care
for aged citizens. Yet the President's views are often communicated

to the nation at large over radio and television. Some statements made under these circumstances will not appear in print, since many newspapers do not report the complete text of speeches broadcast on radio or television.

To make the most of an opportunity to gather speech materials from broadcasts requires much the same kind of preplanning that is done for interviews. You may discover that the Egyptian ambassador is appearing on a public-affairs broadcast. Because you are preparing a speech in which the background of Arab-Israeli conflict is pertinent, you will plan to listen. If you have done some early planning in your speech, you will know the kinds of things to listen for.

Public lectures, not broadcast, are information sources less often available than broadcasts, but their content is often especially valuable. Even college lectures may supply excellent speech material.

Note taking is an important skill to acquire. Anyone who can write can take notes of one sort or another. Taking good notes requires not only the ability to listen well, but it also demands some general background in the subject at hand. Otherwise, it is difficult to make a proper distinction between what is essential and what is not. Indiscriminately made notes are either unnecessarily voluminous because they are filled with unimportant data, or they are too sketchy because the notetaker fails to put down important facts.

A practice that is helpful in taking notes is to keep paper and a pencil near at hand. Some people carry a notebook with them at all times so that they can jot down ideas as they occur. In this way, otherwise vagrant and fleeting thoughts, references, examples, and quotations can be captured and preserved.

The Library

By far the richest source of speech materials (indeed, of knowledge of all kinds) is a well-supplied library. Yet for many students a library is like a lost gold mine of fabulous wealth. They want the gold and are willing to work to dig it out, but they can't find the lode. A few nuggets fall into their hands by chance, but the real riches are never uncovered.

Each library has a systematic method of cataloguing and arranging materials, and these methods must become familiar to the one who uses the library. If you do not understand the card catalog, the use of indexes, or the numbering system in your library, ask a librarian to explain them to you. He will be glad to help. Remember that a librarian is much more than a person who charges out books and collects fines when they are overdue. He is in a very real sense a teacher and is professionally trained for his job. He will be glad to help you find specific pieces of information and to help you familiarize yourself with the resources of the library.

We make some general suggestions about how to find speech materials in the library. It would be virtually impossible to list every available source but we can provide a functional classification of basic materials.

USING THE LIBRARY

The Card Catalog

Much of the material you will use in making speeches will be found in books. The card catalog is a device for locating these books. It is an alphabetically arranged collection of cards listing such bibliographical data as title, author, publisher, date of publication, and other pertinent data. Every book is entered in the catalog with an author card. All but the most general are represented by a title card as well, and these cards will be alphabetically arranged. For nonfiction books, one or more subject entries will also be found. Figures VII-1 to VII-5 are samples of several different kinds of card-catalog entries.

When you use the card catalog and cannot immediately find what you want, look for additional cross-references. If you wanted to explain why President Roosevelt kept the atomic bomb a secret from Vice President Truman, you might look not only under such obvious headings as "Franklin D. Roosevelt," "Harry S. Truman," and "atomic bomb," but under such others as "World War—1939–1945," and "U.S.—Politics and Government."

Special Reference Tools

In addition to the general book collection, a library contains many other sources of information. Among these are standard reference works, magazines, newspapers, pamphlets, and government documents. You will probably find yourself using these sources in preparing speeches at least as much as you use the general book collection but you may know less about them and their indexes than you do about using the card catalog for finding information in books. For this reason we have devised six main categories of information

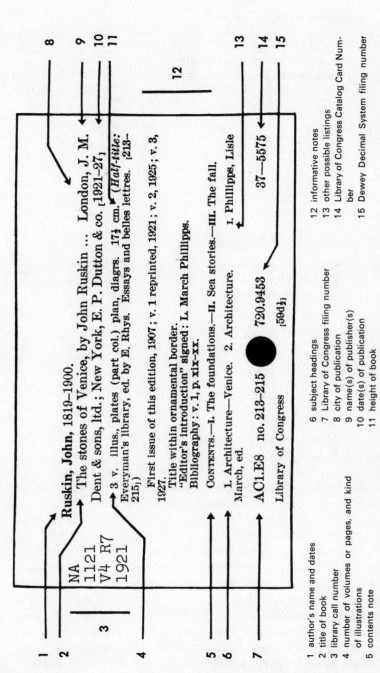

1 — Ruskin, John, 1819–1900.

2 —   The stones of Venice, by John Ruskin ... London, J. M.

3 — NA
1121
V4 R7
1921

Dent & sons, ltd.; New York, E. P. Dutton & co. [1921–27]

4 — 3 v. illus., plates (part col.) plan, diagrs. 17½ cm. *(Half-title:*
Everyman's library, ed. by E. Rhys. Essays and belles lettres. [213–215])

First issue of this edition, 1907; v. 1 reprinted, 1921; v. 2, 1925; v. 3, 1927.

Title within ornamental border.
"Editor's introduction" signed: L. March Phillipps.
Bibliography: v. 1, p. xix–xx.

Contents.—I. The foundations.—II. Sea stories.—III. The fall.

1. Architecture—Venice. 2. Architecture.   I. Phillipps, Lisle
March, ed.

5 —

6 —

7 — AC1.E8   no. 213–215   720.9453   37—5575
                               [59d]

Library of Congress

1 author's name and dates	6 subject headings
2 title of book	7 Library of Congress filing number
3 library call number	8 city of publication
4 number of volumes or pages, and kind	9 name(s) of publisher(s)
of illustrations	10 date(s) of publication
5 contents note	11 height of book

12 informative notes	
13 other possible listings	
14 Library of Congress Catalog Card Number	
15 Dewey Decimal System filing number	

Figure VII–1. A library catalog card, printed for libraries by the Library of Congress. Libraries often add information to these cards and file them under other headings than the author's name, as is explained in other illustrations. The call number is added by the library, according to its own system. When filed in the card catalog at the author's name, as *Ruskin* here, this is the "author" card or the "main entry" card.

Retention as a function of the
method of measurement

BF   **Postman, Leo Jeseph.**
21   Retention as a function of the method of measurement, by
C2   Leo Postman and Lucy Rau. Berkeley, University of Cali-
v.8   fornia Press, 1957.
no.3   217-270 p. diagrs., tables. 24 cm. (University of California publi-
          cations in psychology, v. 8, no. 3)

            Bibliography: p. 269-270.

            1. Memory.   I. Rau, Lucy, 1930–   joint author. II. Title.
          (Series: California. University. University of California publica-
          tions in psychology, v. 8, no. 3)

          BF21.C2   vol. 8, no. 3   154.32   A 57–9951

          California. Univ. Libr
          for Library of Congress   ¡⁵¡†

FIGURE VII–2. A "TITLE" CARD, FOR LIBRARY USERS SEEKING
A BOOK BY ITS TITLE, AS SOME DO WHEN THEY DO NOT KNOW
THE AUTHOR'S NAME. HERE THE TITLE HAS BEEN TYPED ABOVE
THE NAME OF THE AUTHOR; IN SOME LIBRARIES THE TITLE IS
MERELY UNDERSCORED, PERHAPS IN COLORED INK. IN EITHER
CASE THE CARD IS FILED IN ALPHABETICAL POSITION BY TITLE
RATHER THAN BY AUTHOR—THIS CARD WOULD BE AT *Retention*,
NOT AT *Postman*.

which student speakers usually need, and have provided brief ex-
planations of where and how such information is most likely to be
found.

FOR BASIC FACTS AND STATISTICS. The *World Almanac*, the
Information Please Almanac and a number of other such volumes give
a vast amount of specific information. The *Statistical Abstract of the
United States* provides quantitative summary statistics (usually covering 15 to 20 years) on the political, social, and industrial organization of the United States. The *Statesman's Yearbook* gives statistics and
facts on matters which concern the government. *Facts on File* is a
weekly synopsis of world events which, with its index, becomes a
ready reference for a variety of information. The *Congressional
Quarterly* gives a synopsis of federal legislation and the voting records
of senators and representatives.

FOR BRIEF AUTHORITATIVE ARTICLES. For an introductory discussion of a subject, you should go first to an encyclopedia. General
encyclopedias such as the *Britannica* and the *Americana* give information on all phases of human knowledge and their articles usually

Rau, Lucy, 1930-   joint author

BF
21
C2
v.8
no.3

Postman, Leo Jeseph.
    Retention as a function of the method of measurement, by
Leo Postman and Lucy Rau. Berkeley, University of California Press, 1957.

    217–270 p. diagrs., tables. 24 cm. (University of California publi-
cations in psychology, v. 8, no. 3)

    Bibliography: p. 269–270.

    1. Memory.   i. Rau, Lucy, 1930–   joint author. ii. Title.
(Series: California. University. University of California publications in psychology, v. 8, no. 3)

BF21.C2   vol. 8, no. 3   154.32   A 57–9951

California. Univ. Libr
for Library of Congress   [5]†

FIGURE VII–3. A "JOINT-AUTHOR" CARD. THIS CARD IS FILED
IN THE CATALOG AT *Rau*. THE NAME OF THE JOINT AUTHOR
MAY BE TYPED AT THE HEAD OF THE CARD AS HERE, OR MAY BE
MERELY UNDERSCORED. ANOTHER CARD, FILED AT *Postman*, IS THE
"AUTHOR CARD" OR "MAIN ENTRY CARD." CARDS MAY BE PRE-
PARED SIMILARLY, USING INFORMATION ON THE CARD (SEE THE
ARROW), FOR FILING BY THE NAME OF TRANSLATORS, EDITORS,
OR OTHERS, IN ADDITION TO THE "AUTHOR CARD."

include bibliographies to suggest further study. The *Britannica* is
widely considered the best general reference in the humanities while
the *Americana* is thought to be stronger in the areas of science and
technology.

    Specialized encyclopedias are available for more thorough treat-
ment of a subject. To list a representative group we may mention
encyclopedias of *The Social Sciences, Religion and Ethics, World History,
Banking and Finance, The Arts and Sports.* Van Nostrand's *Scientific Encyclopedia,* Grove's *Dictionary of Music and Musicians,* and the *Dictionary
of American History* supply information in the specific areas their titles
name.

FOR MORE EXTENSIVELY DEVELOPED ARTICLES .   Magazines
will probably be your greatest source of current information. The
most common index of such material is the *Reader's Guide to Periodical
Literature.* It indexes a large number of popular periodicals from 1900
to the present. Its entries are arranged in much the same fashion as
the card catalog.

    Except for the card catalog, the *Reader's Guide* is probably the most

Memory

Postman, Leo Jeseph.

BF
21
C2
v.8
no.3

Retention as a function of the method of measurement, by Leo Postman and Lucy Rau. Berkeley, University of California Press, 1957.

217–270 p. diagrs., tables. 24 cm. (University of California publications in psychology, v. 8, no. 3)

Bibliography : p. 269–270.

1. Memory. ɪ. Rau, Lucy, 1930–   Joint author. ɪɪ. Title. (Series: California. University. University of California publications in psychology, v. 8, no. 3)

BF21.C2   vol. 8, no. 3   154.32   A 57–9951

California. Univ. Libr
for Library of Congress   ₍₅₎†

FIGURE VII–4. A "SUBJECT-ENTRY" CARD, USEFUL TO A LI-
BRARY USER WHO KNOWS THE SUBJECT IN WHICH HE WISHES TO
INQUIRE, BUT NOT THE NAMES OF AUTHORS OR TITLES OF BOOKS
IN THE SUBJECT. THIS CARD IS FILED AT *Memory;* THE "MAIN
ENTRY" OR "AUTHOR" CARD IS FILED AT *Postman.* THE SUBJECT
ENTRY IS TYPED OR WRITTEN ABOVE THE NAME OF THE AUTHOR,
SOMETIMES IN RED. IT IS TAKEN FROM THE CARD; NOTE THE ARROW.

used index in the library, but its limitations are too frequently overlooked. Because it indexes only popular magazines, it is of limited
usefulness in investigating more specialized topics. There are too
many specialized indexes to permit a complete enumeration here
but we will list some that should prove useful. The *Social Science and
Humanities Index* (formerly the *International Index*) is an author and
subject index to the scholarly journals in the social sciences and humanities. The *Applied Science and Technology Index* (formerly part of the
Industrial Arts Index) lists articles on business administration, public
administration, and economics. The *Public Affairs Information Service*
indexes a wide variety of books, periodicals, public documents, and
mimeographed material in government, sociology, and business.
The *Agricultural Index*, the *Education Index*, the *Art Index*, and the *Music
Index* catalog periodical literature in their special fields.

The *New York Times* through its index is an especially useful source
of information on current events. This paper prints complete texts of
speeches and documents of public interest. Its treatment of news
items is ordinarily more extensive than that found in other newspapers

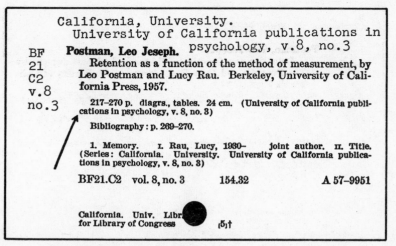

California, University.
University of California publications in
Postman, Leo Joseph. psychology, v.8, no.3
    Retention as a function of the method of measurement, by
Leo Postman and Lucy Rau. Berkeley, University of Cali-
fornia Press, 1957.

    217–270 p. diagrs., tables. 24 cm. (University of California publi-
cations in psychology, v. 8, no. 3)

    Bibliography: p. 269–270.

    1. Memory.   I. Rau, Lucy, 1930–   joint author. II. Title.
(Series: California. University. University of California publications in psychology, v. 8, no. 3)

BF21.C2   vol. 8, no. 3   154.32   A 57–9951

California. Univ. Libr
for Library of Congress   ₍5₎†

FIGURE VII–5. A "SERIES-ENTRY" CARD. THE SERIES ENTRY IS
A FILING DEVICE USED TO BRING ALL WORKS WHICH BELONG TO A
SERIES TOGETHER UNDER THE NAME OF THAT SERIES AS A HEAD-
ING. THIS CARD IS FILED AT *California*. THE "AUTHOR" OR
"MAIN ENTRY" CARD IS FILED AT *Postman*. THE SERIES HEADING
IS ADDED BY THE LIBRARY FROM INFORMATION ON THE CARD;
SEE THE ARROW.

and in the news magazines. Most libraries subscribe to the paper and
keep it on microfilm. The *New York Times Index* locates specific items
in the paper and is an excellent reference tool.

FOR BIOGRAPHY. *Current Biography* is a publication which gives
short useful biographies of living persons. A wide variety of *Who's
Who* books give brief biographical sketches. Webster's *Biographical
Dictionary* contains very brief biographies of a great number of dis-
tinguished persons of all countries and all times. The *Dictionary of
American Biography* sketches the lives of prominent Americans and the
Dictionary of National Biography includes data on the lives of notable
Englishmen. Moreover, all of the specialized encyclopedias men-
tioned earlier contain biographical studies.

The *Biographic Index* is helpful in locating more extended biographies. It is cross-referenced according to the profession or occupation as well as the name of the personages listed and it indexes biographical periodical articles as well as books.

FOR DATES. Dictionaries will supply many of the dates you will
need. The *World Almanac* has a chronological listing of the events of

Basic principles of conservatism
Clinton Rossiter
The conservative says that man is a composite of good and evil. He is not perfect
nor perfectible. No matter what he does he
can never throw off such qualities as
irrationality and selfishness.

Clinton Rossiter, Conservatism in
America, 1955, p. 21.

FIGURE VII–6. A NOTE CARD TO RECORD AN AUTHOR'S IDEA IN WORDS OTHER THAN HIS.

the year previous to its publication. The *New York Times Index* provides the data of events reported in the newspapers.

FOR QUOTATIONS. John Bartlett's *Familiar Quotations* is the best-known source of short quotations. It is arranged chronologically by authors and has a fine index of topics as well. Another source of quotations, Burton E. Stevenson's *Home Book of Quotations*, contains a larger number of entries than Bartlett's book. It is arranged by topics.

METHODS OF RECORDING MATERIAL

The information you wish to consider for your speech should be collected on cards or slips of paper, about 4 × 6 inches. It is perfectly satisfactory to cut $8\frac{1}{2} \times 11$ sheets of paper into four pieces and use these, or you can buy cards at any bookstore. Four items of information should be entered on these cards: (1) a label to identify the material, (2) the author, (3) the information you wish to use, and (4) the necessary bibliographical data. If you prepare note cards carefully, you will need to check the original source only once.

Three useful kinds of cards are illustrated by examples as Figures VII-6, VII-7, and VII-8.

Natural tendency of our economic life is to combination — Justice Oliver Wendell Holmes "It is plain from the slightest consideration of practical affairs, or the most superficial reading of industrial history, that free competition means combination, and that the organization of the world, now going on so fast, means an ever increasing might and scope of combination. It seems to me futile to set our faces against this tendency. (over)

Whether beneficial on the whole, as I think it, or detrimental, it is inevitable, unless the fundamental axioms of society, and even the fundamental conditions of life, are to be changed."

Catherine Drinker Bowen, *Yankee from Olympus*, 1945, p. 330.

FIGURE VII–7. A NOTE CARD RECORDING THE EXACT WORDS OF THE SOURCE MATERIAL.

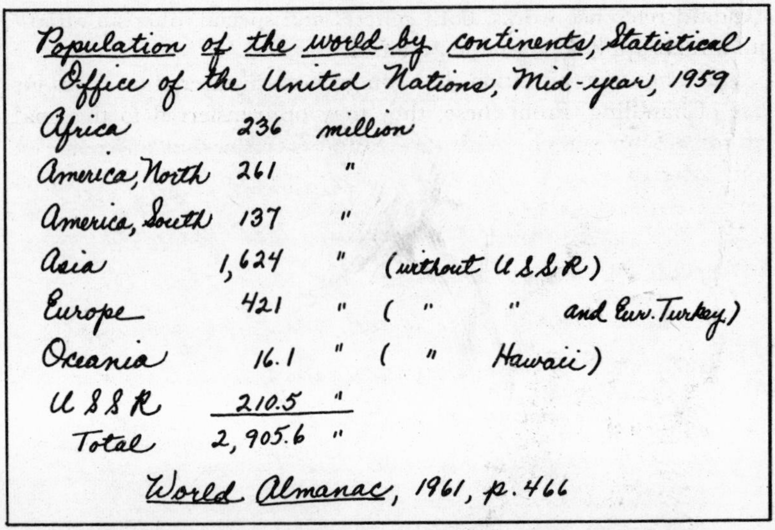

Population of the world by continents, Statistical
Office of the United Nations, Mid-year, 1959
Africa   236   million
America, North 261   "
America, South 137   "
Asia   1,624   "   (without U.S.S.R.)
Europe   421   "   ("   "   and Eur. Turkey)
Oceania   16.1   "   ("   Hawaii)
U.S.S.R.   210.5   "
Total   2,905.6   "
          World Almanac, 1961, p.466

FIGURE VII–8. A NOTE CARD RECORDING FACTUAL DATA FROM
THE *World Almanac*, A SECONDARY SOURCE. THE PRIMARY SOURCE
IS ALSO RECORDED: STATISTICAL OFFICE OF THE UNITED NATIONS.
THE INFORMATION ON THIS CARD IS PART OF A TABLE PRINTED
IN THE *World Alamanc*.

Because the information you gather from all the sources we have
listed may eventually find its way into the outline of your speech,
you will want to make it as easy as possible to handle. Putting each
item on a separate card makes it easy to rearrange the sequence of
cards without excessive rewriting or checking back to your notes.
When the rough draft of your outline has been prepared, you can
decide where the data on each card properly fit into the outline.
When you use note cards in this manner, much of the work in preparing an outline is done automatically, painlessly, and easily.

SUMMARY

The supporting materials for a speech are found in one or the other
of two main sources of information: personal experience or the experience of others. The latter, also called secondary experience, comes
partly from talking with others in conversations and interviews,
and from listening to lectures or to programs on radio or television.
By far the most fruitful source of secondary speech material is the
vast collection of data to be found in any good library. The card
catalog, a great variety of published indexes, and a large number of

standard reference works, both general and special, offer an almost unlimited supply of valuable material.

The items of information that you gather are entered on cards for ease of handling. From these, they may be transferred to the final outline of your speech. With the kind of material that will come to hand when you look diligently and prepare conscientiously, you can make sure that your speeches will show you know what you are talking about. Then you can claim the right to speak and can expect the respectful attention of an audience.

QUESTIONS

1. What is the value of your own experience as a source for supporting material?
2. What is secondary experience?
3. Can a speaker give an unbiased speech?
4. Explain how to go about setting up and conducting an interview.
5. On what basis are books classified in a card catalog?
6. Where would you go to learn basic facts and statistics?
7. What is the value of an encyclopedia?
8. Where are magazines indexed?
9. Draw up a sample note card which records an idea.

EXERCISES

1. Develop a three- to five-minute speech in which the supporting materials are based on personal experience.
2. Develop a three- to five-minute speech in which the supporting materials have been collected in interviews.
3. Answer the following questions using the sources available in the library:
   (a) Where does the phrase "sounding brass" appear in the King James Bible?
   (b) What are the title, publisher, and date of publication of a book by Giles W. Gray and Claude M. Wise?
   (c) What was the date of the first successful fly-by of the planet Mars?
   (d) What was the population of Baltimore in the 1960 census?

(e) Who said, "A great social and economic experiment, noble in motive and far-reaching in purpose," and to what was he referring?

(f) Whom did Ronald Reagan support for the Presidency in 1960?

(g) Where did Robert Kennedy get his undergraduate education?

(h) What football team won the Orange Bowl game in 1958?

(i) How would you describe (briefly) the California condor?

22. Nixon's plan for the U.S. and the world in the '70's.

OUTLINING

I. The purpose of the outline
II. Types of outlines
   A. The scratch outline
   B. The complete-idea outline
      1. Complete sentence
      2. Telegraphic style
   C. The topic outline
III. Techniques of outlining
   A. Parts of the outline
      1. Introduction
      2. Body
      3. Conclusion
   B. Subordination and coordination
      1. Subordinate ideas
      2. Coordinate ideas
      3. Symbols of subordination and coordination
   C. Number of headings
   D. Checking the outline
      1. Logical consistency
      2. Formal correctness
      3. Content completeness of informative outlines
IV. Important technical principles
   A. Each heading a statement
   B. Each heading a single idea
   C. No more than one symbol for any one heading
   D. Headings discrete
   E. Normally at least two coordinate headings at each level
V. Revising the outline
VI. Summary, questions, and exercises

VIII   *OUTLINING*

The ideas and materials of a speech usually come to a speaker in helter-skelter fashion. He gathers his information, arguments, and evidence as he comes across them. When he communicates these to an audience, however, he will certainly profit from presenting them in coherent and orderly sequence and form. Interestingly enough, coherence and order are not essential to communication because everything one says will communicate *something* to an audience. Indeed, it is even possible that an audience will interpret a jumbled message to mean what the speaker intends it to mean. Common sense strongly suggests, however, that if an audience must grasp in perhaps five minutes a message that a speaker may have had five days or even five weeks to prepare, a reasonable sequence and form will improve his chances of being understood *accurately*. Moreover, the *efficiency* of his communication will certainly be increased because the audience requires less effort to understand what a speaker means when he presents his ideas in a coherent order. The greater the ease with which the audience can listen and understand, the greater the chance its interest will be maintained. A valuable method for achieving order and coherence is to outline the speech.

THE PURPOSE OF THE OUTLINE

The basic function of an outline is to make visible to a speaker's eye the relationships his mind sees among the ideas and materials of his speech. It represents on paper the division of ideas suggested by his analysis of the subject; it suggests by the manner in which it groups related materials the logical connections among them; it manifests the coherence, sequence, and form which the speaker's sense of rhetorical effectiveness imposes upon the ideas and materials encompassed by his subject and his purpose. The outline is the speaker's blueprint for his speech.

119

TYPES OF OUTLINES

The Scratch Outline

Almost any group of ideas can be jotted down on paper and called an outline. Such a *scratch* outline might be helpful in beginning to think about a topic but it would serve only poorly as a final means of organizing ideas. Instead, there are two other types of outline which are more useful than the scratch outline at all stages of preparation and in the delivery of the speech.

The Complete-Idea Outline

In the first of these, the *complete-idea* outline, the contents of the outline are fully developed. The complete-idea outline appears in two forms: (1) each idea is stated as a grammatically complete sentence; (2) the full sense of each heading is expressed in a brief telegraphic style similar to that used in newspaper headlines.

> 1. Slums are a serious problem in American cities.
> 2. Slums a serious American problem

The Topic Outline

A second type of useful outline, the *topic* or phrase outline, is written in topic phrases instead of in complete ideas:

> 1. Slums in America

Each of these two forms has its uses. The complete-idea outline is better adapted to a speaking situation that demands close attention to specific statistics, verbatim quotations, and exact language, such as in a formal, detailed report. In its entirety, such an outline will reconstruct for a reader the substance of the speech, even if he did not hear it delivered. Despite these merits, however, the complete-idea outline is inherently susceptible to the danger that the speaker may put into it too much of the language of his speech and thus lose some of the extemporaneity which his speaking ought to have. The topic outline, on the other hand, allows a speaker greater flexibility in detail and language, and is useful in most of the informal speaking situations he meets. In almost all instances, a topic outline will make little sense to anyone except the speaker himself. In general, the more formal a situation, the more complex the material, and the more exact the language required, then the more valuable the complete-idea outline will be. The more informal the situation and the more flexible the material, then the better the topic outline will serve.

TECHNIQUES OF OUTLINING

Parts of the Outline: Introduction, Body, Conclusion

All speeches, assuming them to be substantive in content and substantial in length, have three identifiable parts: a beginning, a middle, and an end. Outlines for speeches mirror these three essential parts in what are called, respectively, an introduction, a body, and a conclusion. A speaker uses each of these parts for its appropriate function.

Though people hear a speaker, they do not inevitably listen to him. But since no speaker can be effective until hearers begin listening, his first job is to make them listen. The devices he uses to catch their attention and arouse their interest, the things he says to make them listen, are included in the first part of the speech and of the outline. Included also are the subject sentence he uses to indicate his purpose in speaking, and any necessary background material. These elements that together make up the first part of the outline are called the *introduction*. After his introduction, the speaker develops his specific purpose in the *body* of the speech. Here he either informs, persuades, or entertains the audience in accordance with his purpose. Finally, he rounds out the speech in the *conclusion*. The following example illustrates the general format of the outline and its parts:

INTRODUCTION
   I. Attention and interest material
  II. Subject sentence of the speech
 III. Background material if necessary
BODY
   I. First main point
  II. Second main point
 III. Third main point
     [And so on]
CONCLUSION
   I. Brief summary of the main points
  II. Restatement of the subject sentence
 III. Remarks that will bring the speech to a graceful close

Subordination and Coordination

The symbol (I, II, 1, 2, A, B, a, b, or the like) that marks each main head and subhead shows the relationship of that heading to others in the outline. The symbol used, and also the degree to which a statement in an outline is indented, indicate the superior, subordinate, or coordinate rank of the statement.

SUBORDINATE IDEAS.   If one idea is derived from another, or is dependent upon another, or is used to support another, it is said to be *subordinate* to the other.

> I. A main head is superior to its subheads.
>   A. Subheads are subordinate to their main heads.

The indenting of the subhead and the use of a different symbol series indicates the subordination to the eye. In the outline, subordinate heads *always follow* the main head.

> *Wrong:* I. Evidence or supporting material, (therefore)
>   A. Main idea
>
> *Right:* I. Main idea (because)
>   A. Evidence or supporting material

This same principle holds true at no matter what level of subordination you are outlining. If, for example, the subhead in the illustration just above were itself in need of further explanation or support, the material used to support it would be placed after A, indented from it, and given a different symbol series to indicate subordination:

> I. First main head
>   A. Support or explanation for I
>   1. Support or explanation for A

For persuasive effect the speaker may wish to develop an idea by presenting first the subheads and then the main head. First, realize that the conventional procedure is far more often used. The danger in the evidence-first plan of outlining, that the speaker may become lost in detail and cause the audience to overlook the main head, cautions against using it without good reason.

However, if a speaker decides to arrange one point in this way he will not materially change from the conventional outline. A change in outline form might be confusing to the eye. Note in the following example the confusion when only a change in a letter, not any change in symbol form or indentation, marks the break from one main idea to another.

    I. First main head
        A. Support for I
        B. Further support for I
        A. Support for II
        B. Further support for II
   II. Second main head
  III. Third main head

The outline is clearer and easier to control if the speaker keeps it in conventional form and adds an arrow to the margin of the paper to remind him that the sequence of delivery is reversed.

    I. First main head
        A. Support for I
        B. Further support for I
   II. Second main head
        A. Support for II
        B. Further support for II
  III. Third main head

COORDINATE IDEAS. If ideas are of equal weight or importance, or if they support the same larger heading, they are said to be coordinate. To illustrate:

    I. First main head
        A. Support or explanation for I
           1. Support or explanation for A
           2. Further support or explanation for A
        B. Further support or explanation for I
           1. Support or explanation for B
           2. Further support or explanation for B
   II. Second main head
        [And so on]

In the outline illustration just above, A and B are coordinate divisions. Statements 1 and 2 under A are in turn coordinate with each other, and by the same token, 1 and 2 under B are coordinate with each other. In every instance, all of the coordinate ideas under the same heading are given an equal degree of indentation and are labeled with consecutive symbols of the same type.

SYMBOLS OF SUBORDINATION AND COORDINATION. The symbols used to show subordination and coordination are purely arbitrary, but custom has established a fairly general usage. Main heads are designated with Roman numerals, first-level subheads with capital letters; then follow Arabic numerals and lower-case letters in that order for further subordination. Any intelligible system of symbols is perfectly satisfactory, provided they are consistent for all of the ideas in a coordinated series, and provided they distinguish subordinate from coordinate ideas. The sequence may be as follows:

> I. First main heading
>   A. Clarification or proof of I
>   1. Clarification or proof of A
>   a. Clarification or proof of 1
>   (1) Clarification or proof of a
>   (a) Clarification or proof of (1)
>   (b) Further clarification or proof of (1)
>   (2) Further clarification or proof of a
>   b. Further clarification or proof of 1
>   2. Further clarification or proof of A
>   B. Further clarification or proof of I
> II. Second main heading
>   [And so on]

Number of Headings

The process of arranging the materials of a speech into a series of main heads and subheads that show proper coordination and subordination, will raise the question as to how many headings may be used at any given level of subordination. There is no definite answer beyond saying that the number of headings depends entirely upon what a speaker thinks will accomplish his purpose. For the main heads this number will usually be somewhere between two and five. It is quite possible, however, for a very brief speech to develop a single main head to explain one aspect of a subject in informative speaking, or to develop a single argument in persuasive speaking. Using more than five main headings will ordinarily make it difficult for an audience to remember very many details of what the speaker has said.

Checking the Outline

As the outline develops, it should be checked for logical consistency and formal correctness.

LOGICAL CONSISTENCY. Since the major purpose of outlining materials is to blueprint a speech and to put order into ideas, logical
consistency is an absolute requirement for the outline itself. It is
met by making sure that the coordination and subordination indicated by the outline are present in the ideas themselves. Suppose, for
example, that a speaker arguing for the creation of a metropolitan
transit authority were to organize a section of his outline thus:

    I. Residents of Los Angeles are facing a crisis in trans-
       portation.
      A. Responsible and informed citizens agree some-
         thing must be done.
        1. . . . .
        2. . . . .
        3. . . . .
      B. Traffic congestion is at a breakdown point.
        1. . . . .
          a. . . . .
          b. . . . .
        2.   Approximately 600,000 automobiles enter
           and leave the downtown area of Los Angeles
           every 24 hours.
          a. Most cars carry only one person: the
            average is 1.4 persons per car.
          b. More than half come and go between 7
            and 9 a.m. and 4 and 6 p.m.
          c. Rush-hour traffic is mainly one way.
            (1) Morning traffic mostly inbound
            (2) Evening traffic mostly outbound
          d. Cars are expensive to operate.

This organization would have told us that d is subordinate to 2 and
that idea d helps to support or clarify idea 2. Clearly, though, the
idea that cars are expensive to operate has no direct connection with
the idea that a number of automobiles enter and leave downtown
Los Angeles every day. Nor does the idea that driving a car is expensive help to show the truth of the idea B that traffic congestion is at a
breakdown point. In no logical sense, then, is d subordinate to either
2 or B. Instead, the idea that cars are expensive to operate is much
more directly connected with the idea in the main head I. Its logical
purpose in the speech is to help show the urgency and magnitude of
the problem itself. Its place in the outline should correspond. Since
it has the same purpose as A (agreed citizenry) and B (traffic conges-

tion), subhead d under 2 is really coordinate with A and B and should become C in the outline.

The corrected outline would then look like this:

I. Residents of Los Angeles are facing a crisis in transportation.
   A. Responsible and informed citizens agree something must be done.
      1. . . . .
      2. . . . .
      3. . . . .
   B. Traffic congestion is at a breakdown point.
      1. . . . .
         a. . . . .
         b. . . . .
      2. . . . .
         a. . . . .
         b. . . . .
            (1) . . . .
            (2) . . . .
   C. Cars are expensive to operate.

FORMAL CORRECTNESS. Many of the problems of logical consistency can be eliminated in the process of making the speech outline formally correct; they can be, that is, if the techniques of outlining are properly used. And the formal correctness of all speech outlines can be checked effectively by a simple and mechanical method.

To see how, begin by observing and reviewing the organization of the persuasive speech. The purpose of the speech is to build acceptance of a proposition. In the outline, main ideas are listed as main heads and are followed by supporting subheads. Main heads (I, II, and so on) are subordinate to the proposition itself. All coordinate divisions of the outline, taken together, should prove the heading to which they are in common subordinate. To illustrate:

The speaker's propostion should be accepted *for*
   I. The first main argument supports it. [The first main argument I is true] *for*
      A. The first subhead supports I. [The first subhead A in turn is true] *for*
         1. This piece of evidence supports A, *and* [A is true also because]

    2. This piece of evidence likewise supports A,
       and [I is true also because]
  B. The second subhead supports I. [The second sub-
    head B in turn is true] *for*
    1. This piece of evidence supports B, *and* [B is
       true also because]
    2. This piece of evidence likewise supports B, *and*
       [the speaker's proposition is true also because]
II. The second main argument supports it. [The second
  main argument II is true] *for*
  [And so on]

To check the outline of a persuasive speech, <u>add the word</u> *for* to
<u>the end of each statement</u> in the outline *which is followed immediately
by a subordinate point.* Add the word *and* to the end of each statement in
the outline *which is followed immediately by a <u>coordinate</u> point or by a larger
heading.* The skeleton looks like this:

    The proposition should be accepted *for*
    I. Helps to prove the proposition *for*
      A. Helps to prove I *for*
        1. Helps to prove A *and*
        2. Also helps to prove A *and*
      B. Helps to prove I *for*
        1. Helps to prove B *and*
        2. Also helps to prove B *and*
    II. Helps to prove the proposition *for*
    [And so on]

This word *for* signifies the various expressions associated with the
logical relation of subordinate points to their superior head. If *for*
seems incongruous when it is applied as a test, apply one of these
other expressions: *because, for instance, in the same way that, as is shown by,
as authorities agree.*

Checking an outline by this *for-and* scheme is relatively simple.
If the outline is in topical form, the complete ideas must be imagined.

The outline of an informative speech can be <u>tested for formal cor-</u>
rectness by mentally adding in front of subordinate points such con-
<u>nective phrases</u> as *for example* and *that is to say.* In coordinate positions
use such words as *moreover, furthermore, in addition.*

CONTENT COMPLETENESS OF INFORMATIVE OUTLINES. The
outline of an informative speech can also be tested by a system of add-

ing ideas. The coordinate headings taken together should add up to no more and no less than their superior head. Consider the following:

Specific purpose
I. . . . .
      A. . . . .
      B. . . . .
            1. . . . .
            2. . . . .
II. . . . .
      A. . . . .
      B. . . . .

$$\text{I.B.1.} + \text{I.B.2.} = \text{I.B}$$
$$\text{I.A} + \text{I.B} = \text{I}$$
$$\text{II.A} + \text{II.B} = \text{II}$$
$$\text{I} + \text{II} = \text{Specific purpose}$$

The following outline would be found faulty because it has more in it than the specific purpose sets forth:

Specific purpose: To inform the audience of the species of trout in the Sierra Nevada Mountains.

   I. My trip to the Sierra last summer
  II. How to fish for trout
 III. Rainbow trout
 IV. Brook trout
  V. Brown trout
 VI. Golden trout

The first two points, while they may be interesting, are pieces of major material that make the six points, when added, total to more than the specific purpose.

The body of the same speech might be so divided that it would total to less than the specific purpose.

   I. Rainbow trout
  II. Brook trout
 III. Brown trout
 IV. Golden trout

This outline does not include enough: lacking such items as "cutthroat trout" (among several others), it totals only to "*some* species of trout," not to "*the* species of trout."

The speaker may have reason for not discussing the omitted point.

It could well be the lack of speaking time. But where time or other conditions force a speaker to exclude a point, this fact should be accounted for in the background material or by a narrowed subject sentence.

Unless a speaker uses this system of testing by addition, he may also produce an outline which contains both too much and too little, in that it includes extraneous items and omits others that are essential:

> *Specific purpose:* To inform the audience of the species of trout in the Sierra Nevada Mountains.
>
>   I. How to fish for trout
>   II. Rainbow trout
> III. Brook trout
> IV. Brown trout

The examples given here are of main points as they relate to the specific purpose. The same principle applies to lower levels of subordination.

IMPORTANT TECHNICAL PRINCIPLES

Each Heading a Statement

Each of the points in an outline, both main heads and subheads, should be a statement. Do not use a question as an outline heading. The major fault with questions in the outline is that there can be no clear relationship between a question and either a superior or a subordinate point. Because a question makes no definite statement, it cannot be proved and it cannot be used as supporting material to clarify or to prove. Moreover, if a heading is phrased as a question, none of the suggested methods of testing the outline can be applied. The injunction against questions *in the outline* does not mean that you should avoid rhetorical questions *in the delivery of your speech.* An outline, however, shows the logical structure of a speech. As such, it should answer questions, not ask them.

> *Wrong:* What are the two basic types of evidence?
> *Right:* There are two basic types of evidence.

Each Heading a Single Idea

Each of the headings in an outline should contain a single idea. An outline is not an essay with numbered paragraphs. Moreover,

the purpose of the outline is to show the <u>logical relationships</u> among
the individual ideas. These relationships are not properly shown if
more than one idea is put into a single heading.

Wrong:
1. A six-year traffic survey in Los Angeles demonstrates an interesting paradox. Though approximately the same number of persons daily come in
   and out of the downtown area, traffic has increased
   20 percent.

Wrong:
1. A six-year traffic survey in Los Angeles demonstrates the interesting paradox that approximately
   the same number of persons daily come in and out
   of the downtown area, but that traffic has increased
   20 percent.

Right:
1. A six-year traffic survey in Los Angeles demonstrates an interesting paradox.
   a. Approximately the same number of people daily
      come in and out of the downtown area.
   b. Traffic has increased 20 percent.

No More Than One Symbol for Any One Heading

To label a single item in the outline as both I and A or both A and 1
is illogical. It suggests that a subordinate point is its own main head,
which is, of course, impossible. When a double symbol is used, it
ordinarily means that the writer of the outline has a series of subordinate points and senses that they need a head, but has not devised
it.

Wrong:
I. A. . . . . . .
   B. . . . . . .

Right:
I.   . . . . .
   A.   . . . .
   B.   . . . .

Wrong:
I.   . . . . .
   A. 1. . . .
      2. . . .
   B.   . . .

Right:
I.   . . . . .
   A.   . . . .
      1.   . . .
      2.   . . .
   B.   . . . .

Headings Discrete

There should be no overlapping among the divisions of an outline. Advocating the repeal of child-labor laws, one speaker argued that other cities in the nation might derive the benefits Philadelphia got from its work-school program initiated to combat the labor shortage of the Second World War. Here is a part of the argument:

I. The wartime work-school program was of great value in Philadelphia.
   A. The program helped reduce the number of dropouts from school.
   B. The program taught initative and responsibility.
   C. Young people gained a new sense of importance from contributing to the family's resources.
   D. Discipline problems at home and at school diminished.

Notice that subpoint B overlaps both C and D. These two points (C and D), instead of being coordinate with B, are really pieces of evidence to show that B is true. They are effects of B. They should be subpoints 1 and 2 subordinated *under* B.

Normally at Least Two Coordinate Headings at Each Level

The purpose of subordinate statements in an outline is to break down the idea contained in the main head, to show its parts or to show how it was arrived at. When an outline contains a single subheading it is not usually a true logical division of the idea to which it is subordinated. Instead, it is most often a restatement of the same idea with greater specification of detail.

Wrong:
   A. The President threatened to veto the bill increasing social-security payments if the increase was too big.
      1. He said the increase must not be more than 7 percent.

Right:
   A. The President threatened to veto the bill increasing social-security payments if the increase was more than 7 percent.

The general exclusion of one-point subordinations does not necessitate exclusion of evidence. You may want to furnish a single piece of evidence or supporting material, an example, or a statistic. By all means do so. In such instances it is quite proper to use a one-point subhead.

Right:
  A. Most cars on the freeways in Los Angeles carry only 1 person:
     1. The average is 1.4 persons per car.

Right:
  A. Americans are often chauvinistic:
     1. American tourists frequently belittle the customs of the countries they visit.

REVISING THE OUTLINE

The first outline of a speech is usually weak. Oftentimes it is little more than the scratch outline mentioned earlier. Usually, when you begin to think about a topic, you lack detailed information and often fail to see the ideas in clear perspective. Moreover, as you gather information and as your ideas develop, you see that relationships you first perceived do not exist. New ideas come into the picture and less adequate ones are discarded. As your knowledge and understanding develop, you see the need for revision of the outline, both for clarity and for forcefulness of presentation. A constant examination of the outline will be necessary, even to the actual moment of speaking.

SUMMARY

In outlining, keep the following points in mind:

1. A complete-idea outline is preferable.
2. Partition the main ideas into a series of distinct, coordinate headings.
3. If a heading is not an immediately self-evident and self-explanatory statement, develop it with a minimum of two subheads.
4. Use statements, not questions, to express ideas.
5. Use proper indentations and symbols to show coordination and subordination accurately. Use one symbol per idea, one idea per symbol.
6. Check the outline for logical consistency and formal correctness.

7. Check the informative outline for completeness by applying the test of addition.
8. Revise the outline as necessary for greater clarity and force.

QUESTIONS

1. What is the purpose of an outline?
2. When is a complete-idea outline the best and when is a topic outline better?
3. Give the general format of a speech showing what goes into the Introduction, the Body, and the Conclusion.
4. Explain subordination and coordination.
5. How should the speaker mark his outline to help him where he wants to deliver the evidence before stating the idea it supports?
6. What is the customary order of subordination in which the various symbols are used?
7. How many main headings should a speech have? Why?
8. How can the outline be tested by a system of adding ideas?
9. The text gives five technical principles for outline development. Explain the three you feel are most important.
10. How much should an outline be revised?

EXERCISES

1. Using the following points, make an outline for the body of a speech showing subordination and coordination by the use of correct symbols and indentations. First find your main heads (there are two of them), then look for the subheads, then proceed to further levels of subordination.

Specific purpose: To inform the audience about the major activities open to students on a college campus

1. Students attend classes
2. Pamphlets
3. There are extracurricular activities
4. Plays
5. Students plan and attend their own social events

6. College football team
7. College fencing team
8. Volleyball
9. They take tests
10. Periodicals
11. Students have a variety of cultural activities outside the classroom
12. College track team
13. Art exhibits
14. Softball
15. Dances
16. College basketball team
17. The primary activities on a college campus are curricular
18. Books
19. College wrestling team
20. Golf club
21. Parties
22. College baseball team
23. Students use the library as a source of information
24. Clubs and fraternities have a league
25. They write papers and deliver speeches
26. Maps
27. Touch football
28. Concert series
29. Tennis club
30. They listen to lectures by the instructor
31. Students attend athletic events as spectators and participants
32. Swimming club
33. Intercollegiate athletics
34. Lecture series
35. Minor sports
36. They engage in class discussions
37. Major sports
38. After-school sports are available
39. Intramural athletics

2. State the specific purpose of the following speech and then outline it. This speech was delivered by President Lyndon B. Johnson at the University of Michigan Commencement, June 1964.

THE GREAT SOCIETY

President Hatcher, Governor Romney, Senators McNamara and Hart, Congressman Meader, and Congressman Staebler, other members of the fine Michigan delegation, members of the graduating class, my Fellow Americans:

It is a great pleasure to be here today. This University has been coeducational since 1870, but I do not believe it was on the basis of your accomplishments that a Detroit high school girl said, "In choosing a college, you first have to decide whether you want a coeducational school or an educational school."

Well, we can find both here at Michigan, although perhaps at different hours.

I came out here today very anxious to meet the Michigan student whose father told a friend of mind that his son's education had been a real value. It stopped his mother from bragging about him.

I have come today from the turmoil of your Capitol to the tranquility of your campus to speak about the future of our country. The purpose of protecting the life of our Nation and preserving the liberty of our citizens is to pursue the happiness of our people. Our success in that pursuit is the test of our success as a nation. For a century we labored to settle and to subdue a continent. For half a century we called upon unbounded invention and untiring industry to create an order of plenty for all of our people. The challenge of the next half century is whether we have the wisdom to use that wealth to enrich and elevate our national life and to advance the quality of our American civilization.

Your imagination, your initiative and your indignation will determine whether we build a society where progress is the servant of our needs, or a society where old values and new visions are buried under unbridled growth. For in your time we have the opportunity to move not only toward the rich society and the powerful society, but upward to the Great Society. The Great Society rests on abundance and liberty for all. It demands an end to poverty and racial injustice, to which we are totally committed in our time. But that is just the beginning. The Great Society is a place where every child can find knowledge to enrich his mind and to enlarge his talents. It is a place where leisure is a welcome chance to build and reflect, not a feared cause of boredom and restlessness. It is a place where the city of man serves not only the needs of the body and the demands of commerce, but the desire for beauty and the hunger for community.

It is a place where man can renew contact with nature. It is a place which honors creation for its own sake and for what it adds to the understanding of the race. It is a place where men are more concerned with the quality of their goals than the quantity of their goods. But most of all, the Great Society is not a safe harbor, a resting place, a final objective, a finished work. It is a challenge constantly renewed, beckoning us toward a destiny where the meaning of our lives matches the marvelous products of our labor.

So I want to talk to you today about three places where we begin to build the Great Society—in our cities, in our countryside, and in our classrooms. Many of you will live to see the day, perhaps fifty years from now, when there will be 400 million Americans; four-fifths of them in urban areas. In the remainder of this century, urban population will double, city land will double, and we will have to build homes, highways and facilities equal to all those built since this country was first settled. So in the next forty years we must rebuild the entire urban United States.

Aristotle said, "Men come together in cities in order to live, but they remain together in order to live the good life."

It is harder and harder to live the good life in American cities today. The catalogue of ills is long: There is the decay of the centers and the despoiling of the suburbs. There is not enough housing for our people or transportation for our traffic. Open land is vanishing and old landmarks are violated. Worst of all, expansion is eroding the precious and time-honored values of community with neighbors and communion with nature. The loss of these values breeds loneliness and boredom and indifference. Our society will never be great until our cities are great. Today the frontier of imagination and innovation is inside those cities, and not beyond their borders. New experiments are already going on. It will be the task of your generation to make the American city a place where future generations will come, not only to live, but to live the good life.

I understand that if I stay here tonight I would see that Michigan students are really doing their best to live the good life.

This is the place where the Peace Corps was started. It is inspiring to see how all of you, while you are in this country, are trying so hard to live at the level of the people.

A second place where we begin to build the Great Society is in our countryside. We have always prided ourselves on being not only America the strong and America the free, but America the beautiful. Today that beauty is in danger. The water we drink, the food we eat, the very air that we breathe, are threatened with pollution. Our parks are overcrowded. Our seashores overburdened. Green fields and dense forests are disappearing.

A few years ago we were greatly concerned about the Ugly American. Today we must act to prevent an Ugly America.

For once the battle is lost, once our natural splendor is destroyed, it can never be recaptured. And once man can no longer walk with beauty or wonder at nature, his spirit will wither and his sustenance be wasted.

A third place to build the Great Society is in the classrooms of America. There your childrens' lives will be shaped. Our society will not be great until every young mind is set free to scan the farthest reaches of thought and imagination. We are still far from that goal. Today, eight million adult Americans, more than the entire population of Michigan, have not finished five years of school. Nearly 20 million have not finished eight years of school. Nearly 54 million, more than one-quarter of all America, have not even finished high school.

Each year more than 100,000 high school graduates, with proved ability, do not enter college because they cannot afford it. And if we cannot educate today's youth, what will we do in 1970 when elementary school enrollment will be five million greater than 1960? And high school enrollment will rise by five million. College enrollment will increase by more than three million. In many places, classrooms are overcrowded and curricula are outdated. Most of our qualified teachers are underpaid, and many of our paid teachers are unqualified. So we must give every child a place to sit and a teacher to learn from. Poverty must not be a bar to learning, and learning must offer an escape from poverty.

But more classrooms and more teachers are not enough. We must seek an educational system which grows in excellence as it grows in size. This means better training for our teachers. It means preparing youth to enjoy their hours of leisure as well as their hours of labor. It means exploring new techniques of teaching, to find new ways to stimulate the love of learning and the capacity for creation.

These are three of the central issues of the Great Society. While our government has many programs directed at those issues, I do not pretend that we have the full answer to those problems. But I do promise this: We are going to assemble the best thought and the broadest knowledge from all over the world to find those answers for America. I intend to establish working groups to prepare a series of White House conferences and meetings on the cities, on natural beauty, on the quality of education, and on other emerging challenges. And from these meetings and from this inspiration and from these studies we will begin to set our course toward the Great Society.

The solution to these problems does not rest on a massive program in Washington, nor can it rely solely on the strained resources of local authority. They require us to create new concepts of cooperation, a creative federalism, between the national capitol and the leaders of local communities.

Woodrow Wilson once wrote: "Every man sent out from his university should be a man of his Nation as well as a man of his time."

Within your lifetime powerful forces, already loosed, will take us toward a way of life beyond the realm of our experience, almost beyond the bounds of our imagination. For better or for worse, your generation has been appointed by history to deal with those problems and to lead America toward a new age. You have the chance never before afforded to any people in any age. You can help build a society where the demands of morality, and the needs of the spirit, can be realized in the life of the Nation. So will you join in the battle to give every citizen the full equality which God enjoins and the law requires, whatever his belief, or race, or the color of his skin? Will you join in the battle to give every citizen an escape from the crushing weight of poverty? Will you join in the battle to make it possible for all nations to live in enduring peace as neighbors and not as mortal enemies? Will you join in the battle to build the Great Society, to prove that our material progress is only the foundation on which we will build a richer life of mind and spirit?

There are those timid souls who say this battle cannot be won, that we are condemned to a soulless wealth. I do not agree. We have the power to shape the civilization that we want. But we need your will, your labor, your hearts, if we are to build that kind of society.

Those who came to this land sought to build more than just a new country. They sought a free world.

So I have come here today to your campus to say that you can make their vision our reality. Let us from this moment begin our work so that in the future men will look back and say: It was then, after a long and weary way, that man turned the exploits of his genius to the full enrichment of his life.

Thank you. Goodbye.

ATTENTION AND RESPONSE

I. The nature of attention
  A. Attention factors
    1. Intensity
    2. Change
    3. Unity
    4. Familiarity
    5. Novelty
    6. Repetition
  B. Principles in the use of attention factors
    1. Attention factors should appear throughout the speech
    2. Attention factors should be emphasized in the introduction
    3. Attention factors should be pertinent to the speech
    4. Attention factors should be appropriate to the interests of the audience
II. Determinants of response
  A. Habits
  B. Set
  C. Values
  D. Suggestion
  E. Projection
III. Summary, questions, and exercises

IX

ATTENTION AND RESPONSE

From a psychological standpoint, a book about speech is a study of perception. It examines the ways in which a speaker may encourage a listener to receive sensory impressions and then to perceive their meanings. The speaker has an idea; he wants his listeners to understand it. He wants that idea to be reproduced in the listener's awareness in such a way that it will have essentially the same meaning and significance for the listener that it has for him.

The speech serves as a kind of map. It is a complex series of reference points made up of literally thousands of visual and auditory impressions which merge to form for the listener a single, over-all interpretation of the idea. The listener's perception of the speaker's idea is analogous to the traditional psychological concept of stimulus-response.

When a psychologist uses these terms, he is speaking of a single unit of energy directed at a single receptor to which the receptor will respond in some observable way. The speaking situation, however, is a complex of interacting stimulus-response relationships. The speaker initiates whole complexes of stimuli to which he asks the audience to attend and eventually respond. The listener's response is no less complex than the speaker's stimulus. From each momentary complex of stimuli, a listener abstracts and selects what he will respond to on the basis of his needs, attitudes, and expectancies. His responses take a multitude of forms ranging from overt action to contemplation. A new speaking situation is created every time the complex of stimuli presented by a speaker or the response of the audience changes.

Two aspects of perception, then, are important to a speaker: the stimuli which he conveys, and the response which the audience makes to them. The success of the speaker's communication depends upon the extent to which he can command the attention of the audience and control the audience's selection of the parts of the speaker's message to which it will respond.

This chapter will consider these two aspects: the factors which determine the attention value of the stimulus complex conveyed by the speaker, and the role of the listener's needs, attitudes, and expectancies in determining his response.

THE NATURE OF ATTENTION

In every speaking situation, a listener has a multitude of stimuli to which he might give attention. He is being continually bombarded by stimuli from the room, the seating, the temperature, the outside noises, the people around him, and his own objective and subjective concerns apart from the speaking situation. The speaker's problem is to cause the listener to give attention to the particular group of stimuli he provides. The speaker must make himself (and his message) the predominant element in this ocean of sensations. He must stand out as a striking figure against a pale background. To do this he must make use of factors in his speech which focus the attention of the audience on what he has to say.

But attention span is quite short. No person can completely concentrate on a single group of stimuli for more than a brief time. Thereafter, his attention will wander and the speaker will be pushed into the background by competing sensations whose attention values had previously been ignored. For this reason, the speaker must provide a continuing pattern of stimuli which command the listener's attention.

In the moment of perception, the listener's interests leap out to anticipate and mix with the speaker's presentation so that a unification of stimulus and response occurs. For purposes of analysis, however, the speaker's presentation can be examined apart from the listener's interpretation. This presentation, the stimuli initiated by the speaker, can make use of certain intrinsic characteristics of stimulation which command attention apart from the listener's interests. Let us examine these attention factors now.

Attention Factors

Six factors will normally command attention regardless of the selectivity of the listener. These are: intensity, change, unity, familiarity, novelty, and repetition.

INTENSITY. Among a group of stimuli, listeners will tend to respond to those which are most intense. Thus, a loud noise, a bright light, or a strong smell will attract attention. To the speaker, this means that the stimuli he conveys must be the most intense in the room. He must be louder than the general babble around him. He must be more forceful in stating his case than his competitors.

Intensity here does not mean just loudness or gross physical gesture. It includes, also, the speaker's attitude toward the situation and his subject. If his attention seems to wander, if he looks out the window, if his arguments sound copied without interpretation from last month's *Reader's Digest*, if the total impression which the audience gets is that he doesn't really care, he can be said to lack intensity. If he wants an audience to pay attention to what he says, a speaker must show that the subject he discusses is of concern to him and that he has a commitment to his own convictions.

CHANGE. If intensity were the only criterion, then the loudest, most positive, and most physically active speaker would get the most attention. You know that he does not. You know that unrelieved intensity in speakers frequently makes listeners tired of hearing them. The intensity of loudness, for instance, can be so constant that it becomes a general characteristic of the occasion. It has nothing about it which sets it apart from the background and it is, therefore, no longer useful in differentiating the speaker from competing stimuli. The audience's attention moves as yours does when you are studying in your room and someone begins to use the typewriter. It attracts your attention because it is different from the stimuli you have become used to. As you become habituated to the sound, however, it fades into the background and as you study you do not even hear the typewriter. This fading is an example of the way we attend to *changes* in the nature and intensity of stimuli more than we do to a continuous level of stimulation.

Not all stimulation which involves change will command attention. A repeated pattern of flashing lights, like a neon sign above a grocery store, fades into the background of attention after the viewer becomes habituated to the patterned change. A speaker with a sing-song pattern of speech changes his pitch and quality but, once the listener finds the pattern, the speaker's rhythmic patterned changes command as little attention as a monotone.

Speakers make use of change to build attention and thus give greater emphasis to ideas. If, at certain points in the speech, you

seem more intent, argue more carefully, and heighten the motivational aspects (more about these in Chapter XI), your audience will
give more attention to those points. You can thus direct the attention
of the audience to your major ideas. But observe care not to emphasize
minor points in this way, or the audience will pay more attention
to them. You would be putting them in the foreground of your listeners' observation and relegating your major points to the background. Frequently a speaker is confused by the listener's insistence
that he did not "hear" a point when the speaker is sure that he "said"
it. Both listener and speaker are right. The speaker "said" what he
thought he said, but not in a way that made the listener "hear"
it. The listener did not perceive from the speaker's manner that the
point was important, so he either ignored it or forgot it.

UNITY.   If speaking were like the visual perception of a bright
light, which is a single stimulus, intensity and change could be
regulated more conveniently. But speaking is not this simple. It
involves subtle abstractions of language and logic; it involves a
visual image which is not a single strong light but many different
stimuli which reach the eye from clothes, stance, facial expression,
and movement. The vocal characteristics of pitch, force, time, and
quality also provide multiple impressions. Over and above such
external stimuli as the hard seats, the ventilation, the whispering
in the row behind him, the listener receives millions of stimuli from
the speaking situation. If he is to comprehend them, they must be
organized. The speaker must, therefore, order his actions so that at
any given moment the listener will receive all the discrete stimuli
as if they were one.

Ideally, every movement and change in voice should support the
speaker's idea. There must be a focusing of attention: the diverse
stimulus components must be so related to one another that they may
be taken as a whole. An analogous element in visual attention is
sharpness of outline. The speaker must assure himself that all the
stimuli at any given moment focus on a central idea.

It is with the purpose of helping speakers to achieve this focus that
teachers caution against unnecessary physical movements, unusual
patterns of speech, or irrelevant ideas. Unless all stimuli are linked
together as a unified stimulus field, the listener will respond to distracting elements which stand out. These distracting sensations will
produce injurious reactions like: "He kept fumbling with his keys."
"She sounded as if she were 'preaching' to us." "What was all that

talk about his uncle's farm for?" Unless there is unity, the listener may well fail to perceive the central purpose of the speech.

FAMILIARITY. Things which are familiar to an audience will frequently command attention. When the ideas in a speech are unfamiliar to the listeners, their minds will tend to wander, to look for more understandable stimuli, in which they are already interested. The speaker must, therefore, relate his subject to what is familiar to his audience. "You may not know or care what a differential is, but if your car didn't have one you wouldn't be in class today," said one student speaker. "The Chinese food you get in a restaurant is not the same food the people in China eat," said another. In each case the speaker was trying to link his subject to what was familiar to his audience.

NOVELTY. A habitual cigar smoker might give his attention to the sight of a man smoking a cigar. What kind of cigar is he smoking? How many does he smoke per day? Questions like these occur to the cigar smoker; the man who does not smoke cigars is likely to say, "Who cares?" But anyone will pay attention to a woman smoking a cigar. That sight is novel.

The out-of-the-ordinary will almost always attract attention. A student speaker brings a strange machine to class. The members of the audience look up. "I wonder what that is all about," they say to themselves.

While novelty will get immediate attention, it must be linked to the familiar if interest is to be sustained. Most listeners will cease paying attention to a thing after they become aware that it has little to do with their interests.

In Chapter XVI (Speaking to Entertain), the principles of humor will be discussed in greater detail. But it can be noted here that the attention-getting quality of humor is based on its novelty.

REPETITION. Since attention span is short and listeners are continually attracted by competing stimuli, it is quite common for main ideas to be forgotten, even those which have been forcefully stated. One method of reinforcing a listener's attention to an idea is repetition.

Judicious repetition of ideas and phrases will strengthen the speech. The speaker can make use of repetition through parallel sentence structure and phrasing. In one section of his Annual Message of January, 1936, President Franklin D. Roosevelt used fourteen consecutive rhetorical questions beginning with the word "Shall." Ten of the fourteen questions begin with the words "Shall we say." (This passage is quoted at length on pages 222–223.) "That government of the people, by the people and for the people shall not perish from this earth," has a repetition of phrase pattern and words which holds attention. The speaker who weaves each new point into the pattern of his speech by associating it with the central thought uses repetition to reinforce his main idea.

If, however, repetition is used too much or wrongly, it is likely to become all the listener hears; it will draw attention away from important ideas and make the audience conscious only of the repetition. Unconscious periodic repetition of distracting mannerisms like "ah" and "uh" reinforce the unnecessary and force the main idea of the speech into the background.

Principles in the Use of Attention Factors

The factors of attention are valuable in selecting and developing the materials of a speech. These factors are not the only criteria for choosing material, for your first obligation is to select materials that support the central idea of your speech. (Chapter VI has discussed this matter.) But having determined what you want to say, you use the attention factors to help you in achieving your purpose. Look now at some of the principles which should control that use.

ATTENTION FACTORS SHOULD APPEAR THROUGHOUT THE SPEECH.   A speaker needs the attention of his audience through his entire speech. When and if attention lags, something important may be lost. Because the span of attention is quite limited, it must be constantly renewed by the speaker. Material should be selected, points should be organized, and delivery should be used to sustain the attention of an audience from beginning to end.

ATTENTION FACTORS SHOULD BE EMPHASIZED IN THE INTRO-DUCTION.   The first and perhaps the most important point at which attention must be developed is in the introduction of the speech. When a speaker arises, he is, in a sense, a blur of movement, unfocused in the attention of his audience. As he goes to the speaking stand and arranges his notes, he becomes a human being; he has distinctive clothing and a distinctive face. Then he begins to talk. If the audience continues to see just a human being with dark hair, black shoes, blue suit, white shirt, and blue tie, the speaker will not hold attention. So it is that the introductory part of his speech must direct the attention of his hearers to his main idea. If the speaker fails to seize the attention of the audience at the beginning of his speech, it will be extremely difficult to do so later on.

ATTENTION FACTORS SHOULD BE PERTINENT TO THE SPEECH. It is easy for a speaker to catch attention by using methods that are completely extraneous to the ideas in the speech. A young man began a speech one day by holding out his hand at arm's length and dropping a large number of glass marbles on the floor. The marbles made a marvelous flash of color as they rattled and rolled and danced around the room. The audience was immediately and completely attentive— to the marbles, not to the speaker. To make it worse, as soon as they discovered the marbles had nothing to do with the speech, their attention was lost. Such *involuntary* attention is like the response to a sudden bright light, or the firing of a shot. It will not last long and is of little use to a speaker.

Listeners will also give a kind of *voluntary* attention which is motivated by something extraneous to the speech itself. For example, a student may voluntarily set himself to hear a dull lecture because he wants to get a good grade in a class, or a workman will force himself to listen to instructions that he must have in order to hold his job. Outlandish attention techniques will send listeners away remembering the technique and not the idea. "Boy, was he loud!" was a remark we once heard from a listener leaving a lecture hall. "That was really a funny joke he told. I have to remember to tell my wife when I get home," said one man after a political speech. Such reactions as these indicate that what may be popularly regarded as a "good speech" may actually be a poor one because the idea of the speaker is lost in the techniques of attention. The speaker wants responses to his *ideas*. He must be sure, therefore, that his attention techniques complement rather than overshadow the ideas.

ATTENTION FACTORS SHOULD BE APPROPRIATE TO THE INTERESTS OF THE AUDIENCE. The kind of attention a speaker gets when he appeals to the habitual concerns of an audience is the most useful. He must look for the best attention factors in a speech and not just the obvious ones. He looks for the factors which will be close to the experience of the audience, for the ones to which the audience can most easily respond.

DETERMINANTS OF RESPONSE

To this point, our discussion has concerned itself with the speaker's active part in controlling the audience's perception of his ideas.

Through the proper attention factors, he influences the selection and interpretation of the stimuli that compete for the attention of the audience. There are, however, other conditions in the audience itself which help to determine its response. These may be referred to as the determinants of interest.

Five major conditions determine the stimuli to which a member of an audience will respond: habits, set, values, suggestion, and projection.

Habits

People perceive objects and ideas as they have been in the habit of perceiving them. When a sensitive critic looks at a poem, he sees form, idea, quality of language. A dullard sees in poetry only words, and perhaps dull words at that. The one responds to the beauty of the poem, the other to its dullness. The poem is different only in the habitual response of its two readers. Much of education is a process of developing new habits of looking at things. Students learn new habits of perceiving a picture, a microscopic organism, an event in history, a novel, a business organization.

A speaker may change some of his listener's habits but he cannot, with a speech, expect to construct new systems on the instant. Since audiences have certain habits of perception, a speaker must make some adaptation to those habits.

Politicians have learned to say "federal health insurance," instead of "socialized medicine." Psychologists, psychiatrists, and social workers use the term "mental illness" in discussing what used to be called "insanity." Words like "health" and "insurance" evoke favorable habitual responses, while "socialism" and "insanity" tend to evoke habitual negative responses.

Set

The habits in an audience are the personalized, internal dispositions of the individual listeners. The set of the audience is a generalized, external predisposition. Listeners tend to have certain predispositions about what should come from a speaking situation. Their interpretations of what a speaker says are determined in part by their expectations, by their set. We know a man, a clever, witty speaker, who frequently addresses groups of high school students to explain to them, among other things, the entrance requirements of the college he represents. He knows his business and he speaks well.

At the same time, he always manages to amuse the young people he addresses and, as a result, has acquired the reputation of being a very funny man. Some time ago he was invited to deliver the commencement address at the graduation of a high school he had visited on several occasions. He prepared what he intended to be a straightforward and serious set of remarks appropriate to such an occasion. His audience laughed at virtually every sentence he uttered. After some uncomfortable moments of surprise and chagrin, he realized that his audience, many of whom knew him by reputation and many of whom had heard him speak before, *expected* him to be funny and so laughed at everything he said. The lesson to be learned here is that a speaker either must meet the anticipations of his audience or must change its set. If he does not do either, he will be misinterpreted and the response he gets will not be the one he wants.

How would you like to be introduced to an audience of a thousand people in a strange town this way: "And now I give you Miss Mary Watkins, whom we all know as one of the most inspirational speakers of our times. We are all anxious to hear what Miss Watkins has to say to us for we know that our lives will be enriched by her message." If you wanted to fall through the floor at that moment no one could blame you. The chairman establishes a set in the audience which you know you cannot meet. Apropos, a word of warning to chairmen of meetings: give the audience a set which will help the speaker. When you introduce the speaker and his topic, create a favorable impression for them both. But do not make the audience expect too much.

Values

A listener's values will affect his response to a speaker's ideas. Value differences have been demonstrated by an experiment with children and coins. A group of children were shown various coins. A beam of light was then projected on a screen and the children were told to adjust the circle of light to the size of the coins. Invariably, the children from poorer families perceived the coins as larger than they actually were. The coins had a greater value for them than for the other children.

Some audiences see greater value in religious ideas than others. Some audiences will give higher values to athletics, agriculture, politics, or books than others do. A skillful speaker understands the system of values which is operative in an audience and adapts his speaking to it. He may be able to change those values somewhat, but he must not ignore them lest his listeners reject him and lose interest in his ideas.

Suggestion

Suggestion is an important part of the conditioning of an audience. It means simply that a listener is influenced by those around him. One form of political suggestion is known as the "bandwagon" technique. A candidate for office tries to create the impression that there is no doubt he will be elected. If this notion can be established, other politicians and some voters may support him because they want to be on the winning side. In one well-known experiment, an audience was told that a bottle contained a fluid with a strong odor. Each member of the audience was asked to hold up his hand when he could smell the odor. Then the bottle was opened. Actually, there was nothing in the bottle. The most suggestible members of the audience soon put up their hands and others followed. Some never did. One significance of the experiment is the fact that the people who raised their hands later were clustered in groups around the more suggestible whose hands had gone up first. This reaction seems to indicate not only that some people are more suggestible than others, but also that they help to influence those around them.

This fact is important to a speaker. When several individuals agree, they reinforce each other's convictions and modify, by suggestion, the ideas of other listeners in the group.

Projection

Perhaps the most frequently overlooked determinant of a listener's response is the phenomenon of projection. You are aware of the projective techniques used by psychologists. The Thematic Apperception Test presents a series of pictures which are deliberately vague. When a viewer is asked to tell a story based on a picture, he will project himself into the picture and express his underlying values and attitudes. An auditory form of projection technique is the "tautaphone," an instrument which produces meaningless sounds. When a listener is asked to interpret these, he projects his own ideas into the meaningless sounds.

If purposely vague pictures and sounds have meaning because a listener or viewer projects his own ideas into them, is it not also to be expected that listeners will do the same with a vague speech? Listeners not only *accept* or *reject* what a speaker says because of habits, set, values, and suggestions; they actually *change* his ideas to make them mean what they want to hear. The more vague the speech, the more the listener will "hear" you say what his prior notion of you leads him to believe you will say.

For a speaker, the implications of this phenomenon are clear. He must make sure that ideas and words are concrete. He must repeat his main ideas and use specific examples, for if the speaker is vague in word and idea, the listener will fill the gaps with what he wants or expects to hear. Experiments have been conducted with classes of college students who were read a meaningless speech like the one in Chapter XII, "Cooperation—An Opportunity and a Challenge." When asked to explain it, most of the students who thought they understood the speaker's point had heard ideas which were compatible with their own. An overly technical speech will also encourage projection. If a speaker's language is so technical as to be unclear, then a listener who desires to find meaning will project his own meaning, perhaps an incorrect one, into what the speaker says.

Projection can also work to a speaker's advantage. Realizing that a listener has certain interests in an idea, a speaker knows that he need not go into great detail. In argument, for example, some of the steps in the reasoning process are omitted. The audience will fill them in. It is a necessary condition of the speaking situation that no speaker can completely develop all his ideas. Listeners would become bored if they were subjected to every detail. "The Anti-Defamation League," a speaker says, "does a real service for America because it fights discrimination," and the listener projects the essential but missing part of the argument, "discrimination is bad." But note that the possible projections here are limited. Suppose the speaker had said, "The Anti-Defamation League, which does a lot of things, is interested in discrimination, and that is a very controversial topic."

A speaker must know his listeners and build a framework that will cause them to project those ideas which are compatible with the speaker's ideas.

SUMMARY

In addressing an audience, a speaker initiates systems of stimuli which a listener accepts, rejects, or interprets in terms of his own interests. In order that the listener may perceive the speaker's ideas correctly, the speaker uses certain devices to focus the attention of his audience on the central idea of his speech. These devices are called attention factors:

1. Intensity
2. Change
3. Unity
4. Familiarity
5. Novelty
6. Repetition

To make his communication effective, the speaker uses these attention factors throughout the speech, but he applies them with particular care in the introduction. He chooses attention factors that are appropriate to the ideas in his speech and pertinent to the interests of his audience.

Five conditions influence the response which an audience will make to a speaker's message and help to determine whether listeners will select the stimuli the speaker intends them to select:

1. Habits
2. Set
3. Values
4. Suggestion
5. Projection

QUESTIONS

1. How do both speaker and listener affect the way an act of communication takes place?

2. The chapter discusses six different attention factors. What three do you consider most important? Why?

3. How is a singsong pattern of speech like a monotone?

4. What principle of attention is in danger from unnecessary physical movement, unusual patterns of speech, or irrelevant ideas?

5. Why should attention factors be emphasized in the introduction?

6. How valuable to a speaker is involuntary attention in an audience?

7. How do listeners' habits affect their responses?

8. What is set?

9. What kind of a speech will invite the greatest listener projection?

EXERCISES

1. Report some experiences that show how people are suggestible.

2. Develop and bring to class the outlines of two or three different introductions to the same speech, emphasizing different attention factors in each.

3. Write a paper in which you analyze a specific audience, explaining what values you believe would be most significant to them. Consult Chapter V in writing this paper.

4. Evaluate some speech delivered in class in terms of what the speaker did, or failed to do, to arouse your attention and sustain your interest.

ARGUMENT: RATIONAL FUNCTIONS

X

ARGUMENT: RATIONAL FUNCTIONS

Consider two men, neighbors, living side by side for years in friendship and harmony. Assume that these two men hold opinions which make them almost as different as men can be. One drives a Chevrolet; the other prefers a Ford. One is a Dodger fan; the other supports the Braves. The one is a Republican; the other a Democrat. They belong to different churches. One owns his own small business; the other works for wages and, at the place where he is employed, is a union shop steward.

In spite of their thoroughly differing views on these and many other subjects, two such persons might spend years in quite close contact as friends, neighbors, colleagues, or business associates without a word of controversy. The many differences between them will persist without being a source of controversy, however, only as long as neither of them is motivated to change an opinion of the other so that it agrees with his own. At whatever moment either of the two feels the necessity for concurrence between them, passive difference becomes active disagreement. In that moment, arguments are presented and an occasion for persuasive speaking has been created.

Noise, wrangling, and ill temper have come to be so closely associated with argument that it is frequently identified with quarreling. Certainly the effort to resolve differences can be carried on in an atmosphere of harsh, angry words and raised voices, but these are not necessary to disagreement; they are not constituents of argument.

In persuasion, a speaker tries to bring about concurrence with his views by stating and defending the position he holds. The expression he uses to state his position is called a proposition. We have already discussed (Chapter III) the three kinds of propositions which may be advocated by a speaker: propositions of fact, value, and policy. Each of these says what the speaker believes to be the proper answer to the corresponding kind of question. Each of them requires to be justified, for merely expressing an attitude or a belief does not always make it acceptable to others. The process of defending a proposition, of getting it accepted by an audience, is called argumentation. In order to create belief in his proposition, a speaker advances arguments to support it. An argument may be defined as a statement or a group of statements intended to support a proposition.

But let us say a word at this point about what it means to support a proposition. People often talk of "proving" propositions. But the word "prove" or "proof" can be misleading. To prove a mathematical theorem is something different from proving that the state of Indiana is a great place to live.

The difference between the two situations is best understood by distinguishing two different kinds of propositions: The first of these is called *analytic*. We may say, for example, that every angle of a triangle must be less than 180 degrees. Whatever one may mean when he makes such a statement must be understood in relation to what he means by triangle. But the meanings one has for the word triangle (for example, that the sum of its angles is 180 degrees) are such that if he understands what the statement means, he knows it must be true. And that is what it means to say that a statment is analytic: To decide that it has meaning is to know that it is true. To deny the truth of the statement would be a contradiction.

Other propositions are *synthetic*. These are not necessarily true; they need to be verified. "There are more registered Democrats than Republicans in California." "The quarterback is the most important member of a football team." And so on, to include any proposition that might normally be the subject of a speech.

Now, notice the difference between these statements and the kind we have called analytic. To decide that a synthetic statement has meaning, one does not have to admit that it is true. If one understands that the sum of the angles of a triangle is 180 degrees, he would contradict himself by denying that any one angle must be less than 180 degrees. On the other hand, to decide that a synthetic statement has meaning does not require one to admit that it is true. To affirm or deny the statement that the quarterback is the most valuable member of a football team may be either correct or incorrect; it may agree or disagree with whatever evidence exists or with whatever meanings one has for "quarterback," but nothing in the form of the statement makes a denial of it an inherent contradiction. This lack of self-contradiction is the nature of the synthetic statement. From what we have said about analytic and synthetic statements, it is clear that the following statement is analytic: The propositions of persuasive speeches are synthetic.

Even though the propositions of persuasive speeches are synthetic (and therefore require justification), many propositions of policy, of value, and of fact cannot be evidenced as *true*. Many of these, nonetheless, are *believed*. What the arguments of persuasion are intended to do, then, is to *create belief*.

PERSUASION ON RATIONAL AND NONRATIONAL GROUNDS

Assume that a speaker is convinced that segregationist attitudes are diminishing in the South, or that our deficit in the international balance of payments is the most serious economic problem America faces today, or that to combat Communism in Asia, the United States should encourage mutual agreement among Asian nations. When he sets out to persuade others to agree with him, he will find in his audience attitudes, opinions and beliefs which are in conflict with his. These conflicting positions in the audience, however, are not based upon entirely rational grounds. The fact that one can believe a proposition which he cannot know is true, and the fact that he can be led to this belief by what someone else says, clearly indicate that there must be grounds for belief other than reason alone. Human beings have needs, wants, and desires which significantly influence the decisions they make about what to do and the judgments they make about what is good or bad and true or false. The arguments of persuasion, therefore, must meet the demand for both rational and nonrational satisfaction that seems to form the basis for most of what people believe and do: Arguments perform nonrational as well as rational functions. Please note carefully, however, that we are speaking not of what arguments *are* but of what they *do*. To think of one argument as rational and another as nonrational, or to call one argument "logical" and another "emotional" is sheer nonsense. All arguments, in varying proportions, have both properties. It is a matter of *convenience* that we look at the rational and nonrational functions of arguments in separate chapters. Do not let this separate consideration of the two functions arguments perform mislead you into the notion that arguments are of separate, distinguishable kinds. Our purpose in the present chapter is to see how the rational part of argument operates in persuasive speaking.

PROBABILITY AND PROOF

Under ideal conditions, the arguments a speaker uses to persuade would constitute conclusive proof of his proposition. Actual conditions are such, however, that conclusive proof is an unobtainable goal. If certainty were available, persuasion would not be needed, for investigation would bring knowledge and no one can disbelieve what he knows with certainty to be true. Thus, the subjects of persuasive speeches will have at least two sides. Is a factual judgment true or false? Does a person or condition have an alleged merit or lack it? Should a proposed policy be adopted or rejected? Any answer to questions such as these is likely to be controversial. When it is, it will be because the evidence on both sides is so limited and so divided that clear-cut decision is difficult. Consequently, proof in persuasion will not have the force of logical or mathematical demonstration. That is to say proof will not be absolute, for no matter how firmly a conviction may be held, there is always the possibility that it may be wrong.

But on the other hand, it is not enough to prove only that a proposition *can* be true. An audience may readily agree that a candidate elected from one political party *might* be more beneficial to the country in the presidency than the candidate from another. But an honestly concerned voter will normally want stronger grounds than "can" or "might" to vote for either candidate. Therefore a speaker's efforts in persuasion are aimed at proving that his proposition is *probably true*. An audience looks at the two sides of a given proposition, recognizes that there is evidence and argument on both sides, and then gives its assent to the side which seems to have the weight of probability in its favor.

In demonstrating the probability of a proposition, "making a case for it," there is a wide range in the strength the case may have. The proposition can be made to seem only plausible; that is, the audience can agree that there is some reason to believe it might be true. A stronger case is one that shows the proposition is likely to be true. The stronger the likelihood, the stronger the case. An audience is completely satisfied when a speaker's case is so strong that his proposition can be accepted as *true*. In these instances, the listener feels that the proposition is more than likely, that it has more than a good chance of being true. He is convinced; he believes; for him, the proposition is true. This same listener may shift his position later, or new evidence may prove him wrong, but at the moment his decision is reached, he is convinced that the speaker's proposition is true.

For a speaker to win such a reaction from an audience is a goal he should not hope to win on every occasion, or from every audience, or from every member of any given audience. An audience's reactions are not dichotomous—it does not accept or reject the speaker's position in such a degree of black or white. Instead, listeners tend to respond along a continuum of shades of gray. That is to say, instead of expecting an audience to fall into two clearly distinguishable groups, those who agree and those who disagree, a speaker must see his task is to shift attitudes, opinions, and beliefs in the direction he advocates. Thus "possibility," "plausibility," "likelihood," and "assurance" are all reasonable goals for the speaker to seek, depending on his particular audience. Consequently, when a speaker faces an audience hostile to his position, his speaking can be called successful if he produces only a measure of indecision in his listeners' devotion to their opposing point of view.

THE STRUCTURE OF ARGUMENT

It is not totally unreasonable to define logic in persuasive arguments as anything which makes a listener think, "That's logical." And since proof is in the mind of the listener, the definition is indisputable. Perhaps most important for a speaker to remember is that his speaking has effects. He is changing the way people view the world and, like a brain surgeon, he has no right to dabble around in someone's head without the highest qualifications. For the speaker in our culture, this means having the strongest possible evidence and the most rigorous reasoning.

The part that logic plays in persuasive argument is suggested by Bertrand Russell. He says in *The Analysis of Mind* that logic is not interested in what people actually believe but only in the conditions which determine the truth or falsehood of what they might believe. But since so many of the propositions that people do in fact believe cannot be proved true or false, logic has severe limitations as an instrument for determining whether the beliefs of people are right or wrong.

In persuasion, then, a speaker presents *arguments* which are, as we have said, statements or groups of statements purporting to *justify* his position by giving his listeners *reasons to believe* what he says is *true*. But there is a difference between a "good reason" for, or a "justification" of a proposition, and "proof" of it in an absolute sense. The part logic plays in the process is not to determine whether what the speaker says is in fact true but rather to determine whether his arguments embody adequate *rational* grounds for believing it to be true.

Every argument in persuasion performs an identifiable operation: it presents (or suggests) evidence and specifies the implications of that evidence. The common practice is to speak of the evidence as the "premises." The implications are stated in what is called the "conclusion."

Traditionally, arguments are considered to be of two types: deductive and inductive. For both kinds of arguments the claim is made that their premises provide evidence for the conclusion, that the conclusion follows from the premises. Only in the case of deductive argument, however, is the claim made that the premises provide *conclusive* evidence. In a properly formulated deductive argument, the conclusion follows *necessarily* from the premises. Inductive arguments are those whose premises offer *some* evidence of the truth of the conclusion. The degree to which the premises of an inductive argument support the conclusion will vary with the amount and quality of the evidence. In no case, however, will an inductive argument provide conclusive proof of the conclusion. Here is a brief examination of the structure of these two kinds of argument.

Deduction

We have said that a deductive argument is one whose premises are claimed to provide conclusive proof of the conclusion. This is not to say, however, that the conclusion of any deductive argument is necessarily true. It means merely that in a valid (that is, a properly constructed) deductive argument, the conclusion is necessarily implied by the premises. The premises of the argument may be true or untrue and the argument itself may be valid or invalid. Only when the premises are true and the argument is valid must the conclusion be true.

Deductive arguments take several forms. Among these, the one most commonly used to illustrate deduction is the categorical syllogism. You have surely seen the classic example that has been appearing in textbooks for perhaps twenty centuries:

All men are mortal.
Socrates is a man.
Therefore, Socrates is mortal.

To illustrate the relationship between the premises and the conclusion of this syllogism, we first draw a large circle to represent *all
mortal beings*. The circle is intended to include not only men but all
animals, birds, trees, insects, fish, and anything else that lives and is
subject to death. Next, we represent *men* with a smaller circle inside the
large one. The smaller circle has to be inside the larger because inductive experience has shown that men, as a class, do die and therefore
are a part of the larger group. Finally, we come to the specific instance
in the form of the individual, *Socrates*, whom we represent by a third
circle. Since Socrates belongs to the class of men, this third circle
must be inside the one representing men. Diagrammed, the syllogism
looks like the structure below.

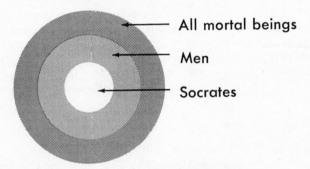

FIGURE X–1. THE CATEGORICAL SYLLOGISM

Immediately, it becomes evident that Socrates could not be classified as a man without at the same time being included in the group
of mortals. It is easy to see why deduction is such an effective form of
argument.

The categorical syllogism is only one of several forms the syllogism
may have, and the syllogism is itself by no means the only form a
deductive argument may take. Consequently our discussion of deductive argument is merely illustrative. It is certainly not intended to
be exhaustive.

But again we say that proofs in persuasion are not absolute. It is
true that the conclusion of a valid deductive argument follows neces-

sarily from the premises. This says nothing, however, about whether the conclusion is *true*. When speakers deliberate on policy decisions and on judgments of fact and value, the premises which provide evidence for their conclusions are themselves debatable. The conclusions of a deductive argument can never be more probable than the premises. The implication of this fact is illustrated with splendid clarity in Lincoln's refutation of an argument used by Stephen A. Douglas in one of their famous debates on the question of slavery in the United States.

Nothing in the constitution or laws of any state can destroy a right distinctly and expressly affirmed in the Constitution of the United States.

The right of property in a slave is distinctly and expressly affirmed in the Constitution of the United States.

Therefore, nothing in the Constitution or laws of any state can destroy the right of property in a slave.

I believe that no fault can be pointed out in that argument; assuming the truth of the premises, the conclusion so far as I have capacity at all to understand it, follows inevitably. There is a fault in it as I think, but the fault is not in the reasoning; but the falsehood in fact is a falsehood of the premises. I believe that the right of property in a slave *is not* distinctly and expressly affirmed in the Constitution. . . .

Induction

By inductive argument we mean this: From the fact that something is true of certain examined members of a class, the conclusion is drawn that the same thing will be true of unexamined members of that class also. The conclusion can be applied to an unlimited number of the unexamined members of the class. Thus induction is often a reasoning process that moves from particulars (or the less general) to the universal (or the more general). Another induction may extend the conclusion to a limited number of unexamined members of the class, for example to the next one which appears. In this case, the induction moves from known particulars to a new unknown particular. The process of induction can be described as taking place in three steps:

1. *Isolated facts, conditions, or phenomena are experienced.* As an amateur entomologist, you collect various species of butterflies. The first butterfly you find proves to have a fine powder on its wings.

2. *Similarities appear among the specific instances which you examine.* Your second specimen is also seen to have a powdery substance on its wings. You observe that the same condition exists in all the butterflies that make up your collection.

3. *A conclusion is drawn.* You conclude that what has been true of all the butterflies you have found thus far will be true of butterflies in general, and that any butterfly you find in the future will have powder on its wings.

It is obvious that such a conclusion is no more than probable. Adding more and more evidence to support it does no more than increase the probability.

PERSUASIVE FORMS OF ARGUMENT

More than 2,000 years ago, Aristotle observed that when a speaker uses arguments to prove a proposition, he uses deductive and inductive reasoning in forms especially adapted to persuasion. To these forms he gave the names that students of rhetoric still use to label the different kinds of arguments found in persuasion. Rhetorical deductions he called *enthymemes*. Rhetorical inductions are termed *examples*. Here is a closer look at the way enthymemes (rhetorical deductions) and examples (rhetorical inductions) operate when they are used by a speaker to build proof.

Deduction in Persuasion—Enthymeme

When a speaker uses deductive inferences in persuasion, he may on occasion put his arguments into syllogistic form. Most often, he will not. Logically, a syllogism is an ordered structure of simple beauty, but stylistically, its formal and often stilted language leaves much to be desired. Speakers almost always put their arguments into the ordinary language of conversational speech. Instead of using complete syllogisms, they use syllogisms in an elided or abbreviated form. That is, they omit whatever premises the audience can infer for itself, and give only those parts of the argument that are necessary. The name "enthymeme" is given to deductive arguments that appear in this shortened form. According to Aristotle, who gave enthymemes their name, deductive arguments are not only abbreviated in structure but, like inductive arguments, they are also probable rather than certain proofs.

The reason for stating deductive arguments as enthymemes is mainly one of style. The attention and interest of an audience are so important that a speaker must do everything he can to retain both. If he forces the audience to plod through every detailed step of his arguments, he tires them, he bores them, and often he gives the impression of talking down to them. Consequently, he says only what must be said to make the argument clear.

Wendell Willkie, in his "Loyal Opposition" speech, delivered after his defeat for the presidency by Franklin Delano Roosevelt, defended the right of the minority to debate issues in those dangerous times just prior to World War II. Note that the premise upon which the argument depends, the proposition that any totalitarian idea should be rejected utterly, is not expressly stated. Instead, the speaker assumes that the audience will supply the missing proposition. Here is what Willkie said.

It has been suggested that in order to present a united front to a threatening world, the minority should now surrender its convictions and join the majority. This would mean that in the United States of America there would be only one dominant party—only one economic philosophy—only one political philosophy of life. This is a totalitarian idea—it is a slave idea—it must be rejected utterly.

Willkie's argument not only illustrates the tendency of a speaker, for the sake of style, to elide the deductive arguments he uses, but it also exemplifies the second characteristic of the enthymeme—the fact that the proof it elicits is only probable. It is in no sense an absolute truth that any totalitarian idea should be rejected. Mr. Willkie could safely assume, however, that his audiences would accept the proposition as being probably true. Consequently, the argument was effective.

When a speaker uses deductive reasoning in persuasion, his inferences take the form of *argument from sign* or *argument from cause*.

ARGUMENT FROM SIGN.   In using argument from sign, a speaker observes directly some fact or condition. Using this as evidence, he draws the conclusion that some other fact or condition, not immediately observable, is true. A good example of inference based on signs is the diagnosis a physician makes. When he examines a patient, the doctor cannot directly observe the disease. Instead, what he looks for are symptoms, a set of conditions which are directly observable. These symptoms are a set of signs from which he can infer the presence of some disease.

Argument from sign may be thought of as deductive. It is always based on a generalization either explicit or implied, and can be put into syllogistic form. This generalization alleges a relationship between an observed sign and what it shows. It asserts that the observed phenomenon and the condition it signals always occur together, that the former does not occur without the latter. If the alleged relationship is accepted or believed by an audience, and if the condition taken as a sign is known or believed to exist, the conclusion follows without question.

The Londoner of Shakespeare's day knew that he could see a play whenever a flag was raised over the Globe Theater. The presence of the flag was taken as a sign that a play would be presented. The conclusion is drawn from two premises: "A flag on the theater always signals the production of a play," and "The flag is flying." From these two propositions, the conclusion necessarily follows that a play is to be produced.

A student speaker, defending the proposition that the United States should continue to support UNESCO, contended that UNESCO has been instrumental in preserving art. In support of this contention, he offered these occurrences as signs that UNESCO has indeed labored to preserve works of art:

1. It advised the Austrian government on the restoration of a number of old paintings.
2. It helped Yugoslavia restore murals and frescos.
3. It advised Syria and Lebanon in their efforts to restore ancient monuments and archeological sites.
4. It helped Peru in the restoration of her historical monuments.

On December 8, 1941, the day after the Japanese attack on Pearl Harbor, Franklin Delano Roosevelt delivered the famous speech in which he asked the Congress to declare that a state of war existed between the United States and Japan. In that speech, the President said:

Yesterday, December 7, 1941—a date which will live in infamy—the United States of America was suddenly and deliberately attacked by naval and air forces of the Empire of Japan. . . .

Yesterday the Japanese Government also launched an attack against Malaya.

Last night Japanese forces attacked Hong Kong.

Last night Japanese forces attacked Guam.

Last night Japanese forces attacked the Philippine Islands.

Last night the Japanese attacked Wake Island.

This morning the Japanese attacked Midway Island.

Japan has, therefore, undertaken a surprise offensive extending throughout the Pacific area. The facts of yesterday speak for themselves.

The President was right. The signs of a Japanese surprise offensive were incontestable.

TESTING SIGN RELATIONSHIPS.   In argument, the sign relationship alleged by a speaker must be accepted by his audience. It is the crucial point in the argument. Consequently, before an argument from sign is used in persuasion, the reliability of the generalization upon which the argument depends must be examined in the light of three questions.

1. *Is there a reliable relationship between the observed fact and the conclusion drawn?* An accidental relationship is no sure basis for argument from sign. The conclusion you draw in such cases is likely to be a coincidence or just plain superstition.

A little boy, returning from an afternoon at the beach with his parents, sees another car on the street. He says, "Look, those people have been to the beach, too." He bases his inference on the fact that two long, pointed sticks protrude from the trunk of the other car. They look to him like poles for a pair of beach umbrellas. The basis for the inference is quite tenuous, because even if his supposition is correct, and the pointed sticks are a sign that there is a beach umbrella in the back of the car, their presence is by no means a certain sign that the people in the other car are returning from the beach.

There may be a splendid correlation between the number of smogless days in Los Angeles and the number of days of rain in Phoenix, Arizona, but a smogless day in Los Angeles is nonetheless a poor sign of rain in Phoenix. Perhaps you have heard it said that when more boys than girls are being born at any given time the fact is a sign of impending war. Such a condition is about as trustworthy a sign of coming war as left-handedness is of superior intelligence.

2. *Do changed circumstances of time or place alter the relationship between sign and conclusion?* The reliability with which one condition can be taken as the sign of another condition can be altered by time and place. In the first half of the nineteenth century, the fact that a Southern farmer was a man of means would be a very reliable sign that he was a slaveowner. Today, no amount of wealth would be a sign that such a man owned slaves.

3. *Is the conclusion supported by the concurrence of other signs?* A single sign may often be insufficient evidence of the condition it seems to point to. Additional corroborating signs are frequently needed to support the conclusion of an argument from sign. Circumstantial evidence in a criminal case is an example. To say that a man is guilty of burglary because he was in the vicinity at the time the crime was committed is a weak argument. To show, in addition, that he was seen leaving the burglarized home and was arrested with stolen articles in his possession is to offer further and more substantial signs of his guilt.

In problems as complex as those that arise in human society, a single sign will seldom be a sure indication of a given fact or condition. Much more often than not, several are required to establish probability. Stock-market analysts make forecasts based on very tenuous data. What kinds of facts are such predictions based on? In July of one year, employment set a new record and unemployment dropped. For the second quarter of the year, the gross national product increased $5,000,000,000 over the first quarter. Personal income for the first seven months of the year is 1.06 times that for the same period in the year before. Now, do these facts *prove* that the over-all economy is in a healthy state? They may justify the proposition for some; for others not. At any rate, the conditions described are *signs* that indicate something about the condition of business. From them, one can draw inferences about the present and future states of the economy.

ARGUMENT FROM CAUSE. Every effect must have a cause, and no agent can properly be considered a cause unless it produces an effect. The two are inevitably associated. When an occurrence or condition is the direct result of an antecedent occurrence or condition, the relationship between them is said to be that of cause and effect. The one that exists prior in time and operates to bring about the other is said to be the cause. The one that exists as a direct result of the first is said to be the effect. Inferences based on causal reasoning appear either as arguments *from cause to effect* or as arguments *from effect to cause*.

1. *Cause to effect.* In a recent classroom speech, the speaker proposed that the state government should operate clinics to dispense narcotics at low cost to addicts. His speech contained these examples of argument from cause to effect: Lack of availability, plus the greed of peddlers, causes the price of narcotics to be high. High prices cause

narcotics addiction to be very expensive. The expense of being an addict forces addicts to turn to crime for money to support their habit. He argued further that the clinics he proposed would reduce the cost of addiction, thus removing the cause of a large proportion of present-day crime, and would, at the same time, eliminate narcotics peddlers by removing their source of profit.

Do you remember Mark Antony's funeral oration over the body of Caesar? Shakespeare has Antony use this *cause-to-effect* argument.

> It is not meet you know how Caesar loved you.
> You are not wood, you are not stones, but men:
> And, being men, hearing the will of Caesar,
> It will inflame you, it will make you mad.

Arguments of this kind move forward in time. That is, in reasoning from cause to effect, a speaker infers from one event or condition that a second event or condition will follow, the first being the cause, the second its result. This kind of reasoning is used to support an appeal for or against an increase in taxes, the choice of a man for public office, a program of disarmament, or any specified course of action.

2. *Effect to cause*. The second kind of argument from causal relation moves backward in time from a given condition and attempts to establish a probable cause. This kind of reasoning determines why the Roman Empire fell, why there has been a war, what causes juvenile delinquency, what causes a high divorce rate, or the cause of any other of the host of society's problems. Only an intelligent understanding of probable causes will permit more than temporary, symptomatic relief in any situation that demands improvement. Aspirin may stop a headache, but it will not stop the eyestrain that causes the headache. Not knowing that eyestrain is present may lead to effects even more serious than headaches.

In the British House of Commons, in 1780, Charles James Fox delivered a speech in which appears the following clear example of argument from effect to cause.

It is this cursed American war that has led us, step by step, into all our present misfortunes and national disgraces. What was the cause of our wasting forty millions of money, and sixty thousand lives? The American War! What was it that produced the French rescript and the French War? The American War! What was it that produced the Spanish Manifesto and Spanish War? The American War! What was it that armed forty thousand men in Ireland with arguments carried on the points of forty thousand bayonets? The American War! For what are we about to incur an additional debt of twelve or fourteen millions? This accursed, cruel, diabolical American War!

Patrick Henry used reasoning of this kind in the "Liberty or Death" speech which patriotic tradition attributes to him.

I ask . . . , sir, what means this martial array, if its purpose be not to force us to submission? Can gentlemen assign any other possible motive for it? Has Great Britain any enemy in this quarter of the world, to call for all this accumulation of navies and armies? No, sir, she has none. They are meant for us; they can be meant for no other.

TESTING CAUSAL RELATIONSHIPS. Arguments from cause, like arguments from sign, should be thought of as deductive. They, too, depend upon a stated or implied generalization—in this case, that in all instances a given event or set of circumstances can be expected to bring about a second event or condition as a direct result. Here again, as in the case of inference from sign, it is essential to the argument that the audience accept the premise which states the causal relationship upon which the speaker's conclusion depends. If the causal relationship stated or implied by the speaker is accepted by the audience, and if conditions described by the speaker are known or believed to exist, arguments from cause will be accepted as conclusive proof. In order to avoid the many dangers inherent in causal arguments, test their rhetorical soundness before you use them in persuasion.

1. *There must really be a causal relationship.* We have said that a cause always precedes its effect. That is, it comes earlier in time. This one characteristic is often an occasion of the fallacy called *post hoc, ergo propter hoc*—"after this, therefore on account of this." The fact that one event follows another does not mean that the second is the result of the first. Time sequence, then, does not constitute causal relationship. Superstitions are good examples of faulty causal reasoning of this sort. Either a causal faculty they do not possess is attributed to certain occurrences ("Oh, you broke a mirror. Seven years bad luck!") or, on the basis of coincidental time sequence, a causal connection that does not exist is alleged ("I sprained my ankle when I stepped off the curb because I walked under a ladder just before it happened.")

It is easy, but naive, to allege a causal relationship where none really exists; many factors can intervene to destroy a neat chain of causal reasoning. One is often tempted to assert the truth of a conclusion on the basis of an event that he would expect to cause a certain result. He fails to notice that other causal factors intervene. Having the engine in an automobile overhauled should result in improved performance and economy of the car. But if the driver tries to economize further by using paint thinner for fuel, he introduces another factor that will completely prevent the engine overhaul from having the desired effect. By the same token, a fisherman plagued by mosquitoes can expect little help from an insect repellant if he washes it off because he doesn't like the smell.

2. *Avoid oversimplification in determining cause and effect.* Rarely, if ever, are cause and effect found in simple one-to-one ratio. Most often, an effect comes about through the operation of a whole series of contributing causes. It is quite simple to say that a president *caused* a depression or a war. It is also quite foolish to make such an assertion. The tremendously complex nature of social ills makes oversimplification both a temptation and a danger. If, however, a speaker undertakes to show that a president's policies made a substantial contribution to certain unfortunate events, he is on safer and also more reasonable ground.

More often than not, a cause generates, or at least influences, multiple effects. Any course of action, when put into operation, has results; that is, it becomes a cause operating to bring about effects that may be good, bad, or indifferent. If a speaker argues that juvenile delinquency results from bad comic books (itself a thoughtless analysis), he may conclude that censorship of reading materials would cause a reduction of juvenile delinquency. But censorship involves side effects which may very well be worse than any good it accomplishes.

Determining cause and effect is usually a complicated and difficult process. Yet causality may be the most important concept in the whole of argumentation.

DISTINGUISHING BETWEEN SIGN AND CAUSE. Arguments from sign and from cause are often difficult to distinguish. For one reason, English has a limited number of logical connectives such as "because," "since," "hence," and "therefore." These or similar words are used to indicate argument and conclusions to argument regardless of whether a speaker is basing his inferences on sign or on cause. Moreover, if argument from sign is to be effective, there must be some kind of causal relationship between two events when one is the sign of the other. Otherwise, signs are merely accidental.

An argument from sign is called a *ratio cognoscendi*—a way of knowing that a proposition is true. When you see a flock of geese pointing northward across the sky, you know that spring will soon be here. If a man buys a new car every year, wears expensive clothes, and lives in an exclusive section of town, you take these indications to mean he suffers no immediate lack of money. In each of these instances, the signs are interpreted to mean that the conclusion drawn from them *is* true. No attempt is made to say *why* it is true: why spring is coming, or why the man in question is wealthy.

Arguments from cause, on the other hand, lend credibility to propositions by offering reasons that will explain *why* they are true. This kind of inference is a *ratio essendi*, a way of accounting for the existence of something.

The example of the physician's diagnosis helps to show the difference between these two forms of argument. When someone is ill, the physician reasons from signs *that* his patient is ill. In order to know *why* the patient is ill, the doctor must look to the germ, virus, or condition that *caused* the illness. The major distinction, then, between arguments from sign and arguments from cause is in what they attempt to show. An argument from sign, making no use of causal relationships, attempts to show *that* a condition has existed, does exist, or will exist. An argument from cause assumes the condition and offers to explain *why* it is so.

Induction in Persuasion—Example

In describing the structure of inductive arguments, we said that their conclusions can be extended to either a limited or an ulimited number of unexamined members of a class. Each of these two possibilities serves as a basis for argument in persuasion. If the conclusion is unlimited in its extension, a generalization is made about the whole class. When a speaker makes such a generalization and offers evidence to support it, he uses *argument by generalization.* When the conclusion to an induction is limited in its extension and is applied to some particular unexamined member of the class, the speaker uses *argument by analogy.*

ARGUMENT BY GENERALIZATION. The generalization a speaker makes in persuasion may be either true or false. For our purposes, it must be assumed that the speaker himself believes them to be true and that he would not otherwise bring them to bear in an argument. Many of the generalizations that are useful to a speaker are propositions which an audience already holds to be true. Such propositions may vary widely, from the rashest kind of generalization to highly credible beliefs carefully distilled from intelligent interpretations of broad experience. In other instances, when an audience cannot be expected to know, understand, or readily accept propositions that are important in a speech, the speaker may establish them inductively through argument by generalization.

Suppose in arguing against socialized medicine you were to contend that the quality of medical service under such a system could always be expected to be poor. You might adduce a number of specific instances in which socialized medicine has afforded medical care of poor quality. On the basis of these specific instances, you would conclude that what is true of the known examples cited would be true of all other unexamined instances of socialized medicine, even those not yet in existence.

A large number of examples is not always necessary in effective rhetorical induction. It is quite possible that a single case in point might be sufficient to create belief in a proposition. In the example just cited, although there are several countries where socialized medicine has been adopted as a policy, instead of listing a number of instances wherein the government pays the cost of medical care, you might develop an extended and detailed description of its failure in one specific place. It is evident that in drawing a universal conclusion from no more than one specific instance there is grave danger of forming a hasty and untenable generalization. If such an argument is to have the desired persuasive force, it must be drawn from a carefully selected and well-developed example which an audience can easily accept as truly representative of the proposition it supports.

Since generalizations depend upon the examples that support them, the critical element in them is the quality of the examples themselves. These examples are precisely the kind of supporting material described in Chapter VI (Supporting Material: Types and Use) and must meet the criteria described there. Here is a brief list of these criteria.

1. The examples must be representative.
2. Negative instances must be accounted for.
3. The examples must be sufficient in number.

ARGUMENT BY ANALOGY. Confusion sometimes arises over the term analogy because it is used in two ways: In the first sense, the word refers to the language device a speaker may use to illustrate or clarify an unfamiliar idea by comparing it to a similar idea with which his audience is familiar. For example, you might say that the gills of a fish serve much the same purpose as the lungs of an animal, or that a world federation of nations would be quite like the United States in its political structure. An illustrative analogy has great merit not only for clarifying an idea but also as a means of lending vividness to the idea. "We all know," says Emerson, "that as the human body can be nourished on any food, though it were boiled grass and the broth of shoes, so the human mind can be fed by any knowledge." To the extent that clarity and interest are necessary in any speech, an illustrative analogy may be useful in persuasion. It may also serve to create belief.

In a second sense, analogy is used to mean the reasoning process by which a speaker infers that what is true of one specific instance will also be true of a similar specific instance. No one has to learn to drive each of the makes of automobiles separately. Automobiles are enough alike in the way they operate for a driver to be able to move easily from one to another and drive it without learning how to operate each new one that comes along. Even if he learned to drive in a Chevrolet, and has driven only this one car, he knows by analogy that he will be able to drive a Ford should the occasion arise.

An analogy draws a conclusion about two items, events, or conditions which belong to the same class. It is a prediction that because two things are alike in certain known respects they can be expected to be alike in other respects where the similarity is as yet unknown. Using this kind of reasoning, a speaker argues that because socialized medicine has operated succesfully in Great Britain it would operate successfully in the United States, or that since two cities are nearly equal in population, have similar kinds and amounts of industry, and are alike in other important respects, they may be expected to equal each other in say, wealth, or number of children of school age, or some other point of comparison.

Franklin Delano Roosevelt used this analogy in his "Arsenal of Democracy" speech, December 29, 1940.

Tonight, in the presence of a world crisis, my mind goes back eight years to a night in the midst of a domestic crisis. It was a time when . . . the whole banking system of our country had ceased to function. . . . I tried to convey to the great mass of American people what the banking crisis meant to them in their daily lives. Tonight I want to do the same thing, with the same people, in this new crisis which faces America. We met the isssue of 1933 with courage and realism. We face this new crisis—this new threat to the security of the nation—with the same courage and realism.

Suppose you were trying to prove that part-time students, taking all their classes at night, ought to meet the same rigorous standards set for day students. You might say:

"Look at it this way. A swing-shift worker can't be any less capable and efficient than a fellow on the day shift. The work he turns out has to be just as good. What if you had a part-time job on the swing shift at Norco Aircraft? You wouldn't last a week if you did poor work there. If you ever told your boss the work you turn out shouldn't have to pass inspection because you're there only part time, how long do you think you'd last? Well, the same thing is true in school. The fact that you are a part-time student and take only late afternoon and evening classes doesn't mean you can get by with low quality work."

The chief benefit of drawing an inference by analogy is that it allows one to profit from experience; the chief danger lies in the fact that some important difference may have been overlooked in making the original comparison. The driver who has operated only late-model cars with automatic transmissions will not be able to drive a car with a standard shift solely on the basis of his earlier experience. The British system of socialized medicine can be expected to operate successfully in the United States only if the two countries are similar in respects that are important to government operation of a medical program.

It is clear, then, that an analogy is any argument of the form, "Event A is like Event B." One customarily hears the comment that all analogies are false. A more accurate appraisal would be that any analogy whatsoever may be true or false but no one knows how to tell which is so. Any two events whatever have an infinite number of properties in common. To take two at random: a Ranger satellite and Miss America of 1968. What do these have in common? Among other things, both are more than ten feet from the moon. Therefore, it is true to say that Ranger satellite and Miss America of 1968 are alike (in this and an infinite number of other ways). But it is equally true to say that any two events are different in an infinite number of ways: Miss America of 1968 is, for example, closer to you than a Ranger satellite.

Consider the following as properties ascribed to two events:

Event A: $a \ b \ c \ . \ . \ j \ . \ . \ n$
Event B: $a \ b \ c \ . \ . \ . \ . \ n$

Now pair the proper ties the two events have in common. It is reasoned that since A and B have properties $a, b, c, \ldots n$ in common, and since Event A has property j, then Event B has property j also. There is, however, no way of telling whether j is among the infinite number of properties the two events have in common or whether it is in the list of properties which A has and B lacks.

Now someone is likely to say that it is silly to ascribe to Miss America the property of being more than ten feet away from the moon. This statement is not so silly, however, as a property of a Ranger satellite. Nor does it seem so silly for Miss America to be closer to you than a Ranger satellite. The point is this: These are idiosyncratic judgments and are relative to the value system of the one who makes them. Hence, an analogy says nothing about the events it compares but only about the person who makes it. Some similarities are significant; some are not. Some differences make a difference; some do not. The crucial problem in analogy, therefore, is in choosing events for comparison wherein one can specify a set of "significant" properties which the two have in common and whose differences are *not* "significant." Since this requires the judgment of some person, the probative value of any analogy depends upon the minds of the audience because a listener may regard what the speaker considers to be significant similarities as trivial, or his few significant differences as important. Proof, as we have seen, is in the mind of the audience. A few years ago, colleges were debating the topic of a guaranteed annual wage. A speaker used the following analogy to defend his contention that labor was unwise in demanding a guaranteed income.

The labor movement has made tremendous strides in this country since the pioneering days of Samuel Gompers. At the same time, labor has made many enemies who distrust unions as the weapon of the laboring man's greed. Right now, when the unions themselves are shot through with corruption, it would be foolish for labor to demand a guaranteed annual wage. Do you remember the story of the dog with the bone? He saw his reflection in a pond. It looked to him as if the dog he saw had a bigger bone, so he dropped his bone to take the bigger one—and lost both. If the workingman insists upon reaching for the bigger bone of a guaranteed annual wage, he may lose many of the advances labor has made up to now.

Obviously, this analogy compares items that are not at all alike in any literal sense. The argument draws its force from the fact that it establishes an apparent or plausible ratio: The greed of the dog bears the same relationship to his loss of the bone that the laboring man's greed would bear to his loss of hard-won advances.

In the Cooper Institute address, Abraham Lincoln addressed a portion of his remarks to Southern politicians:

In [the] event [that a Republican President is elected], you say, you will destroy the Union; and then, you say, the great crime of having destroyed it will be upon us! That is cool. A highwayman holds a pistol to my ear, and mutters through his teeth, "Stand and deliver, or I shall kill you, and then you will be a murderer!"

In 1850, John C. Calhoun clashed in a debate with Henry Clay and Daniel Webster over the question of extending slavery into territory recently acquired from Mexico. The great call of Webster and Clay was for Union. Calhoun answered, "The cry of 'Union! Union! The glorious Union!' can no more prevent disunion than the cry of 'Health! Health! glorious Health!' on the part of a physician can save a patient lying dangerously ill."

A good analogy may be worth ten thousand syllogisms, much as a picture is worth ten thousand words.

SUMMARY

Controversies arise when one person is motivated to change an opinion of others so that it agrees with his own. In so doing, he uses arguments to justify belief in his point of view. The arguments he uses will be examples of either inductive or deductive inference. If the former, they will be said to offer *some* evidence of the truth of the conclusion. Inductive arguments help to establish the probability of the conclusion drawn. Deductive arguments, on the other hand, are said to provide conclusive proof. That is, if the argument is valid, the conclusion is necessarily implied in the premises.

Although the conclusion of a valid deductive inference follows necessarily from the premises, this consequence says nothing about whether the conclusion is true. Only when the premises are certainly true *and* the argument is valid is the conclusion certainly true. But when speakers deliberate on proposed policies, judgments of value, and allegedly factual conditions, the premises that provide evidence for their conclusions are only probable. Hence, the proofs in persuasion are only probable. The arguments a speaker offers, then, are used to give a rational basis to belief. They do not constitute absolute proof.

Deductive arguments appear in persuasion either as arguments from sign or arguments from cause. The first of these is called a *ratio cognoscendi*, a method of knowing *that* some statement is true. An argument from cause, *ratio essendi*, provides a reason for being, by offering to explain *why* a statement is true.

Inductive arguments in persuasion appear either as generalizations or as analogies. In making generalizations a speaker presents evidence in the form of examples to justify the belief that what is true of the instances cited will be true of all unexamined instances of the same phenomenon. An argument by analogy does not use its premises as evidence that exemplifies something about a whole class. Instead, it concludes that what is true of examined instances will be true of another *particular* instance of the same class of phenomena.

QUESTIONS

1. What conditions set up an occasion for persuasive speaking?
2. What is an argument?
3. Why are analytic statements not used in persuasion?
4. What is meant by: "a speaker's efforts in persuasion are aimed at proving that his proposition is probably true"?
5. What are the two points of view from which arguments are evaluated?
6. What are the steps in the process of induction?
7. Explain the categorical syllogism as a form of deductive argument.
8. What must a speaker do to establish a persuasive generalization from a limited number of examples?
9. Differentiate between analogy as argument and analogy as a stylistic device.
10. How are inferences drawn by analogy?
11. What is an enthymeme?
12. What is argument from sign?
13. Explain two of the tests of sign relationships.
14. Differentiate between argument from sign and argument from cause.

EXERCISES

1. Write a short essay (no more than three double-spaced type-written pages) in which you explain how the principle of probability is applied to some problem in your major field of study. You need not go into extensive detail. Write the paper so that it reflects the general understanding of experts in the field. The following topics might suggest the kind of subject you should choose:

    (a) Can history predict future events?

    (b) What is the nature of probability theory in genetics?

    (c) How much do intelligence tests and intelligence quotients tell an elementary-school teacher about her students?

    (d) To what extent does chemistry provide absolute truths?

    (e) What is the theory behind minority rights in a democracy?

    (f) In what sense is human personality predictable?

    (g) Is mathematics an absolute science?

    (h) How do economists know when a country is in a depression?

2. Examine the texts of several speeches delivered in the last presidential campaign. (See the *New York Times*, *Vital Speeches of the Day*, or *Representative American Speeches* for texts of many of these.) Find the specific proposition the speaker is advocating and decide whether it is a proposition of fact, of value, or of policy.

3. In the editorials of such news magazines as *The Reporter* and *U.S. News & World Report* (or in newspaper editorials), find samples of arguments from example, from analogy, from sign, and from cause. For inductive arguments (example and analogy), evaluate the evidence presented; for deductive arguments (sign and cause), evaluate the generalization upon which the argument is based.

4. Collect examples of arguments you hear in conversation and evaluate them as in exercise 3. Here are some samples of what you might listen for:

"I didn't think you were at home. I didn't see your car in the driveway."

"My eyes are bothering me. I must have been studying too much."

"Don't make so much noise; you'll wake your mother."

"All the best television viewing times are filled with westerns. Look at Saturday night's schedule."

Incidentally, can you tell what kind of argument is used in each of the examples given in this exercise? How would you counter these arguments if you disagreed?

ARGUMENT: NONRATIONAL FUNCTIONS

I. Motive appeals
   A. Types of motive appeals
      1. Self-preservation
      2. Happiness
      3. Self-esteem
      4. Well-being of family and friends
      5. Financial well-being
      6. Preservation of the society
   B. Using motive appeals
      1. Make the motive appeals a product of the ideas of the speech and not an end in themselves
      2. Choose the motive appeal which is best adapted to the audience
      3. Use multiple motive appeals where appropriate
      4. Keep the motive appeals consistent throughout the speech
      5. Let the materials of the speech develop the motive appeals
      6. Avoid overusing motive appeals

II. The *ethos* of the speaker
   A. Credibility
   B. Elements of *ethos*
      1. Trustworthiness
      2. Competence
      3. Good will toward the audience
   C. Using *ethos*
      1. Be temperate in showing trustworthiness, competence, and good will
      2. Build *ethos* indirectly
      3. Use the credibility of others to support your own *ethos*
      4. Sometimes use candor to disarm a hostile audience
      5. Use a chairman's introduction to build *ethos*

III. Summary, questions, and exercises

XI

ARGUMENT: NONRATIONAL FUNCTIONS

If listeners could be persuaded by logic alone, this world would probably be much better organized. It would probably be much duller also. The fact is, however, that people are *not* so persuaded, that the world *is* largely disorganized, and that it is surely *not* dull. In view of these conditions, a complete undersanding of what happens in a persuasive speaking situation will not be found in the study of logic. Speakers and audiences act and react according to patterns of thought which are not always logical in any strict sense. Persuasion is to be understood psychologically. The necessary psychological insights can be gained only if each speaking situation is viewed as a unique event in which the speaker and the audience cooperate at a particular moment in the act of persuasion.

In the preceding chapter, we said that proofs in persuasion are only probable, and that it is the audience which determines what is probable and what is not. Even so, a listener's door to objective reality is no more open than is the speaker's. He knows the world only as he perceives it. His perceptions of what is probable are colored by all his experiences; by the set of values he gained from his parents, the impressions he received while he was growing to maturity, his reactions to contacts with other people in the streets, in schools, in the army, on athletic teams, or where have you. All these experiences influence his perception and lead him to conclusions about life which have not undergone the tests of rigorous logic but which, nonetheless, are fervently held convictions.

The convictions a person has about men in general, about groups, about events, and about himself may be called assumptions. When anyone sits as a member of an audience, his own assumptions are rarely up for debate. Instead, they serve him as measures of the acceptability of a speaker's ideas and arguments. In order to persuade his audience, therefore, a speaker must argue within the framework of the assumptions of the audience.

We do not say that persuasion is nonlogical; it is logical within the framework of the opinions, attitudes, and beliefs of the listener. But the term logical has come to mean some application of external criteria to the language phenomenon that is independent of the audience. In this sense when we say something is "logical" or "illogical," we are probably telling more about ourselves than we are about the act being described. We more nearly mean that a speaker is "correct" or "incorrect," "truthful" or "untruthful."

Perhaps it would be well to begin by saying that the extent to which one's behavior is consistent with his perceptions of the world around him is the extent to which he is logical. The person who "knows" that smoking is injurious to his health and still smokes is not illogical. His behavior merely indicates that he is not subject to a single motivation. He may regard the "pleasure" of smoking as greater than the "harmfulness." He may consider smoking a sign of manliness. Or, he may even regard it as a challenge: "Other people may get cancer from smoking but not me." Although the probabilities of scientific evidence make it seem "illogical" for one to think that he is somehow biologically resistant to disease because of his greater will power, the person with this belief is not illogical if he *reasons* that because of his resistance he can smoke without harm to himself. He may be wrong or he may be foolish and he may even die because of this reasoning, but he is not *illogical*.

The audience has, therefore, a consistency (a logic, if you will), but to understand it a speaker must understand what motivates listeners. Chapter V examined the factors which tend to make audiences what they are and to respond as they do. The preceding chapter on the rational functions of persuasion examined the structures of reasoning which systematize the process of argument and inquiry. This chapter is concerned with the elements of the speaking situation whereby a speaker can effect some changes in an audience by identifying his proposal with what influences his listeners. These elements are two: the appeals which excite motivations already in the listener and the evidences of *ethos* which increase the credibility of the speaker himself.

MOTIVE APPEALS

In addition to rational bases, people have other grounds for their behavior. They do things in order to achieve some desired goal—to attain something perceived or judged to be good, to avoid something considered bad. These grounds we may call motives. They are the product of opinions, attitudes, and beliefs, and they affect one's perceptions of the world. A motive is an inner state which will impel someone to take action to change a situation which causes him stress.

Some motives are biological. The desires to avoid hunger, pain, or death are obvious ones. Others are learned. Such learned motivations as protection of family, ego-enhancement, and financial well-being, may or may not be derived from biological motives, but to a speaker this is not a vital question. The vital question for him is: How does he excite the inner state that causes a listener to take the action the speaker desires?

For this purpose the speaker looks to particular combinations of language symbols which will put the listener under stress so that he will be receptive to the speaker's message as a means of relieving that stress.

Types of Motive Appeals

Since learned motives arise from an infinite variety of circumstances, a list of potential motive appeals is limited only by the imagination and endurance of the compiler. It is nearly impossible to classify them. Consequently, the definition of appeals which will excite these motivations is a frustrating task. Furthermore, when one attempts to limit the number he runs the danger of speaking so generally as to say little of value. This second alternative is the one we risk now. In view of this limitation, as the speaker chooses motive appeals he will do well to adopt them more specifically to the listener than the following statements might seem to indicate.

The general motive appeals which become immediately identifiable are those which relate to a listener's self-preservation, his happiness, his self-esteem, the well-being of those close to him, his own financial condition, and the well-being of the society to which he belongs.

SELF-PRESERVATION. Perhaps the strongest motive appeal is to a listener's desire for his own well-being. On this ground, he is encouraged to drive more safely, to have a cancer check-up, or to give up smoking. Self-preservation is not always the strongest possible motivation, but it is a human drive so powerful that it is a primary basis for many of the persuasive appeals we hear.

HAPPINESS.   When the basic drive of self-preservation has been satisfied for the individual, he will make his own happiness a basic objective. He will want to find the best place to take a vacation, the right kind of car for his enjoyment, the kind of job he will like best.

SELF-ESTEEM.   Frequently a listener will take action to enhance his self-esteem, even at the sacrifice of personal safety. Men may even give up their lives in personal sacrifice to achieve a desired goal. Others give up high-paying positions to work for the government or a charity for a dollar a year. In part, they do these things from a desire to help bring about some social good, but they also do it for self-satisfaction. Men want to see the organization to which they belong become recognized for its excellence. At least a part of their motivation is their self-satisfaction. In short, a man may feel that on a given occasion, self-esteem is more important than self-preservation or happiness.

WELL-BEING OF FAMILY AND FRIENDS.   Closely related to self-preservation and self-esteem is the desire to provide a better life for family and friends. Even when a man knows that what he does will not benefit him, he may do it for the good of his family and friends. On these grounds he buys insurance and fights a "war to end wars." A person is willing to sacrifice now to prevent suffering among his descendants. This feeling is, of course, closely related to self-preservation; it is often difficult to separate the two motivations. People want to preserve themselves and to preserve those whose loss would bring them pain.

FINANCIAL WELL-BEING.   Surely many would deny that the acquisition of physical goods is their primary motivation. To some people, money means little but, on the other hand, some members of an audience will measure almost everything by its monetary value. Although these two conditions are extremes, they serve to illustrate the variety to be found in attitudes toward financial security. It must be agreed, nonetheless, that financial well-being is an important motivation to which substantially all Americans react, although with differing degrees of intensity.

PRESERVATION OF THE SOCIETY.   Almost by nature men are conservative; they want to preserve what is familiar to them. Even the radical has such an association with other radicals that, although he may wish to topple the general society, he wishes to preserve and expand the society of radicals to which he adheres. Thus, when one speaks of preserving the society, it means more than sustaining the city, ethnic group, state, or nation. The listener you are trying to motivate may be a member of all of these but at the same time he may give active allegiance to some other group. He may be more a Republican than a Chicagoan, more a laboring man than an Italian. Many people give only passive allegiance to their country. For such people, patriotism is not a great motivation. With those who give active allegiance to a church, an appeal to religion will probably tend to be more effective than it will be with those whose church membership is passive. Thus when you make an appeal on the basis of the common good of the group, you need to be sure to motivate in the name of the group whatever has the greatest allegiance of the audience.

USING MOTIVE APPEALS

The following six principles are helpful to the speaker in selecting motive appeals.

1. Make the motive appeals a product of the ideas of the speech and not an end in themselves.
2. Choose the motive appeal which is best adapted to the audience.
3. Use multiple motive appeals where appropriate.
4. Keep the motive appeals consistent throughout the speech.
5. Let the materials of the speech develop the motive appeals.
6. Avoid overusing motive appeals.

MAKE THE MOTIVE APPEALS A PRODUCT OF THE IDEAS OF THE SPEECH AND NOT AN END IN THEMSELVES. We have noted that a listener's motivations are excited when he is under stress. He is under stress because he becomes aware that his desire for some end is frustrated or unfulfilled. In such a state the listener will try to relieve the stress. A listener who is made to realize that his own self-preservation is involved in whatever policies America develops toward Communist China will feel a need to find some means to alleviate this stress. If, in fact, such a motivation is aroused, then any proposal a speaker recommends must be consistent with that motivation; the listener must perceive it as a means of relieving the stress brought about by the threat to his well-being. For this reason the speaker must be sure that he provides a motive appeal which grows out of his own particular solution to a problem. If a motive appeal merely creates stress in a listener, he may choose a solution which is quite different from the one advocated by the speaker. Arousing fear of Communist China, for instance, without directing that fear toward a specific goal may result in the listener's concluding that we should go to war now when the speaker would have cautioned restraint. The motive appeal must, therefore, be developed not only in terms of exciting the listener's concern but also in directing it toward an acceptable solution. Motive appeals not related to specific ideas will cause greater disorganization for the listener with less predictability of behavior. The speaker who arouses feelings toward injustice without showing a means for the relief of injustice may, in extreme cases, inadvertently be producing a riot.

Furthermore, society will usually judge unkindly the speaker who puts the motivation of an audience above his concern for ideas which help to resolve problems. Such a person in time is labeled a "rabble-rouser" and eventually his views may be ignored.

A final point is perhaps one of ethics rather than of rhetoric. The first responsibility of a speaker is to tell the truth as he sees it, not to pursue the false god of temporary success. Above all, be honest with your audiences and true to yourself. Don't be like the student who truly believed that capital punishment ought to be retained but elected to argue against it in order to curry favor with his instructor and his class.

CHOOSE THE MOTIVE APPEAL WHICH IS BEST ADAPTED TO THE AUDIENCE.   A representative of the police department speaking on highway safety to a high-school audience might use the appeal of self-preservation. Frequently, however, adults have lectured teen-agers on such a subject only to discover that this appeal had no effect. Why? Because young people don't have the same fears of death which adults have. The solemn warnings of adults seem to teen-agers to be pretended fears intended to thwart youth's natural independence and interest in adventure. The motive appeal of self-esteem might be more meaningful to an audience of young people. The speaker would better say, in essence:

No doubt about it, you are old enough to make your own decisions on what you should do. Adults have already put a lot of responsibilities on you and in return we should be willing to give you some deserved privileges. Everyone should be allowed to clown a little, but you can see that too much fooling around in cars can be dangerous.

It's up to you to police yourselves. Tell the fellow who goes too far and endangers others that he is not the kind of person you want to associate with. It is the few of that kind who make it tough on the great majority of high-school drivers who are a real credit to themselves.

This argument bases its motivation on an appeal that is more likely to move the audience. Too many speakers use motive appeals they think should be effective. But if an audience is not religious or patriotic or acquisitive, then it will not respond to those motives. Build appeals on the motivations your listeners actually feel. You can do so only when you have made an accurate evaluation of what an audience thinks and feels about the subject of your speech. Here again the importance of audience analysis becomes clear.

USE MULTIPLE MOTIVE APPEALS WHERE APPROPRIATE. You may wish to tell a group at a service club that support for the Children's Camping Fund will benefit the community and at the same time increase the stature of the club and its members. Thus, you use both social and personal appeals to win their support.

Multiple motive appeals are useful in meeting the problem of possible differences within audiences. An audience may contain those with an emotional concern for the community and others impervious to this appeal but susceptible to self-esteem. One appeal reaches one listener and a second reaches another and so both may be persuaded.

KEEP THE MOTIVE APPEALS CONSISTENT THROUGHOUT THE SPEECH. Remember that motive appeals must be consistent throughout the speech, and be sure when you use two or more appeals that they are compatible. It is compatible to support a camping fund by offering the good of the community and enhancement of the listener's self-esteem as motive appeals because the listener fulfills his ego needs by doing what is "right" for the community. But suppose a speaker were to urge the retention of capital punishment on the grounds that it protects the listeners against murderers and also saves them tax money by eliminating the cost of keeping convicted murderers in prison. These motivations are not compatible because the second motivation runs precisely counter to the same antipathy toward taking human life that gives the first motivation its appeal. Thus the speaker who uses this inconsistent double appeal counters his own motivation. In essence, he expects the listener to respond to an appeal to self-preservation (a notion of the value of life) and also to a second appeal which, if accepted, denies the significance of life at least as compared with money. Motivation must be activated in the audience without establishing grounds for arousing those same emotions *against* the proposition.

When multiple motivation is appealed to, be sure that the consistency among the appeals is clear. Allow them to develop together so that they become, in a sense, parts of one motivation. Do not jump from one appeal to another.

LET THE MATERIALS OF THE SPEECH DEVELOP THE MOTIVE APPEALS.   A speaker cannot gracefully say to an audience, "And I tell you this for your own self-preservation." Effective appeal is developed through the concrete details of the speech. Persuasive speaking is not made up of some magic combination of words. Such misconceptions are perpetuated by those lovers of language who ignore the fact that words have persuasive force only because they call up meanings which excite the motivations of the listener. If you wanted to arouse a man to some action concerning an automobile accident, which of the following would you do?

1. Discuss the emotion of those who give speeches about auto accidents?
2. Discuss the emotion of those who view auto accidents?
3. Discuss the emotions of those who are in auto accidents?
4. Show a picture of an auto accident?
5. Show a picture of an auto accident in which someone dear to the viewer was injured?

This list obviously moves from the less to the more personal. At the same time it moves from what is less concrete to what is more concrete. The more personal and the more concrete an idea, the greater is the capacity to be motivated by the abstractions of a speaker. To be successful as a speaker you must select those examples, statistics, and comparisons and contrasts with which your listener can identify.

AVOID OVERUSING MOTIVE APPEALS.   In one sense this principle is a contradition in terms because overuse of motive appeal is no motive appeal. The member of the college club or fraternity who sees all small crises as major catastrophies or the politician who sees every occasion as a time to defend "home, flag, and mother" lose their effectiveness because listeners learn to discount what they say. At a time when the case demands powerful motive appeals such speakers, like the boy who cried "wolf," will be ignored.

What is the overuse of motive appeal? That question is determined by the audience. The history of oratory is resplendent with examples of great speeches with highly developed motive appeals by such men as Demosthenes, Cicero, John Donne, Daniel Webster, Abraham Lincoln, Woodrow Wilson, Franklin Roosevelt, Adlai Stevenson, or John F. Kennedy. One can also find great speeches with considerably more modified appeal, frequently by the same men. The key to the greatness of an orator is his ability to adapt to his audience.

THE ETHOS OF THE SPEAKER

We have already observed that proofs in rhetoric are only tentative—that argument, supporting detail, and motive appeals develop only probable truths in the listener's mind. At this point we can add another factor which makes ideas more probable—the credibility of the speaker.

Credibility

People are more inclined to believe what is told them by someone they trust, a principle that seems simple enough. Credibility is established in a variety of ways. Authority figures, for example, tend to have greater credibility. No matter how much the President of the United States may be distrusted by some people, he generally has more credibility than the fellow who occupies the classroom seat next to you.

At times authority figures have trouble gaining trust. The current popular term for this problem is "credibility gap." The Mayor, Senator, Cabinet member, Governor, or President who lacks the credibility he might wish to have, has done something to make himself less believable.

To a large extent credibility, or the lack of it, is established by what a person says. When the city council says it will improve rubbish collection and does not, when a candidate for the state legislature says he will support open-housing legislation to one group and tells another he will oppose it, when anyone's word is contradicted by his other words or actions he will lose credibility for the listener who perceives this.

While the problems of credibility for a public figure are interesting, those of the college student are quite different, though not generically so. The student has varying degrees of credibility depending on whether he talks to his speech class, social club, parents, or sociology professor. His problem is most likely to be one of building credibility through the speech itself. The proof which a speaker develops during a speech to enhance his credibility and, therefore, his persuasiveness, is called *ethos*.

The concept of *ethos* (sometimes unfortunately called "ethical proof") is not to be confused with *ethics*. The most outrageous liar, for example, can deceive a listener and foist off on him thoroughly untrue assertions if the listener accepts the speaker as a person worthy of trust. The very name "confidence man" suggests the importance of winning the trust of others, even for a swindler.

Ethos may thus be defined as that part of a speaker's persuasiveness which results from the audience's favorable impression of him as a spokesman for the truth. Whether or not he actually is speaking the truth is another matter.

Elements of Ethos

It is generally agreed that if a speaker is to be persuasive he must demonstrate to his listeners by his words and by his conduct that he is trustworthy and competent, and that he bears good will toward his audience.

TRUSTWORTHINESS.   Listeners are more inclined to accept the views of a speaker who appears to them to be trustworthy. Statements which he makes need to be believable to an audience and when his statements are likely to be questioned, they should be backed up with supporting details which will tend to establish the probability of what he says.

The admonition to bolster assertions with evidence has been given elsewhere. In the present context, however, supporting details are considered as lending more than clarity, interest, and rational proof. Adequate support is also important in establishing *ethos* because if a listener feels that a speaker is untrustworthy on one given point, that feeling will tend to include other points. If a speaker hides some essential facts, distorts or takes things from context at some time, a knowledgeable listener will readily believe that he will do this at other times.

Audiences who disagree with a speaker are particularly prone to be critical of what he says. Indeed, hostile audiences search for reasons to reject speakers. A speaker has achieved at least a small measure of success if he can get even some members of a hostile audience to say, "I don't agree with what he said but he certainly is honest and sincere." While there seem to be no meaningful measures of the persuasiveness of sincerity, a listener who applies this term to a speaker obviously is more well disposed toward the speaker than he might be and his recognition of the speaker's trustworthiness indicates that the speaker has communicated his meaning even if the listener doesn't agree.

COMPETENCE. The speaker must show his audience that he has intellectual tools adequate for the problem on which he speaks—both general intellectual capacity and specific knowledge of his subject. In some cases, credibility based on competence is established before the speech. Listeners go to hear an "authority" speak or they listen because the speaker is known as an "intelligent man." When you consider one of your professors intelligent, your opinion is influenced by your attitude toward his position and by what other students have said about him.

That part of credibility which is generated by the speaker's intelligence must also be built during the speech. A speech should reveal that the speaker has knowledge and insights that are of value to the listener. If the signs of the speaker's intelligence are not obvious, the listeners may pay little attention to what he says. Your classmates have little reason to believe that you are an authority on any subject. Consequently, you will need to indicate the background, reading, and thinking which qualify you to talk. To enhance your *ethos*, your speech should reveal your knowledge of the subject under discussion, evidence a rigorous logical development, and display what is frequently called common sense.

GOOD WILL TOWARD THE AUDIENCE. An effective public speaker indicates to his audience that he advocates a proposal for their good as well as for his own. He shows, either directly or indirectly that he is unbiased, has no ax to grind, possesses no ulterior motive. Without overdoing direct praise, he shows that he regards his listeners as intelligent and good people. In short, the speaker will show his audience that he wants them to be there; that he regards them as worthy of what he has to say, and that he wants the best for them.

Using Ethos

Five principles may help you to use *ethos* in a speech.

1. Be temperate in showing trustworthiness, competence, and good will.
2. Build *ethos* indirectly.
3. Use the credibility of others to support your own *ethos*.

4. Sometimes use candor to disarm a hostile audience.
5. Use a chairman's introduction to build *ethos*.

**BE TEMPERATE IN SHOWING TRUSTWORTHINESS, COMPE-
TENCE, AND GOOD WILL.**   While a speaker must show his listeners
that he is worth listening to, he has the potential for injuring his
ethos if he creates the impression that he is too self-centered. Frequently, a speaker will avoid this problem by specifically down-
grading his experience humorously. Here is a professor of economics
speaking before a businessman's club.

I appreciate your introduction, Mr. Trautman, and I am pleased
to be here to give you some of my observations of the problems of the
small businessman during cyclical changes. I have spent many years
studying this problem. I was also foolish enough to write a book on
business cycles a few years back. I'm sometimes afraid that the more I
study the less I know and I'm sure you're all aware of the old saying
that if all the economists in the world were placed end to end they
wouldn't reach a conclusion.

Direct, heavy-handed attempts to impress listeners with one's own
qualifications, to speak like the salesman who keeps insisting that he
has no personal reason for making a sale when the customer knows
that he does, can be injurious.
BUILD ETHOS INDIRECTLY.   Much of the *ethos* of a speaker is built
by the fact that he shows through his thoroughness, accuracy, and
careful thought that he *is* competent rather than by *telling* listeners
that he is competent.

In a very real sense we see here how all the factors of the speaking
situation go together. Credibility and *ethos* help to make argument,
evidence, and motive appeal more believable and thus more persuasive. Conversely, the speaker who organizes, supports, and uses
language well to develop his speech strengthens his *ethos*.
**USE THE CREDIBILITY OF OTHERS TO SUPPORT YOUR OWN
ETHOS.**   To a large extent quotations from sources which rank high
in the estimation of the listener help to make a speaker more believable. He associates himself and his message with others of high
credibility and thus wins a kind of reflected or secondary *ethos*.
SOMETIMES USE CANDOR TO DISARM A HOSTILE AUDIENCE.
So much emphasis is placed on not offending hostile listeners that one
may think it is always best to hide his true views from such an audience. But many speakers are so successful through candor that that

technique cannot be ignored. Several years ago an Assemblyman in California spoke to a regional meeting of the California State Employees' Association and said in effect, "There is no need to disguise the truth many of you know. I voted against your pay raises this year and it's only fair to tell you that I will do it again if I feel that it is against the interests of the state." To this day, persons who were at that meeting comment on his statement and remark, "He may not agree with you but at least he's a man who isn't afraid to tell you where he stands." Candor in that case built *ethos* by contradicting the all-too-prevalent notion that a politician is one who skirts issues.

USE A CHAIRMAN'S INTRODUCTION TO BUILD ETHOS. The chairman's introduction can build the credibility of a speaker by giving relevant facts which will be significant to the audience. When the chairman is better known to the audience than the speaker, he can frequently do a better job of building credibility for the speaker than the speaker himself can. Remember this situation when you are called upon to chair a meeting and plan your introductions carefully with it in mind.

SUMMARY

Persuasion is a product of a combination of proofs. In addition to logical proof (argument), psychological proofs help to persuade. These proofs take the form of motive appeals and the *ethos* of the speaker. Motive appeals provide a basis for arousing in the audience motivation toward the acceptance of a proposition. The six types of motive appeals discussed in this chapter represent several major motivations which people have: self-preservation, happiness, self-esteem, well-being of family and friends, financial well-being, and preservation of the societies to which they belong.

In using motive appeals, a speaker should follow these principles: The appeals should be a product of the ideas of the speech and not an end in themselves. The motivation should be consistent throughout the speech, even when motivation is multiple. The motives used should be compatible with one another to insure consistency of effect. The materials of the speech should carry the motivation and the speaker should avoid overusing motive appeals.

A speaker creates a favorable *ethos* for himself by the clues he gives to his own credibility. A speaker's credibility established before he begins to speak will effect his persuasiveness, but more important to us is how he uses this situation to build *ethos*, what clues to his character he gives his audience during the speech itself. He gives these clues to show that he is trustworthy and competent and has good will toward his listeners. In giving these clues the speaker should be temperate, indirect, associate himself with the credibility of others, and sometimes use candor. The chairman of a meeting can often enhance the credibility of a speaker he introduces.

QUESTIONS

1. Which kind of motive appeals do you suppose are most often effective with college students? Why?

2. What is wrong with finding a good basis for motivation and then selecting a subject to fit it?

3. What is the danger of using a large number of different motive appeals in a speech?

4. How can multiple motive appeals be effective?

5. How obvious should you be in identifying for your audience the motivation you use?

6. Give an example of overused motive appeals.

7. What is *ethos*?

8. How does *ethos* differ from ethics?

9. How do credibility and *ethos* differ?

10. What are the three characteristics which a speaker must evidence in order to have good *ethos*?

EXERCISES

1. Consider some prominent public speaker you have heard recently. What did you know about his reputation before you heard his speech that affected your reception of his ideas? What did his speech do to confirm or deny your opinion of him? Write a short paper explaining your reactions.

2. Which do you consider more important to a speaker's effectiveness, motive appeals or *ethos*? Why?

3. Examine two of the three speeches following Chapter XVIII. What motive appeals does the speaker use? How well do you think he adapted his appeals to his audience?

4. Examine two of the three speeches following Chapter XVIII. How well does the speaker develop *ethos* according to the principles discussed in this chapter?

LANGUAGE AND ORAL STYLE

I. How language works
  A. Symbolism
  B. Meaning
    1. Denotation
    2. Connotation
    3. Syntax
    4. Context
  C. Emotional coloring
II. Style
  A. Written style and spoken style
  B. Characteristics of good oral style
    1. Propriety
      a. Shoptalk
      b. Slang
      c. Taboos
      d. Formal English
      e. Informal English
    2. Precision
      a. Accuracy
        (1) Avoid exaggeration
        (2) Avoid ambiguity
      b. Concreteness and specificity
        (1) Avoid meaningless qualifiers
        (2) Avoid abstract terms
        (3) Avoid general terms
    3. Simplicity
    4. Directness
    5. Originality
  C. Making style vivid
    1. Figures of speech
    2. Parallel structure
    3. Antithesis
    4. Rhetorical questions
III. Improving language and style
IV. Summary, questions, and exercises

XII

LANGUAGE
AND ORAL
STYLE

The outline of a speech has on occasion been likened to the skeleton of a human body. The comparison is useful insofar as it suggests the relationship of parts to whole in functional order. Moreover, if outline is to speech as skeleton is to body, it is clear that a speech is not wholly represented by its outline. In much the same sense that the human skeleton requires ligaments, muscles, and nerves to function, a speech becomes a complete and living thing only when the sinews and flesh of language are added.

At least one further comparison can be made. The muscles of the human body are either weak or strong, flabby or firm. Language, too, is either weak and flabby or firm and strong. In this chapter, we will consider how language is used to give movement and strength to a speech by adding to the skeleton of the outline the firm, strong muscles of effective oral style.

HOW LANGUAGE WORKS

When a speaker addresses an audience, the understanding he wants his listeners to have or the proposition he wants them to accept cannot be transplanted directly from his mind into theirs. The speaker's meaning is not a material currency which can be circulated from hand to hand. Instead, he must use some medium of transmission. Language is instrumental in formulating such a medium.

Symbolism

Language may be defined as a system of visual and audible symbols, verbal and nonverbal, which one uses to encode a message. Such a message is transmitted by a speaker to an audience in order to evoke meanings in his listeners. But not just any meanings. He wants to evoke meanings which are similar enough to his own that it may be said his audience understands what he intends to say.

The use of language as a means of communication is an enormous feat of symbol-making. To cite a fairly simple instance, the word *and* is widely symbolized by the mark "&" (and has been ever since 63 B.C.). The mark itself is called an ampersand, and this is a further verbal symbolization. So you see that a man can not only devise things which stand for other things, but he can also devise words that are names for these new things.

Words may be represented by graphic signs in writing or by combinations of sounds in speaking. Whether the set of graphic signs looks like

W. Va.   or   West Virginia,

it is represented by roughly the same combination of sounds when put into speech. We say "roughly" because the sound signs, too, may undergo some variation, depending on the accent and dialect of the speaker. But despite differences in spelling (British *kerb* vs. American *curb*) or in spoken renderings (*tomayto* vs. *tomahto*), verbal symbols are created to describe or refer to the things they name.

Not all language is verbal. Certain kinds of communication dispense with words: a skull and crossbones on the label wrapped around a bottle will tell you something important about the contents as quickly as the verbal symbol *Poison*. The cross and the star of David are almost universally known symbols, but neither of them is verbal language. Shaking a clenched fist communicates something quite clearly to a large part of the world's population, but it is not a word. Verbal language, however, is the primary means by which human beings have recorded and transmitted the accumulated experience and wisdom of the past. And, for the most part, speakers depend on verbal symbols to communicate ideas. A speaker uses language to tell his listeners what is in his mind. Since the language is not his ideas, but only stands for them, an enormous part of the effectiveness of any speaker's communication depends upon his ability to use language well. The problem in using language is to choose the right symbols to evoke the intended response.

Meaning

Because word-symbols stand for things and ideas, we tend to think that words are the basic units of meaning, but words in themselves have no meaning. The answer to the apparently simple question, "What does *slip* (or *hand* or *sack* or *pool*) mean?" is, equally simply, "Nothing!" The meanings, that is, the various senses in which these or any other words are used, are never in the words themselves. They exist only in the people who use and receive them. But the meanings for the one who hears words are never precisely the same as the meanings for the one who speaks them.

The point is that all meaning is idiosyncratic; it is only in somebody's mind and it is peculiar to him who has it. Hence the exact duplication of meaning, the evocation of the same meanings by a verbal stimulus in two people, could occur only if their two brains were identical, cell for cell, synapse for synapse, nerve for nerve. In addition, each of the two people would have to have had identical experiences with the phenomenon that the verbal symbol names. These conditions cannot be met. Consequently, the meanings evoked in two people by the same symbol must be different. However, since people who have words which they use in common also have over-lapping meanings for these words, communication is impaired only to the extent that the dissimilarities in their meanings create confusion. A couple of examples will suggest the kinds of differences which cause confusion.

If someone proposes to tell a group how to make raisin cookies, each person in his audience will have somewhat different meanings for "raisin." The object that the name "raisin" denotes to each member of his audience is, however, likely to be pretty much the same sort of thing. It could happen that one might buy muscat raisins and another white raisins so that their cookies would not be exactly alike, but that difference isn't very serious.

In other cases different meanings create confusion. The superintendent of a highway construction crew says, "Make sure that everyone is out of the area before you set off the dynamite." In this message situation, the speaker doesn't want to say later in the afternoon while he picks up pieces of the crew, "What do you mean, you looked around and didn't see anybody? Is that your idea of making sure?" Therefore, the superintendent is likely to take pains to satisfy himself that both he and the dynamite crew have very much the same meaning for the term, "Make sure."

In view of the fact that meanings are in people, not in words, you can readily see, despite popular misconceptions to the contrary, that the dictionary does not govern the language. The function of a dictionary is not *to define* any given word, but merely *to record* the many senses in which people have used the word to express their meanings in various contexts at various times.

Theoretically, one may define a word in any way he chooses and then use it in that sense. If this use of the word fails to stir up overlapping meanings in the one who hears it, or if it runs too far counter to his meanings for the word, communication suffers. Here's an example of what we mean.

In this book, the word *proposition* is used to name a statement which expresses a judgment concerning fact, value, or policy. This is an ordinary use of the term in rhetoric. In logic, however, the word has quite a different meaning. To avoid possible confusion, we thought we might use the word *conclusion* instead of *proposition*. After all, a speaker's proposition is the conclusion of his line of argument and it is the conclusion at which he wants his listeners to arrive. The word conclusion was abandoned, however, after one of us tried to define it in class one day. A student objected to the definition quite vigorously, saying, "You can't use the word conclusion that way. It really means something else." This student must have felt as Alice did when talking with Humpty Dumpty.

"There's glory for you!"

"I don't know what you mean by 'glory,' " Alice said.

Humpty Dumpty smiled contemptuously. "Of course you don't— till I tell you. I mean 'there's a nice knock-down argument for you!' "

"But 'glory' doesn't mean 'a nice knock-down argument,' " Alice objected.

"When *I* use a word," Humpty Dumpty said, in rather a scornful tone, "it means just what I choose it to mean—neither more nor less."

"The question is," said Alice, "whether you *can* make words mean so many different things."

Somewhere between the rigid confusion of Alice, who tries to make *words* (instead of people) "mean" something (and then always mean the same thing), and the arbitrary nonsense of Humpty Dumpty, who should not hope to be easily understood, lies a way of using words to let someone know what you have in mind.

To understand something about the way language works, consider for a moment some of the relationships among words and reality and people. Four important notions are involved in this consideration: *denotation, connotation, syntax,* and *context.*

DENOTATION. The denotation of a word is the object, event, or concept which it names. When people think and talk, they need some way of pointing to or signifying things they can't carry around in their hands. Words, then, are used as symbols which stand for, which *denote*, the things people want to refer to in conversation. An "automobile," a "monarchy," and a "unicorn" are, in varying degrees, difficult to designate by pointing out. Yet, for one reason or another, one may want to talk about them. The word used to name each thus becomes a way of pointing to the thing it names. Other events, such as those named by words like "speak," "take," or "be," are named by words which are intended to denote the event. Denotation may be said to name the relationship between a word and the world outside a speaker's head. Words become necessary in communication directly in proportion to the difficulty one would have in pointing to the object, event, or concept they are used to name. But what about "unicorn?" Can that word be used to refer to anything outside the user's mind? The answer is, "Yes, the word unicorn denotes a small, horselike animal with a single horn in the center of its forehead."

"Show me one."

"I can't. I don't think there ever has been, is now, or will be a single instance of a unicorn in the whole world. If there ever were to be one, that one, or any other like it, would be what the word would denote."

CONNOTATION. Not only do people have denotative meanings for words, which, as we have seen, grow out of the relationships words have with objective reality, but, in addition, they develop connotative meanings for the words as well. These latter meanings do not develop as a result of the relationship between the words and *reality*, as in the case of denotations; instead they result from the relationships *people* have with words and what the words name.

It is possible for two users of the same language to have very much the same understanding of the objects, events, or concepts which words in that language are used to name, such as "socialized medicine," "guaranteed annual wage," or "federal aid to education." But in addition to this denotative meaning, each individual has other meanings which he does not, indeed cannot, share with any other person. These meanings are internalized, personalized, attitudinalized. They result from the fact that every experience one has with a word, whether he uses it himself or someone else does and every experience he has with what the word is used to name, adds to and changes his meanings for the word by changing his attitude toward the thing. These meanings, which develop from the relationships among people, words, and things, are called connotations.

To say it another way: Denotative meanings are externalized; they are unaffective (unemotionalized), impersonal, and, for the most part, common among all the users of a language. Connotative meanings, on the other hand, may be thought of as internalized; they are affective, pesonal, and particularly idiosyncratic.

SYNTAX.   Words may also elicit meanings in a third manner. This way results from the relationships words bear to other words when they are used in accordance with the grammatical customs of a language. That is, the *syntax* a speaker uses, the way in which he structures his sentences, gives clues to what he means. Consequently, a speaker ought to follow the grammatical practices accepted in the language and expected by his audience. If he does not, he runs a double risk: He is likely to lose credibility (have the audience think less well of him, think him less worth listening to), and he is less likely to be understood in the sense he intends.

CONTEXT.   A fourth and final dimension of meaning is found in context. Syntactical meaning has to do with the way words elicit meaning by virtue of their placement in a sentence. It is a function of grammar, of the relationship of words to other words. Contextual meaning refers to the meaning words evoke by virtue of the subject matter that surrounds them. We said earlier in this chapter that words are not the basic units of meaning. With few exceptions they are ambiguous; they can be taken in any of several senses. Even when they are formulated into syntactically correct sentences, they often fail to encode a speaker's meaning in such a way that it will be accurately understood. Have you ever seen a dog run? Of course! But are you sure? Sometimes the word "run" denotes an enclosure within which domestic animals may range about. So we ask again whether you have ever seen a dog run. Perhaps and perhaps not. This example helps to explain the difference between syntactical meaning and contextual meaning. At the same time, it helps to show how the context within which a word appears gives clues to what a speaker means. The question we asked about the dog run was phrased in perfectly acceptable syntax. Yet that syntax points to one set of meanings while the question was intended to elicit another. Only when the question is surrounded by other words, put into a context, will it say what the user intends.

Emotional Coloring

Language serves not only to transmit fact and opinion to an audience but also to communicate a speaker's affective attitudes as well. In some instances, it is useful to report facts with as little emotional coloration as possible. Informative speaking, for instance, is intended to communicate an idea in such a way that it will be *understood* and *remembered*. Consequently, the speaker's language should be objective. To the extent that his language is also interesting and clear, it will serve him even better.

At other times, understanding and retention are only part of a speaker's goal. In persuasive speaking particularly, language has the additional function of creating attitude. On these occasions, a speaker deliberately chooses emotive or attitudinal language— language that will influence the emotional reactions of his audience regarding the ideas he discusses, for language has great power to evoke emotional response. The affective responses a speaker's language evokes are instrumental in shifting his audience's meanings toward his own and thereby help the speaker to create in the audience the attitudes, opinions, and beliefs he wants it to have.

Language, however, also has great power to lie or to deceive because it encapsulates a whole complex of attitudes and reactions into a single word. When that word is honorific, it is called a euphemism; when the word is pejorative, its use is said to be name-calling. Both euphemism and name-calling have bad reputations and, for the most part, rightly so. They are two widely used substitutes for adequate evidence and sound argument. And herein lies the danger of emotive language. When attitudes and feelings are severed from evidence and reasoning, the results are frequently to the disadvantage of the speaker and his audience as well.

The names that people apply to things always tell more about the people than about the things. Professor Felix Cohen, noted philosopher of law, once remarked that if he were to be called an unbeliever, an infidel, and a Gentile, he would know that the people using these terms would be, repectively, a Christian, a Mohammedan, and a Mormon. When a speaker argues against the extension of social security to include hospitalization and health benefits by referring to such a proposal as "socialized medicine," we know more about his attitude than about the proposal.

But there is a proper use for emotive language. Once a speaker is convinced that he has a clear and correct understanding of the subject he discusses, then his language becomes a tool for communicating that understanding to others. Since the speaker's attitudes are a part of the truth as he sees it, he cannot properly be denied the use of whatever language will accurately and efficiently communicate his attitudes, as parts of his thinking, to others. Neither moral laxity nor intellectual fuzziness is involved when a speaker takes advantage of the emotive connotations of words to supplement the logical elements of his proof.

To put the whole matter briefly, attitudinal and connotative language is frequently a necessary and desirable tool of effective public speaking. It helps to communicate ideas and attitudes clearly, vividly, and interestingly. And this is precisely what a speaker tries to do.

We add, almost (but not entirely) parenthetically, the well-intentioned advice that although the history of oratory offers many examples of speakers who have used language to create bias; who have given emotional coloration to subjects requiring objective treatment; who have substituted additudinal language for evidence and sound argument, nonetheless *you*, following the tradition and the example of the just and honorable speakers of all time, should use the powerful weapon of language in a manner acceptable to your own conscience and to the ethical dictates of society as well.

STYLE

Any number of speakers may talk on the same subject. They may use the same sources of material, indeed the same materials. Further, they may organize their materials and ideas in the same manner. Yet when these speakers deliver their talks, no two speeches will be alike in every detail. Ignoring differences in voice, in physical appearance, and in such visual aspects of delivery as posture, stance, and gesture, there will still be one noticeable and substantial difference among the several speeches. This difference will be in the use of language. No two speakers will choose the same words to express what may be essentially the same idea. That variety in language which distinguishes one expression of an idea from another may be called style.

Style is defined in a variety of ways. Put simply, it is the choice of words a person makes to communicate what is in his mind. To use language well is to clothe the speech in suitable garments. Good oral style is that use of language which meets the intellectual and emotional demands of speaker, speech, audience, and occasion. In the following portion of this chapter, it will be our purpose to identify, as clearly as we can in brief treatment, those elements of style which make for an effective use of language in speaking. As a first step toward understanding the style of oral communication, let's see how it differs from written discourse.

Written Style and Spoken Style

In writing, the expression of ideas is directed toward the eye. Some importance is ordinarily attached to the ability of a reader to comprehend a passage of writing quickly and easily. In general, however, there is relatively little demand on him to grasp an idea instantly when it is presented in written form. Under ordinary circumstances, a reader may examine a page at leisure. Whenever he wishes, he may pause to reflect on what he has read, to think about the ideas, and to absorb them at any rate he finds comfortable. He can reread a passage any number of times his understanding requires and his interest allows. In short, the goal of a writer is to make his ideas ultimately intelligible to a reader.

A listening audience, on the other hand, has no such opportunity for leisurely consideration of the ideas presented to it. A listener cannot go back to rehear. If he pauses to reflect, he breaks the tightly woven chain of the speaker's organization, loses connection with the speaker's development, and is left behind. Often, he is completely lost as a listener. Consequently, whereas a writer must be ultimately intelligible to his readers, a speaker must be instantly intelligible to his listeners.

Characteristics of Good Oral Style

In the use of language, as in all other aspects of speaking, clarity and interest are indispensable qualities. That is to say, the task of language in a speech is to make ideas instantly, clearly, and accurately intelligible, and to do so in a manner that engages the continuing attention of the audience. The language usage that best attains this end constitutes good oral style. It will display these characteristics: propriety, precision, simplicity, directness, and originality.

PROPRIETY.   Style is appropriate to the extent that the speaker's language is adapted to his audience and to the occasion of his speech. As a matter of fact, in daily life one constantly adjusts his speech practices to different audiences without ever thinking of the process. During the course of a day, a man will talk to his children, his wife, his colleagues, his boss, his neighbors, casual acquaintances, total strangers, old friends: no two listeners are exactly alike. In each of these situations the process of audience analysis automatically and unconsciously precedes the speaker's selection of vocabulary, sentence structure, and figure of speech. A political orator speaking to members of his own party will use one kind of language and even certain terms which he will take pains to avoid when addressing an audience which also includes people of another political persuasion. That a man would address his wife in the same way he addresses the salesman who tries to sell him an insurance policy is highly unlikely. A man who is signalling an S.O.S. doesn't use scientific or technical terminology, nor does he use the language of the *Congressional Record* when making love.

The choice of language, then, is habitually determined by the audience and the occasion. One of the hallmarks of an ineffective speaker is his inability to adapt his language to these two elements of the speaking situation. Linguistically ill-equipped, he is as handicapped as an automobile that can travel in one gear only.

Shoptalk. The phenomenon of "shoptalk" illustrates one aspect of language propriety. Many occupations and activities have what amounts to a private system of language signals, a jargon incomprehensible to all but those participating in the activity.

Shoptalk sometimes provides a speaker with useful verbal shortcuts which immediately identify him with his audience. Used thus, it may gain him a vital psychological advantage. The limitations of such language usage are apparent. The jargon of the trade is useful only for talking to the trade.

Slang. Other language forms have even more limited usefulness than shoptalk. These forms should be considered totally inappropriate. Among them is slang. There is nothing wrong with the motive that generates slang. It grows out of the attempt to find a fresh, colorful, sharp, or humorous expression of an idea. Usually, however, slang is shortlived. If it does last, either it becomes a part of standard speech and is no longer slang, or it becomes the hackneyed, impoverished language of the speaker who is illiterate or too lazy to find language that says what he really means. A speaker may justify using slang on the ground that it adds vividness to his expression, but he runs the danger that it will add a jarring note to what he says.

Taboos. Even more to be avoided than slang is language that violates the taboos of the speaker's audience. These are many.

Among them are profanity, vulgarity, and obscenity. Language of this sort may communicate very effectively—profanity, for example, is notoriously expressive!—but it is not socially acceptable.

Linguistic taboos are more often applied to what are considered improper word forms or improper occasions than they are to subject matter. Certain tribes avoid naming their gods for fear of offending them, but they will use circumlocution to talk about the gods. Two terms with the same denotation will often flourish side by side because one of them has connotations that make it taboo and improper in public discourse. Examples are certain words that refer to the functions of excretion and reproduction. Whatever the taboos of his audience are, a speaker who violates them exposes himself to reproof and a consequent loss of effectiveness.

Formal English. At another extreme from shoptalk, slang, and linguistic taboos is a language style which a subject, audience, and occasion sometimes require a speaker to use. It is called *formal* English. This term is used to denote the variety of language used for communicating with people who demand precise expression either because they are exacting in their language usage or because the matter communicated is highly important. The language used in a Supreme Court proceeding, for example, must be formal in tone and precise in meaning—informality or flippancy would be highly inappropriate, imprecision a source of confusion. The English of a United Nations debate or report needs to be formal because formal English will come closest to evoking the same meanings in all the people who use English for communication—a few being the Australians, Canadians, Ceylonese, Ghanaians, Indians, Irish, Jamaicans, Maltese, Pakistanis, and delegates from the United States. Moreover, formal English is better suited than colloquial English is for accurate translation into French, Russian, Chinese, and the other languages used at the United Nations. Although relatively few situations call for a strictly formal usage, it is to the student's advantage to know how to operate at this level, for certainly in college he will be expected to write (and even to deliver orally) academic reports, reference papers, and, at the graduate level, seminar papers and theses. All of these situations customarily require formal English.

Informal English. All the styles of language we have been examining are of limited usefulness for public speaking: Shoptalk is for specialists only, slang is normally inappropriate, linguistic taboos must not be violated, and formal English is used in the kind of speaking that is rarely heard in the course of ordinary life. What style of English, then, is widely and generally appropriate?

Stephen Leacock described it in his remark about the use of "English" for literature and "American" for speaking. Conversation is conducted in "American" or informal English. Informal English admits many words and sentence constructions that formal English excludes, words and forms customarily found in the casual speaking of educated people. Since such people are at ease in this language, a speaker may well use it in addressing them. Compilers of dictionaries label some of its words "colloquial," as indeed they are. But "colloquial" need not suggest inferiority or incorrectness; it is merely a descriptive label. Colloquial language is not necessarily incorrect and may be highly appropriate.

Informal English includes that large body of words and expressions employed by educated people in carrying on the public and private business of the contemporary world. This language is found in communications aimed at general listeners and readers: speeches, magazine articles, newspaper columns, and the like. This is the language that will be appropriate in the majority of speeches you will be called upon to make while in college and after graduation.

PRECISION.   For all his bumbling speech, Polonius knew well the functions of language. It was clear to him that Hamlet was reading *more* than "Words, words, words." Polonius understood that words are used to communicate meaning, or, as he put it, "matter." You may smile at his clumsiness, but you should admire the old man's efforts to be clear and precise in what he said.

To be precise in language is to choose the right words for expressing an idea. The right words are those that say clearly what a speaker has in mind. They put his ideas sharply into focus and minimize the chance of confusion on the part of a listener.

We have said that good oral style is designed to make a speaker's ideas instantly intelligible. But a speaker will say clearly only what he has clearly in mind. Consequently, the first requirement for clear language is a clear idea. Assuming, though, that a speaker knows what he wants to say, his problem is to say it well.

Language must have two major characteristics to be precise (and thus clear). The first of these is accuracy; the second is concreteness.

Accuracy. The two most important obstacles to accuracy in speaking are exaggeration and ambiguity.

Avoid exaggeration. Hyperbole is the name given to the kind of exaggeration that is used for dramatic effect. This sort of exaggeration is an acceptable figure of speech and is not likely to cause confusion or lack of clarity. When you say, "My car is as old as the hills," no one will take the statement literally. Such deliberate and intentional inaccuracies in language add vividness to expression. But this use of hyperbole is noticeably different from what happens when a woman says, "*Everyone* just *raved* about my new dress!" It may very well be true that one or two of her friends made some polite remark about the dress but her statement is literally meant and is expected to be literally taken. This sort of exaggeration introduces unnecessary and thoughtless imprecision into what should be an accurate statement of fact.

The advertising vocabulary contains the most obvious offenses in using the kind of exaggeration that robs a statement of accuracy. "Big" isn't *big* enough, so advertisers use, in progression, "gigantic," "colossal," and, not even ultimately, "supercolossal." This kind of thinking leads toothpaste manufacturers to identify as their "large" size the smallest tube of toothpaste available through retail channels. When the supersuperlatives have been exhausted, what next?

To exaggerate for emphasis has been called an American trait. It is more nearly universal. But exaggeration fails to achieve its effect when it is used unceasingly, as the habit of using too much spice makes normally seasoned food seem flat.

Avoid ambiguity. Ambiguity is found in contexts, not in words. A statement is ambiguous when either of two meanings is possible and the context does not make clear which is intended. Grammatical ambiguity (often called *amphiboly* or *amphibology*) results from an uncertain grammatical construction. Newspapers offer frequent examples of amphiboly. More amusing than confusing, it is, nonetheless, an example of inaccuracy in the use of language:

"Throw the horse over the fence some hay."

"I like teaching more than my wife."

"Her hair was pulled back in a bun while at her throat which complemented her navy-blue tailored dress was a multistrand of beads."

"The restaurant is famous for its *foie gras* made from goose livers and its fine chef."

News notes about members of a woman's club: "We are sorry to report that our Past President, Mrs. Gertrude Sturtevant, is at home recuperating from an operation."

A headline: "Drowning dampens spirits at beach party."

Story on a society page: "A few youths swam in the chill night air."

A second kind of ambiguity grows out of the fact that a word may evoke a number of potential meanings and the context fails to make clear which of these is intended. The lawyer who phoned his wife to say he would be late for dinner because he was delayed by a bar meeting was guilty of (deliberate?) ambiguity.

Concreteness and specificity. The greatest enemy of precision in language, other than a lack of accuracy, is vagueness. It resides in the words, not in their contexts. Once the speaker's meaning for a word is determined within a context, ambiguity is removed and his meaning is usually clear. A vague word, on the other hand, is one so broad that no matter what its context, left unaided, it will tend to be imprecise. We will mention three classes of words that lead to vagueness; meaningless qualifiers, abstract terms, and general terms. The implication is that you avoid using them whenever possible.

Avoid meaningless qualifiers. Many words give the impression of qualifying or quantifying when really they don't. What does one mean, for example, when he says that a man is "fat," "thin," "tall," "short," "middle-aged," or "bald"? The terms are so relative that they mean virtually nothing except with reference to some scale or some exact criterion. The images listeners get from such terms as these will vary widely and also differ widely from what the speaker intends to convey. How many is "some," "few," "several"? How much is "lots," or "very"? Whenever you can (and this will be nearly always), give precise information.

Avoid abstract terms. An abstract term is one that names a quality apart from any material instance of it. By their very nature, abstract terms must be vague because they refer to no tangible object. Abstract terms, like other vague words, lack precision because they can mean so many things. A speaker can hardly avoid talking about such abstractions as *justice, honesty, democracy, virtue,* and the like, but to do so without definition or without clear examples that convey a precise image is to be vague.

Abstract terms are tempting for several reasons. Most obvious of these is the fact that it is easier to use an abstract term than it is to force oneself to make clear distinctions among a number of borderline cases all of which are comfortably covered by the abstract term. A speaker can condemn "gambling" but avoid mentioning or thinking about church bingo parties. He can deprecate "obscene" books and let his hearers think of *Lady Chatterley's Lover* or something else. He can denounce "undemocratic nations," and let his hearers put the government of Transcisalpuria into that category if they wish. He can deplore "corruption" in "unions"; he need not then stigmatize Local 4321 of International XYZ.

Another reason abstract terms are tempting is that they make it possible to avoid definite commitments. When governments "rattle sabers," they do not make blunt threats but rather veil the threatened consequences in vague language. No government would say, "Stop putting missile bases in the countries around our border or we'll knock your head off." Instead, the language of diplomacy leaves enough room for doubt so that maneuvering is possible and backtracking causes no loss of face. "Inconsistent with national safety," "will strongly oppose any attempt," "lead to serious consequences." Analyses of conditions and forecasts of trends made by some stock-market analysts are splendid examples of precisely this sort of vagueness.

Avoid general terms. The use of general terms is a third cause of vagueness in expression. A comedian, whose name we have forgotten, makes fun of the practice of using what he calls the "vague specific." Good examples of the "vague specific" are found in several of the phrases student speakers seem to like to use: "authorities agree . . ."; "in my research I found that . . ."; "in an article I read . . ." Other examples of general terms: "A large midwestern city," "noted chemist (physicist, theologian, or whatever)," "government sources," "statistics show . . ."

The solution to problems of vagueness in language is to make the language as precise as possible. The way to do this is to use concrete rather than abstract terms, to use specific rather than general terms, to formulate meaningful definitions, to give clear examples.

Developing a sensitivity to language will make a speaker aware of the subtle shadings in idea and emotional coloration that may be achieved in his use of words. Moreover, it will make him intensely aware of the linguistic practices that exist in his own speaking. He will begin to strive for the word or phrase that carries the exact shade of meaning that he intends, and he will not be content with one that is only a near approximation.

SIMPLICITY.   A naive but common assumption is that "big" words are somehow better because they are more impressive than their ordinary and familiar counterparts. Acting on this assumption, speakers often sound pompous when they mean to be dignified. Nothing is more damaging to one's purpose than feeble elegance. Henry David Thoreau, whose own style is marked by economy and simplicity, commented that long words had a paralysis in their tails. (Thoreau said that he went for walks along the river, not on riparian excursions.) Far from being an elevated variety of English, self-conscious formality is pretentious and unnatural.

Former Representative Maury Maverick coined the term "gob-bledygook" as a label for writing or speaking that is pompous, wordy, involved, and full of long, Latinized terms. Gobbledygook is almost totally destructive of clarity. What did the college ad-ministrator mean who listed these aims for education?

. . . the development of intellectual consistency, the creation of aesthetic awareness, the liberation of the personality, the awakening of nonverbal and nonrational sensibilities to amplify adult experience, and the structure of an insight into the eternality of human aspiration and frustration.

Multisyllabic words from Latin and Greek roots may seem im-pressive to the one who uses them, but for English-speaking listeners one- and two-syllable words of Anglo-Saxon origin are better. As we recall, it was Thomas Aquinas who said that simplicity is the essence of beauty. Impressiveness in style is a part of its beauty, but pomposity is too easily mistaken for impressiveness. A young woman comparing the relative merits of two spools of thread said she found it "monetarily advantageous to purchase the larger spool." Her listeners might have been less amused to hear that it was "cheaper in the long run to buy the larger spool."

Lack of simplicity often robs style of propriety and precision. First, propriety suffers when language is too technical. The doctor who warns a patient of "an incipient carcinomatous condition in the duodenum immediately inferior to the pylorus" would be much clearer (to the layman) if he spoke of "the first stages of cancer at the upper end of the small intestine." Second, an attempt to use "im-pressive" language can often lead to embarrassing mistakes in ac-curacy. In Sheridan's play, *The Rivals*, the now famous Mrs. Malaprop gave her name ("Malapropism") to this kind of mistake:

Observe me, Sir Anthony.—I would by no means wish a daughter of mine to be a progeny of learning; I don't think so much learning becomes a young woman; for instance, I would never let her meddle with Greek, or Hebrew, or Algebra, or Simony, or Fluxions, or Paradoxes, or such inflammatory branches of learning—neither would it be necessary for her to handle any of your mathematical, astronomical, diabolical instruments:—But, Sir Anthony, I would send her, at nine years old, to a boarding-school, in order to learn a little ingenuity and artifice. Then, sir, she should have a supercilious knowledge in accounts;—and as she grew up, I would have her instructed in geometry, that she might know something of the contagious countries;—but above all, Sir Anthony, she should be a mistress of orthodoxy, that she might not mis-spell, and mis-pronounce words so shamefully as girls usually do; and likewise that she might reprehend the true meaning of what she is saying. This, Sir Anthony, is what I would have a woman know;—and I don't think there is a superstitious article in it.

To achieve simplicity, use not only short, forceful words, but also as few words as possible to accomplish your purpose. Notice we say *to accomplish your purpose*, and not just to be understood, because your purpose includes being understood in a certain way.

DIRECTNESS.   The style of public address is much more direct and personal than written style. A speaker uses first and second person pronouns "I," "you," "we," to a much greater extent than a writer. On July 26, 1952, Adlai E. Stevenson accepted the Democratic party's nomination to run for the Presidency. In the following excerpt from his acceptance speech, observe not only the directness and personalness of his style, but the simplicity as well.

Mr. President, Ladies and Gentlemen of the Convention, my Fellow Citizens:

I accept your nomination—and your program.

I should have preferred to hear those words uttered by a stronger, a wiser, a better man than myself. But after listening to the President's speech I even feel better about myself.

None of you, my friends, can wholly appreciate what is in my heart. I can only hope that you understand my words. They will be few.

ORIGINALITY.   Change of pace is as important in speaking as it is in pitching a ball game. Nothing destroys interest or dulls attention as effectively as monotony. You remember that in Chapter IX we identified change as being one of the characteristics of a stimulus that make it attract attention. Originality in style is a form of skillful change, one that helps to avoid monotony in language. Instead of using trite expressions, try to bring freshness and vigor to your speaking through saying what you have to say without the use of clichés, hackneyed phrases, and figures of speech that are tired from overuse.

William H. Whyte, Jr., constructed a composite business speech built out of some sixty badly overused expressions and constructions. It is an example of what Whyte says can be called *reverse* gobbledygook which "lends a powerful straight-from-the-shoulder effect to ambiguity and equivocation." Look at the style of that speech.

Cooperation—An Opportunity and a Challenge*
An Address

It is a pleasure and a privilege to be here with you today. These great annual meetings are always an inspiration to me, and doubly so today. After that glowing introduction by our toastmaster, I must confess, however, that I'd like to turn the tables and tell a little story on Chuck. When I say it's about the nineteenth hole and a certain gentleman whose baritone was cracked, those of you who were at the Atlanta conference last year will know what I mean. But I won't tell it. Chuck Forbes is too good a friend of mine and, seriously, I know full well we all realize what a tower of strength his yeoman service has been to the association in these trying times.

Yes, gentlemen, trying times. So you'll pardon me if I cast aside the glib reverberation of glittering generalities and the soothing syrup of sugar-coated platitudes and put it to you the only way I can: straight English.

We're losing the battle!

From every corner the people are being weaned from the doctrines of the Founding Fathers. They are being detoured from the high-speed highways of progress by the utopian highwaymen.

Now, the man in the street is a pretty savvy fellow. Don't sell him short. Joe Doakes may be fooled for a while, but in the end he wants no part of the mumbo jumbo the global saboteurs are trying to sell him. After all, he is an American.

But he has to be told.

And we're not telling him!

Now let me say that I do not wish to turn the clock back. None of

---

* William H. Whyte, Jr., "The Language of Business," *Fortune* (November, 1950), 114. Courtesy of *Fortune* Magazine.

us do. All forward-looking businessmen see themselves as partners in a team in which the worker is a full-fledged member. I regard our employees as our greatest business asset, and I am sure, mindful as I am of the towering potentials of purposeful energy in this group of clear-sighted leaders, that in the final analysis, it is the rock foundation of your policies, too.

But the team can't put the ball across for a first down just by wishing it. The guards and the tackles can't do their job if the quarterback doesn't let them in on the play. And we, the quarterbacks, are muffing the ball.

How are we to go over for a touchdown? My friends, this is the $64 question. I don't know the answers. I am just a plain-spoken businessman. I am not a soothsayer. I have no secret crystal ball. But I do know one thing: before we round the curve into the homestretch, we have a job to do. It will not be easy. I offer no panaceas or nostrums. Instead I would like to suggest that the real key to our problem lies in the application of the three E's.

What are the three E's?
ENTERPRISE! ENDEAVOR! EFFORT!

Each and every one of us must appoint himself a salesman—yes, a missionary, if you will—and get out and do some real grass roots selling. And when we hit the dirt, let's not forget the customers—the greatest asset any business has.

Now, much has been done already. But let's not fool ourselves: the surface, as our chairman has so wisely said, has hardly been scratched. The program is still in its infancy. So let me give it to you straight from the shoulder. The full implementation, gentlemen, depends on *us*.

So let's get on the beam! In cracker-barrel fashion, let's get down to earth. In good plain talk the man in the street can understand, let's remind Joe Doakes that the best helping hand he will ever find is the one at the end of his own shirt sleeve.

We have the know-how.

With sights set high, let's go over the top!

Making Style Vivid

The most important function of style in language is to give vividness to the ideas the language conveys. Language brings clarity and interest to a speech only if the speaker's style makes his ideas not only instantly intelligible but also vividly perceptible. Language which has the good qualities already discussed in this chapter will do much to make a speaker's expression vivid. We now turn our attention to a number of special devices which a speaker may use to reinforce the effectiveness of the language he uses.

FIGURES OF SPEECH.   Figurative language uses words to convey meanings beyond their literal meaning. It makes some change in the meaning or use of a word and thereby adds color and vividness to expression. The language of everyday conversation is abundantly sprinkled with figures of speech.

Of the many forms that figurative language takes, the most common are *metaphor* and *simile*. Both of these figures are formed by comparing one object with another. A simile makes a comparison between two things and ordinarily indicates the comparison with such a word as *like* or *as*. When a sports broadcaster told how spectators left a stadium during a dust storm, he said the event "looked like a mob scene being sandblasted off a billboard." This kind of comparison of the two events constitutes a simile.

If the things compared are closely alike, a simile is not vivid. If the broadcaster had compared the dust-driven spectators to people running indoors from a rain, he would have had a dull simile.

Adlai E. Stevenson said, "The world at our mid-century is, as someone has said, like a drum—strike it anywhere and it resounds everywhere."* Robert G. Ingersoll said of a speech by William McKinley that "he handled his facts as skillfully as Caesar marshaled his hosts on the field of war." Senator J. W. Fulbright said America was shocked to discover that "the newly emerging nations of Asia and Africa were awake and struggling like new children to grow up."† Senator Fulbright also said on the same occasion, "We are treating our relationship to the world of the twentieth century like a quack doctor who prescribes aspirin for tuberculosis."‡

A metaphor, like a simile, is based on comparison. But whereas in a simile the comparison is explicit, a metaphor is an implied comparison. The difference between the two figures is that while simile says one thing is *like* another, the metaphor says one thing *is* another. In October, 1896, Robert G. Ingersoll used this metaphor in a speech: "I know that labor is the Atlas on whose shoulders rests the great superstructure of civilization and the great dome of science

---

* Adlai E. Stevenson, *Call to Greatness* (New York: Harper and Brothers Publishers, 1954), p. 4.

† *Vital Speeches of the Day*, 26:24 (October 1, 1960), 74.

‡ *Ibid.*

adorned with all there is of art." Henry Clay said that the Union
formed by the Constitution was "a marriage that no human authority
can dissolve or divorce the parties from."

Similes and metaphors, used intelligently, can add greatly to
the vividness of a speech. They will detract from it, however, when
they are abused. Trite similes and far-fetched metaphors are fatal to
effective expression.

Trite expressions in the speech of others are much more noticeable
than are those one uses himself. Examples of tired speech abound.
Here are a few instances of the sort of similes and metaphors that fail
to interest because they have been used too much.

Mad as a wet hen
Nervous as a cat
Slow as molasses in January
White as a sheet
To stick like a leech
To be a bookworm
Good as gold
Fat as a pig

Avoid these and any other comparisons that have become hackneyed. Language is like a flashlight battery. It illuminates better
when it is fresh.

Overstatement, understatement, and *irony* (identified as forms of
humor in Chapter XVI) are used also as figures of speech to heighten
the vividness of an idea without seeking to arouse laughter. Overstatement has already been referred to in this chapter under the name
of hyperbole.* It consists in using a stronger word than is necessary
to convey an idea. The result of this usage is to exaggerate, but for
vividness, not deception. Observe the several examples of overstatement in the following excerpts from a single paragraph in a lecture
by Adlai Stevenson.†

I am not a historian, but I doubt if anyone will dispute the *in-
comparably* dramatic qualities of the twentieth century. . . . In fifty
years, distance has been *obliterated* by a technological revolution that
has brought *all mankind* cheek to jowl, and that has released the creative and obliterative power of the atom. . . . National independence

---

* See also page 284.
† *Op. cit.,* p. 209. Our italics.

and democracy have scored *spectacular* victories and suffered *shocking* defeats. . . . Two new *colossi*, the United States and the Soviet Union, have *suddenly* emerged. Ideas, on which the West has had an export *monopoly* for centuries, are now also flowing out of the East and colliding *everywhere* with our Western ideas.

Understatement* is the opposite of exaggeration. It deliberately says less than what might be said and thus calls attention to an idea. To say of a man one considers thoroughly dishonest "He is not the most scrupulous person I know," is to understate the case.

Irony† uses language to say one thing but to imply quite another. It is often found in the same context with either exaggeration or understatement. Note the combination of irony, understatement, and overstatement in the following passage. The speaker, Robert G. Ingersoll, is arguing *in favor of* the demonetization of silver.

In 1816 Great Britain demonetized silver, and that wretched old government has had nothing but gold from that day to this as a standard. And to show you the frightful results of that demonetization, that government does not now own above one-third of the globe, and all the winds are busy floating her flags.

There is no question that figures of speech add vividness to the expression of a speaker's ideas. But a word of caution. Figures can be used to excess. When they are, style becomes not vivid, but "purple." It becomes flamboyant, flowery, and weak. Here, in a press release from the office of a Congressman, is an example of what can happen.

If we throw stones of criticism we will break the glass houses and the idols with feet of clay will be toppled from their pedestals of self-exaltation by the angry winds created by the righteous indignation of Americans sacrificed on the cross of gold by selfish, greedy men and their stooges in high places.

Another example of the overuse of figures of speech is a portion of a letter written to the editor of a newspaper:‡

If the country's listing ideal isn't soon righted people will someday find that an even keel is so far out from underneath that no counterweight thrown against a rotten ship of state can vindicate the cause

---

* See Chapter XVI, p. 284.
† See Chapter XVI, p. 284.
‡ From a letter to the editor of the Bernardsville (New Jersey) *News*, quoted in *The New Yorker* (December 25, 1965), p. 50.

of freedom without rending permanently some plank in the bulwark that this society has always taken for granted as being there, being somewhere, but which won't exist at all once debasement gives way to disjunction, and a bright hope born in 1776 founders and becomes part of the memory of that mass of other toppled nations which spell in grotesque form the failure of man to govern himself.

PARALLEL STRUCTURE. Another method of making ideas vivid is to repeat phrases of identical or similar construction. The effect of the repetition is to draw the attention of the audience to the speaker's ideas. A well-known example appears in Lincoln's Gettysburg Address. "Government of the people, by the people, for the people." In his first inaugural address, President Franklin Delano Roosevelt used this parallel structure.

Our greatest primary task is to put people to work. . . .

The task can be helped by definite efforts to raise the values of agricultural products and with this the power to purchase the output of our cities.

It can be helped by preventing realistically the tragedy of the growing loss, through foreclosure, of our small homes and our farms.

It can be helped by insistence that the Federal, State and local governments act forthwith on the demand that their cost be drastically reduced.

It can be helped by the unifying of relief activities which today are often scattered, uneconomical and unequal. It can be helped by national planning for a supervision of all forms of transportation and of communications and other utilities which have a definite public character.

And in his second inaugural address, President Roosevelt said:

I see millions of families trying to live on incomes so meager that the pall of family disaster hangs over them day by day.

I see millions whose daily lives in city and on farm continue under conditions labeled indecent by a so-called polite society half a century ago.

I see millions denied education, recreation and the opportunity to better their lot and the lot of their children.

I see millions lacking the means to buy the products of farm and factory and by their poverty denying work and productiveness to many other millions.

I see one-third of a nation ill-housed, ill-clad, ill-nourished.

ANTITHESIS. Antithesis is the opposing or contrasting of ideas. Not only is antithesis widely and commonly used, but it is also among the oldest of the consciously practiced rhetorical techniques. (Incidentally, the familiar English construction "Not only . . . but also . . ." used in the preceding sentence and often throughout the book is a familiar example of antithesis.) Antithesis was a favorite stylistic device among the orators of ancient Greece. Listen to the magnificent language of Demosthenes, considered by many to be the finest speaker the world has ever known. In his speech *On the Cheronese*, he gives us a splendid example of antithesis, combines it with parallel structure and, as he balances idea against idea and clause with clause, he builds toward the climax of a passage of exceptional power and grace.

It was not safe in Olynthus to speak in behalf of Philip until the fruits of his capture of Potidaea had been bestowed on the Olynthian people; it was not safe in Thessaly to speak in behalf of Philip until the mass of the Thessalians had been helped by Philip's expulsion of their tyrants, and his restoration of the Pylaea to them; it was not safe in Thebes, until he had restored to them Boeotia and uprooted the Phocians; but at Athens, when Philip has not only robbed us of Amphipolis and the Cardian land, but is preparing Euboea as a rampart against you, and is now moving on to Byzantium, it is safe to speak in behalf of Philip.

Perhaps the most famous instance of antithesis in the oratory of modern times is in John Fitzgerald Kennedy's inaugural address: "Ask not what your country can do for you. Ask what you can do for your country."

RHETORICAL QUESTIONS. A question is "rhetorical" when a speaker expects no direct answer to it from his audience. He knows the answer; he uses the question not to elicit an overt response but to add vividness to the expression of his ideas. A direct question, even one that requires no answer from a listener, engages his immediate, personal attention to a degree that statement often will not.

Rhetorical questions may be the speaker's method of forcing his listeners to formulate explicit (but silent) answers to his questions. In his famous "Compromise Speech," delivered to the Senate in February, 1850, Henry Clay used rhetorical questions in this fashion. In the paragraph quoted below, Clay refers to the first of eight resolutions he had proposed as a compromise between North and South over the question of slavery.

The first resolution, Mr. President, as you are aware, relates to

California, and it declares that California, with suitable limits, ought to be admitted as a member of this Union, without the imposition of any restriction either to interdict or introduce slavery within her limits. Well now, is there any concession in this resolution by either party to the other? I know that gentlemen who come from slaveholding States say the North gets all that it desires; but by whom does it get it? Does it get it by any action of Congress? If slavery be interdicted within the limits of California, has it been done by Congress—by this government? No sir. That interdiction is imposed by California herself. And has it not been the doctrine of all parties that when a State is about to be admitted into the Union, the State has a right to decide for itself whether it will or will not have slavery within its limits?

A rhetorical question may be used to summarize a point developed by a line of argument. "What better way, then, is there to destroy peace than by preparing for war?" The answers a speaker wants to these kinds of questions are obvious. They do not have to be put into words, though they may be answered by the speaker himself.

President Franklin Delano Roosevelt used rhetorical questions very effectively. In a campaign speech, delivered in Chicago, October 14, 1936, the President said,

To [the business men of America] I say:
Do you have a deposit in the bank? It is safer today than it has ever been in our history. It is guaranteed. Last October first marked the end of the first full year in 55 years without a single failure of a national bank in the United States. Isn't that on the credit side of the government's account with you?

Are you an investor? Your stocks and bonds are up to a five and six year high level.

Are you a merchant? Your markets have the precious life-blood of purchasing power. Your customers on the farms have better incomes and smaller debts. Your customers in the cities have more jobs, surer jobs, better jobs. Didn't your government have something to do with this?

Are you in industry? Industrial earnings, industrial profits are the highest in four, six, or even seven years! Bankruptcies are at a new low. Your government takes some credit for that.

Are you in railroads? Freight loadings are steadily going up and so are passenger receipts because, for one reason, your government made the railroads cut rates and make money.

Are you a middleman in the great stream of farm products? The

meat and grain that move through your yards and elevators have a
steadier supply, a steadier demand and steadier prices than you
have known for years.

In his annual Message to Congress, January 3, 1936, this same
master of style put rhetorical questions into combination with the
device of parallel structure to achieve a striking effect:

Shall we say that values are restored and that the Congress will,
therefore, repeal the laws under which we have been bringing them
back? Shall we say that because national income has grown with
rising prosperity, we shall repeal existing taxes and thereby put off
the day of approaching a balanced budget and of starting to reduce
the national debt?

Shall we abandon the reasonable support and regulation of banking? Shall we restore the dollar to its former gold content?

Shall we say to the farmer—"The prices for your product are in
part restored, now go and hoe your own row"? Shall we say to the
home owners—"We have reduced your rates of interest—we have
no further concern with how you keep your home or what you pay
for your money, that is your affair"?

Shall we say to the several millions of unemployed citizens who
face the very problem of existence—yes, of getting enough to eat—
"We will withdraw from giving you work, we will turn you back to
the charity of your communities and to those men of selfish power
who tell you that perhaps they will employ you if the government
leaves them strictly alone"?

Shall we say to the needy unemployed—"Your problem is a local
one, except that perhaps the Federal Government, as an act of mere
generosity, will be willing to pay to your city or to your country a
few grudging dollars to help maintain your soup kitchens"?

Shall we say to the children who have worked all day—"Child
labor is a local issue and so are your starvation wages; something to
be solved or left unsolved by the jurisdictions of forty-eight states"?

Shall we say to the laborer—"Your right to organize, your relations with your employer have nothing to do with the public interest;
if your employer will not meet with you to discuss your problems and
his, that is none of our affair"?

Shall we say to the unemployed and the aged—"Social security
lies not within the province of the Federal Government, you must
seek relief elsewhere"? Shall we say to the men and women who live
in conditions of squalor in country and in city—"The health and the
happiness of you and your children are no concern of ours"?

Shall we expose our population once more by the repeal of laws to protect them against the loss of their honest investments and against the manipulations of dishonest speculators?

Shall we abandon the splendid efforts of the Federal Government to raise the health standards of the nation and to give youth a decent opportunity through such means as the Civilian Conservation Corps?

IMPROVING LANGUAGE AND STYLE

Facility in language and felicity in style increase the fidelity of communication. Neither of these is innate, and neither of them is easy to achieve. Your style will be what it becomes over the years, and it will be what you make it. We offer here a few suggestions to guide you in doing what every speaker must do—build his own style through the experience of years. But start now!

Become aware of your own use of languge. Listen to yourself. Record your speeches whenever you can. Instead of forgetting about a speech once you have delivered it, use it for practice material. Your primary concern in preparing a speech is with the ideas it conveys, and with the organization and materials that will make the ideas interesting and clear. In delivering the speech, with the ideas firmly at hand, and with notes to refresh your memory, you are free to give consideration to the language you use. This is the essence of extemporaneous speaking.

Be curious about words. As you read and listen, never let an unknown word pass you by. Make it identify itself. Examine its etymology and its usage. Then add it to your vocabulary. A good dictionary is one of the most valuable reference books you can own. But to keep a word in your vocabulary, you have to use it. If you do not, you will soon lose the word.

Study the language of others. Listening carefully to the speeches you hear in class is one good way of making a start toward being habitually aware of the language others use. An even better procedure is to read printed texts of speeches, to study them thoughtfully, to examine their structure and their materials and to analyze the speaker's use of language.

Practice writing and speaking. No matter how much you may learn about style, your own use of words will improve little without practice. The speaking you do in class is, of course, only a beginning. The most significant progress comes through experience. Through practice in both writing and speaking you can work toward developing an artistic use of language that functions with the ease of habit.

SUMMARY

The ideas a speaker communicates are not a material substance that can be passed from hand to hand like money; nor can they be poured into a listener's head like water from a cup. Instead, ideas are "stirred up" in an audience by the symbols the speaker uses to *stand for* the ideas. Almost all the word-symbols a speaker uses can convey many different ideas; that is, each one can elicit many potential meanings. The meanings a word will actually elicit are determined by four relationships:

1. *Denotation*—the relationship of words to *reality*.
2. *Connotation*—the relationship of *people* to words and the objects, events, and concepts the words are used to name.
3. *Syntax*—the relationship of words to *other words* in grammatical structures.
4. *Context*—the relationship of words to the *passage* or *discourse* in which they are used.

Style in language is the way words are put together to express thought. Oral style differs from that of written discourse mainly in that the language of a speaker must make his ideas instantly, clearly, and accurately intelligible to his listeners.

Good oral style has these distinguishable characteristics: propriety, precision, simplicity, directness, originality. Language is appropriate when it is properly suited to the audience and the occasion of a speech. Informal English, as it is normally used by educated people in the majority of their writing and speaking, is the most widely appropriate. To be precise, language should be both accurate and concrete. Exaggeration, ambiguity, and vagueness are the natural enemies of precision in language.

Simplicity in style is best achieved by avoiding flowery, impressive-sounding language in favor of short, forceful words of Anglo-Saxon origin. Simplicity also demands brevity, using as few words as possible to say accurately what is meant.

In their everyday communication, audiences use a liberal sprinkling of personal pronouns, contractions, and direct quotations. Their ears are attuned, therefore, to the relaxed idiom of informal conversation. A speaker lends directness to his style by using this same kind of informality and personalness in his language.

Clichés, trite expressions, and hackneyed, overused phrases rob a speaker's style of originality. Originality in style is best achieved by avoiding tired words and phrases in favor of language with freshness and variety.

The most successful style is that which makes a speaker's ideas come alive for his audience. We have mentioned only four of the several devices a speaker may use to give his style the vividness effective speaking requires: figurative language, parallel structure, antithesis, and rhetorical questions. There are many others you should know and use.

To improve the style of your speeches, do these four things:

> Become aware of your own use of words.
> Be curious about words.
> Study the language of others.
> Practice writing and speaking.

A critical and responsible speaker understands that words may be weapons, not to be used without full knowledge of the consequences of their being uttered. He understands clearly the linguistic implements at his disposal. He neither uses them unscrupulously to make his points easily nor is he himself mastered by them. He is always in full and firm control.

QUESTIONS

1. Define language.
2. What kind of language is the primary means of human communication?
3. How do words communicate?
4. What is denotation? Connotation?
5. How do syntax and context give clues to a speaker's meaning?
6. Under what conditions can a speaker be criticized for improper use of attitudinal and connotative language?
7. What is style?
8. What are some of the differences between written style and oral style?
9. What usefulness is there in shoptalk?
10. When is exaggeration used improperly?
11. What three classes of words lead to vagueness? Give examples.
12. What is a malapropism? Give examples.
13. What is parallel structure? Give examples.

14. How does antithesis make more vivid the expression of an idea?
15. What is a rhetorical question? How is it used?
16. What should the speaker do to improve his style?

EXERCISES

1. Construct a sample vocabulary of the jargon used in at least one occupation. Translate each word or phrase into language appropriate for a general audience.

2. Select an essay written in "formal" English style and convert one or more paragraphs into acceptable, informal, oral style.

3. Find the mistakes in Mrs. Malaprop's comment (p. 213) and suggest a more accurate word for each.

4. Note examples of vague terms used in classroom speeches (meaningless modifiers, abstract words, general words) and show how they may be made more precise through illustration and definition.

5. Write down trite expressions in one round of classroom speeches and suggest a phrase that expresses each idea more vividly.

6. This chapter considers only a few of the many widely used figures of speech. Make a list of several figures not mentioned and find examples of each in printed texts of speeches. For example: metonymy, synecdoche, personification, apostrophe.

7. Record a brief extemporaneous speech. Transcribe it and then polish the style.

DELIVERY: PSYCHOLOGICAL ELEMENTS

I. Communication and catharsis
  A. Cathartic elements of speech
  B. Communicative elements of speech
II. Factors affecting adjustment to a speaking situation
  A. Culture
  B. Past experience
  C. Conditioning
  D. The person addressed
III. The conflict of cathartic and communicative elements
IV. Some practical suggestions
  A. Don't blame yourself
  B. Adopt a conversational attitude
  C. Realize the importance of experience
  D. Prepare thoroughly
  E. Practice consciously the positive aspects of the speech role
V. Summary and questions

XIII

DELIVERY:
PSYCHOLOGICAL
ELEMENTS

Speaking demands the immediate physical presence of the person communicating in a way that writing, painting, sculpture, and other forms of communication do not. His presence affects the audience. The importance of solid content in a speech is not diminished, however, by saying that good communication demands good delivery. For a listener, delivery is not only the vehicle for communication but also an important measure of the sincerity of a speaker and the significance of his ideas. Recall some of the times you have given your attention to a poised, self-confident speaker and withheld it from a halting and unsure one.

Such experiences are unfortunately frequent. Many worthwhile ideas are lost because of the inability of a speaker to give them the vitality they need. And many worthless trinkets have been accepted as sound ideas because they were delivered with enthusiasm and directness. But even though delivery is so important to effective speaking, competence in delivery will not by itself bring success; success will be elusive, however, if this competence is lacking.

Skillful delivery implies an understanding of some of its psychological, vocal, and visual elements. The next three chapters will examine these in that order. The present chapter will consider the relationship between a speaker's attitudes toward the total speaking situation and his effectiveness.

COMMUNICATION AND CATHARSIS

Speech is a human behavior, one of the behaviors which people perform to bring their environments and themselves into equilibrium. The fact that the audience is clearly a part of the speaker's environment explains his desire to minimize the entirely natural anxiety he feels about the reactions of his listeners. Such anxiety springs from the fact that communication, whether in private conversation or formal public speaking, is an eminently personal ego-involving situation. The act of speaking satisfies two different needs: cathartic needs and communicative needs.

Cathartic Elements of Speech

Some speaking serves to meet the personal needs of the speaker alone. On such occasions the speaker is not concerned about what kind of a reaction he will get from others; he wants to express his fears as a way of eliminating them: to experience a catharsis. Everyone has had the experience of talking to himself, has had thoughts which he must express if he is to maintain satisfying emotional equilibrium. He makes sure he is alone and then "tells off" the wise guy in the political-science class, saying the things that social training would not allow anyone to say to the wise guy's face: how obnoxious he is, how he disrupts the class with useless questions, how he insults people with whom he disagrees. The speaker, having vented his spleen through cathartic speech, achieves a personal satisfaction. The next time he meets his obnoxious acquaintance face to face, he can smile and say, "Good morning."

Although such speech is used only to release feelings without trying to influence the attitudes and conduct of others, it is not always addressed to oneself. The principle of catharsis has long been recognized as a valuable psychological experience both by religious leaders and by psychotherapists. It is an essential part of everyone's life. A person often tells his feelings to a friend not because he feels that the friend can do something about them but because he has the need to express his feelings to someone—to get them out.

Feelings that invite catharsis evidently arise from problems that reside in the speaker rather than in his listener—audience, psychologist, confidant, or friend. Other feelings that reside in the speaker are his anxiety over being ridiculous, his embarrassment, his worries about his clothes or his haircut or his facial contours. All speakers have these feelings in some measure.

Communicative Elements of Speech

In this book we are less interested in cathartic elements of speech than in the kind of speaking which communicates something else, the sort of speaking which serves as a means of gaining a socially significant response from a listener. It is a social act; both speaker and listeners are involved. Cathartic speech, in contrast, is not social; it is personal, often individual.

FACTORS AFFECTING ADJUSTMENT TO A SPEAKING SITUATION

The total speaking situation—an interaction of speaker, speech, audience, and occasion—is a transaction in much the same sense that what happens between a merchant and a customer is a transaction. Speakers not only change the audience but the audience also changes them. The relationship between speaker and audience is more than one in which the speaker initiates a stimulus to which the listener responds. As soon as a speaker begins to initiate stimuli, the listener begins to respond; this response in turn stimulates the speaker as he speaks. A dynamic circular relationship of stimulus-response is set up. There are so many factors in the total speech situation that any attempt to decipher individual patterns of stimulus and response would be quite useless. There are, however, several general social factors which affect the speaker's attitude toward the act of speech and his perceptions of audience reactions.

Culture

A speaker's ability to cope with a listener's reactions are determined in part by the subculture from which he comes. Some cultural and subcultural groups emphasize the ability to use language in a sophisticated way and thus demand of their members a level of success which puts pressure on them. Even when parents in our society do not make specific demands on their children, the children whose parents' professions generally require a high degree of language skill, such as lawyers, ministers, and teachers feel that they are under pressure to develop language skills.

Certainly the general American culture, committed to solving society's problems through persuasion, puts a high priority on effective communication at all levels of the society. The tremendous success of Dale Carnegie courses and Toastmaster and Toastmistress clubs testifies to the significance of communication in our society. Some will respond favorably to the influence while others will seek to avoid the speaking situation or search for easy ways to satisfy its requirements.

Past Experience

Past experience has an important influence on a speaker's attitudes. This is the reason that satisfactory experiences in communication should be provided for students in the elementary schools. This is not the time to define good elementary-school experiences but we may certainly say that unfortunate experiences in the past affect one's response to the present. We can all understand the problem of the awkward junior high school boy who is called upon to recite in class and forgets his memorized poem. If he is treated unsympathetically by his teacher and is laughed at by his classmates, he may remember that experience and avoid all other speaking situations whenever he can.

The influence of past experience is not limited to the schoolroom. All one's experience with language, all the responses one receives from his listeners, parents, teachers, and friends can affect his approach to any new speaking situation.

Conditioning

The process of conditioning can make the speaking situation more difficult. Anxiety arises when one sees a difference between what he expects to happen and what he perceives actually happens. Thus, the speaker who wants to sound like Daniel Webster, or Reverend Martin Luther King, Jr., or even the boy next door, but who perceives that he does not meet this standard will take a different path the next time he speaks. He will keep trying something new until his behavior is reinforced—until he gets satisfaction from the experience —until his expectations and perceptions are the same. From then on he will tend to do those same things so long as he receives the reinforcement. Thus he is conditioned to a particular way of preparing and delivering a speech.

When a speaker on consecutive occasions attempts some new way of meeting the situation, each time without success, he becomes increasingly frustrated and his anxiety increases. Finally, a new kind of conditioning sets in and he finds that the only way to escape the frustration and anxiety is to avoid the experience altogether. When compelled by circumstances to give a speech, such a person will be quite anxious in the situation.

The Person Addressed

Another social influence which affects adjustment to the speaking situation is the amount of anxiety aroused in the speaker by the person spoken to. Many teachers who are very nervous before an audience of adults have no difficulty whatsoever when speaking before their classes. They have learned to expect favorable responses from children but not from adults. Sometimes a speech class poses a problem because the student speaker knows he will be graded by his instructor. His classmates, when the instructor is absent, do not constitute a threat and, therefore, are not the source of concern that they are when they are in the classroom situation.

Culture, past experience, conditioning, and the person being addressed are by no means the only elements which affect the attitude a speaker will have toward a speaking situation. Many other social influences affect him. We have discussed these four to point up the fact that although each experience is unique, the social elements in a situation cause one to generalize about his experiences, frequently to his own disadvantage. They teach him to expect success or failure and thus establish attitudes toward the speaking situation before it is ever confronted.

THE CONFLICT OF CATHARTIC AND COMMUNICATIVE ELEMENTS

For a speaker, one of the most annoying reactions to a speaking situation is fear. The outward signs of a speaker's fear and anxiety are called "stage fright." In its milder form it is known as "nervousness." It may involve stumbling over words, vocalizing pauses (the injection of "uh" and "er" without regard to meaning), trembling hands and knees, or the inability to look directly at members of the audience. The type and extent of the symptoms differ from person to person. Regardless of the form the symptoms take, the fear reaction can be said to result from the fact that cathartic elements in the speaking situation are interfering with the communicative purpose of the speech.

Obviously, a person who cares only about fulfilling his expressive (noncommunicative) needs in public speaking has a problem which a speech class cannot hope to cure. It is highly doubtful that such a person would remain long in a speech class. The notion that such a person might exist, however, helps to show what is behind fear reactions. Each fear reaction indicates a tendency for a speaker to concern himself with his personal ego needs rather than with the effectiveness of his talk. He worries not about how well his listeners understand his ideas, nor how persuasive his arguments are, nor how much the audience enjoys his humor. Instead, he frets about how they evaluate him, how he looks, and whether they are laughing at him rather than with him. In short, his anticipations about the audience are reinforced by a glance, a whispered comment in the back of the room, a cough. In most situations the audience is not making such an evaluation. A speaker should not come before an audience feeling he is to be judged on such personal grounds. He comes to share an idea with them. We might say that a speaker's anxiety and fear are proportional to the extent to which he questions his personal acceptability rather than the acceptability of the idea he espouses.

Needless to say, no speaker can entirely divorce his person from his attempt to persuade. Nor should he try. No one has ever been a speaking machine. A speaker's personal involvement with his ideas is essential to the kind of enthusiasm which helps build satisfactory audience response. For this reason, even the most experienced speakers are anxious about the speaking situation. A competent speaker expects such anxiety, uses it by designing his speech so as to clear away as much anxiety as he can, and lives with the remnant of anxiety that no speaker can eliminate.

SOME PRACTICAL SUGGESTIONS

Understanding why fear and anxiety are present in a speaking situation will help you to develop proper attitudes toward speaking in public. Here are some practical suggestions to help you put this knowledge to work.

Don't Blame Yourself

Speakers who find themselves subject to some of the physical reactions of fear and anxiety will frequently enlarge the problem by becoming angry with themselves. But stage-fright reactions cannot really be voluntarily controlled. If the speaker understands how powerless he is, he may be able to cease blaming himself and thus reduce the psychic feedback. He cannot will away the anxiety no matter how much pressure he puts on himself. A speaker who learns to live with his anxiety has gone a long way toward relieving himself of fear.

Adopt a Conversational Attitude

One of the most helpful attitudes to develop is the idea that public speaking is an expanded and formalized version of conversation. People speaking to a group of friends in informal surroundings have little difficulty in saying what they want to say. The person who thinks of public speaking as something enormously greater and more formal than private conversation burdens himself with pressures which are not a part of the informal situation. The more one can think of public speaking as conversation, the easier public speaking will be. The same direct, friendly, enthusiastic kind of communication which is so enjoyable in a friendly get-together is what makes public speaking effective.

Realize the Importance of Experience

Just as unhappy experiences can condition a person to fear public speaking, so also can favorable experiences condition him to enjoy it. To attain this goal, a speaker must banish from his ideas about speaking as much of the mystery as possible: He must know what good speech is and he must study the methods of organizing speeches, supporting them, and delivering them. He must also realize that in the cafeteria, the hallway, or at the dinner table he is continually making speeches and that it is his perception of a speaking situation, rather than the actual situation, which makes it threatening. When he sees that making a good speech has no requirements which he cannot master, and that an effective speaker is an intelligent craftsman rather than a miracle worker, he can begin to have the kind of experiences which build confidence. Each favorable experience will reinforce the others.

Prepare Thoroughly

It seems obvious that anxiety will attack the speaker who isn't sure of what he wants his speech to do or whether his speech will do it. In the presence of these uncertainties, he is insecure about how his audience will react. Careful preparation is the only realistic solution to this problem. A speaker must study his subject well. He must be sure to understand the limited topic on which he will speak and he should also build a broad circle of information around it.

There are certain laxities that effective speaking does not allow:

"I'm not too sure about this but I think you understand what I mean." "I think it is pronounced . . ." "I understand that Professor Kernaghan has a different view on this but I couldn't find his book in our library." "I had to work late last night so I didn't have a chance to check all the facts." These and similar statements merely say that the speaker is not expert on the subject. Listeners ask, "Why should I listen to him?" A speaker's confidence grows out of knowing that he is well prepared and out of seeing that his audience realizes he is qualified to speak on his subject.

Practice Consciously the Positive Aspects of the Speech Role

There is much value in deliberately adopting the pose of good adjustment to the speaking situation. Psychologists tolerate the view that the acceptance of a role makes a person do things which are compatible with it. A speaker may feel more composure because he adopts the body set and delivery of one who is composed. Actors have long recognized that audiences tend to do and feel what they see being done and felt. When they see someone in pain on the stage they "feel" pain. When the actor is happy they "feel" happy. This reaction is called *empathy*. Empathy is useful to a public speaker. If listeners perceive an alert speaker, they will tend to be alert. The speaker, seeing a favorable audience response, tends to become more confident.

Here are a few specific actions you can practice to help give you the appearance of emotional control.

Walk briskly to the platform. Walk directly and resolutely to the rostrum and put down your notes. Don't slouch or shuffle along the way. Don't glance nervously at the audience or fumble with your papers or clothing.

Look directly at the audience. When you reach the rostrum and have assembled your notes before you, look directly at the audience for a brief time before beginning your speech. Think of this as a moment when you "meet" the audience and make your first friendly contact with them. During the speech, concentrate on looking directly at the members of the audience. The speaker who seems unable to look directly at his listeners gives a sure sign of anxiety. Eye contact is perhaps the most important factor in good delivery. It will be discussed in more detail among the visual elements of delivery in Chapter XV.

Use a good attention factor in your introduction. Your introduction may set the tone for the reactions you will get to the rest of the speech. For this reason, you will want to get off to a good start. Make sure to plan an opening which will arouse the interest of the audience; then deliver it as you planned it. Don't let any anxiety you feel make you rush into the main body of the speech and so slide over the interest-gaining use of the attention factor. Attention factors have been discussed in Chapter IX, and further discussion appears in Chapter XVII under the heading "Gaining Attention."

Control the rate of delivery. When nervous fear strikes a speaker, his first reaction is to get his unpleasant experience over with as soon as possible. This reaction is understandable because the human organism always tries to avoid unpleasant stimuli. Your effectiveness can be hurt by the perfectly normal desire to escape an unpleasant situation. To avoid this reaction, measure the rate of your delivery. Talk more slowly than you might be inclined to, especially at the beginning of the speech.

Keep your nervousness to yourself. No matter what happens, don't tell your audience that you are nervous. Far too many speakers do this, as a defense. They try to break the ice by saying something like, "Well, I hope you're more relaxed about this speech than I am." Or when they fumble with words or have muscle spasms they look self-conscious or apologize or giggle. You might be able to gain sympathy this way, but you won't win respect.

If a speaker tells his listeners about his troubles, they will give him sympathy but they will withhold from him the very important thing he seeks—support for his ideas. Audiences can feel sympathy for a speaker in distress, but they will not follow one who finds it necessary to lean on his listeners.

If a speaker is obviously nervous, his listeners know it without having to be told. When a speaker has difficulty, empathy makes the audience suffer with him. Furthermore, there is some reason to believe that feeling sympathetic makes an audience uncomfortable. This discomfort can very easily turn to annoyance directed at the person who makes the request for sympathy. If the speaker fights out his problem his audience will react favorably to his perseverance. Many will admire him for doing what they feel they cannot.

SUMMARY

Speech is used, often at one and the same time, to communicate an idea to someone, to elicit a response, and to fulfill personal needs without concern for a response.

Many factors influence the way each speaker adjusts to a speaking situation but all cases of poor adjustment come about because cathartic elements break through into the social or communicative purpose of the speech. For this reason a speaker must do all he can to concentrate on the social purpose of his speaking and not on his personal needs.

Speech classes are not designed to resolve feelings of insecurity. If those feelings are relatively insignificant, a course in speech may be the means whereby they can be resolved. The practical suggestions offered in this chapter make no pretense toward performing psychotherapy. They are designed to help speakers learn how to control the disruptive interference of their personal needs so that the speaking they do will fulfill its primarily social aim. Students do learn to speak well in spite of the perfectly normal anxieties that assail all speakers.

QUESTIONS

1. Differentiate between a speaker's cathartic and communicative needs.

2. What do you consider to be your greatest source of anxiety in the speaking situation?

3. What is conditioning? How is it significant to a speaker?

4. What false emphasis is the basis of fear reactions in a speaker?

5. The text mentions some practical suggestions which will help alleviate nervousness. Which two do you consider most important? Why?

DELIVERY: VOCAL ELEMENTS

I. Voice production
   A. Respiration
   B. Phonation
   C. Resonation
   D. Articulation and pronunciation
      1. Pronunciation
      2. The speech alphabet
      3. Articulation
II. Elements of voice
   A. Pitch
   B. Force
   C. Time
   D. Quality
III. Using the voice to communicate meaning
   A. Emphasize the important words
   B. Make clear distinctions among the ideas
   C. Make words sound like what you mean
   D. Speak in a conversational manner
IV. Summary, questions, and a list of special readings in voice

XIV

DELIVERY: VOCAL ELEMENTS

One important means of making and keeping contact with the world is the sense of hearing. Through it come a large proportion of the stimuli that influence thought and action. These stimuli come to the ear in the form of sound. As far as the ear is concerned, sound is made up of four elements: pitch, force, time, and quality. It is these elements that the ear hears and transmits to the brain, where they are interpreted and given meaning. The ear is capable of distinguishing a wide range of variation in the pitch, force, time, and quality of the sounds that come to it.

The ear hears voice, as it hears any sound, in terms of these same four elements. Consequently, pitch, force, time, and quality are basic considerations for the speaker who wants to use his voice effectively. In order to explain clearly the function of each of these elements in good speech, we must examine the process through which speech is brought about.

VOICE PRODUCTION

For the production of sound, two conditions are necessary. First, there must be an elastic system, that is, a body capable of vibration, and, second, there must be a force outside the elastic body to set it into motion. When these conditions occur, the oscillation of the vibrating body causes disturbances which are transmitted through some medium to the ear. In the voice, the part that vibrates (the elastic system) is the vocal folds. The force that sets the vibrators into motion is the breath stream controlled and supplied under pressure by the muscles of the breathing mechanism. The transmitting medium is ordinarily the atmosphere. The sound produced by a speaker is resonated in the chambers of his throat, mouth, and nose and is thus given the quality characteristic of that particular speaker's voice. Finally, this vocal sound is modified by the articulators into the various sounds of speech. Thus, four steps are involved in producing any given speech sound. These are respiration (breathing), phonation (vocal-fold vibration), resonation, and articulation.

Respiration

There are many misconceptions about breathing in speech. The best way to avoid these false impressions is to understand how respiration helps to produce vocal sounds.

In breathing, both the air and the lungs are inert. They do not take an active part in respiration. It is muscles that do the work. Air moves into and out of the lungs, not through any power of its own, and not because the lungs pull or push the air, but because the muscles of the body serve to bring about changes in air pressure within the lungs.

Because the ribs are curved, and because they are fastened to the framework of the body, when they are raised through muscular action they tend to move outward from the center line. Put your hands in the center of your chest and press your elbows to your side. Now raise your elbows without moving your hands. Notice that as your elbows rise, they move away from your body and the distance between them increases. The ribs act in somewhat the same way. They are raised by muscles between the ribs and by other muscles fastened to the ribs from other parts of the skeleton. The rising action tends to increase the lateral dimensions of the rib cage. (See Figure XIV–1.)

The vertical dimension of the thorax (rib cage) is also increased in breathing. Separating the lungs from the abdominal cavity is the diaphragm, a somewhat convex or dome-shaped partition of muscle and tendinous fiber. When the muscular portion of the diaphragm is tensed, the convex shape of the diaphragm is, to a degree, flattened. This action increases the vertical dimension of the thorax, enlarging the space within. (See Figure XIV–2.)

Because the lungs within the thorax are elastic and open to the atmosphere, as the space that confines them is enlarged, they enlarge to keep the space filled. The pressure of air outside the body forces air to enter the lungs.

Inhalation is always an active process. That is, muscular activity is always required to bring air into the lungs whether it will be used for speaking or not. Exhalation, on the other hand, is not so active a process in quiet breathing. When one is not "out of breath," or when the breath stream is not used to vibrate the vocal folds, the muscles

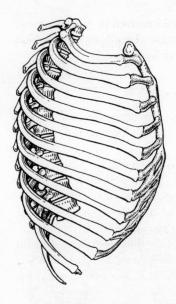 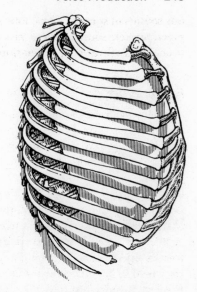

FIGURE XIV–1. SIDE VIEWS OF THE RIB CAGE. *Left:* POSITION OF THE RIBS AFTER EXHALATION AND BEFORE INHALATION BE-GINS. *Right:* POSITION OF THE RIBS AFTER INHALATION AND BE-FORE EXHALATION BEGINS. OBSERVE THE INCREASE IN THE VOLUME OF THE CHEST CAVITY.

ordinarily used in exhalation can remain passive. The weight of the body itself (the force of gravity acting on the walls of the chest and on the abdomen) tends to make the thorax contract and creates enough pressure on the lungs to force the air out.

Speaking requires greater muscular activity than does quiet respiration. Otherwise, the breath stream will not be under enough pressure to vibrate the vocal folds strongly enough to produce a sound of desirable quality and sufficient strength. The additional pressure needed for good speech comes from muscles that surround the abdominal area of the torso. By contracting, these muscles force the viscera upward to press against the bottom of the diaphragm. As the diaphragm rises, it decreases the space within the rib cage. Other muscles pull the ribs down. These actions compress the air inside the lungs and expel it under pressure past the vocal folds, causing them to vibrate.

The muscles of respiration are quite strong and when they are used

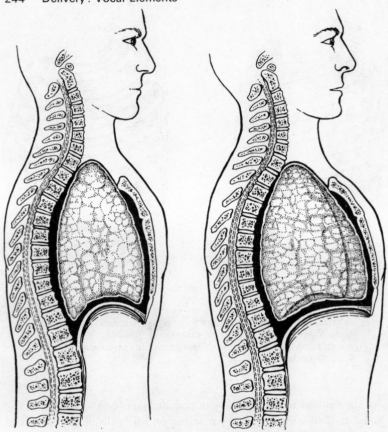

FIGURE XIV–2. SECTIONS OF THE THORAX (*left*) BEFORE IN-
HALATION AND (*right*) AFTER INHALATION OBSERVE THE FLAT-
TENING OF THE DIAPHRAGM AND THE EXPANSION OF THE THORACIC
CAVITY WHICH THE LUNGS OCCUPY.

vigorously they can make the voice quite loud. Under ordinary conditions, however, sheer loudness of voice is not nearly so important as
the control exercised over it. Coordination of muscular activity
rather than simple muscle power achieves the necessary control.

As a final point in our very brief sketch of the breathing process, let
us say one more word about the diaphragm. For many years the
prescription has been constantly repeated that for proper use of voice
one must "breathe from the diaphragm." To avoid unnecessary confusions and errors, this injunction must be clearly understood. There
is little doubt that the diaphragm is one of the chief muscles used in

inhalation. But other muscles must be used actively and directly to expel air from the lungs. The injunction to "breathe from the diaphragm" has little meaning, therefore, except as a psychological aid to voice production. The diaphragm is active primarily in inhalation. Physically, the most it can do in exhalation is to oppose the other muscles in their effort to expel the air and thus help to control the outgoing air stream.

Phonation

The vocal folds are housed in a structure called the larynx. It is situated at the top of the windpipe, or trachea, and is clearly evidenced in men by the protrusion in the neck commonly called the "Adam's apple." What we refer to as the "Adam's apple" is in reality one of the nine cartilages that make up the larynx. These cartilages are joined together and to the body by ligaments and are operated by a nicely balanced set of opposing muscles. Two of the cartilages of the larynx are called the *arytenoids*. These are shaped somewhat like pyramids and are arranged so that they can pivot on their base. Connecting the arytenoids and the thyroid cartilage (the "Adam's apple") are two muscles called the *thyro-arytenoids*. It is the thyro-arytenoid muscles that form the major portion of the body of the vocal folds. When certain other muscles (mainly the crico-arytenoid and the arytenoid muscles) are tensed, they pivot the arytenoid cartilages and bring them closer together. In this manner the thyro-arytenoid muscles are also brought together. (See Figure XIV–4.) This action closes off the passage that leads from the lungs to the outer air and impounds air in the lungs. When the muscles of exhalation force air out of the lungs, the pressure that is built up under the vocal folds forces them aside so that a puff of air escapes. As the air escapes, pressure is reduced. Elasticity and muscular tension in the folds causes them to close off the passage again. Immediately pressure builds up and the folds are forced aside. This open-and-close action sets the passing stream of air into vibration and produces vocal sound. The speed at which the vocal folds vibrate can be seen from the fact that to produce the pitch A above middle C they would have to open and close 440 times a second.

A complete theory of vocal-fold vibration has yet to be developed and there have been for many years widespread differences of opinion about the exact nature of their movement. It is clear, however, that

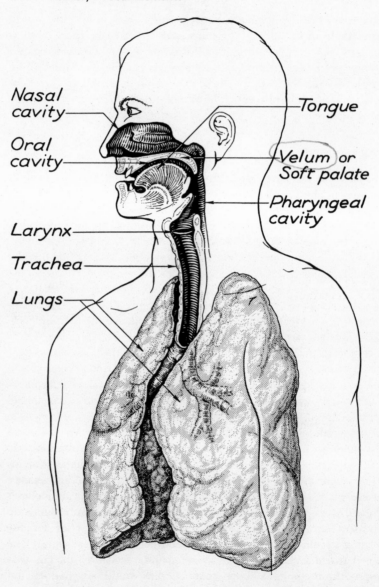

Nasal cavity

Oral cavity

Larynx

Trachea

Lungs

Tongue

Velum or Soft palate

Pharyngeal cavity

FIGURE XIV–3. THE PRINCIPAL ORGANS OF SPEECH. THE RIBS, DIAPHRAGM, AND THORACIC MUSCLES ARE NOT SHOWN.

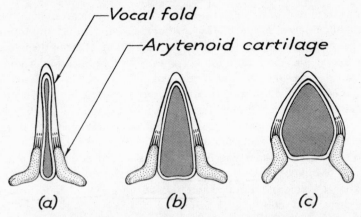

Vocal fold

Arytenoid cartilage

(a)   (b)   (c)

FIGURE XIV–4. THE VOCAL FOLDS AND THE ARYTENOID CAR-
TILAGES. *Diagram a:* THE VOCAL FOLDS CLOSE TOGETHER, AS IN
PHONATION. *Diagram b:* THE VOCAL FOLDS PARTLY OPEN, AS
IN WHISPERING. *Diagram c:* THE VOCAL FOLDS RELAXED AND
ENTIRELY OPEN, AS IN DEEP BREATHING.

the vocal folds are not to be visualized as strings similar to those of a
violin. Nor are they to be likened to the reed of a clarinet. A much
closer analogy is to be found in the lips of a trumpet player when he
sets into vibration the column of air in that instrument.

Resonation

A simple experiment will help to explain resonance.

The sound produced by blowing across the top of an empty bottle
has a definite pitch. Partly fill the same bottle with varying amounts
of water and a stream of air across the top will produce, for each level
of water, a different pitch. The reason for these differences is that at
each level, the liquid in the bottle leaves only a certain amount of
room for air. As the volume of air in the bottle changes, the frequency
at which it vibrates changes and the pitch is changed. In other words,
each column of air has a natural frequency at which it tends to
vibrate. For this reason, an organ maker chooses pipes of varying
lengths and girths to produce the pitches he desires.

Holding a vibrating tuning fork over the mouth of the bottle will
also set the air inside into vibration. In this latter case, however, instead of vibrating at its own natural frequency (as a stream of air
across the top would cause it to do), the air will vibrate in the bottle
at the approximate frequency of the tuning fork. The sound of the
tuning fork thus is amplified (made louder) because the sound from

the vibration of air in the bottle is added to it. By using tuning forks of different pitches, it can be shown that the more closely the tuning fork matches the natural frequency of the column of air in the bottle, the louder the resultant sound becomes. This amplification of sound is called *resonance*, and the bottle acts as a *resonator*. The specific instance described is an example of *cavity* resonance. Putting the handle of a vibrating tuning fork against a table top will produce an example of what is called *sounding-board* resonance. Here again, the more closely the tuning fork approximates the natural frequency of the surface, the louder will be the total sound produced. Through cavity resonance, and to some extent through sounding-board resonance, the voice is amplified as it passes from the vocal folds through the throat and mouth.

Resonance is not to be confused with reverberation. Reverberation occurs when sound is reflected from a surface such as the wall of a room. It is, in other words, an echo. When you stand at some distance from a surface that reflects sound and shout, or clap your hands, you can hear the sound coming back to you after it has bounced off the reflecting surface. In a room, reverberations are usually undesirable because the reflected sound is mixed in with the original and distorts its quality. The booming sounds one hears in a large church with a vaulted ceiling, which distort the music of the choir and make it difficult to understand the words of a sermon, are examples of the disrupting effect of reverberation. Resonance, on the other hand, takes place mainly within the cavities formed by a speaker's throat, mouth, and nasal passages. Instead of distorting the sound, resonance gives the speaker's voice its characteristic quality.

Articulation and Pronunciation

Once the processes of respiration, phonation, and resonation have been accomplished, a speaker has (at the tip of his tongue, literally) the raw material of speech. Vocal sound does not become connected discourse until the speaker has modified the vocal tone into the sounds that make up whatever dialect he speaks. Articulation and pronunciation, then, are significant in the production of good speech. *Pronunciation* is the sum of all the audible characteristics of the word: the individual sounds, the order in which they occur, their duration, the stress given to syllables, and so on. *Articulation* is the process by which the individual sounds are formed and connected into speech. Decisions about what sounds should make up a word must be made before

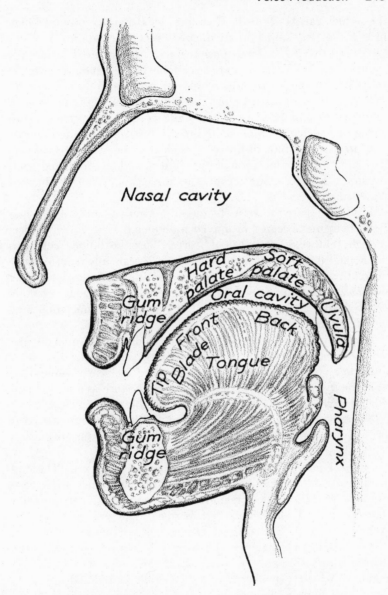

FIGURE XIV–5. THE ARTICULATORS AND RESONATORS.

the sounds can be formed. Therefore, let's consider pronunciation first, and then examine briefly the process of articulation.

PRONUNCIATION. Good pronunciation is achieved when the sounds a speaker articulates are acceptable in the standard version of the dialect he speaks. In other words, it is quite possible for a speaker to have very precise articulation and still be guilty of poor pronunciation. If, for example, he pronounces the word *can't* as "cain't," even though his articulation of each sound in the word is quite accurate and precise, and though the word is clearly understood by all who hear him, his pronunciation of this word should be considered poor, because it is not the one accepted by the vast majority of educated Americans.

Dictionaries are the most obvious authoritative source of information about the accepted or agreed pronunciation of words. Notice, though, that we do not speak of "correct" pronunciation. As long as a language is spoken, it changes. Dictionaries can only report what is current usage at the time they are printed and printing a word does not freeze its pronunciation for all time. But since language changes occur slowly, a dictionary's report of standard pronunciation may be safely accepted.

English is spoken in a large number of dialects throughout the world. Speakers from England, Canada, Australia, New Zealand, and other parts of the English-speaking world are clearly distinguishable one from the other. Persons who learn English as a second language will also ordinarily use a distinguishable pronunciation.

Not only will English be pronounced differently in different parts of the world, but within the borders of one country a variety of dialects will be heard.

In the United States, there are many dialect regions. Three of these include a large enough portion of the population to be considered the major dialect regions of this country. The three major dialects of the United States are Eastern, Southern, and General American English. Each of these is recognized as a "standard" dialect, and is considered to be preferable to any other speech pattern in the area in which it is used. Deviations from the standard dialect of the region in which a speaker lives are generally considered "substandard" and ought to be avoided.

THE SPEECH ALPHABET. To study the sound system of any language, or any dialect of a language, some accurate method of notation is necessary. English spelling is notoriously untrustworthy as a means of indicating the pronunciation of a word. A single letter of the alphabet may be used to spell a variety of sounds. The letter *a*, for example, spells a different sound in each of the following words: *hat, late, calm, above, courage*. The same sound, on the other hand, may be spelled in several different ways. Look at the word *courage*, for instance. The letter *a* in this word spells the same sound as the *i* in *hit*, the *o* in *women*, the *e* in *exist*, and both the *u* and the *y* in *busy!*

A very useful system for circumventing the vagaries of spelling is found in the International Phonetic Alphabet, a set of symbols that may be used to indicate with precision and uniformity the sounds that appear in the spoken language. Using symbols from the I.P.A., one may put into written form the essential elements of any word in English.

Many of the symbols in the phonetic alphabet appear exactly like the letters you are familiar with in the printing of an ordinary book. Several others are likely to be unfamiliar. These are taken from the alphabets of other languages such as Greek, or are arbitrarily created, or are variations of familiar symbols. In any case, the symbols are easy to understand, easy to learn, and easy to use. Their most important usefulness lies in the fact that each symbol has a uniform meaning. A given sound, no matter how it may be spelled in a word, is always indicated by the same symbol in phonetic transcription; and a given symbol, no matter where it appears in a phonetic transcription, always stands for the same sound.

The following list includes the symbols that are used to transcribe the standard sounds of American English. The symbol ['] in a phonetic transcription means that the syllable which *follows* it should be stressed.

Vowels

Phonetic Symbol	Key Word	Phonetic Transcription
i	meet	[mit]
ɪ	hit	[hɪt]
e	chaotic	[ke'atɪk]

Depending on such factors as its position in a syllable, stress, and duration, the vowel [e] in English words frequently becomes the diphthong [eɪ]. See the list of diphthongs that follows.

Phonetic Symbol	Key Word	Phonetic Transcription
ɛ	net	[nɛt]
æ	bad	[bæd]
a	A satisfactory key word for this vowel is hard to find. It may be considered an intermediate sound between [æ] and [ɑ]. Some Eastern speakers use [a] instead of [æ] or [ɑ] in "broad a" words. For example, path is [paθ] instead of [pæθ, pɑθ]. Perhaps you have heard President Kennedy's pronunciation of the words *last* [last], *path* [paθ], or *grass* [gras]. The sound [a] is most commonly heard in the standard diphthongs [aɪ] and [aʊ] which are listed below.	
ɑ	calm	[kɑm]
ɒ	hot	[hɒt]
	(as pronounced by Southern British and some Eastern American speakers)	
ɔ	ball	[bɔl]
o	location	[loˈkeɪʃən]
	Like the sound [e], and under the same general conditions, this vowel also frequently becomes a diphthong [oʊ]. See the list of diphthongs that follows.	
ʊ	look	[lʊk]
u	pool	[pul]
ɝ	bird	[bɝd]
	(as heard in General American English)	
ɜ	bird	[bɜd]
	(as heard in the East and South)	
ɚ	father	[ˈfɑðɚ]
	(as heard in General American English). [ɚ] is always an unstressed vowel.	
ə	father	[ˈfɑðə]
	(as heard in the East and South). Like [ɚ], the vowel [ə] is always unstressed. Not only is [ə] the Eastern and Southern variant of [ɚ], it is also one of the most frequent vowels in English. It appears as the pronunciation of many vowels in unstressed syllables.	
ʌ	love	[lʌv]

Phonetic Symbol	Key Word	Phonetic Transcription
		Diphthongs[1]
aɪ	kite	[kaɪt]
aʊ	cow	[kaʊ]
eɪ	gay	[geɪ]
oʊ	go	[goʊ]
ɔɪ	boil	[bɔɪl]
		Consonants
b	be	[bi]
p	pit	[pɪt]
t	tag	[tæg]
d	dog	[dɔg]
k	cake	[keɪk]
g	go	[goʊ]
m	meat	[mit]
n	no	[noʊ]
ŋ	sing	[sɪŋ]
f	fun	[fʌn]
v	vain	[veɪn]
s	six	[sɪks]
z	zoo	[zu]
θ	thin	[θɪn]
ð	then	[ðɛn]
ʃ	ship	[ʃɪp]
ʒ	measure	['mɛʒɚ, 'mɛʒə]
h	hit	[hɪt]
ʍ	white	[ʍaɪt]
		This sound is sometimes transcribed as [hw], thus [hwaɪt].
tʃ	chin	[tʃɪn]
dʒ	judge	[dʒʌdʒ]

[1] A diphthong is a complex of vowel sounds within the same syllable. It begins with a recognizable vowel sound, glides through several intermediate positions, and ends with another recognizable vowel. The average listener usually hears a diphthong as a single sound. There are many diphthongs in American English. The five listed here are considered major.

Phonetic Symbol	*Key Word*	*Phonetic Transcription*
l	lull	[lʌl]
r	red	[rɛd]
w	wet	[wɛt]
j	yes	[jɛs]

Many of the symbols in the phonetic alphabet are familiar to you, while several of them are quite strange. Get to know all of them. Try writing words, phrases and sentences in phonetic symbols. The more aware you become of the sound system of English, the more conscious you will be of your own speech and of the precision with which you pronounce your words.

ARTICULATION.   Articulation has been identified as the process whereby vocal tone is modified into the sounds of oral communication. Figure XIV–5 shows what the articulators are. Let's see briefly how they help to produce clear speech.

The major factor in the articulation of vowel sounds is the position of the *tongue* in the mouth. The best illustration of this position effect is the vowel diagram, a formalized, schematic representation of the interior of the mouth with the lips to the left and the pharynx to the right as indicated in Figure XIV–6.

The dots on the diagram suggest for each vowel the approximate position of the highest part of the tongue when the vowel is pronounced. The tongue position indicated for each vowel sound by the dots is no more than approximate because each individual speaker varies. Moreover, the diagram tends to be more nearly descriptive of *conversational* speech than it does of the sort of speaking one may expect to use in public address. Public speaking normally demands greater loudness. The degree of mouth opening is affected and this in turn tends to cause shifts in tongue position. The diagram is useful, nonetheless, in that it illustrates the fact that tongue position is significant in the formation of vowel sounds.

Look, for example at the words *sit*, *seat*, *set*, and *sat*. The spellings, of course, are all different. When you listen to each word, however, you can tell that what distinguishes one from another is the vowel sound. The initial and final sounds, [s] and [t], are the same for all. Say each of the words and notice carefully how you cause this difference. You will observe that in each case the vowel sound is dif-

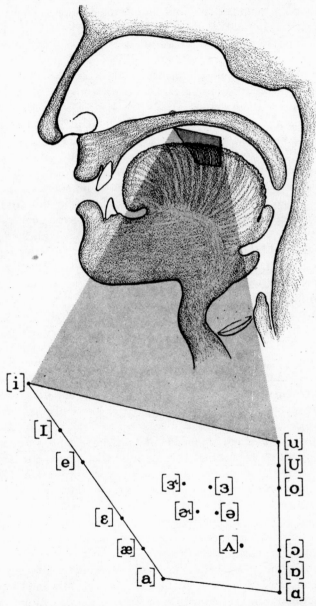

FIGURE XIV–6. TONGUE POSITION IN FORMING CERTAIN VOWELS. (*adapted from Eisenson*)

ferent for one main reason—you change the position of your tongue. The vowel [i] in *seat* [sit] is distinguishable from [ɪ], [ɛ], and [æ] because the position and tension of your tongue are different from what they are when you say the other vowels.

The *lips* become significant in forming the back vowels [ɒ], [ɔ], [o], [ʊ], and [u] because the lips are normally rounded in the proper articulation of these sounds. In a sense, the *lower jaw* may be considered an articulator as well. It would be difficult to produce a good [ɑ] or [ɔ] sound without dropping your lower jaw to give room in your mouth for proper articulation of these vowels.

All parts of the articulatory mechanism help to fashion the consonant sounds. A few simple examples will show how each of these works. When you say a [b], an [m], or a [p], your lips are lightly pressed together to give each of these part of its characteristic sound. Thus the lips are important. [θ] and [ð] are made with the help of the tongue and the teeth, and the lower lip and the teeth cooperate on [f] and [v]. The *teeth*, then, are important. The *upper gum ridge* becomes an articulator when the tip of the tongue touches it in [t], [d], [n], and [l]. For [m], [n], and [ŋ], the *soft palate* (velum) must be relaxed so that air can pass through the nose. In all other English sounds, the soft palate should be raised to close off the nasal passage. Finally, the *vocal folds* themselves are important articulators. Except for factors not important here, the only significant difference between [s] and [z] or between [f] and [v] is that the [s] and [f] are produced without vibrating the vocal folds, whereas the [z] and the [v] require that the vocal folds vibrate. The same is true of several other "voiced" and "voiceless" pairs of consonants.

Think for a moment about the total physiological process of voice production. Muscles of the chest and abdomen must be tensed and relaxed at the proper moment and for just the right sustained period of time to provide air at just the proper pressure. The vocal folds must be lengthened and shortened, tensed and relaxed discretely to produce desired pitches. The resonating cavities must be modified in shape by the articulators at a rapid rate and at precisely the right moment to form accurately the different sounds of speech. The fact that intelligible speech can occur at all seems almost miraculous.

Actually, this complex mechanism works so rapidly and each part is so thoroughly integrated with every other that an attempt to isolate and improve any single part of the process should be guided by a highly skilled professional. A knowledge of the physiology of the vocal mechanism is of value in the classroom primarily in order to dispel some of the untrue notions about speech. It is easy to see that a speaker seriously oversimplifies the process when he looks for the solution to speech problems in "diaphragmatic breathing," "lower pitch," or "more careful articulation." In a public speaking class, only the most general problems can be solved.

ELEMENTS OF VOICE

All judgments about a speaker's voice are limited by the ear of the hearer. Since, as we have said, the ear hears a voice in terms of its pitch, force, time, and quality, any meaningful consideration of the voice must be in terms of these four elements. Thus in talking about the voice in isolation from other factors in delivery, it is perhaps best to think of the vocal mechanism not only as a means of producing sound, but also as an instrument admirably suited to controlling variation of pitch, force, time, and quality in the sounds it produces. Let us examine each of these elements in order to define it and to discover the part it plays in effective communication.

Pitch

We have said that when an elastic system is set into vibration by some outside force, sound results. The rate at which the vibrations occur (number of vibrations per second) is called the frequency. It is the frequency of vibration which is interpreted by the ear as pitch. To produce the pitch A above middle C, the sound source must vibrate 440 times per second. The faster the sound source vibrates (that is, the higher the frequency), the higher the pitch sounds. As the frequency increases or decreases, the pitch rises and falls. Thus pitch can be defined as the relative highness or lowness of a sound in terms of some musical scale. By using the muscles in the larynx a speaker controls the length and tension of the vocal folds in order to produce variations in pitch.

In order for a sound to be audible to the normal ear, the frequency must be within certain limits. If there are too few or too many vibrations per second, the human ear cannot hear the sound. This principle is utilized in "silent" whistles that are used for signaling to dogs. These are so high in pitch that a man cannot hear them, but a dog's ears respond to such high pitches that the whistle is plainly audible to him.

Force

Perhaps the easiest element of voice to understand is force. For our purposes, we can use this term to refer simply to the loudness of a sound. It is mainly determined by what is called the *amplitude* of the vibration. When the stream of air that vibrates the vocal folds is not strong, the vocal folds move but little and only relatively slight disturbances are set up in the air that transmits the sound to the ear. Consequently, the ear is not strongly stimulated and the sound is heard as a soft tone. When the breath is more strongly expelled from the lungs and the vocal folds are caused to vibrate more vigorously, greater disturbances are set up in the air. These strike the ear more forcibly and the ear records the sound as being loud. There is no necessary connection between force and pitch. Each can vary independently of the other. There is a tendency, however, for pitch to rise as force increases.

Time

There are three ways the ear recognizes time in speech. The first of these is through *duration*. This term refers to the length of time any given sound is made to last. For an example, look at the two words *leap* and *gleam*. The letters *ea* are used to spell the same vowel sound [i] in both words. The vowel is quite short in the word *leap* but in *gleam* the vowel lasts a noticeably greater length of time.

The second factor of time is *rate*, or the number of words spoken per minute. There is no necessary connection between rate and duration any more than there is between pitch and force. The two are independent of each other. That is, the rate of speech can be slow, even though the individual sounds are given short duration. The result is a choppy, staccato delivery. On the other hand, when rate is slow and duration is long, a form of drawl results. By the same token, the duration of individual sounds can be long or short when the rate is fast.

The third factor of time is *pause*: the moments when sound ceases. Pauses are an essential part of speaking: a speaker must breathe, he must rethink his ideas, and he must allow the audience to grasp what he has said before he goes on. The most efficient use of pauses takes place when a speaker makes all three of these objectives coincide. That is, the speaker should pause to breathe and to think at points where it will most benefit his listeners to have an interval for assimilating an idea.

Frequently nervousness will interfere with an effective use of pauses. When a speaker rushes ahead to get the speech over with in the shortest possible time, none of his pauses, whether for breathing, for thought, or for audience assimilation, will make much sense.

Often a speaker feels that if he isn't talking all the time, the audience's impression of his fluency will suffer. Many speakers, oppressed by this notion, will fill what should be pauses with meaningless vocalization, a continued nervous insertion of "er" and "uh" that not only distract from what is being said but also make the speaker appear to be at a loss for ideas and words.

The length of a pause can indicate the importance of a point the speaker has made. In a sense, it tells the listeners how long the speaker wants them to "think that one over." By pausing when he has completed a main point, a speaker can tell the listeners how important the point is; at the same time, he lets them think the idea over, thinks for himself about what he is going to say next, and draws in a good breath of air. When pauses are properly used, they do much to clarify the phrasing in a sentence; they add emphasis to ideas; and they contribute greatly to the audience's impression of the speaker as a mature, thoughtful, and secure person.

Quality

There is a wide variety in the sounds produced by different kinds of vibrating bodies. Among musical instruments, for example, it is easy to distinguish one from another because no two different kinds of instruments sound exactly alike. It is not necessary to know the name of a marimba or a glockenspiel to tell them apart even when they play the same notes. The difference lies in the quality of the sounds they produce. Similar quality differentiations can be made among human voices. Even over the telephone, an instrument designed for intelligibility of transmission rather than fidelity, a voice can usually be recognized. Characteristic articulations as well as pitch and time patterns help to identify it, but its unique quality also helps to single it out. Let's see briefly how vocal quality is determined.

You will remember from an earlier part of this chapter that cavities and sounding boards will best resonate pitches that match their own natural frequencies. This fact helps to explain vocal quality. In voice production, cavity resonance is more significant than sounding-board resonance. Thus the cavities of the throat, mouth, and nose are the most important resonators of the voice.

The sound produced by vibration of the vocal folds is very complex. That is, it has not only a fundamental pitch, but contains many overtones as well. It differs, for instance, from a tuning fork, which produces a pure tone, a fundamental pitch with no overtones. Each of the overtones in the voice is acted upon by the resonating cavities of the throat and head so that it is either increased or decreased in strength depending upon whether the cavities respond to its particular pitch. The result is that each voice acquires its own peculiar characteristic quality or timbre. We can thus say that quality is determined by the number, the frequency, and the relative strengths of the overtones in the voice.

USING THE VOICE TO COMMUNICATE MEANING

A speaker must make his ideas immediately intelligible. Listeners cannot stop to mull over a speaker's idea as they might re-examine an obscure paragraph in an essay. Discourse cannot be meaningful in the sense the speaker intends or to the degree he wants it to be compelling without the kind of delivery which brings his ideas sharply and immediately into focus. Here are some of the ways a good speaker uses his voice to give clarity to his ideas.

Emphasize the Important Words

Although a speaker gives up the writer's advantage of allowing a reader to understand ideas at leisure, the speaker has an advantage which a writer does not. He can use his voice to say instantly what he means. He does not have to depend on such crude symbols as commas, periods, exclamation points, and question marks to carry shades of meaning. If he has good control of his voice, a speaker can give a whole complex of different emphases to a single phrase.

In almost any sentence some words are more important than others; thus the less important one can often be omitted without loss of the basic meaning. Because reader time and newspaper space are both at a premium, newspaper headlines are usually telescoped to as short a form as the writer feels he can use and still accurately communicate meaning. Sometimes an obvious verb will be left out. "Legislative Session Near Close." Such words as *a*, *and*, *the* are seldom used. "Clouds, Fog Lift for Pleasant Day." To say more is unnecessary; to say less would destroy the meaning.

Even in the case of newspaper headlines, however, the words that remain are not of equal importance. A news item may be headed "Pilgrims for Holy Week Come to Old Jerusalem." While all of the words may be needed, some carry a larger burden of the meaning than do others. The word *Pilgrims*, for instance, not only cannot be omitted, but it is obviously more important than the words *for* and *to*. If this headline is read aloud, the word *Pilgrims*, then, must be given somewhat greater stress than either *for* or *to*. The phrase *for Holy Week* refers not to just any week in the year, but to a very particular one. Thus the word *Holy* would be given more stress than either of the other two words. Further, the word *Week* is of greater relative importance than *to*. In terms of emphasis, then, the words in the headline call for something like the following degrees of relative emphasis: "PILGRIMS for HOLY *Week Come* to OLD JERUSALEM."

In the most rudimentary sort of language use, nouns and verbs do the real work. As ideas become more complex, other kinds of words are used to add subtlety to the meaning. A speaker is the only one who knows exactly what he means; he is the one who must decide which of his words carry the burden of his meaning. In every case, he must select these important words that carry his meaning and give emphasis to them.

Emphasis is likely to be identified at first thought with loudness. One way to let an audience know what is important is to make it loud. This is the parent's tried and true method with young children. When mother says, "Come at once," children will frequently wait until the call becomes loud enough to indicate that mother means business. However, the speaker who deals with sophisticated people learns that loudness is the crudest form of stress. The most effective emphasis is created through *variety*, in *all* the elements of vocal delivery: pitch, force, time, and quality.

Make Clear Distinctions among the Ideas

"Catholics make up approximately five per cent of the population in West Virginia compared with thirty per cent in Wisconsin." In this sentence there are at least two and possibly three opposing sets of ideas that must be made separate and distinct. Clearly, *five* per cent is different from *thirty* per cent and this difference should be made clear by the voice. Moreover, West Virginia is not to be confused with Wisconsin. And by the attention to Catholics, a distinction is implied between Catholics and non-Catholics among the populations of the two states. Variety in pitch, force, time, and quality must make audible for the listeners such distinctions among the speaker's ideas.

The same principle applies not only to words that communicate a contrast but also to those that express ideas in a series. Lack of variety in the speaker's voice makes them all sound alike. In a West Coast area the Weather Bureau once made a most unfelicitous assignment of a representative to read the midday forecast. He was well aware of the different words for meteorological phenomena, but his speech habit prevented his listeners from hearing these words clearly. Through its lack of variety, his voice made "clouds," "fog," "rain," "clear," "warm," sound the same; the words might almost as well have *meant* the same. Because they are not the same, variation in pitch, force, time, and quality should have been used to suggest that each of the words in this series was to be distinguished from the others.

Make Words Sound Like What You Mean

There are many words which are an imitation of the sound they name. This is true, for example, in naming the sounds made by birds: ducks quack, geese hiss, sparrows chirp, hens cluck, and so on. Insects buzz and hum. The word *boom* imitates the sound it names. The fact that words often imitate sounds can add color to speech.

The imitation of the sound indicated by a word, however, is only a part of what we are talking about when we say that a word should be made to sound like what you mean. One of the major functions of a speaker's words is to communicate not only the factual and logical notions he has in mind but an emotive qualitative content as well. He can convey attitudes towards the ideas he discusses more clearly if he uses his voice to carry to his listeners the emotional qualities he wants in his words. By the vocal quality he gives to his words, the speaker can make *war* sound heroic or unpleasant, *peace* sound pleasant or weak. His voice can help him to show the goodness or badness he imputes to ideas, their rightness or wrongness, their beauty or ugliness, their merit or lack of it.

Speak in a Conversational Manner

Probably nothing in speaking contributes more importantly to effective delivery than a conversational style. A speaker can conceivably use bad diction or even bad grammar, yet if his delivery is spontaneous, direct, and conversational, his chances of effective communication are better than if he had beautiful diction and perfect grammar but lacked a conversational delivery.

Most Americans do not, as a rule, read aloud very often or at any great length. When they do, they sound much like the child first learning to read. Even when he reads fluently, the words of an inexperienced or untrained reader will most likely sound crated for delivery, boxed in with a variety of stiff patterns, repetitions of pitch cadences, an unvaried tempo, an unchanging degree of force, and a dull quality of monotony that destroys much of the meaning of what is being read. Reading patterns often attach themselves to the speaking of memorized words as well. One mark of a poor actor is his inability to speak in a spontaneous, conversational mode.

A good speaker uses all the means of emphasis at his command and the amount of emphasis he can create through variety is enormous. Considering this fact, it is amazing that so many speakers talk as if they were reading a series of words from a paper. Through monotony and dullness, they throw away one of the most important advantages a speaker has over a writer—the ability to give instantaneous clarity to ideas through variety in the elements of speech.

SUMMARY

Speech is brought about by the operation of four bodily processes: respiration, phonation, resonation, and articulation. Respiration supplies the force for phonation. Phonation produces vocal sound. This sound is resonated by the cavities of the throat, mouth, and head to give each voice its characteristic quality. Finally, the indeterminate vocal sound is transformed into speech by the eight articulators: lips, teeth, tongue, lower jaw, hard palate, velum, upper gum ridge, and voice folds.

Speech is heard by the ear in terms of its four variable characteristics: pitch, force, time, and quality. By controlled variation of these elements, a speaker gives emphasis to his ideas and helps bring clarity to his speech.

In using his voice, a speaker should be guided by four principles:

1. Emphasize the important words.
2. Make clear distinctions among the ideas.
3. Make words sound like what you mean.
4. Speak in a conversational manner.

QUESTIONS

1. Explain the two conditions necessary for the production of sound.

2. How is the diaphragm used in speech?

3. Explain how the vocal folds function to produce a sound.

4. What is resonance?

5. What are the eight articulators? What do they do?

6. Would you agree that a person with good articulation would have good pronunciation?

7. How is acceptable pronunciation determined?

8. Should a Southern dialect be considered a substandard form of American speech?

9. What are the four elements of sound which the ear hears?

10. Discuss how the pause is used in effective speech.

11. What must the speaker substitute in his speech for the punctuation marks used in writing?

12. What is the significance of the conversational mode in speech?

SPECIAL READINGS IN VOICE

Little can be done in a public speaking course to correct specific problems in vocal delivery. If you have such problems, your instructor may refer you to the speech clinic of your college. If there is no clinic on campus, he may want to recommend practice materials that will be of help. There are many good and quite readable books on voice and diction. Each one will have a variety of practice materials. We list a few of these here. Many of them are almost sure to be in your library.

Akin, Johnnye. *And So We Speak: Voice and Articulation.* New Jersey: Prentice-Hall, Inc., 1958.

Anderson, Virgil A. *Training the Speaking Voice.* New York: Oxford University Press, 2nd edition, 1961.

Ecroyd, Donald H., Murray M. Halfond, and Carol C. Towne. *Voice and Articulation: A Handbook.* Glenview, Illinois: Scott, Foresman and Co., 1966.

Fairbanks, Grant. *Voice and Articulation Drillbook*. New York: Harper and Brothers, 1960.

Grasham, John A., and Glenn G. Gooder. *Improving Your Speech*. New York: Harcourt, Brace & World, 1960.

DELIVERY: VISUAL ELEMENTS

I. Physical action in speaking
   A. Eye contact
   B. Posture
   C. Movement
   D. Gesture
II. The use of visual aids
   A. Types of visual aids
      1. Diagrams and graphs
      2. Maps and globes
      3. Pictures
      4. Models and actual objects
   B. Principles for the use of visual aids
III. Summary, questions, and exercises

XV

DELIVERY: VISUAL ELEMENTS

Everything a speaker does, in public or private address, on or off the platform, helps to communicate something. "Everything" includes especially his language, his voice, and the way he uses his body. Each of these elements of the communicative situation is a language and is therefore interpreted by the audience as having some bearing on what the speaker is saying. The more of these languages the speaker puts to use at the same time, the more channels he uses simultaneously to carry his message, the more likely the message is to get through. It is quite apparent that all the languages must be saying the same thing, that all the channels must be carrying the same message. Otherwise, not only will they fail to help him make clear to his audience what he wants it to understand him to mean, but they will actively hinder him by counteracting and contradicting each other. Make sure that your words, manner, gestures, facial expression, visual aids—all of the visible and audible cues and clues you give the audience about your meaning—are saying the same thing at the same time. This chapter will consider the visual cues the speaker gives the audience: the way his body helps him to communicate and the way he uses visual aids.

PHYSICAL ACTION IN SPEAKING

The most significant visual element of a speaking situation is, of course, the speaker himself. It is up to him to see to it that the communication of his ideas is not hampered by the way in which he uses his body when he speaks. That he uses his body implies that he must have his body under control.

Eye Contact

When one speaks, he should *look directly at the audience*. This means something more than not looking at the floor, at the walls, out the window, or head-down into his notes. It means more than sweeping the audience with an occasional glance. It means looking directly and personally into the faces of individual members of the audience, moving the look from person to person in the group, making personal eye contact with everyone to whom he speaks. Now, when a speaker addresses a very large crowd, or speaks in a large auditorium where he is removed from his audience at some distance, looking directly into the eyes of each listener becomes difficult or impossible. He must nevertheless give the impression as best he can that he is doing just that.

Your own experience will tell you that listeners do not respond well to a speaker in public or private who does not look at them. Some people are not aware of this reaction because their own habits of eye contact are poor. But you have met people who avoided your glance. What was your reaction to them? There is no point in trying to make a case for the notion that the man who refuses to look you in the eye is himself shifty or untrustworthy; the important idea here is that you react badly to him when he does.

There is one more important reason for the speaker to look directly at his listeners. A speaker should take advantage of every bit of help he can get. The audience itself is an important source of help. As a rule, people respond to what they see and hear, and their responses tell the speaker what effect he has on them. It would be extravagant for the speaker not to use to advantage the feedback the audience gives him in reaction to his speech. Only by making direct visual contact with individual members of the group can the speaker tell who is alert and friendly, who is bored, who is unconcerned, or who is just not listening.

Posture

An audience's response to a speaker as a person is the most significant factor which determines its response to his ideas. Indeed, it is futile to distinguish between the speaker and his ideas. A speaker's posture is one determinant of an audience's response to him as a person. Consequently, the speaker should stand before his audience in a manner that indicates stability and assurance. His posture should be poised but not stiff, relaxed but not sloppy.

Experienced speakers sometimes lean on a speaking stand, put their hands in their pants pockets, or even sit on the edge of a table. Whether such posture is acceptable depends more on the degree of formality in the speaking situation than it does on "rules" of public speaking. Such obvious casualness is likely to work to the disadvantage of a beginning speaker, for many audiences tend to expect speakers to treat them with a kind of formal respect. Correctly or incorrectly, they consider the speaker who is too relaxed in his posture to be taking liberties with them. A second and perhaps more important reason for not being too casual is that an inexperienced speaker is likely to dramatize his relaxation in the effort to dispel or disguise stage fright. Instead of covering up his nervousness, he points it up. This does his effectiveness more harm than good.

Even so, a speaker can achieve and communicate assurance through control over his body and its posture. Though he may not control the trembling in his muscles, he can control the things he does to try to hide it. If you have any such need, stand straight, balance your weight on both feet, and look directly at your audience. The results will be far better than anything you can do by way of draping yourself over the lectern, crossing your ankles, slouching with your hands in your pockets, sitting on the edge of a desk, or pacing back and forth in front of your audience. Granted, this posture won't do much to keep your hands and legs from quivering, but it will help your nervousness from interfering with your communication. You may not think so but your audience will. And that is the important point. Put the stress where the stress belongs. Remember that you are there to *talk*; to talk about *ideas*, not to model clothes or to make a pretty picture for the audience.

Movement

In general, a speaker should avoid making any movement which is not necessary. Moving from one place to another in the room, pacing back and forth on the platform, are seldom necessary. Many an anxious speaker has used such wandering as a means of working off some of the excess energy that builds up before he begins to speak. But when there is nothing in the *speech* to motivate his pacing, when the motivation is in the *nervousness of the speaker*, his walking around during the speech serves no real purpose as far as the audience is concerned and is therefore only distracting.

A highly important detail of movement is the manner of getting to your designated speaking position and back to your seat when you have finished. An audience will consider these acts a part of your speech and will hold you responsible for everything you do from the time you leave your seat until you sit down again. Your speech begins not when you utter your first words, but when you first stand up. Similarly, your speech is not over with your conclusion; it goes on until the attention of the audience is no longer on you. It is quite conceivable that you will hold the attention of your listeners even after you sit down and until something actually distracts them from you.

Under these conditions, it is only reasonable to conduct yourself in a manner that will not detract from the general effectiveness of your speech. Walk to and from the platform with firmness and poise. A large part of the *ethos* discussed in Chapter XI comes from your giving the audience the impression that you are prepared to speak and that you welcome the opportunity. Preserve your dignity by neither racing nor shuffling to the front of the room. When you have finished speaking, maintain the atmosphere of competence and authority you have built up by returning to your seat quietly and deliberately.

Gesture

Another kind of bodily activity in speech is gesture. Gesture is distinguished from the kind of movement just discussed by the fact that it involves the hands, arms, and head, but does not carry the speaker from one part of the room to another.

If they are to be effective, gestures must appear to be natural and spontaneous. When a speaker is criticized for lack of physical activity, he will often comment that gesturing is not "natural" for him. More often than not, the very remark will be accompanied by an emphatic and decisive gesture. The point is that gesture is quite *natural*, but it is not *habitual* for the beginner in a formal speaking situation. The problem is to carry over into public speech the same freedom of movement the speaker normally gives to hands, arms, and head, and the same mobility of facial expression he uses as naturally in private speech. Obviously, some speakers quite naturally gesture more than others. But every speaker should use gestures at least as extensively as he does in private conversation. Those rare persons who do not gesture at all, even in private speech, should maintain the poise of private speech even in public. They should have no difficulty in finding a place to put their hands. The usual experience has been, however, that most speakers have some movement of the hands and arms but these movements are choppy and incomplete. Beginning speakers frequently have slight movement of the hands as their hands rest at their sides or on the rostrum. The speaker in such cases feels the need for movement but is inhibited from making gestures consistent with the meaning he intends his words to convey. If involuntary or inhibited gesturing is your problem, give some conscious attention to bringing your gestures up and making them deliberate, complete, and forceful.

Gestures made with the hands and arms are of two kinds: those that are used to point up ideas by giving emphasis to the words that carry the ideas, and those that are used for description. There is no set vocabulary of gestures. You may point up an idea with your finger or pound a word home with your fist. You may spread your hands to show size or extend your arm to show place. You will find that when you are enthusiastic about your own ideas and when you have the will to communicate those ideas, your own personal speaking habits will supply you with a spontaneous and varied group of gestures that belong to you.

Facial expression is as significant in delivery as gestures made with the hands and arms. When you speak, your face gives your listeners very clear cues on your own reactions to what you are saying. Audiences tend to read your face as closely as they listen to your words. Therefore, it is up to you to give them accurate cues. A lively mobility of facial expression is such a natural part of spontaneous oral communication that even though the speaker with the stiff, dead-pan face may be thoroughly engaged in what he is saying, the audience tends to interpret his lack of facial expression as a lack of enthusiasm for his own ideas.

THE USE OF VISUAL AIDS

We conclude these chapters on delivery with a brief section on the use of visual aids. These mechanical aids which a speaker brings to the speaking situation are sometimes quite useful in making an idea clear. It is our intention only to mention the various types of aids which are available and to indicate some common-sense rules for using them.

Types of Visual Aids

Most visual aids can be classified into four categories: (1) diagrams and graphs, (2) maps and globes, (3) pictures, and (4) models and actual objects.

DIAGRAMS AND GRAPHS.   Diagrams are useful when the speaker wishes to explain some process. When a speaker talks about the basic operation of a spring motor or an internal-combustion engine, a schematic diagram will help him to show the relationships among the various parts and functions of the object under discussion. See Figure XV–1.

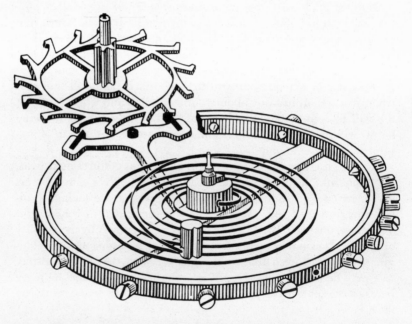

FIGURE XV–1. A SIMPLE DIAGRAM THAT CAN BE ENLARGED FOR VIEWING BY AN AUDIENCE OR SHOWN BY A PROJECTOR. Courtesy of *Hamilton Watch Company.*

Graphs provide a means for showing relationships among statistical data, such as the yearly crime rate, the federal government's tax collections, or the increasing school population. Such graphs are generally of three types. *A line graph* will give the viewer an idea of a general trend over a period of time. A *bar graph* shows comparative quantities clearly where the comparison is among a relatively small number of years, companies, nations, or what have you. It is simple to make. Figure XV–2 shows a bar graph.

**Divorces in the United States from 1890 to 1965
per 1,000 Population**

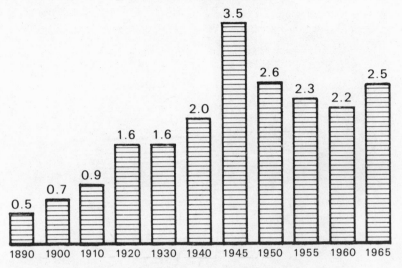

FIGURE XV–2. A BAR GRAPH MADE FROM DATA COMPILED BY
THE NATIONAL CENTER FOR HEALTH STATISTICS. MOST GRAPHS
PUBLISHED IN BOOKS, REPORTS, AND MAGAZINES REQUIRE REDESIGN
TO MAKE THEM SATISFACTORY AS VISUAL AIDS FOR SPEAKERS. THIS
ONE IS RELATIVELY SIMPLE AND CLEAR. IT COULD BE ENLARGED FOR
EASEL DISPLAY OR PROJECTED ON A SCREEN.

A *pie graph* is useful for showing how the parts of a whole are divided.
See Figure XV–3.

MAPS AND GLOBES.   Maps will frequently help a speaker to explain geographical relationships. Globes are ordinarily less useful to a
public speaker than maps because of the distance that is likely to
separate the speaker from his audience. If listeners are gathered about
a speaker, a globe may be useful; otherwise, a globe is difficult for all
to see and for the speaker to use. When a speaker needs to give particular emphasis to the shape of the earth and to the relationships
which are brought about because of that shape, a globe becomes a
functional visual aid.

PICTURES.   It is not always true that "a picture is worth a thousand
words" because a picture has a particular disadvantage which graphs
and maps do not have. Whether it is a drawing, a painting, or a
photograph, whether it is shown directly or projected as a slide, a pic-

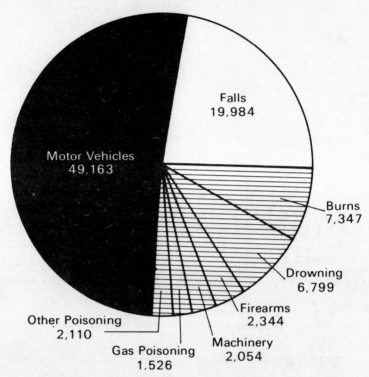

Principal Types of Accidental Death in 1965

FIGURE XV-3. A PIE GRAPH. WHEN THESE AIDS ARE USED FOR
WALL DISPLAY OR PROJECTION, THE SECTIONS SHOULD BE CLEARLY
DISTINGUISHED BY COLOR OR BY STRONG CONTRASTING SHADING.
THIS GRAPH WAS PREPARED FROM 1965 DATA OF THE NATIONAL
CENTER FOR HEALTH STATISTICS.

ture necessarily encompasses a narrower scope of material than a
graph or diagram. Furthermore, it does not make comparisons and
contrasts immediately comprehensible as do graphs. A picture becomes most useful when it portrays an object that is unfamiliar to an
audience.

MODELS AND ACTUAL OBJECTS.   When a speaker wishes to explain some object, displaying the object itself or a model of it during
the speech will help an audience visualize what he is saying. Like
pictures, however, these visual aids often seem more useful than they

actually are. The mere presence of an object does not make its explanation more clear. To explain the aerodynamic principle of lift, a diagram of an airplane wing showing lines of air flow is probably more illustrative than a small model of an airplane. If a speaker wanted to explain the functioning of the *f* stop and the time mechanism on a camera, he could do a better job with a diagram than with the actual camera because the latter is so small that the members of the audience couldn't see it nearly as well.

Principles for the Use of Visual Aids

A little common sense is about all one really needs to use visual aids properly. Here are some common-sense principles to keep in mind when you design and use visual aids.

1. The visual aid must be large enough to be easily seen by all the members of the audience. If it is too small it is of no help.
2. The speaker should talk to the audience and not to the aid.
3. The speaker's language should be as vividly descriptive as if there were no model, map, or diagram. The visual aid should support the language of the speaker and not be a substitute for language.
4. The speaker should avoid blocking the audience's view of the visual aid.
5. The speaker should be sure that his visual aid has only enough detail to make his point. The visual aid should be as simple as is practical.
6. The visual aid should be at the intellectual level of the audience. Clarifying notations which the audience would already know should be omitted.
7. The relationships among various items on the visual aid should be clearly indicated.
8. The visual aid should be an integral part of the speech. The speaker should avoid using pictures, models, and the like unless they clearly add to his main idea. Remember, an attractive visual aid which is not related to the main purpose of the speech will do much to draw attention away from the speech.
9. In using a blackboard for diagrams to be made during the speech, the speaker must draw well enough to get a favorable response from his diagrams and he must be sure that he doesn't take too much time doing it.
10. When the speaker is finished with his visual aid he should put it

out of view of the audience. Otherwise, it will be a continuing distraction.

SUMMARY

A speaker's physical action is as much a part of the speech as his ideas or his vocal delivery. An audience judges a speaker and his ideas by what it sees almost as much as by what it hears. Consequently, controlled physical action is an important part of effective delivery. Perhaps the most significant visual aspect of communication is eye contact; a speaker should look directly at his audience. He should stand before the audience with a relaxed yet not too casual posture. The movement of the speaker to and from the speaking position helps to manifest his vitality, but he should not pace around the room during his speech. The gestures he uses should be full and complete rather than choppy and underdeveloped, definite rather than vague.

A speaker may also add to his speech effectiveness by visual aids. Most visual aids can be classified as diagrams and graphs (among which are the line, bar, and pie graphs), maps and globes, pictures, and models and actual objects. The rules for using visual aids are largely matters of common sense. Keep these points in mind:

1. Make the aid large enough.
2. Speak to the audience, not to the aid.
3. Continue to use descriptive language; the aid is not a substitute.
4. Avoid blocking the view of the members of the audience.
5. Try to keep the aid as simple as possible but be sure to use enough detail to cover all the points which must be covered.
6. Keep the aid at the intellectual level of the audience.
7. Indicate relationships clearly.
8. Make the aid an integral part of the speech.
9. Take special care with preparation and practice if you plan to use the blackboard for visual aids.
10. When you are finished with the aid, put it out of sight of the audience.

QUESTIONS

1. Why is eye contact important?
2. How much should a speaker gesture?

3. Explain the nature of the different kinds of diagrams and graphs mentioned in the text.

4. What is the potential disadvantage to using models?

5. The text lists ten principles for the use of visual aids. Which five do you consider most important?

EXERCISES

1. There are many opportunities to observe, analyze, and evaluate the part physical activity plays in communication: the public platform, the pulpit, the theatre (drama, dance, pantomime), the legislative assemblies, and the like. Observe one of these instances of communication and write a 500-word paper analyzing and evaluating the effectiveness of the part played by physical action in helping the speaker or performer say what he meant.

2. Prepare a five-minute informative speech in which you use visual aids to clarify the main purpose of the speech. Be sure that the speech you choose needs visual aids and that the aids are essential to the whole speech, not to just a part of it.

SPEAKING TO ENTERTAIN

I. Topics
II. Organization
III. Humor
    A. Sources of humor
    B. Forms of humor
       1. Overstatement
       2. Understatement
       3. Irony
       4. Unexpected turns
       5. Play on words
       6. Burlesque
    C. Making humor effective
       1. Be objective
       2. Show kindliness
       3. Use good taste
       4. Learn to laugh at yourself
       5. Let the humor label itself
       6. Stop when you're ahead
IV. Heightening the interest
    A. Suspense
    B. Conflict
    C. Vividness
    D. Novelty and familiarity
V. Summary, questions, and exercises

XVI

SPEAKING TO ENTERTAIN

Every effective speech, regardless of the ultimate response the speaker wants, must be clear and interesting to his audience. The two-fold requirement of clarity and interest has been repeatedly stressed in this book. The present chapter and the two following will show how this requirement may be satisfied in working toward each of the three general ends of speaking. Our specific subject now is speaking to entertain.

On occasion, a speaker's purpose is to interest, divert, or amuse his audience. A fairly obvious example of such an occasion is the after-dinner speech. Someone once introduced an after-dinner speaker by asking the audience to divert its attention from a turkey stuffed with sage in order to hear a sage stuffed with turkey. It would be a brave man who dared approach that audience hoping for their serious consideration of a weighty topic. But what kind of topics are suitable for you when you want to entertain?

TOPICS

Look primarily to personal experience for the subject of a speech to entertain. Nearly everyone has had adventures, exciting experiences, or just experiences that will make good speech subjects. You may have made trips to interesting parts of the country, or to foreign countries. You may have had interesting jobs, met unusual people, developed unique hobbies, done exciting things. Any of these activities is a potential subject for an interesting and entertaining speech.

To be entertaining, a speech need not be devoid of meaningful ideas. It can have a very real and useful point to it. The speaker who talked about the glories of growing up and described the dubious advantages of maturity—with its responsibilities, debts, taxes, and the like—did have something of a point. But because he had no problem to solve, no proposition to prove, and no lesson to teach, he amused and diverted his audience with an offbeat, deliberately eccentric discussion of the subject. What distinguishes a speech to entertain from one to inform or to persuade is the light touch with which the speaker takes up his subject.

Even if we were to suppose that you had never had any exciting or interesting experiences, you would still not lack an abundance of suitable topics. Being able to entertain others lies not so much in the excitement or amusement inherent in what you have to say as in the exciting or amusing way you look at things and make others see them. If you have never traveled, here or abroad, or fought a war, or had a hobby, you can still find entertaining subjects provided you have a sense of humor. Of course, if you have done nothing, seen nothing, felt nothing, never have been amused or excited, and have no sense of humor, we must admit you face something of a problem. But certainly you don't consider yourself an amoeba. As long as you are alive, you are in a world filled with situations and people—and these are the basis of entertainment. They are the subjects of speeches to entertain.

ORGANIZATION

A speech to entertain is not merely a collection of funny stories. It is a speech and, as such, must have at least a semblance of order. The speaker devises a central idea and then proceeds to "develop" it. Some of the audience's pleasure may come from the insane way the idea is developed, but the speaker must give the appearance of starting from a logical base. Digressions need only seem to be appropriate in order to be perfectly acceptable. But the speaker should be aware of his diversions. Then he can use them consciously as a source of humor.

A lawyer gave a speech that offers a good example of this point. He talked about the problems of forming the then-new American Football League. His starting point was that the initials of the group, AFL, had led to all kinds of confusions—including labor problems. He moved next to the fact that forming the League required the work of many lawyers. Having thus mentioned lawyers, he digressed purposely into a discussion of the evils of having too many lawyers around. As he neared the end, he paused, looked at his audience and said, "I seem to be talking too much about lawyers. I wonder why that is." His audience, knowing that he was a lawyer, laughed with him as he moved into the conclusion of his speech.

Good transitions are a useful device for imposing a sense of order on a speech to entertain. The temptation to say, "That reminds me of a story," is a strong one. Resist it. Look instead for transitions which move the speech from point to point, not from joke to joke. The stories and quips then fall into place with the force of properly used supporting material. If your transitions emphasize the gist and not the jests, the audience will see in your speech a plausible (though perhaps zany) coherence.

HUMOR

There has been strong implication in what we have said so far that much of a speaker's success in entertaining speeches spring from his ability to use humor well. It does, indeed. Therefore, we must say something about the use of humor.

Humor is as universal as language. It is found in the gentle teasing of a friend, in subtle quips understandable only to a few, in bitter satire that strikes at folly and vice. The things that cause amusement range widely from the most highly intellectual delicacies of wit to the broadest sort of slapstick, custard-pie comedy. In life's most serious moments, laughter intrudes to break tension. The grim jests of war are clear proof that individuals need release and frequently seek it in humor.

Just what it is that makes humor has often occupied the thoughts of psychologists, rhetoricians, philosophers, and philosophical comedians. Quintilian, who taught speech at Rome in the first century of the Christian era, said,*

I do not think that anybody can give an adequate explanation, though many have attempted to do so, of the cause of laughter, which is excited not merely by words or deeds, but sometimes by touch.

and further:

There are no specific exercises for humor nor professors to teach it.

But if there are no professors of humor, there are students of humor, or at least students. And professors can offer an introductory discussion and suggestions that may move the students to reflection about humor and to further study.

---

* *Institutio Oratoriae*, VI, 3. Translated by H. Rackham. Loeb Classical Library.

Sources of Humor

Whatever other points may be at issue about the nature of humor, one must agree that it is exclusively a human characteristic. Only men among all living creatures laugh. Human beings have even been defined as "animals that laugh." Upon no more than casual examination, it becomes evident that what seems to be laughter in animals is only a caricature of human amusement. Probably the simplest explanation for man's sole proprietorship over laughter lies in the fact that it requires intelligence somewhat above that of a chimpanzee, a horse, or a dog to understand the things that cause amusement.

It has also been said that the comical does not exist outside of what is strictly human.* To borrow examples from Bergson, landscapes may be dull, or beautiful; they are never laughable. Human beings laugh at animals only when the latter exhibit some human characteristic, attitude, or expression. A hat is "funny" not of itself but because of the human whimsy that gave it a shape out of the ordinary.

Bergson's observations lead him to two other conclusions which are of interest here. First, emotions tend to silence laughter. Disinterestedness, emotional detachment, seems to be a necessary condition for amusement. The comical appeals only to intelligence. Bergson points out, secondly, that laughter needs an echo. It is social; it occurs in a *group*. Regardless of how large it may grow, the circle of those who laugh is a closed one. Those not privy to a joke feel no desire to laugh.

There seem to be many different kinds of laughter, only one of which is the sort that arises out of amusement. J. C. Gregory has attempted to show that laughter of all kinds springs from one form or another of relief.† Among these is the laughter caused by tickling, said to be relief springing from the recognition that an attack on the sensitive areas of throat or ribs is not made by fangs but by friendly fingers. Again, there is the laugh of greeting, which arises from relief felt when a potential enemy is seen to be a friend. Laughs of contempt, superiority, and self-congratulation may arise out of relief one feels at victory and an end to danger, or at escaping the misfortunes that befall another. Gregory rather pointedly denies Bergson's contention

---

* For a more thorough discussion of ideas merely sketched in this paragraph and the next, see Henri Bergson, *Laughter* (New York: The Macmillan Company, 1911).

† J. C. Gregory, *The Nature of Laughter* (New York: Harcourt, Brace & Co., Inc., 1924).

that emotion is absent from the reaction to what is comical. It need not be of great concern which of the two theories is correct. If emotion accompanies laughter, it is human emotion and it is clear that intelligence is needed to appreciate humor.

Despite the modesty with which students of humor approach an attempt to isolate the sources of humor and its constituents, there is some agreement as to what these are. Whether other elements may be present in comic situations, in amusing language, or in droll characters, *incongruity* and *surprise* seem to be sufficient to cause laughter. The humor springs from recognition of the incongruity or from the failure of an expected outcome to be realized.

It is not always possible to judge what will cause amusement in an individual. The great German philosopher Schopenhauer is said to have chuckled when he saw a tangent to a circle. The straight line of the tangent led him to expect it to meet another straight line at an angle but the curving circumference of the circle failed to follow through. To Schopenhauer, this unexpected geometry seemed ludicrous. Who could anticipate this reaction?

A speaker faces a somewhat analogous situation. The specific instances of circumstance or language that will amuse an audience are not always anticipated by the speaker. A young lady launching a vigorous attack on the foreign-aid policy of the United States offered evidence of its wastefulness by citing the amount of money spent in India to build grain elevators that are "better than our own." "But," she said, "they are empty." When her audience laughed, a look of surprise crossed her face. She seemed a little vexed to find such levity in the audience. She was talking about *quite* serious matters. Recovering her poise, she went on to show that money had also been spent "to build elaborate cotton mills in Korea. But cotton doesn't grow there." When the audience laughed again, she was quite disconcerted. She looked out over the group with a puzzled frown, and then as she realized the incongruity in the conditions she described, her expression gave her listeners still another moment of unintended delight. Had she seen the incongruity in the situation sooner, she could have used it to advantage.

Forms of Humor

The list of things that bring laughter is long and varied. We will mention here six types of humor that seem especially useful in speaking to entertain.

OVERSTATEMENT. Stories about the New Jersey mosquito are as numerous as the little monsters which inspire them. But no New Jersey mosquito can compete with the variety that inhabit Minnesota.

A party of campers were sleeping in the Minnesota woods. One of the group, Harold Erickson, heard a commotion near him as he dozed in his sleeping bag. Then he realized that someone or something was pulling one of his companions, sleeping bag and all, off into the brush. Erickson crawled after the retreating sleeping bag some hundred yards. He reached a rise and looked down into a gully to see two mosquitoes standing over his friend.

"Let's drag him back a little further," said one.

"No," said the other, "let's eat him here before the big ones come and take him away from us."

It is well to understand that humor is not always pleasant or funny. Recognizing incongruity or being surprised by an unexpected outcome can cause laughter under grim conditions as the following example of overstatement shows.

A young man driving a car around Rim of the World Highway near Crestline, California, drove off the road and down the side of the mountain. When the accident was discovered, a police car and an ambulance were dispatched to the area. While the ambulance attendants were giving what comfort they could to the battered young man, a zealous policeman badgered the poor fellow with questions. The officer seemed to be particularly concerned about speed and kept forcing the question, "How fast were you driving when you went over the cliff?" Finally the injured man looked up at the policeman and said, "Three hundred and seventy-five miles an hour."

UNDERSTATEMENT. If one may believe them, the stories that are told about President Calvin Coolidge make him the champion understater of all time. "Silent Cal" wasn't much of a talker anyway and what little he had to say didn't tend toward elaboration.

Mr. Coolidge returned home from church one Sunday morning and was asked by Mrs. Coolidge what the minister had talked about.

"Sin."

"Well, what did he have to say?"

"He's against it."

IRONY. *Intending a meaning which is the opposite of the literal sense of the words.* According to Abraham Lincoln:

A politician of less than ideal quality so aroused the citizenry of a small midwestern town that they decided to tar and feather him and ride him out of town on a rail. As they put him on the rail, he remarked, "If it weren't for the honor of the thing, I would just as soon walk."

UNEXPECTED TURNS.   A Texan and an Ohioan were riding through the Middle West on a train. The Texan spent considerable time telling his fellow passenger about the vastness of the state of Texas, "Why" he said, "do you know that in Texas you can ride all day and all night and all the next day and never leave the state of Texas?"

"I know what you mean," said the Ohioan, "the trains are terribly slow in Ohio, too."

PLAY ON WORDS.   One evening during a terrible storm on the English countryside, a knight rode up to an inn on a greyhound dog. He inquired of the innkeeper whether he could find a place to sleep. The innkeeper at first told him that there was no more space. It looked as if the knight would have to go back out into the storm. But then the innkeeper noticed that the greyhound was sorely fatigued and in general quite the worse for wear. So he changed his mind, saying, "I wouldn't send a knight out on a dog like this."

"Oh Mr. Gilbert," said a wealthy lady to William Gilbert at a dinner party, "your friend Mr. Sullivan's music is really too delightful. It reminds me so much of dear Baytch [Bach]. Do tell me: What is Baytch doing just now? Is he still composing?"

"Well, no, madam," Gilbert returned, "just now, as a matter of fact, dear Baytch is by way of decomposing.*

BURLESQUE.   *Ludicrous treatment of the sensible and sensible treatment of the ludicrous.* Ambrose Bierce† had this way of dealing with Ben Franklin's sayings from *Poor Richard's Almanac.*

A penny saved is a penny to squander.
A man is known by the company he organizes.
A bad workman quarrels with the man who calls him that.
What is worth doing is worth the trouble of asking somebody to do it.
Think twice before you speak to a friend in need.

---

* Hesketh Pearson, *Gilbert and Sullivan* (Baltimore: Penguin Books, 1950), p. 93.

† As quoted in R. P. Falk, *The Antic Muse* (New York: Grove Press, 1955), p. 27. This book is worth consulting.

Making Humor Effective

The following suggestions will help to get the best results from your use of humor in speaking.

BE OBJECTIVE.   Overriding all use of humor should be a sense of the speaker's objectivity toward the situations and people he pokes fun at. Listeners must feel that the weaknesses a speaker sees in them and others are the normal weaknesses of human beings. Outlandish techniques may be used to point up these foibles, but listeners can laugh more freely if they are confronted with what is at base a true picture (though drawn in caricature), presented impartially and without prejudice.

SHOW KINDLINESS.   Speakers are constantly tempted in using humor to be sarcastic, to ridicule some person, group, or idea. Sarcasm and ridicule are properly classed as forms of humor and they are effective weapons in the arsenal of a persuasive speaker. But in a speech meant to entertain, they strike a sour note. Barbed attacks may seem to find favor with an audience, but the truth is that though they may please they do so by inviting the audience toward smugness and the speaker toward insolence. The speaker also runs the danger of offending his listeners or of having them realize that they have been cheapened by their part in the act. Pointing out incongruities is not in itself an act of unkindness. But to do so with bitterness is out of place in a speech to entertain. Raillery and banter lack the bitterness of sarcasm and ridicule. These may be used in a spirit of good will.

USE GOOD TASTE.   Good taste is difficult to define and audiences differ in what they consider to be acceptable. Therefore, arbitrary prescriptions to avoid jokes about nationality, race, religion, and sex do not always hold true. A good rule to follow is that if any bit of humor is at all likely to offend, avoid it. On the public platform, therefore, avoid any humor which even hints at vulgarity or obscenity. The stock in trade of the burlesque stage comedian has no place in the kind of speaking that is of interest to us here. The world is full of fine humor which can be drawn upon without invading areas which may give offense. The cost of a laugh is too high if the price you pay for it is making yourself offensive.

LEARN TO LAUGH AT YOURSELF.   One way a speaker reveals both objectivity and kindliness in humor is to laugh at himself. Before he can find effective humor in the weaknesses of others he must first sense the foibles in himself.

LET THE HUMOR LABEL ITSELF. There is no joke that has to work so hard for a laugh as the one that is introduced with the suggestion that it is intended to be funny. If a speaker lets it appear that he is working at being witty, he will never make it. The humor that is worth using needs no identification by the speaker. Then, too, some audiences are strangely perverse in that if a speaker tells them he has an amusing incident to recount, they either expect too much or set themselves (unconsciously or not) to resist. The most effective humor slides into the mind without announcement or fanfare.

STOP WHEN YOU'RE AHEAD. There are few things for which people develop a taste more easily than applause. And the taste for applause is virtually insatiable. It is difficult to stop when you know you are doing a good job, when an audience is responsive and you feel that you could hold it indefinitely. There is always a tendency to exploit the favorable reaction of the audience just a little more. But just those few extra stories or jokes may be all it takes to push the speech past its peak of effectiveness. From then on, it goes downhill. It is much better to quit while you're winning. Paradoxically, your listeners will be better satisfied if you leave them feeling that they still want more.

HEIGHTENING THE INTEREST

Humor is only one of the sources from which entertainment is derived. Any device a speaker uses to heighten the interest of his audience in what he says can contribute to the success of a speech to entertain. Some of these devices demand brief mention now. Several of them have already been noted either in Chapter IX (Attention and Response) or in Chapter XII (Language and Oral Style). It is proper that they should have been, for there is no way of separating these methods of heightening the effect of a speech from the principles of attention and interest or from the element of language.

Suspense

Curiosity, the desire for information, is not the exclusive property of monkeys, cats, and children. Every normally alert person has some degree of inquisitiveness. In human beings, curiosity evidences an eagerness to learn. This fact can be used by a speaker to catch and hold the attention of an audience and to heighten its interest in what he has to say. If listeners want information, they will be interested in the source from which it may come to them: the speaker and his speech. The "information" they want can be about the outcome of some point at issue, the identity of the murderer in a crime story, or the punch line of a joke.

Suspense is created when the speaker withholds from the audience for a time the information required to forecast the final outcome of what he is talking about. As long as he can keep his listeners guessing, he can keep them interested. Suspense is thus a means of heightening their interest.

Conflict

An interest in conflict seems to be natural. The enormous popularity of westerns on television is a case in point. All sports involve competition in one form or another and the essence of competition is conflict, hence the popularity of sports. The more obvious competition is, the greater the interest becomes. Anything that suggests a fight draws interest whether it is a schoolyard brawl, a chess game, professional boxing, or athletic teams in competition. The interest of plays and stories is almost always in some kind of conflict. A similar interest can be created by a speaker when the materials he uses suggest conflict or struggle. A conflict has an outcome; listeners want to know the outcome of stories and situations a speaker uses. Thus conflict heightens the audience interest in a speech. Moreover, by timing his revelation of the outcome to create suspense, the speaker can heighten the interest still further.

Vividness

The more vividly a scene or incident can be visualized, the more colorful it becomes. Adding concrete details to the telling of a story heightens interest by making the ideas immediately clear and easy to grasp. Language that is vague, general, and abstract makes the audiences struggle for the ideas it is supposed to communicate; and they quickly cease to struggle. Specific language, on the other hand, builds images that make the ideas sharp and clear.

Dialogue and dialect also lend vividness to the telling of a story. If, instead of translating what is said, a speaker lets his characters talk in their own words, they come alive in a way they otherwise would not. If the characters speak in a regional or other dialect, the speaker can use it to add another dimension of reality and vividness to the telling—

provided his rendition of the dialect is accurate enough to be believable. Using dialects well is not a skill that comes naturally; it must be developed through practice. Moreover, it requires a good ear for the sounds of language and for the tone and the tempo patterns of speech. Lacking this, a speaker will do better to ignore a dialect rather than imitate it poorly.

Novelty and Familiarity

New ideas lose their strangeness and become welcome when they are associated with ideas that are familiar. Something one has never seen or even heard of makes no sense to him until he can join it to something familiar. A distributor for one of the major oil companies, an engineer and a graduate of Princeton University, said that when he first went to a small town in southwest Texas to represent his company, he found it difficult to overcome barriers between himself and the dealers who retail his company's petroleum products. As soon as he learned to talk their kind of language, however, his problem dissipated. At first he had been something wholly novel to their experience; now his language had become a linking familiarity.

Interest in new ideas comes from finding something known in what is unknown. Novelty is effective for heightening interest only when there is a familiar peg to hang it on. Illustrative analogies and apt examples can be used to help listeners see the familiar in novel ideas and situations.

Speakers often have the reverse opportunity: to heighten interest in familiar ideas by giving them a novel treatment. No matter how stale a subject is, a clever treatment and fresh materials can give it a slant that will delight an audience. Here again, as we said earlier, the way a subject is handled is what determines its ability to entertain.

SUMMARY

Virtually any topic that would be suitable and in good taste in a friendly conversation can be converted into an entertaining speech. The central idea may be organized in either a conventional or unconventional way, but the development of the speech should emphasize the central idea rather than lose it among jokes or stories.

The major emphasis in speeches to entertain is ordinarily put on humor. This is found in the recognition of incongruity or in the surprise that springs from an unexpected outcome. Humor takes several forms, among them, overstatement, understatement, irony (saying one thing but meaning the opposite), unexpected turns, plays on words, and burlesque (giving ludicrous treatment to sensible subjects and sensible treatment to ludicrous subjects).

For greatest effectiveness, a speaker's humor should be objective, without malice, and in good taste. If he learns to laugh at himself and his own shortcomings, the speaker will be better able to enjoy and help audiences enjoy the foibles of others. Humor that is labeled as such will tend to have less effect. The best humor will identify itself without being labeled. Plan the speech to entertain so that it reaches its peak of reaction in the audience very near the end. Letting a humorous speech drag on after this peak has been reached may destroy the whole effect.

Other than humor, there are several devices that one may use to heighten the effectiveness of his speaking. These devices stimulate the interest of an audience: suspense, conflict, concreteness, novelty, and familiarity.

QUESTIONS

1. What is the purpose of an after-dinner speech?

2. What is the primary source for topics for the speech to entertain?

3. Comment on the notion that the speech to entertain should avoid the discussion of meaningful ideas.

4. What is the function of the transition in a good speech to entertain?

5. Comment on the idea that "the comical does not exist outside of what is strictly human."

6. Do you believe that humor is an intellectual and not an emotional experience?

7. What are the two basic constituents of humor?

8. Define the six forms of humor discussed in the text.

9. Why should sarcasm be avoided?

10. Should a speaker let an audience know he intends to be humorous? Explain your answer.

11. Comment on the idea that a speaker should exhaust the humor in a situation before closing his speech.

12. Explain three of the four methods discussed in the text for heightening interest.

EXERCISES

1. The following speech by renowned humorist Mark Twain was delivered in Hartford, Connecticut, at a dinner honoring an Englishman named Cornelius Walford. Read the speech, and then write a brief paper discussing the following points:
   (a) What seems to be the specific nature of the occasion?
   (b) Who would seem to make up the audience?
   (c) What is the structure of the speech?
   (d) What are some of the forms of humor the speaker uses?
   (e) Can you see any serious purpose underlying the speaker's use of humor?

ACCIDENT INSURANCE—ETC.*

Gentlemen,—I am glad, indeed, to assist in welcoming the distinguished guest of this occasion to a city whose fame as an insurance centre has extended to all lands, and given us the name of being a quadruple band of brothers working sweetly hand in hand—the Colt's arms company making the destruction of our race easy and convenient, our life-insurance citizens paying for the victims when they pass away, Mr. Batterson perpetuating their memory with his stately monuments, and our fire-insurance comrades taking care of their hereafter. I am glad to assist in welcoming our guest—first, because he is an Englishman, and I owe a heavy debt of hospitality to certain of his fellow-countrymen; and secondly, because he is in sympathy with insurance, and has been the means of making many other men cast their sympathies in the same direction.

Certainly there is no nobler field for human effort than the insurance line of business—especially accident insurance. Ever since I have been a director in an accident-insurance company I have felt that I am a better man. Life has seemed more precious. Accidents have assumed a kindlier aspect. Distressing special providences have lost half their

---

* From *Mark Twain's Speeches*, with an introduction by William Dean Howells (Harper & Brothers Publishers: New York, 1951), pp. 249–251. Copyright 1923, 1951 by The Mark Twain Company. Reprinted by permission of Harper & Row, Publishers.

horror. I took upon a cripple now with affectionate interest—as an advertisement. I do not seem to care for poetry any more. I do not care for politics—even agriculture does not excite me. But to me now, there is a charm about a railway collision that is unspeakable.

There is nothing more beneficent than accident insurance. I have seen an entire family lifted out of poverty and into affluence by the simple boon of a broken leg. I have had people come to me on crutches, with tears in their eyes, to bless this beneficent institution. In all my experience of life, I have seen nothing so seraphic as the look that comes into a freshly mutilated man's face when he feels in his vest pocket with his remaining hand and finds his accident ticket all right. And I have seen nothing so sad as the look that came into another splintered customer's face when he found he couldn't collect on a wooden leg.

I will remark here, by way of advertisement, that that noble charity which we have named the HARTFORD ACCIDENT INSURANCE COMPANY is an institution which is peculiarly to be depended upon. A man is bound to prosper who gives it his custom. No man can take out a policy in it and not get crippled before the year is out. Now there was one indigent man who had been disappointed so often with other companies that he had grown disheartened, his appetite left him, he ceased to smile—said life was but a weariness. Three weeks ago I got him to insure with us, and now he is the brightest, happiest spirit in this land—has a good steady income and a stylish suit of new bandages every day, and travels around on a shutter.

I will say, in conclusion, that my share of the welcome to our guest is none the less hearty because I talk so much nonsense, and I know that I can say the same for the rest of the speakers.

SPEAKING TO INFORM

I. Determining the specific subject of the speech
   A. Limiting the subject
      1. Narrowing the scope to limit a subject
         a. Limit the subject in time
         b. Limit the subject in space
         c. Narrow the subject to a subproblem
         d. Discuss a portion of a process
      2. Treating a series of narrowed aspects of a subject
   B. Formulating a statement of purpose
II. Organizing the body of the speech
   A. Patterns of arrangement
      1. Chronological pattern
      2. Geographical or spatial pattern
      3. Topical pattern
      4. Pattern of definition
      5. Pattern of comparison and contrast
      6. Pattern of cause and effect
   B. Using multiple patterns of arrangement
   C. Number of points in the body of the speech
III. Adding supporting detail
IV. Preparing the conclusion
V. Preparing the introduction
   A. Gaining attention
   B. The subject sentence
   C. Background material
VI. Practicing the delivery
VII. Summary, questions, and exercises

XVII

SPEAKING TO INFORM

Of all the talking that goes on in the world, an enormous part of it is done to accomplish such ends as clarifying ideas, transmitting facts, or giving instructions. At home, at school, and at work, as well as on the public platform, much communication has as its purpose giving information to others. In every case, what an audience understands a speaker to say, rather than what he intends to say, is the significant criterion of what, in fact, he has said. If a message is to be given with clarity, therefore, it must be prepared in such a manner that the speaker can best hope it will be received with accuracy. To accomplish this end, prepare an informative speech using the following six steps:

1. Determine the specific subject of the speech.
2. Organize the body of the speech.
3. Add supporting materials.
4. Prepare the conclusion.
5. Prepare the introduction.
6. Practice the delivery.

DETERMINING THE SPECIFIC SUBJECT OF THE SPEECH

Before he can make an outline, and even before he can begin to gather materials, a speaker must do two things: first, he must determine the scope or breadth of his subject and, second, he must formulate a precise statement of what his specific subject will be.

Limiting the Subject

NARROWING THE SCOPE TO LIMIT A SUBJECT.   More often than not, determining the scope of a speech means limiting or narrowing the subject so that the speaker can develop his ideas in sufficient detail within the time limit of his speech. Here again, as in every other aspect of speaking, the influence of the audience is paramount. What it wants or needs to know determines in large measure the extent to which and the methods by which a speaker fixes the scope of his subject. There are several means of narrowing a topic:

1. *Limit the subject in time.* Such a general subject as "American Presidential elections" might be restricted to a discussion of "The disputed election of 1876," or "The war-time elections of 1864 and 1944."
2. *Limit the subject in space.* A speech on American foreign trade could be narrowed to a consideration of trade with a selected country or to the most significant foreign products which enter through the Port of New York.
3. *Narrow the subject to a subproblem.* Select as the specific topic of the speech a part of some larger question or controversy. Instead of discussing the general question of labor-management relations, for example, isolate the subproblem of labor difficulty on the San Francisco or New York waterfront and deal only with this.
4. *Discuss a portion of a process.* The unloading of a cargo ship on the New York waterfront is a topic restricted in scope to give the speaker ample time for detailed development of the subject.

Overambitious students frequently complain that an adequately limited subject isn't broad enough, that nothing can be said about topics that are so narrow. Industrious and imaginative research, however, will discover a variety of instructive ideas in the most narrowly restricted subject. The speaker who begins by thinking a subject is too narrow appears on the day he is to speak with the concern that he has too much material.

The kind of limitation you give to a subject must first be decided in terms of the subject itself and then be modified by what the audience needs and wants to know; choose the narrowing principle that will best clarify the ideas. While you might use no more than one of these methods in limiting many subjects, in restricting others you will want to use more than one. It is not necessary to narrow a subject by all of these methods, but here is what might be done with a single topic, using all four methods of limitation.

> *General subject:* Civil disobedience
> *Narrowed in time:* Summer, 1967
> *Narrowed in space:* Detroit, Michigan
> *Narrowed to a subproblem:* Rioting

Narrowed to a portion of a process: The attitudes of local
Black leaders toward the Detroit riots in the summer of 1967

Because every speech must ultimately end, even if the only limitation is the physical endurance of the speaker, we have stressed the
desirability of narrowing the subject so that the ideas may be developed in whatever detail is warranted.

TREATING A SERIES OF NARROWED ASPECTS OF A SUBJECT.
Sometimes, however, an audience or occasion can prevent a speaker
from narrowing his subject in the conventional manner just described.
A naval officer, for example, assigned to brief a group of civilian government officials on combat landings, might not want to restrict the
scope of his talk by any of the four methods suggested. Nevertheless,
the same demands for clear exposition must be met in these circumstances as in those that permit subjects to be narrower in scope.

When a speaker must cover a broad subject, he can do it successfully
by putting together a series of treatments of *narrow aspects* of the
broader subject. An example will help to clarify the distinction between the two methods of limitation. A student wanted to select a
speech topic from the general subject the Catholic Church. Using
conventional methods of narrowing the scope of his subject, he might
have arrived at this topic: "The rites of ordination to the priesthood of
the Catholic Church." Instead, this speaker chose to present the
Church in a much broader aspect. In his speech he maintained the
over-all broadness of view of the general subject, but he selected three
specific points which he felt would not only increase his audience's
knowledge of the Church but would also be of interest to a group of
non-Catholic listeners: the Mass as the central act of worship, the
practice of confession, and the doctrine of papal infallibility.

Formulating a Statement of Purpose

The general end of an informative speech is, as was said in Chapter
III, to bring about understanding of something. Before you can begin
to organize the speech, however, and even before you begin to gather
materials, you must make for yourself a clear statement of precisely
what this something is. The most common procedure for making
such a statement is to formulate an infinitive phrase which says
clearly what response you want from your audience. Such a phrase
simultaneously identifies the general end of the speech, specifies the

subject of the speech, and sets its precise scope. The resulting expression of what you intend to accomplish in your speech is called a statement of specific purpose or, more simply, a statement of purpose. It identifies for you exactly what idea you want to clarify for your audience. Going back for a moment to the subject of civil disobedience as it was limited in the example on page 296, here is the statement of purpose for a speech on that topic:

> To inform the audience of the attitudes expressed by local Black leaders about the Detroit riots in the summer of 1967.

The statement of purpose should be put in writing so that you can refer to it as a guide for your speech. It will serve as a test to help you decide what material belongs in the speech and what does not. Every speaker can find many interesting ideas and tempting pieces of material to put into a speech. His great problem is one of selection: admitting those items which are essential to the specific purpose and rejecting those which are not. Sometimes even the most interesting material must be omitted, if the essential unity of the speech is to be preserved. To be useful, speech materials must be more than interesting; they must be directly related to the central idea of the speech as expressed in the statement of purpose and they must serve to make the idea clear. Once it is formed, the statement of purpose should be used as a rigorous standard by which to eliminate unneeded materials. In the case just cited, the statement of purpose was not so used.

Recently, a student gave a speech with the specific purpose of informing his audience about the basic teachings of Siddhartha Gautama, founder of the religion now known as Buddhism. The speech was developed through four main points: (1) Hindu influence, (2) the "Four Noble Truths" that explain the cause and cure of human suffering, (3) the "Noble Eight-Fold Path" by which the cure of human suffering can be established, (4) the concept of Nirvana. Unfortunately, in the course of the speech the speaker allowed himself to drift into a lengthy discussion of Gautama Buddha's life. Now, without doubt a close connection exists between the life history of a man and the religious-philosophical system he establishes. Nonetheless, in this instance it was apparent that the speaker included this material because it was *interesting* and not because it was *necessary* to accomplish the specific purpose of his speech. Had the speaker wished, he could have formulated his purpose in a manner to justify a discussion of the life of Buddha. In this instance, his altered statement of purpose would have served as his guide to the selection of materials in the same way that the original statement should have guided him.

ORGANIZING THE BODY OF THE SPEECH

From the days of the earliest writers on public speaking, order has been recognized as an essential ingredient in good communication. Note that we say "good" communication. No matter how badly a speaker may jumble his ideas and materials, he will still communicate something. He has very little assurance, however, that what he means and what his audience thinks he means will bear much resemblance to each other. If a speech is to make the impression the speaker desires, its parts should be so related that the speech as a whole is easy to understand and easy to remember.

A well ordered speech has three basic divisions: introduction, body, and conclusion. These have been referred to in earlier chapters. All the essential material implied in the statement of purpose is contained in the body of the speech. The introduction and the conclusion help the audience to perceive accurately what the speaker means in the body of the speech. Since the body is the essential part of a speech, it is organized first.

Patterns of Arrangement

The process of organizing the body of a speech may be looked at from two points of view. The first of these is analytical. The speaker examines his subject to determine what kind of logical division or partition he can impose upon it. Dividing the subject into parts is necessary (as we saw in Chapter II) because the whole of the subject cannot be communicated at once. The component ideas must be given to the audience one at a time. It is the function of the analytic process to determine what these components are.

A part of the analytic process in the organization of an informative speech is directed toward making decisions about what we may call the rhetorical requirements of the speaking situation. This means that the speaker must not only decide what kind of partition the subject demands, he must also make judgments about what kinds of information are needed to satisfy audience demands. Journalists long ago developed a rule of thumb to test the completeness of a news story.

If the opening paragraph does not answer the questions Who? What? When? Where? Why? and How? the writing is considered faulty. One who makes an informative speech will profit from examining the content of his speech with a journalistic eye.

In the discussion of outlining (Chapter VIII) the comment was made that the main points of an informative speech should "add up" to the subject proposed by the statement of purpose. The notion involved here is somewhat similar but includes the additional dimension that a speaker may partition his speech adequately with respect to the subject and yet fail to meet the demands of the audience. For example, it is not uncommon to hear a quite competent discussion of a complex operation, procedure, concept, or piece of machinery. The question "how?" is satisfactorily answered, yet the speech is unsatisfying because nothing is done to relate the idea, action, or object described to any function or purpose. The "why?" is ignored. No suggestion is made here that every informative speech will demand attention to all of the who-what-when-where-why-how questions. In any instance, one or several of these may be totally irrelevant. Our advice is simply to be aware of them, to consider them, and to make a judgment about how many of them must be answered to make what you want to say interesting and clear to your audience.

The second aspect of organization is the process of synthesis. The speaker decides how to arrange the parts of the subject into a pattern which he thinks will best meet the expectations aroused in the audience by the subject sentence of the speech and by the attention factor he has used to enlist the interest of the audience.

In deciding what will be the main points in the body of your speech, look for the organizational pattern which will best help your audience understand and remember what you say. There are several methods of arranging an informative speech to achieve clarity and retention. We will comment on the chronological pattern, the geographical or spatial pattern, the topical pattern, the pattern of definition, the pattern of comparison and contrast, and the pattern of cause and effect. Select for your speech the pattern which best fits your subject and which best meets the expectations of the audience.

CHRONOLOGICAL PATTERN.   Many subjects will yield easily to a historical or chronological sequence of presentation. In the following example, the basic steps in the development of the table of atomic weights are clarified by using a chronological partition as the means of ordering the main ideas.

Statement of purpose: To inform the audience about the basic steps in the development of the periodic table.

I. Scientists observed certain similarities in the behavior of groups of elements.

II. Mendelyeev found that the elements could be arranged in an order of increasing atomic weight to bring the elements of these groups into columns.

III. Ramsey completed the organization by assigning atomic numbers.

IV. Later atomic chemists related the atomic numbers to the distribution of electrons in the shells of the various atoms.

GEOGRAPHICAL OR SPATIAL PATTERN. Another common pattern of arrangement is by location. Such an order provides the opportunity to develop a subject in terms of the relation of one point to another in space. In the following outline, the speaker explained the parallel between latitudinal life zones by using a geographical pattern of arrangement. This example is particularly interesting from two points of view; first, two geographical principles actually are at work in one speech and, second, no better pattern or organization is immediately apparent for this subject. Geographical order in this case is virtually essential. A speech on the subject of the pollution in America's rivers might be organized into (a) rivers of the East, (2) rivers of the Midwest, (3) rivers of the West. Such an organization, however, would not be the best for understanding the problem of pollution. Geographical order is useful only when the essential ideas are best divided and best understood on that basis.

Statement of purpose: To inform the audience of the parallel relationship between the plant life of a region and the region's altitude and distance from the equator

I. Tropical forests flourish near sea level and near the equator.
   A. Climatic conditions.
   B. Typical plants.

II. Deciduous forests occur in temperature zones at low altitudes.
   A. Climatic conditions.
   B. Typical plants.

III. Coniferous forests grow at higher altitudes and far from the equator.

      A. Climatic conditions.
      B. Typical plants.
  IV. Mosses, lichens, and low herbaceous growths are characteristic of the far north and areas above timber line.
      A. Climatic conditions.
      B. Typical plants.
   V. Ice and snow caps the highest mountains and both polar regions.
      A. Climatic conditions.
      B. Typical plants.

TOPICAL PATTERN. Any method of partitioning which divides a subject into its component parts can be called a topical pattern. In this sense, both the chronological and the geographical patterns or organizations are forms of topical arrangement. The latter is considered as a separate method of organization to accommodate natural or traditional classifications that are neither chronological nor geographical. Many such classifications are familiar to you: animal, vegetable, and mineral; political, social, and economic; strings, percussion, woodwinds, and brass. Any subject which can be analyzed into component parts can be organized by the method of typical arrangement. Here is an example of topical partition according to function.

    Statement of purpose: To inform the audience of the part played by each of the three services to make the Normandy landing in World War II a success

   I. The Army Air Force softened up the area and protected the troops.
  II. The Navy guarded the troopships and softened up the beach.
 III. The ground forces went ashore to make and hold a beachhead.

PATTERN OF DEFINITION. A fourth method of division is definition. Speeches intended to answer such questions as "What is radioactivity?" or "What is a depression?" or "What is a Socialist?" can often be made meaningful by using as main heads methods of definition selected from among those discussed in Chapter VI. One may properly ask whether this pattern of organization is clearly distinguishable from others, such as the topical arrangement or that by comparison and contrast. Nonetheless, it is easy to see how it gets its name and how it can be profitably used.

Statement of purpose: To inform the audience of the essential nature of jazz

   I. Jazz is a form of popular music indigenous to the United States.
     A. Jazz originated in New Orleans.
     B. Jazz began just after World War I.
  II. Jazz differs from other popular music.
     A. It differs from Spirituals.
     B. It differs from Western Music.
     C. It differs from Folk Music of the hill country.
 III. Jazz takes several forms.
     A. Dixieland.
     B. Blues.
     C. Progressive jazz.

PATTERN OF COMPARISON AND CONTRAST. Speakers frequently make use of the similarities and differences between two items or concepts when an audience is familiar with one of them and not familiar with the other. Comparison and contrast are not only rhetorical forms of definition and forms of supporting material (see Chapter VI), but they can also serve as organizational principles for an informative speech.

Statement of purpose: To inform the audience of the characteristics of a good teacher

   I. A good salesman must have three kinds of knowledge.
     A. He must be familiar with his product.
     B. He must understand the demands and requirements of his customers.
     C. He must know the principles of persuasion.
  II. A good teacher will have similar kinds of knowledge.
     A. He will know his subject thoroughly.
     B. He will understand the needs of his classes.
     C. He will be skilled in the principles of effective communication.
 III. A good salesman and a good teacher have similar personality traits.
     A. Enthusiasm.
     B. Honesty.
     [And so on]

PATTERN OF CAUSE AND EFFECT.   When a speaker wants to explain a topic in terms of what caused an event or when he wants to
explain the consequences of some event, he will use a cause-and-
effect order. You would employ this pattern to explain either the
causes for the stock-market crash of 1929 or the *effects* of radioactivity
on the human body. In the following example, both cause and effect
are combined in the same organizational pattern in order to clarify
the subject more fully.

> *Statement of purpose:* To inform the audience of the problem
>   of smog in the Los Angeles Basin
>
> I. Effects of smog.
>   A. Smog is harmful to the human body.
>   B. Eleven billion dollars per year in property dam-
>   age is incurred.
>   C. Agricultural losses are sustained.
>   1. Plants and crops.
>   2. Livestock.
>   D. Visibility is limited.
>   E. The area loses tourist trade.
> II. Causes of smog.
>   A. Chemical.
>   1. Automobiles.
>   2. Industrial plants.
>   B. Climatic.
>   1. Temperature inversion.
>   2. Weak winds.

Using Multiple Patterns of Arrangement

In organizing an informative speech, you are not only trying to
find *some* method of arrangement that will pull the points of the
speech together, but you are also trying to find *the* method that best
expresses and emphasizes the most natural sequence of ideas.

You need not confine your partitioning of an informative speech
to a single method. It is quite possible that your ideas will become
clearer if you combine two (or even more) of the methods mentioned.
In some instances, the nature of the subject itself demands multiple
levels of arrangement. When, for example, you explain the step in
building an automobile on an assembly line, you will necessarily
combine chronological, spatial, and topical elements in the sequence
of ideas. The following outline includes two methods of arrangement:
topical and chronological.

Specific purpose: To inform the audience of the purpose of the three major honor societies open to speech and drama majors

I. Phi Beta Kappa.
 A. First on campus—1906.
 B. Purpose—to recognize scholarship.
II. Delta Sigma Rho.
 A. On campus—1916.
 B. Purpose—to recognize forensic ability.
III. Alpha Theta Phi.
 A. On campus—1934.
 B. Purpose—to recognize dramatic ability.

The speaker's objective is to classify the purposes of the honor societies, but the chronological element in the arrangement of ideas is valuable in strengthening the unity of the material.

In contrast, notice the lack of order in the following outline:

Statement of purpose: To inform the audience of the essential nature of atheism

I. Early Greeks.
 A. Two meanings for atheism.
  1. Believing in foreign or strange gods.
  2. Believing that there are no gods.
 B. The original Greek word was "atheos."
II. Atheism and Communism.
 A. Associated with international socialist movement.
 B. Part of the state philosophy of the Soviet Union.
III. Atheists and agnostics differ in their beliefs.
 A. Neither is convinced of the existence of God.
 B. Negative evidence sufficient for atheists.
 C. Proof one way or other needed for agnostics.
IV. Atheism today.

Ignoring the lack of coherence in the organization of subheads, look at the basic partition of the main points. The first main point appears to promise a chronological development. The second point shifts ground, however, and introduces what must probably be identified as a topical heading of the central idea. The third point introduces yet another pattern in the form of comparison and contrast. The fourth point returns to the original chronological pattern. The result is a mishmash of tangled ideas. Even if the speaker is successful in making clear each main point individually, his listeners will probably have only a confused notion of what atheism is.

It is clear, then, that imposing multiple patterns of organization on a speech is an advantage only as long as they are compatible and consistent throughout.

Number of Points in the Body of the Speech

No set rule can be given for determining how many points the body of a speech should have because the nature of the subject determines this figure. A reasonable number of main points would be from two to five. More than this number gives the audience too much to remember. Keep in mind at all times that you are trying to give your audience ideas they can carry away with them. The number of main points in the speech should be controlled to a large extent also by the time you have available for speaking. You should allow at least a minute to develop each of the major headings in the body. Thus, if your speech is to be five minutes long, considering the fact that you also need an introduction and a conclusion, four points in the body would be a maximum. Even in a seven-minute speech, three points are not too few. If you have more time, concentrate on extending the development of a few points rather than on increasing the number.

ADDING SUPPORTING DETAIL

After you have established the basic partition through which you will develop the central idea of a speech, you are ready to develop these points by adding supporting detail. The partitioning of a speech creates an orderly structure that helps the audience follow the ideas and see the relationships among them; the supporting details are the sparks that strike fire to the cold logic of the outline. (You might review Chapter VI.)

When you choose supporting material for a speech, always keep in mind the fact that the key element in any speaking situation is the audience. Select material with the audience in mind. Use those materials which will best clarify your ideas and best sustain the interest of your audience.

Listeners usually grasp an idea more readily when it is associated with some object, person, or event which they already know or can easily comprehend. The more vividly your examples, statistics, definitions and quotations revitalize experiences which a listener has had, the better are your chances of making your speech interesting and clear to him. For this reason it is a good beginning rule of thumb to use at least one supporting detail for every idea you bring into a speech.

Variety in supporting detail is a further help toward building interest. A speaker who exclusively uses statistics, or only hypothetical examples, or nothing but quotations, may lose the attention of an audience because his materials lack variety. To be sure, having some supporting material, even if it does lack variety, is preferable to having no material at all, but get variety if you can.

PREPARING THE CONCLUSION

When the speaker has organized his ideas and materials into the body of the speech, he has a unified and coherent view of what he wants his audience to understand. The conclusion of his speech is then prepared. The function of the conclusion is to draw together all the diverse elements of the body of the speech, the main ideas and the supporting materials, in order that the audience may have an understanding of this subject that is as unified and coherent as the speaker's. Whereas in developing his discussion it was necessary to partition the ideas, in concluding the speaker tries to give his audience an overview of the subject; he tries to get them to see the topic as a whole. The conclusion should therefore contain, minimally, a restatement of the purpose and a recapitulation of the main ideas. In short, it should be a summary of the speech. This much is needed to assure clarity.

Clarity, however, is a minimal requirement. The conclusion can also lend a personal touch to the speech and bring it to a graceful close by adding a story, a joke, or a quotation which illustrates the total idea the speaker means to convey. The conclusion is the speaker's last chance to make sure that his audience has understood the central idea of the speech.

PREPARING THE INTRODUCTION

The last step in organizing a speech is developing the introduction. After the central idea has been logically partitioned; after the main points have been developed with clearly organized, interesting, and pertinent supporting materials; and after the conclusion has been planned—then the speaker knows to all intents and purposes what he is going to say. The major part of his preparation has been completed. The introduction of the speech is, in one sense, an added part. It is the part that prepares an audience to listen to the body of the speech. The introduction to an informative speech must accomplish two ends: it must gain the attention of the audience and it must disclose the subject of the speech. This much, then, must be included: material to *gain attention*, and a *subject sentence*.

Over and above these two essential elements, however, some introductions include a third kind of material. These are the additional items of information which may be needed to clarify the subject sentence or to orient the audience before the speaker begins the development of the central idea. Such information is called *background material*.

Gaining Attention

It is often difficult for a speaker to realize that an audience is not ready to listen to him as soon as he is ready to speak. The speaker must *win* the attention of an audience before he can present his ideas. Talking serves no communicative end if the audience is not listening. Material must be provided in the introduction to catch the attention of the audience and direct its attention to the subject of the speech. Any of several means of gaining attention may be used. Here are a few: startling statistics, a story, an anecdote, a quotation, or a reminder to the audience of what it already knows about the subject of the speech. (See Chapter IX again, if you need to.)

Suppose you were planning to give a description of student government at your college. To show the importance of knowing what the student-body officers do, you might begin by pointing out the amount of money collected by the student body each year, and by showing the way this money is spent. Or you might recall the last campus election, or quote an authoritative statement about the importance of student-body government in college life. All of these ideas, and many others, may come to mind as means of gaining attention.

Despite the value of such devices for winning the ear of a listener, the speaker must avoid misusing them. Nothing must be done to interfere with the primary object of a speech—to communicate an idea. The materials used to catch attention must lead the audience *directly* to the central idea of the speech. Avoid the practice of using any introductory device that gains attention but fails to focus this attention on the subject.

A speech student in a class of businessmen persistently used some startling means of getting attention but consistently he failed to relate it to his subject. He would rise, for instance, go to the rostrum and say,

"Bob, I disagree completely with you on that matter. If I've told you once I've told you a thousand times that you just don't know what you're talking about." A pause, and then, "Ladies and gentlemen, how much insurance does an unmarried man need? Here is a question I would like to speak to you about this evening." And so the speech would proceed. Needless to say his audience was bewildered. Bob would sit there waiting (with the rest of the audience) to find out what the speaker's opening remark had meant. They never did find out because it bore no relationship to the subject. It was nothing more than a gimmick to get attention.

A student once came into speech class and sought to catch attention by shooting an arrow over the heads of the students. The missile sent the class diving for the aisles. Another student pointed a gun directly at a girl in the audience and pulled the trigger. The gun had a blank in it but the experience was a great shock to the girl. Another young man caught attention by taking off his pants and ironing them. Many such incidents are fun to recall, but the speeches they introduced are long since forgotten.

The Subject Sentence

The opening a speaker uses to catch attention brings him directly to a specific statement of his subject. The statement of purpose which the speaker formulates serves admirably to guide him in preparing his speech, but stylistically it leaves much to be desired. It will not be used in the speech in the form it originally takes. Instead, it will be replaced by a *subject sentence*. This, in effect, is the statement of purpose recast into a sentence of the sort the speaker might use in conversation.

> *Statement of purpose:* To inform the audience of the legislative, executive, and judicial branches of student government at Howard College

would, in a speech, become a subject sentence somewhat as follows:

> *Subject sentence:* In order to understand how student government works at Howard College, let's look at the functions of the Student Council, Student Body President, and the Student Court.

Background Material

When an audience is not familiar with the subject at hand, it may be necessary to do more than state the subject sentence. When you choose a subject which is new to the listeners, you will often need to orient them to it. For example, when the Inchon landing was in the news there was no necessity for background material on a speech about it, but as the Korean war fades in our memories, it becomes more and more necessary to remind listeners of that earlier time. You would need to tell them, for instance, of the stalemated condition which existed in the war at the time this bold move was planned. By doing this, you give your audience a clearer picture of the main ideas.

Such background material, however, should be limited to a few sentences and must not become an extended discussion. If you are talking about the basic plays of the T formation to an audience with little knowledge of football, you may need to explain the T formation briefly. If the audience knows so little of the subject that it takes a long time to prepare them for your discussion, it would be better to change your purpose to that of explaining the T formation itself. To spend three minutes of a five-minute speech in giving background is a waste of valuable time. If this much background information is necessary for the audience's understanding, then the speaker should revise his statement of purpose and make the background material the subject of his speech.

PRACTICING THE DELIVERY

At all times it is well to remember that until its delivery a speech is a growing thing, representing your increasing awareness of the subject and the specific audience to which you speak. For this reason, your speech will continually change during the time you are working on it. You will be shifting points around, replacing one example with a better one, or considering new principles of partition.

Perhaps because so much of our training in school deals with written rhetoric, we sometimes come to think that a speech is something that we write out and read. As a result of this attitude we are tempted to prepare a careful outline, and then when it is completed to stop revising it and begin to practice the oral delivery. But a speech is different from an essay. It will be judged by the impact its oral delivery has on the audience. Consequently, it should be tried out *orally*, in parts and in the whole, from the early stages of preparation. When the first rough approximation of your speech has been drawn up, begin to "talk it through." As you hear things in the speech you don't like, change them, replace them, improve them. The outline should be developed in the atmosphere of *oral rhetoric*. With this kind of preparation, a speech will come to be part of you; more and more it will grow into a communication that reflects your ideas, your knowledge, and your individual personality.

SUMMARY

Of all the talking that goes on in the world each day, a large part is occupied with the transmitting of information. Informative speaking is an important process and therefore skill in this kind of communication is both necessary and desirable. To insure that the information he gives will be interesting and clear, a speaker should take six steps in preparing an informative speech:

1. *Select and narrow the subject, and formulate a statement of purpose.* The subject may be narrowed either as a whole or in its aspects. The more conventional methods are to narrow the subject to a specific segment of time, or of space, or to a subproblem in a larger controversy, or to a single portion of a process. One or more of these methods of narrowing the subject may be used. A speech topic may also be narrowed by including in the discussion a series of treatments of selected aspects of the whole subject. Narrowing the whole gives a limited view of the subject by developing in detail a very restricted aspect of the subject; narrowing the aspects gives a broader view of the subject without sacrificing specificity and detail.

2. *Choose the basic method of partitioning the subject and determine the main points of the body of the speech.* One or more of several patterns of organization may be used to impose a clear and reasonable sequence on the ideas of the speech, both in the main points and in their subheadings: (a) chronological arrangement, (b) geographical arrangement, (c) topical arrangement, (d) arrangement by definition, (e) arrangement by comparison and contrast, and (f) arrangement by cause and effect. The total number of main points will usually be from two to five.

3. *Add the supporting details.* Use a variety of supporting materials to bring your ideas sharply into focus for your audience.

4. *Prepare the conclusion.* Summarize the main points of the speech, including a restatement of the subject sentence; bring speech to a graceful close.

5. *Prepare the introduction.* Plan to open the speech in a way that will

catch the attention of the audience and, at the same time, lead directly into the subject sentence. When necessary, include background material to orient the audience to the subject of the speech.

6. *Practice the delivery*. Familiarize yourself thoroughly with the ideas and materials of the speech by "talking it through" from the early stages of preparation. With the contents thus firmly in mind, you will be able to deliver the speech with fluency, vigor, and conversational spontaneity.

QUESTIONS

1. List the six steps in preparing a speech.
2. How may a subject be limited?
3. How can a speaker with limited time handle a broad subject?
4. Explain four of the six patterns of arranging the body of a speech.
5. Explain how a speaker gains attention in the introduction of his speech.
6. Differentiate between a specific purpose and a subject sentence.
7. What care must be taken in using background material in the introduction?
8. Explain how to practice the delivery of a speech.

EXERCISES

1. Organize and deliver a five- to seven-minute informative speech on a topic selected from the subject matter of a course you are now taking (other than Speech). Prepare the outline carefully and give your instructor a carbon copy of your speaking outline before you deliver the speech.

2. Select one item from the following list (or one supplied by your instructor) and prepare two statements of purpose for informative speeches on that subject. In the first instance, narrow the scope and limit the subject by using one of the methods explained on pages 295–297. In the second statement of purpose, do the like using another of the methods. Formulate a subject sentence for each statement of purpose.

The liberal arts	Southern hospitality
Biology	The National Forests
The Civil War	College athletics
Summer jobs for students	Student government
Farming	Boating

3. Illustrate with a brief outline each of the six methods of partitioning the body of an informative speech.

4. Select an informative speech by one of your classmates and suggest how you might have tried to gain attention had you delivered his speech. Is your method better than his? Why?

5. With four of your classmates, select a subject for a symposium (each speaker delivers a speech on one specific phase of the general subject). Divide the subject into five subtopics. Let each speaker deliver a five- to seven-minute informative talk on a different one of the subtopics. The symposium topics might be:

    (a) The basic beliefs (nature of man, God, and the relationship between the two) of the five largest non-Christian religions of the world.

    (b) The main responsibilities of the five major executive officers of our state.

    (c) The extent of the five major types of crime in our city.

    (d) The main ideas about writing of five contemporary novelists.

6. The following speech was delivered in a speech class by Charles F. Peters, a student majoring in mathematics. In a brief paper, analyze and evaluate the organization of the speech.

THE HOW AND WHY OF OLD FAITHFUL

When the American mountain men of the early eighteen hundreds, men like Jedediah Smith, Jim Bridger and Hugh Glass, came out of the West they brought with them incredible tales. "High in the Rockies," they said, "was a land where the earth boiled under your feet, where spouts of hot water as tall as a flagpole came roaring out of the trembling ground, and whole valleys steamed with sulphurous fumes as if the lid over Hell itself had been shot full of holes."*

These early descriptions astounded the folks on the eastern seaboard

---

* National Geographic Society, *America's Wonderlands* (Washington, D.C.: The National Geographic Society, 1959).

and taxed their credulity but they cause us no surprise today. What our forebears had watched in awe we know were the geysers of Yellowstone. All of us have read about these. Many of us have actually seen, at least in travel films or pictures if not in person, the most famous, "Old Faithful."

But for many of us the working of this geological phenomenon is just as mysterious as it was to Jim Bridger. It interested me enough to try to find out the how and why of geysers and you may be interested in what I learned about these natural fountains which intermittently erupt, hurling steam, boiling water, and sometimes mud to great heights above the surface. The particular theory I'm going to discuss is not the only explanation of how a geyser works but it's the oldest and most widely accepted. It was proposed in 1847, interestingly enough, by Robert Bunsen, the German chemist who invented the Bunsen burner.

Beneath the geyser's mouth is the geyser well, which is made up of a network of underground channels. These channels may be from ten to one hundred feet deep. The geyser well usually goes down a short distance as a single channel and then branches into many offshoots. These offshoots may be contorted and twist about each other. They may be jagged and narrow in some places, and broad enough to form large subterranean cavities in others. Most passages are between one and five feet in diameter.

Molten igneous rock material beneath the geyser well furnishes the heat that keeps the well and its water at a high temperature.

All levels of the well have a delicate balance between the temperature of and the pressure on the water. The water temperature on the surface is nearly 100 degrees centigrade, while on the bottom it is above 270 degrees. The hotter water near the bottom of the well does not boil or vaporize because of the pressure caused by the water above it. This variation of temperatures within the well is possible only because there is no *convection* to transfer the temperatures around evenly. That is, there can be no mass movement or currents because of the contorted and restricted nature of the passages that form the well. If there were convection, we would have a boiling spring, where all the water boils evenly, instead of a geyser, where the variable pressure situation causes an eruption. The eruption itself occurs when the temperature of the water near the bottom of the well becomes great enough to vaporize the water, and the resulting bubbles of steam become trapped in the crooked passages near the bottom. Under these conditions one cubic inch of water will vaporize into fifty cubic inches of steam. Thus, some water wells up and runs over at the mouth of the geyser. This loss of water eases the pressure throughout the entire column and permits water at all levels of the well to flash into steam.

The enormous pressure caused by the new steam forces the boiling water out of the channel network and into the air, sometimes as high as two hundred feet.

After the eruption the well immediately begins to refill. Some of the erupted water drops back into the well. Subsurface water seeps into the well through permeable rocks and fissures, or water may run into the well from a nearby hot spring. When this new water flows into the well, it does not immediately boil: If it did we would have nothing but a steaming vent. Rather, the water goes back into the pressure relationships I have already described and the cycle begins again.

The interval between eruptions varies from ten minutes to several weeks. Its length depends upon such things as the rate at which the channel network refills, the proximity of the well to its source of heat, the amount of constriction in the well passages, the size of the entire channel network, and the amount of steam that escapes through the rocks that form the geyser well.

It would seem that the eruption of a geyser, then, is neither a mysterious nor an unexplainable occurrence as the early mountain men thought, but is rather an ordered process of nature where the balance between temperature and pressure in a geyser well and the peculiar configurations of the channels of that well determine how frequent, how high, and how faithful Old Faithful's eruptions will be.

SPEAKING TO PERSUADE

I. The nature of persuasion
   A. Identification and disassociation
   B. Persuasion uses a variety of proofs
   C. The limitation of objectives
II. Organizing the speech to persuade
   A. Persuasive organization in general
      1. The introduction
      2. The body
      3. The conclusion
   B. Types of persuasive organization
      1. The proposition-to-proof pattern
      2. The problem-to-solution pattern
      3. The reflective pattern
   C. Determining the best persuasive order
   D. Determining the placement of arguments
III. Summary, questions, and exercises

XVIII

SPEAKING

TO PERSUADE

THE NATURE OF PERSUASION

To persuade someone is to cause him to believe or act in a predetermined way. In persuasion, a speaker presents to his listeners
impelling proofs which cause them to do or believe something. The
effectiveness of persuasion depends upon a speaker's ability to satisfy
his audience that the mode of conduct, the value judgment, or the
factual condition he proposes is expedient or good or true. In order to
do this, he must offer proofs. The proofs are not rigorous, however, in
the mathematical or scientific sense, because proofs in rhetoric are
to a greater or lesser degree tentative. There is, in other words, no
fund of absolute knowledge on which a speaker can draw; neither
can he develop absolute proof. The tentative nature of rhetorical
proof is discussed in Chapter X as the concept of probability.

The materials a speaker uses, the examples he chooses, the definitions he formulates, the comparisons and contrasts he draws must be
within the scope of his listeners' comprehension. The thesis he de-
fends must likewise be advocated within the framework of the existing
ideas, opinions, attitudes, and beliefs of his audience.

Identification and Disassociation

Here the term identification becomes useful. Let us think of persuasion as a process whereby a speaker identifies his cause with the
opinions of his audience. Everyone is, as we have said, a complex of
these mental postures. They are either positive or negative and one
clings to them with varying degrees of tenacity. In the same sense
that a weather forecaster may say there is a sixty percent chance of
rain, so a man may be 60 (or 50 or 80) percent in favor of the Democratic party, open housing, fraternities, or the Methodist Church.
In similar varying degrees, he will be negatively inclined toward
other subjects. Thus a speaker tries to make his proposal consonant

with the way his audience views the world. When he is successful, his audience will identify the speaker's position with their own.

When, for example, a speaker proposes adoption of the local school-board budget to a listener who values calm, careful consideration of all sides of a subject, the speaker will stress the hours of thoughtful study which have gone into preparing the budget.

Again, suppose a speaker favors massive spending in poverty areas. Addressing an audience negatively disposed toward taxation, he will have to give his listeners some ground upon which to identify with what he proposes: for example, that poverty spending will result in general economic benefits, or that it will aid law and order, or that it is supported by men who are generally known to oppose increased taxes.

The counterpart of identification is disassociation. At the same time the speaker identifies his proposal with positive attitudes in the audience, he will disassociate it from negative ones.

Thomas Jefferson came to the Presidency in 1801 after some stormy political conflicts. Many Federalists feared that he would institute repressive actions against them. After a campaign and a close election that had to be decided in the House of Representatives, Mr. Jefferson had to allay Federalist fears. In his Inaugural Address he disassociated himself from the rancor of the past by characterizing it as the natural excess of political campaigning and identified his Presidency with such widely accepted values as unity, law, and reason.

During the contest of opinion through which we have passed the animation of discussions and of exertions has sometimes worn an aspect which might impose on strangers unused to think freely, and to think and write what they think; but this being now decided by the voice of the nation, announced according to the rules of the constitution, all will of course arrange themselves under the will of the law, and unite in common efforts for the common good. All too, will bear in mind this sacred principle, that though the will of the majority is in all cases to prevail, that will, to be rightful, must be reasonable; that the minority possess their equal rights, which equal laws must protect, and to violate which would be oppression. Let us then, fellow-citizens, unite with one heart and one mind. . . . We have called by different names brethren of the same principle. We are all Republicans; we are all Federalists.

Persuasion Uses a Variety of Proofs

A speaker will use a variety or combination of proofs to bring about persuasion. The rational and nonrational elements of proof combine to influence audience response. Indeed, they are so closely intermingled in any persuasive speech that only the critic who is consciously looking for them can isolate one aspect of the proof from another. In a single statement, the critic will often find evidence of each. As an example, when Winston Churchill became Prime Minister of England in the dark days of 1940, he assumed the fearful responsibilities of his office with a statement of policy that we know as the "Blood, Sweat and Tears" speech. The conclusion of this famous speech illustrates the intermingling of the different kinds of proof. Churchill says:

> You ask, what is our policy? I say it is to wage war by land, sea and air. War with all our might and with all the strength God has given us, and to wage war against a monstrous tyranny never surpassed in the dark and lamentable catalogue of human crime.
> That is our policy.
> You ask, what is our aim? I can answer in one word. It is victory. Victory at all costs—victory in spite of all terrors—victory, however long and hard the road may be, for without victory there is no survival.
> Let that be realized. No survival for the British Empire, no survival for all that the British Empire has stood for, no survival for the urge, the impulse of the ages, that mankind shall move forward toward his goal.
> I take up my task in buoyancy and hope. I feel sure that our cause will not be suffered to fail among men.
> I feel entitled at this juncture, at this time, to claim the aid of all and to say, "Come then, let us go forward together with our united strength."

Look at the individual sentences. Which parts are rational appeals, which are motive appeals, and which rely upon the audience's acceptance of the speaker? Each sentence is a mixture of each kind of proof.

The Limitation of Objectives

The extent to which a speaker can hope to be persuasive must be kept in proper perspective. It is a misconception to think that a speech to persuade may be counted successful only if it causes an audience to change its ways. The dramatic picture of a speaker who meets a hostile audience and during the course of a half-hour address converts it into an audience of friendly partisans is not accurate. The concept of the spellbinder who can mold audiences to his will on any subject is a myth. The persuasive speakers most celebrated in history have frequently had to be satisfied with the knowledge that they moved the members of the audience only a little way. As a persuasive speaker, your objective is to move listeners in your direction, however short the journey may be, or to stop, if only for a short time, their movement in another direction. In many instances to expect more than this is to open the door to harsh disappointment.

ORGANIZING THE SPEECH TO PERSUADE

On September 11, 1941, President Franklin D. Roosevelt delivered from the White House a speech which has since been called "The Freedom of the Seas." In this speech, the President announced it to be the policy of the United States government to attack any German or Italian warship which entered what the United States had defined as her defensive waters. Previously, the policy of the United States had been to defend only her own ships from attack, but now she would protect all shipping in her defensive waters by sinking on sight any Axis submarine or surface raider. But notice the order in which the President presented his ideas.

He opened his speech with a detailed discussion of a number of unprovoked attacks on American vessels. He characterized these attacks as "international lawlessness" and as the manifestation of a design on the part of the Axis "to abolish the freedom of the seas and to acquire absolute control and domination of these seas for themselves." Next, he discussed the implications for America of the Axis plan. He pointed out that in time Germany would, through controlling the seas, be able to subjugate the United States. He said that something must be done: "When you see a rattlesnake poised to strike, you do not wait until he has struck before you crush him."

Only after he had elaborated this kind of background, building a strong case against the depredations of the Axis navies, did Roosevelt propose and defend the policy he had formulated. Why did he approach the subject in the way he did? Why did he withhold his statement of the proposition of his speech until so near the end? Why did he not state, bluntly and tersely, the policy of the American government? Because in September of 1941 a considerable segment of the American population felt that if the United States could stay neutral, and would attack Axis ships only when and if they attacked her own, she could avoid becoming entangled in the war and live in peace with whatever victor emerged.

Three months later, the United States was brought into the war by the Japanese attack on Pearl Harbor. After this time, a policy of attacking the ships of the Axis powers could be set forth bluntly. There would be less need to prepare the audience to give favorable hearing to such a policy. But in September, the President had to adopt a speech organization that took into account the desire of his audience to avoid conflict. The organization he chose helped his audience to disassociate from the then current policy of defense and to identify with his newly established policy.

This example not only shows the importance of organization in a speech to persuade, but it also indicates that the organization of a given speech will depend upon the temper of a given audience. Let's examine this latter concept in some detail.

Persuasive Organization in General

The general structure of the speech to persuade is the same as that for the speech to inform. Each has an introduction, a body, and a conclusion.

THE INTRODUCTION. A speaker uses an introduction to focus attention on his subject and to arouse the interest of his audience in it. In many instances, a speaker will include in his introduction a clear statement of the proposition he wishes to prove. In other instances, the speaker may want to withhold for a time the specific thesis. (Franklin D. Roosevelt's speech on the freedom of the seas is an example). In such cases the speaker substitutes for a clear revelation of his proposition a more general statement to let the audience know what the speech will be about.

John F. Kennedy's introduction to his speech to the Greater Houston Ministerial Association during the 1960 Presidential campaign indicates clearly to his audience the subject of his speech.

I am grateful for your generous invitation to state my views.

While the so-called religious issue is necessarily and properly the chief topic here tonight, I want to emphasize from the outset that I believe that we have far more critical issues in the 1960 election: the spread of Communist influence, until it now festers only ninety miles off the coast of Florida—the humiliating treatment of our President and Vice President by those who no longer respect our power—the hungry children I saw in West Virginia, the families forced to give up their farms—an America with too many slums, with too few schools, and too late to the moon and outer space.

These are the real issues which should decide this campaign. And they are not religious issues—for war and hunger and ignorance and despair know no religious barrier.

But because I am a Catholic, and no Catholic has ever been elected President, the real issues in this campaign have been obscured—perhaps deliberately in some quarters less responsible than this. So it is apparently necessary for me to state once again—not what kind of church I believe in, for that should be important only to me, but what kind of America I believe in.

Both in Roosevelt's speech on the freedom of the seas and in Kennedy's speech on religion in government, the introduction is used to help the listener know what the speech is about, but only in Kennedy's introduction is the specific purpose revealed to the audience.

THE BODY.   In the body of a persuasive speech, arguments are stated and supported. The arguments and their supporting material are selected with an eye to influencing the audience to believe or act in a specified manner.

THE CONCLUSION.   The conclusion of a speech to persuade will rarely be like the conclusion of an informative speech—a summary of the ideas in the body. It will usually be a climax which summarizes only in the sense that it is the final outcome of all that has come before. The Reverend Martin Luther King, Jr., founder and President of the Southern Christian Leadership Conference, delivered his speech, "I Have a Dream," at the Lincoln Memorial on August 28, 1963, at the climax of the Civil Rights March on Washington. He told of the failure of the nation to make good on its "promissory note." He called for the nation to continue to advance civil rights, for Negroes to continue to press for their rights. Then he gave a series of nine statements beginning "I have a Dream," followed by five statements containing the phrase "Let freedom ring," and ended:

When we let freedom ring, when we let it ring from every village and every hamlet, from every state and every city, we will be able to speed up that day when all of God's children, black men and white men, Jews and Gentiles, Protestants and Catholics, will be able to join hands and sing in the words of the old Negro spiritual, "Free at last! free at last! thank God almighty, we are free at last!"

Such a steady building makes it almost impossible to say where the conclusion begins. It could begin with the first "I have a dream" or with the first "Let freedom ring." The whole section is climactic.

The last phrase is a summary, not of content but of attitude—"we are free at last!"

The conclusion to William Jennings Bryan's speech at the Democratic National Convention in 1896 was a metaphorical statement which, in a sense, summarized his whole argument in favor of the free silver plan, in the platform:

. . . [We] will answer their demands for a gold standard by saying to them: You shall not press down upon the brow of labor this crown of thorns, you shall not crucify mankind upon a cross of gold.

James B. Conant, former President of Harvard University, speaking in Washington, D.C. on May 24, 1961, to a national conference on the unemployed, out-of-school youth, concluded his more analytical speech with more of a content summary:

In conclusion, let me repeat my sense of shock as I contemplate conditions in our big cities with respect to youth in slum neighborhoods. The problems are the result of a social situation the roots of which run back to the days of slavery and the result of an economic problem which is in part a reflection of the total unemployment situation and in part a result of racial discrimination among labor unions and employers. To improve the work of the schools requires an improvement in the lives of the families who inhabit these slums, but without a drastic change in the employment prospects for urban Negro youth, relatively little can be accomplished. I close by urging that our large-city problems be analysed in far more detail than in the past and with a far greater degree of frankness. Neighborhood by neighborhood we need to know the facts, and when these facts indicate a dangerous social situation the American people should be prepared to take drastic measures before it is too late.

In these three examples one can see how differences of occasion and audience call out different kinds of conclusions. Dr. Conant speaks to a conference of experts who are aware of the problem. His speech (and its conclusion) has a more informative tone. Mr. Bryan concludes his speech as a part of a debate on the resolution. He is more conscious of the need to reinforce argument. The Reverend Mr. King is building an attitude; he wants, not an acceptance of a specific proposal, but an identification with a way of life.

Types of Persuasive Organization

Any persuasive speech in support of any proposition may be organized in any one of three patterns. A speaker chooses the one which he thinks will make his arguments most effective with a specific audience and for a specific proposition. The question of which format to use requires some discussion and the discussion requires that you understand more fully what the three patterns are.

The patterns of arrangement discussed in Chapter XVII (Speaking to Inform) are usually unsatisfactory for a persuasive speech because they emphasize understanding and clarification. In persuasion, the emphasis is on influencing the way an audience will think or act. For this purpose, there are other ways of organizing a speech. Three of these methods are widely enough applicable and of sufficiently general character to warrant specific mention. In using the first of these, a speaker identifies his proposition *early* in the speech and then presents his supporting arguments. We may call this the *proposition-to-proof* pattern. It is frequently referred to as a deductive pattern or organization. The term deductive is probably unfortunate because it invites confusion with the kind of reasoning that bears the same name. In the other two patterns, the speaker identifies his propostion *later* in the speech. In varying degrees, these two patterns use what may be called a proof-to-proposition order. They are frequently called inductive organization, although the use of inductive has the same disadvantages inherent in the practice of calling proposition-to-proof order deductive. When these patterns are used, at least a portion of the speaker's supporting proof is presented before his proposition is identified. These patterns are named, respectively, the *problem-to-solution* pattern and the *reflective* pattern.

THE PROPOSITION-TO-PROOF PATTERN. A proposition-to-proof pattern of organization is one in which the speaker states his proposition in the introduction of his speech and then develops a series of supporting arguments in the body. The main idea is revealed from the very beginning and the proofs are developed and heightened by building up subpoints. The speech concludes with an appeal for acceptance of the proposition.

Suppose you were to speak in favor of a compulsory student-body fee to support extracurricular activities at your college. You look over your arguments and you find several good reasons for adopting the fee.

1. It will provide more opportunity for participation by all of the students.
2. It will provide a program of higher quality.

3. It will provide finances for some smaller activities which would not exist at all without funds from such a source.
4. It will mean better public relations for the college.

You also note that the one strong argument against this proposal is its unfairness to those who would not participate in student activities.

1. Students who aren't interested in student activities will have to pay for something they don't intend to use.

You recognize your reply to this objection:

1. Even those who do not use the student-body card benefit indirectly through the improved public relations of the school. (Note the relationship to this to Point 4 above.)
2. It is the democratic principle that everyone must share in the expense of maintaining the group when the membership of the group are agreed by majority vote.

Here you have four arguments in favor of the fee and one against, with the answer to the opposition argument contained within one of the original arguments in favor, and the opposition argument further countered by an appeal to democratic principle. How might these be presented in the proposition-to-proof pattern of organization? The following example is given to show the main points. (Obviously, if you were to give the speech, you would need evidence and supporting detail that are not shown here.)

INTRODUCTION
I. The current student-body election has aroused the interest of us all.
II. I would like to enlist your support in favor of the compulsory student-body fee to support extra-curricular activities.

BODY
I. It will provide more opportunity than now exists for everyone to participate.
II. It will provide financing for the smaller activities.
III. It will provide a program of higher quality than the present one.
IV. It will mean better public relations for the college,

and thus eventually benefit even the students who do not participate in extracurricular activity.

V. The only democratic way to gain these advantages is with a compulsory student-body fee.

CONCLUSION

I. Because of the opportunity it will provide for everyone, the aid it will bring to the smaller activities, and the better public relations it will bring to the college, all of us should agree to the imposition of this compulsory fee.

II. The way to achieve these advantages is for all of us to vote for the fee at the election so that we can all benefit from it.

THE PROBLEM-TO-SOLUTION PATTERN. In using the problem-to-solution order, a speaker first gets the attention of his audience and presents a problem which needs to be solved. He then recommends a course of action and shows how it will solve the problem. He concludes with an appeal to act on the suggestion. The solution which the speaker wishes to propose is withheld from the audience at the beginning of the speech, at least until the problem has been presented. How long it will be withheld is determined by the situation. Here's how the argument in support of a compulsory student-body fee would look in a problem-to-solution pattern:

INTRODUCTION

I. The current student-body election has aroused the interest of us all.

BODY

I. One of the problems of this college is the lack of financial support for student activities.

A. Currently the activities program is so limited that few students can participate.

B. Activity is limited to events like proms and intercollegiate athletics.

C. Little publicity is given to our school in the local newspapers because we lack a program which will draw the attention of people outside the college.

II. The solution to this problem is in a "yes" vote for compulsory student-body fee.

A. It will solve the problems I have already discussed.

B. It will help to put our activities program on a democratic basis with everyone sharing the load equally.

CONCLUSION

I. So support the solution to these problems—vote "yes" next Tuesday.

THE REFLECTIVE PATTERN. A third type of persuasive organization, the reflective pattern, also withholds the presentation of the solution until later in the speech. In using the reflective pattern, a speaker describes a problem situation and suggests several possibilities for solution. Next, he evaluates each of these. Finally, he proposes the one which he presents to his audience as the best. This form is compatible with a thoroughly objective approach to the subject. By the time the speech is prepared, however, the speaker's purpose is quite argumentative. Far from being purely analytical, he knows before he begins to speak exactly what course of action he will advocate. Everything he says is intended to move the audience toward accepting it.

Organized in the reflective pattern, the outline of a speech supporting a compulsory student-body fee would look like this:

INTRODUCTION

I. The current student-body election has aroused the interest of all of us.

BODY

I. One of the problems of this college is the lack of financial support for extracurricular activities.
A. Currently, the activities program is so limited that few students can participate.
B. Activity is limited to events like proms and intercollegiate athletics.
C. Little publicity is given to our school in the local papers because we lack a program which will draw the attention of the people outside the college.

II. The causes for this unsatisfactory condition are two:
A. Receipts from year to year under the voluntary student-activity fee have been uneven.
B. The percentage of students who pay the voluntary fee is small.

III. We need some system which will satisfy two requirements.

    A. It should furnish enough money.

    B. It should furnish a consistent amount of money.

  IV. The choice is between our present system and the proposed compulsory-fee system which will be on the ballot at the next election.

  V. The new compulsory-fee system will best meet our needs and in the most democratic fashion.

CONCLUSION

  I. When you go to the polls Tuesday, vote for the compulsory fee.

With this brief explanation as background, let's see how a speaker makes his decision about which type of persuasive organization he should use.

Determining the Best Persuasive Order

The choice of persuasive order is based on many factors, among them: the complexity of the proposition, the attitudes of the listeners, the speaker's credibility with the audience, and the presence or absence of opposition speakers. The proposition-to-proof order is easier to develop with clarity because the proposition is constantly before the listener and the relationship between the speaker's purpose and his individual arguments can be continually reinforced. Both the problem-to-solution and the reflective pattern, on the other hand, have the advantage of presenting an idea gradually and thus permit a speaker to support his position before the audience can form a clear notion of rejecting it. Although research into this aspect of persuasion is still tentative, here are some general principles which a speaker can keep in mind when he selects his organizational pattern.

1. *Listeners do not like to be undecided.* Consequently, there is a point in every persuasive speech at which the listener decides for or against the speaker. During the course of a speech several such points may occur as the listener changes his mind or shifts along a continuum between credence and disbelief. The listener's initial decision may be made before the speech even begins. An audience whose opinions are contrary to the speaker's will tend to reject his ideas once his position is made known. Therefore, when an audience is opposed to the speaker's position and knows the argument in support of its own view, it will be to the speaker's advantage to delay associating himself with the position his listeners oppose. Obviously, however, such a practice is unprofitable if the audience knows the speaker's position in advance.

In such a case, using the proposition-to-proof order would be a sign of candor, thereby strengthening the speaker's *ethos* and tending to lessen somewhat the listeners' objections.

2. *When listeners already agree with a speaker, he can do little wrong.* Virtually all he says will reinforce the listener's beliefs. The proposition-to-proof order would seem best to give such an audience immediate and continued reinforcement of its views.

3. *Variations in the intelligence, education, and sophistication of audiences influence their response to persuasive order.* Some listeners, regardless of what position they hold, are influenced by an orderly, logical approach. These hearers might be more easily influenced by a proposition-to-proof order. Other listeners respond more readily to the identification the speaker makes with their needs. In the latter case, a problem-to-solution order may be best because it groups together the needs of the listener and emphasizes them at one point in the speech for maximum immediate effect.

4. *The reflective pattern is designed for the situation wherein the audience has little knowledge of the subject.* It creates understanding first and gets to the issues later. Using this order, a speaker can approach the subject in such a way that the listener understands more clearly what kinds of decisions he must make before he makes them. The reflective pattern has another and perhaps more important advantage. In using it, the speaker imposes his analysis of the topic on the audience. Because the audience is thereby conditioned to the speaker's analysis, later speakers will find it more difficult to undo his persuasive effect; to do so, they must contradict not only his conclusions but his analysis as well.

Determining the Placement of Arguments

Once the problem of general arrangement has been resolved, a more specific question arises: "In what order should individual arguments be put?" Some will say that a speaker should save his strongest argument to give his speech a greater impact at the end. Another will claim the contrary, that putting the best argument first gives the speech a strong start. Experimental investigations of the question have produced mixed results. The decision, as in all other questions in rhetoric, depends upon the state of the audience. However, some general, though tentative, principles are worth considering.

1. While disagreement exists over the relative importance of the

first and last positions, arguments presented early and late are clearly better remembered than those presented in the middle of the speech.

2. When one argument depends on another for its meaning, the dependent argument must obviously follow the one on which it depends. It is useless, for instance, to argue that some federal medical plan will alleviate the shortage of physicians in rural areas before your audience believes that such a shortage exists.

3. If the ideas in a speech are sufficiently unrelated, the speech will appear to lack a unifying theme. It becomes something like a grocery list. The advantage of primacy (putting the strongest argument first) has been observed to be considerably weakened on these occasions. When, for example, a political candidate speaks on a number of relatively unrelated points, the audience will give greatest attention to items which it considers most important, regardless of the order in which they are presented.

4. When a speaker has high status in the eyes of the audience, it will tend to see greater strength in arguments presented early in the speech. Listeners have greater expectations of such speakers and it is only after the speaker has failed to reinforce their expectations that they will be less attentive.

5. Generally, arguments against the speaker's position, even when the speaker refutes them, should not be presented first because they tend to build opposition in the listener's mind. Then the speaker must overcome not only the opposition but in addition he must combat whatever mechanisms the audience establishes to permit it to ignore or avoid his arguments. There is an additional danger. Once a listener makes a decision in the course of the speech, he tends to pay less attention to what follows. Thus, even if the opposition arguments are refuted, the listener will be less likely to "hear" the speaker's arguments in his own behalf.

There is an exception to this principle. When an audience has firmly held arguments opposing the speaker's position, it is probably best to refute those arguments early or the listener may rehearse them throughout the speech and ignore the arguments the speaker uses to support his position.

SUMMARY

In persuasion a speaker selects arguments and motivations which will cause a listener to identify the speaker's proposal with what the listener already knows and believes. Proof in a persuasive speech has both rational and nonrational elements. These elements are so thoroughly blended that one can hardly be distinguished from another. Success in persuasion is not always likely to be dramatic. With some audiences, even the most persuasive speaker can win no more than a slight shift toward his position.

Three different types of organization are useful in persuasion: the proposition-to-proof, the problem-to-solution, and the reflective patterns. A speaker determines which of these to use for the over-all structure of his speech on the basis of audience attitude. The complexity of the proposition, the attitudes of the listeners, the speaker's credibility, and the presence or absence of opposition speakers all help to determine the choice of persuasive order. The placement of arguments in a speech influences the ease with which they will be remembered and the degree to which they will reinforce agreement and diminish opposition.

QUESTIONS

1. What is persuasion?
2. What is meant by "identification"?
3. Was the Reverend Martin Luther Ling, Jr., an emotional or a logical speaker?
4. Must a specific statement of what the speaker will prove be made in the introduction to every persuasive speech?
5. What is the nature of a persuasive conclusion?
6. How is the deductive pattern basically different from the problem-to-solution and the reflective patterns?

EXERCISES

1. Organize and deliver a five- to seven-minute persuasive speech. Turn in to your instructor a copy of your outline, a brief analysis of your audience, a brief statement of what motivation you will use and why you will use it, and a brief statement of what organization you will use and why you will use it.
2. Listen to some persuasive speeches in class. What persuasive order did the speakers use? Could you improve the speeches by changing the order?

3. Write a brief analysis of one of your classmates' speeches, evaluating the method of organization and the use of motive appeal in relation to the classroom audience to which the speech is delivered.

4. Formulate a proposition of policy from one of the general topics listed at the end of Chapter III. Sketch the outline of a persuasive speech on this proposition showing each of the three methods of persuasive organization.

5. Examine one of the three speeches at the end of this chapter and write a paper evaluating its persuasive techniques.

6. Examine the three speeches at the end of this chapter and compare and contrast the rhetorical techniques used.

DUTY, HONOR, AND COUNTRY
General Douglas MacArthur

No human being could fail to be deeply moved by such a tribute as this [Thayer Award]. Coming from a profession I have served so long and a people I have loved so well, it fills me with an emotion I cannot express. But this award is not intended primarily to honor a personality, but to symbolize a great moral code—a code of conduct and chivalry of those who guard this beloved land of culture and ancient descent. For all hours and for all time, it is an expression of the ethics of the American soldier. That I should be integrated in this way with so noble an ideal arouses a sense of pride, and yet of humility, which will be with me always.

Duty, honor, country: Those three hallowed words reverently dictate what you ought to be, what you can be, what you will be. They are your rallying point to build courage when courage seems to fail, to regain faith when there seems to be little cause for faith, to create hope when hope becomes forlorn.

Unhappily, I possess neither that eloquence of diction, that poetry of imagination, nor that brilliance of metaphor to tell you all that they mean.

The unbelievers will say they are but words, but a slogan, but a flamboyant phrase. Every pedant, every demagog, every cynic, every hypocrite, every troublemaker, and, I am sorry to say, some others of an entirely different character, will try to downgrade them even to the extent of mockery and ridicule.

But these are some of the things they do. They build your basic

Address to the Cadets at West Point, May 12, 1962, from Representative Speeches of General of the Army Douglas MacArthur, Senate Document 95, Eighty-eighth Congress, Second Session.

character. They mold you for your future roles as the custodians of the Nation's defense. They make you strong enough to know when you are weak, and brave enough to face yourself when you are afraid.

They teach you to be proud and unbending in honest failure, but humble and gentle in success; not to substitute words for actions, not to seek the path of comfort, but to face the stress and spur of difficulty and challenge; to learn to stand up in the storm, but to have compassion on those who fall; to master yourself before you seek to master others; to have a heart that is clean, a goal that is high; to learn to laugh, yet never forget how to weep; to reach into the future, yet never neglect the past; to be serious, yet never to take yourself too seriously; to be modest so that you will remember the simplicity of true greatness, the open mind of true wisdom, the meekness of true strength.

They give you a temperate will, a quality of the imagination, a vigor of the emotions, a freshness of the deep springs of life, a temperamental predominance of courage over timidity, of an appetite for adventure over love of ease.

They create in your heart the sense of wonder, the unfailing hope of what next, and the joy and inspiration of life. They teach you in this way to be an officer and a gentleman.

And what sort of soldiers are those you are to lead? Are they reliable? Are they brave? Are they capable of victory?

Their story is known to all of you. It is the story of the American man-at-arms. My estimate of him was formed on the battlefield many, many years ago, and has never changed. I regarded him then, as I regard him now, as one of the world's noblest figures; not only as one of the finest military characters, but also as one of the most stainless.

His name and frame are the birthright of every American citizen. In his youth and strength, his love and loyalty, he gave all that mortality can give. He needs no eulogy from me, or from any other man. He has written his own history and written it in red on his enemy's breast.

But when I think of his patience in adversity, of his courage under fire, and of his modesty in victory, I am filled with an emotion of admiration I cannot put into words. He belongs to history as furnishing one of the greatest examples of successful patriotism. He belongs to posterity as the instructor of future generations in the principles of liberty and freedom. He belongs to the present, to us, by his virtues and by his achievements.

In twenty campaigns, on a hundred battlefields, around a thousand campfires, I have witnessed that enduring fortitude, that patriotic self-abnegation, and that invincible determination which have carved his statue in the hearts of his people.

From one end of the world to the other, he has drained deep the chalice of courage. As I listened to those songs [of the glee club], in memory's eye I could see those staggering columns of the First World War, bending under soggy packs of many a weary march, from dripping dusk to drizzling dawn, slogging ankle deep through the mire of shell-pocked roads; to form grimly for the attack, blue lipped, covered with sludge and mud, chilled by the wind and rain, driving home to their objective, and, for many, to the judgment seat of God.

I do not know the dignity of their birth, but I do know the glory of their death. They died, unquestioning, uncomplaining, with faith in their hearts, and on their lips the hope that we would go on to victory.

Always for them: Duty, honor, country. Always their blood, and sweat, and tears, as we sought the way and the light and the truth. And twenty years after, on the other side of the globe, again the filth of murky foxholes, the stench of ghostly trenches, the slime of dripping dugouts, those boiling suns of relentless heat, those torrential rains of devastating storms, the loneliness and utter desolation of jungle trails, the bitterness of long separation from those they loved and cherished, the deadly pestilence of tropical disease, the horror of stricken areas of war.

Their resolute and determined defense, their swift and sure attack, their indomitable purpose, their complete and decisive victory—always victory, always through the bloody haze of their last reverberating shot, the vision of gaunt, ghastly men, reverently following your passwords of "duty, honor, country."

The code which those words perpetuate embraces the highest moral law and will stand the test of any ethics or philosophies ever promulgated for the uplift of mankind. Its requirements are for the things that are right and its restraints are from the things that are wrong. The soldier, above all other men, is required to practice the greatest act of religious training—sacrifice. In battle, and in the face of danger and death, he discloses those divine attributes which his Maker gave when He created man in His own image. No physical courage and no greater strength can take the place of the divine help which alone can sustain him. However hard the incidents of war may be, the soldier who is called upon to offer and to give his life for his country is the noblest development of mankind.

You now face a new world, a world of change. The thrust into outer space of the satellite, spheres, and missiles marks a beginning of another epoch in the long story of mankind. In the five or more billions of years the scientists tell us it has taken to form the earth, in the three or more billion years of development of the human race, there has never been a more abrupt or staggering evolution.

We deal now, not with things of this world alone, but with the illimitable distances and as yet unfathomed mysteries of the universe.

We are reaching out for a new and boundless frontier. We speak in strange terms of harnessing the cosmic energy, of making winds and tides work for us, of creating unheard of synthetic materials to supplement or even replace our old standard basics; to purify sea water for our drink; of mining ocean floors for new fields of wealth and food; of disease preventatives to expand life into the hundreds of years; of controlling the weather for a more equitable distribution of heat and cold, of rain and shine; of spaceships to the moon; of the primary target in war, no longer limited to the armed forces of an enemy, but instead to include his civil populations; of ultimate conflict between a united human race and the sinister forces of some other planetary galaxy; of such dreams and fantasies as to make life the most exciting of all times.

And through all this welter of change and development your mission remains fixed, determined, inviolable. It is to win our wars. Everything else in your professional career is but corollary to this vital dedication. All other public purposes, all other public projects, all other public needs, great or small, will find others for their accomplishment; but you are the ones who are trained to fight.

Yours is the profession of arms, the will to win, the sure knowledge that in war there is no substitute for victory, that if you lose, the Nation will be destroyed, that the very obsession of your public service must be duty, honor, country.

Others will debate the controversial issues, national and international, which divide men's minds. But serene, calm, aloof, you stand as the Nation's war guardian, as its lifeguard from the raging tides of international conflict, as its gladiator in the arena of battle. For a century and a half you have defended, guarded, and protected its hallowed traditions of liberty and freedom, of right and justice.

Let civilian voices argue the merits or demerits of our processes of government: Whether our strength is being sapped by deficit financing indulged in too long, by Federal paternalism grown too mighty, by power groups grown too arrogant, by politics grown too corrupt, by crime grown too rampant, by morals grown too low, by taxes grown too high, by extremists grown too violent; whether our personal liberties are as thorough and complete as they should be.

These great national problems are not for your professional participation or military solution. Your guidepost stands out like a tenfold beacon in the night: duty, honor, country.

You are the leaven which binds together the entire fabric of our national system of defense. From your ranks come the great captains who hold the Nation's destiny in their hands the moment the war tocsin sounds.

The long gray line has never failed us. Were you to do so, a million ghosts in olive drab, in brown khaki, in blue and gray, would rise from their white crosses, thundering those magic words: duty, honor, country.

This does not mean that you are warmongers. On the contrary, the soldier above all other people prays for peace, for he must suffer and bear the deepest wounds and scars of war. But always in our ears ring the ominous words of Plato, that wisest of all philosophers: "Only the dead have seen the end of war."

The shadows are lengthening for me. The twilight is here. My days of old have vanished—tone and tint. They have gone glimmering through the dreams of things that were. Their memory is one of wondrous beauty, watered by tears and coaxed and caressed by the smiles of yesterday. I listen vainly, but with thirsty ear, for the witching melody of faint bugles blowing reveille, of far drums beating the long roll.

In my dreams I hear again the crash of guns, the rattle of musketry, the strange, mournful mutter of the battlefield. But in the evening of my memory always I come back to West Point. Always there echoes and reechoes: duty, honor, country.

Today marks my final rollcall with you. But I want you to know that, when I cross the river, my last conscious thoughts will be of the corps, and the corps, and the corps.

I bid you farewell.

I HAVE A DREAM
Reverend Martin Luther King, Jr.

Five score years ago, a great American, in whose symbolic shadow we stand, signed the Emancipation Proclamation. This momentous decree came as a great beacon light of hope to millions of Negro slaves who had been seared in the flames of withering injustice. It came as joyous daybreak to end the long night of captivity.

But one hundred years later, we must face the tragic fact that the Negro is still not free. One hundred years later, the life of the Negro is still sadly crippled by the manacles of segregation and the chains of discrimination. One hundred years later, the Negro lives on a lonely island of poverty in the midst of a vast ocean of material prosperity. One hundred years later, the Negro is still languished in the corners of American society and finds himself an exile in his own land. Se we have come here today to dramatize an appalling condition.

Address at the Lincoln Monument, Washington, D.C., August 28, 1963. From *Representative American Speeches 1963–1964*, edited by Lester Thonssen (H. H. Wilson Company: New York, 1964), pp. 44–48. Reprinted by permission of Joan Daves. Copyright © 1963 by Martin Luther King, Jr.

In a sense we have come to our nation's Capital to cash a check. When the architects of our republic wrote the magnificent words of the Constitution and the Declaration of Independence, they were signing a promissory note to which every American was to fall heir. This note was a promise that all men would be guaranteed the unalienable rights of life, liberty, and the pursuit of happiness.

It is obvious today that America has defaulted on this promissory note insofar as her citizens of color are concerned. Instead of honoring this sacred obligation, America has given the Negro people a bad check; a check which has come back marked "insufficient funds." But we refuse to believe that the bank of justice is bankrupt. We refuse to believe that there are insufficient funds in the great vaults of opportunity of this nation. So we have come to cash this check—a check that will give us upon demand the riches of freedom and the security of justice. We have also come to this hallowed spot to remind America of the fierce urgency of *now*. This is no time to engage in the luxury of cooling off or to take the tranquilizing drug of gradualism. *Now* is the time to make real the promises of Democracy. *Now* is the time to rise from the dark and desolate valley of segregation to the sunlit path of racial justice. *Now* is the time to open the doors of opportunity to all of God's children. *Now* is the time to lift our nation from the quicksands of racial injustice to the solid rock of brotherhood.

It would be fatal for the nation to overlook the urgency of the moment and to underestimate the determination of the Negro. This sweltering summer of the Negro's legitimate discontent will not pass until there is an invigorating autumn of freedom and equality. 1963 is not an end, but a beginning. Those who hope that the Negro needed to blow off steam and will now be content will have a rude awakening if the nation returns to business as usual. There will be neither rest nor tranquility in America until the Negro is granted his citizenship rights. The whirlwinds of revolt will continue to shake the foundations of our nation until the bright day of justice emerges.

But there is something that I must say to my people who stand on the warm threshold which leads into the palace of justice. In the processes of gaining our rightful place we must not be guilty of wrongful deeds. Let us not seek to satisfy our thirst for freedom by drinking from the cup of bitterness and hatred. We must forever conduct our struggle on the high plane of dignity and discipline. We must not allow our creative protest to degenerate into physical violence. Again and again we must rise to the majestic heights of meeting physical force with soul force. The marvelous new militancy which has engulfed the Negro community must not lead us to a distrust of all white people, for many of our white brothers, as evidenced by their presence here today, have come to realize that their destiny is tied up with our destiny and their freedom is inextricably bound to our freedom. We cannot walk alone.

And as we walk, we must make the pledge that we shall march ahead. We cannot turn back. There are those who are asking the devotees of civil rights, "When will you be satisfied?" We can never be satisfied as long as the Negro is the victim of the unspeakable horrors of police brutality. We can never be satisfied as long as our bodies, heavy with the fatigue of travel, cannot gain lodging in the motels of the highways and the hotels of the cities. We cannot be satisfied as long as the Negro's basic mobility is from a smaller ghetto to a larger one. We can never be satisfied as long as a Negro in Mississippi cannot vote and a Negro in New York believes he has nothing for which to vote. No, no, we are not satisfied, and we will not be satisfied until justice rolls down like waters and righteousness like a mighty stream.

I am not unmindful that some of you have come here out of great trials and tribulations. Some of you have come fresh from narrow jail cells. Some of you have come from areas where your quest for freedom left you battered by the storms of persecution and staggered by the winds of police brutality. You have been the veterans of creative suffering. Continue to work with the faith that unearned suffering is redemptive.

Go back to Mississippi, go back to Alabama, go back to South Carolina, go back to Georgia, go back to Louisiana, go back to the slums and ghettos of our northern cities, knowing that somehow this situation can and will be changed. Let us not wallow in the valley of despair.

I say to you today, my friends, that in spite of the difficulties and frustrations of the moment I still have a dream. It is a dream deeply rooted in the American dream.

I have a dream that one day this nation will rise up and live out the true meaning of its creed: "We hold these truths to be self-evident; that all men are created equal."

I have a dream that one day on the red hills of Georgia the sons of former slaves and the sons of former slaveowners will be able to sit down together at the table of brotherhood.

I have a dream that one day even the state of Mississippi, a desert state sweltering with the heat of injustice and oppression, will be transformed into an oasis of freedom and justice.

I have a dream that my four little children will one day live in a nation where they will not be judged by the color of their skin but by the content of their character.

I have a dream today.

I have a dream that one day the state of Alabama, whose governor's lips are presently dripping with the words of interposition and nullification, will be transformed into a situation where little black boys and black girls will be able to join hands with little white boys and white girls and walk together as sisters and brothers.

I have a dream today.

I have a dream that one day every valley shall be exalted, every hill and mountain shall be made low, the rough places will be made plains, and the crooked places will be made straight, and the glory of the Lord shall be revealed, and all flesh shall see it together.

This is our hope. This is the faith with which I return to the South. With this faith we will be able to hew out of the mountain of despair a stone of hope. With his faith we will be able to transform the jangling discords of our nation into a beautiful symphony of brotherhood. With this faith we will be able to work together, to pray together, to struggle together, to go to jail together, to stand up for freedom together, knowing that we will be free one day.

This will be the day when all of God's children will be able to sing with new meaning

> My country, 'tis of thee,
> Sweet land of liberty,
>   Of thee I sing:
> Land where my fathers died,
> Land of the pilgrims' pride,
> From every mountain-side
>   Let freedom ring.

And if America is to be a great nation this must become true. So let freedom ring from the prodigious hilltops of New Hampshire. Let freedom ring from the mighty mountains of New York. Let freedom ring from the heightening Alleghenies of Pennsylvania!

Let freedom ring from the snowcapped Rockies of Colorado!

Let freedom ring from the curvacious peaks of California!

But not only that; let freedom ring from Stone Mountain of Georgia!

Let freedom ring from Lookout Mountain of Tennessee!

Let freedom ring from every hill and molehill of Mississippi. From every mountainside, let freedom ring.

When we let freedom ring, when we let it ring from every village and every hamlet, from every state and every city, we will be able to speed up that day when all of God's children, black men and white men, Jews and Gentiles, Protestants and Catholics, will be able to join hands and sing in the words of the old Negro spiritual, "Free at last! free at last! thank God almighty, we are free at last!"

THE CUBAN MISSILE CRISIS
President John F. Kennedy

Good evening, my fellow citizens. This Government, as promised, has maintained the closest surveillance of the Soviet military build-up on the island of Cuba. Within the past week unmistakable evidence has established the fact that a series of offensive missile sites is now in preparation on that imprisoned island. The purposes of these bases can be none other than to provide a nuclear strike capability against the Western Hemisphere.

Upon receiving the first preliminary hard information of this nature last Tuesday morning (October 16) at 9:00 A.M., I directed that our surveillance be stepped up. And having now confirmed and completed our evaluation of the evidence and our decision on a course of action, this Government feels obliged to report this new crisis to you in fullest detail.

The characteristics of these new missile sites indicate two distinct types of installations. Several of them include medium-range ballistic missiles capable of carrying a nuclear warhead for a distance of more than 1,000 nautical miles. Each of these missiles, in short, is capable of striking Washington, D.C., the Panama Canal, Cape Canaveral, Mexico City, or any other city in the southeastern part of the United States, in Central America, or in the Caribbean area.

Additional sites not yet completed appear to be designed for inter-mediate-range ballistic missiles capable of traveling more than twice as far—and thus capable of striking most of the major cities in the Western Hemisphere, ranging as far north as Hudson Bay, Canada, and as far south as Lima, Peru. In addition, jet bombers, capable of carrying nuclear weapons, are now being uncrated and assembled in Cuba, while the necessary air bases are being prepared.

This urgent transformation of Cuba into an important strategic base— by the presence of these large, long-range, and clearly offensive weapons of sudden mass destruction—constitutes an explicit threat to the peace and security of all the Americas, in flagrant and deliberate defiance of the Rio Pact of 1947, the traditions of this nation and Hemisphere, the Joint Resolution of the Eighty-seventh Congress, the Charter of the United Nations, and my own public warnings to the Soviets on September 4 and 13.

Address to the nation, October 22, 1962, from U.S. Department of State Bulletin, Vol. X.VII, No. 1200 (November 12, 1962), pp. 715–720. Delivered from the White House by television and radio at 7:00 P.M. E.S.T. on October 22, 1962. A White House press release; as delivered text.

This action also contradicts the repeated assurances of Soviet spokesmen, both publicly and privately delivered, that the arms build-up in Cuba would retain its original defensive character and that the Soviet Union had no need or desire to station strategic missiles on the territory of any other nation.

The size of this undertaking makes clear that it has been planned for some months. Yet only last month, after I had made clear the distinction between any introduction of ground-to-ground missiles and the existence of defensive antiaircraft missiles, the Soviet Government publicly stated on September 11 that, and I quote, "The armaments and military equipment sent to Cuba are designed exclusively for defensive purposes," and, and I quote the Soviet Government, "There is no need for the Soviet Government to shift its weapons for a retaliatory blow to any other country, for instance Cuba," and that, and I quote the Government, "The Soviet Union has so powerful rockets to carry these nuclear warheads that there is no need to search for sites for them beyond the boundaries of the Soviet Union." That statement was false.

Only last Thursday, as evidence of this rapid offensive build-up was already in my hand, Soviet Foreign Minister Gromyko told me in my office that he was instructed to make it clear once again, as he said his Government had already done, that Soviet assistance to Cuba, and I quote, "pursued solely the purpose of contributing to the defense capabilities of Cuba," that, and I quote him, "training by Soviet specialists of Cuban nationals in handling defensive armaments was by no means offensive," and that "if it were otherwise," Mr. Gromyko went on, "the Soviet Government would never become involved in rendering such assistance." That statement also was false.

Neither the United States of America nor the world community of nations can tolerate deliberate deception and offensive threats on the part of any nation, large or small. We no longer live in a world where only the actual firing of weapons represents a sufficient challenge to a nation's security to constitute maximum peril. Nuclear weapons are so destructive and ballistic missiles are so swift that any substantially increased possibility of their use or any sudden change in their deployment may well be regarded as a definite threat to peace.

For many years both the Soviet Union and the United States, recognizing this fact, have deployed strategic nuclear weapons with great care, never upsetting the precarious status quo which insured that these weapons would not be used in the absence of some vital challenge. Our own strategic missiles have never been transferred to the territory of any other nation under a cloak of secrecy and deception; and our history, unlike that of the Soviets since the end of World War II, demonstrates that we have no desire to dominate or conquer any other nation or impose our system upon its people. Nevertheless, American citizens have become adjusted to living daily on the bull's eye of Soviet missiles located inside the U.S.S.R. or in submarines.

In that sense missiles in Cuba add to an already clear and present danger—although it should be noted the nations of Latin America have never previously been subjected to a potential nuclear threat.

But this secret, swift, and extraordinary build-up of Communist missiles—in an area well known to have a special and historical relationship to the United States and the nations of the Western Hemisphere, in violation of Soviet assurances, and in defiance of American and hemispheric policy—this sudden, clandestine decision to station strategic weapons for the first time outside of Soviet soil—is a deliberately provocative and unjustified change in the status quo which cannot be accepted by this country if our courage and our commitments are ever to be trusted again by either friend or foe.

The 1930's taught us a clear lesson : Aggressive conduct, if allowed to grow unchecked and unchallenged, ultimately leads to war. This nation is opposed to war. We are also true to our word. Our unswerving objective, therefore, must be to prevent the use of these missiles against this or any other country and to secure their withdrawal or elimination from the Western Hemisphere.

Our policy has been one of patience and restraint, as befits a peaceful and powerful nation, which leads a worldwide alliance. We have been determined not to be diverted from our central concerns by mere irritants and fanatics. But now further action is required—and it is underway ; and these actions may only be the beginning. We will not prematurely or unnecessarily risk the costs of worldwide nuclear war in which even the fruits of victory would be ashes in our mouth—but neither will we shrink from that risk at any time it must be faced.

Acting, therefore, in the defense of our own security and of the entire Western Hemisphere, and under the authority entrusted to me by the Constitution as endorsed by the resolution of the Congress, I have directed that the following initial steps be taken immediately :

First : To halt this offensive build-up, a strict quarantine on all offensive military equipment under shipment to Cuba is being initiated. All ships of any kind bound for Cuba from whatever nation or port will, if found to contain cargoes of offensive weapons, be turned back. This quarantine will be extended, if needed, to other types of cargo and carriers. We are not at this time, however, denying the necessities of life as the Soviets attempted to do in their Berlin blockade of 1948.

Second : I have directed the continued and increased close surveillance of Cuba and its military build-up. The Foreign Ministers of the Organization of American States in their communiqué of October 3 rejected secrecy on such matters in this Hemisphere. Should these offensive military preparations continue, thus increasing the threat to the Hemisphere, further action will be justified. I have directed the Armed Forces to prepare for any eventualities; and I trust that in the interests of both the Cuban people and the Soviet technicians at the sites, the hazards to all concerned of continuing this threat will be recognized.

Third: It shall be the policy of this nation to regard any nuclear missile launched from Cuba against any nation in the Western Hemisphere as an attack by the Soviet Union on the United States, requiring a full retaliatory response upon the Soviet Union.

Fourth: As a necessary military precaution I have reinforced our base at Guantanamo, evacuated today the dependents of our personnel there, and ordered additional military units to be on a standby alert basis.

Fifth: We are calling tonight for an immediate meeting of the Organ of Consultation, under the Organization of American States, to consider this threat to hemispheric security and to invoke articles six and eight of the Rio Treaty in support of all necessary action. The United Nations Charter allows for regional security arrangements—and the nations of this hemisphere decided long ago against the military presence of outside powers. Our other allies around the world have also been alerted.

Sixth: Under the Charter of the United Nations, we are asking tonight that an emergency meeting of the Security Council be convoked without delay to take action against this latest Soviet threat to world peace. Our resolution will call for the prompt dismantling and withdrawal of all offensive weapons in Cuba, under the supervision of United Nations observers, before the quarantine can be lifted.

Seventh and finally: I call upon Chairman Krushchev to halt and eliminate this clandestine, reckless, and provocative threat to world peace and to stable relations between our two nations. I call upon him further to abandon this course of world domination and to join in an historic effort to end the perilous arms race and transform the history of man. He has an opportunity now to move the world back from the abyss of destruction—by returning to his Government's own words that it had no need to station missiles outside its own territory, and withdrawing these weapons from Cuba—by refraining from any action which will widen or deepen the present crisis—and then by participating in a search for peaceful and permanent solutions.

This nation is prepared to present its case against the Soviet threat to peace, and our own proposals for a peaceful world, at any time and in any forum in the Organization of American States, in the United Nations, or in any other meeting that could be useful—without limiting our freedom of action.

We have in the past made strenuous efforts to limit the spread of nuclear weapons. We have proposed the elimination of all arms and military bases in a fair and effective disarmament treaty. We are prepared to discuss new proposals for the removal of tensions on both sides— including the possibilities of a genuinely independent Cuba, free to determine its own destiny. We have no wish to war with the Soviet Union, for we are a peaceful people who desire to live in peace with all other peoples.

But it is difficult to settle or even discuss these problems in an atmosphere of intimidation. That is why this latest Soviet threat—or any other threat which is made either independently or in response to our actions this week—must and will be met with determination. Any hostile move anywhere in the world against the safety and freedom of peoples to whom we are committed—including in particular the brave people of West Berlin—will be met by whatever action is needed.

Finally, I want to say a few words to the captive people of Cuba, to whom this speech is being directly carried by special radio facilities. I speak to you as a friend, as one who knows of your deep attachment to your fatherland, as one who shares your aspirations for liberty and justice for all. And I have watched and the American people have watched with deep sorrow how your nationalist revolution was betrayed and how your fatherland fell under foreign domination. Now your leaders are no longer Cuban leaders inspired by Cuban ideals. They are puppets and agents of an international conspiracy which has turned Cuba against your friends and neighbors in the Americas—and turned it into the first Latin American country to become a target for nuclear war, the first Latin American country to have these weapons on its soil.

These new weapons are not in your interest. They contribute nothing to your peace and well being. They can only undermine it. But this country has no wish to cause you to suffer or to impose any system upon you. We know that your lives and land are being used as pawns by those who deny you freedom.

Many times in the past Cuban people have risen to throw out tyrants who destroyed their liberty. And I have no doubt that most Cubans today look forward to the time when they will be truly free—free from foreign domination, free to choose their own leaders, free to select their own system, free to own their own land, free to speak and write and worship without fear or degradation. And then shall Cuba be welcomed back to the society of free nations and to the associations of this Hemisphere.

My fellow citizens, let no one doubt that this is a difficult and dangerous effort on which we have set out. No one can foresee precisely what course it will take or what costs or casualties will be incurred. Many months of sacrifice and self-discipline lie ahead—months in which both our patience and our will will be tested, months in which many threats and denunciations will keep us aware of our dangers. But the greatest danger of all would be to do nothing.

The path we have chosen for the present is full of hazards, as all paths are; but it is the one most consistent with our character and courage as a nation and our commitments around the world. The cost of freedom is always high—but Americans have always paid it. One path we shall never choose, and that is the path of surrender or submission.

Our goal is not the victory of might but the vindication of right—not peace at the expense of freedom, but both peace and freedom, here in this hemisphere and, we hope, around the world. God willing, that goal will be achieved.

GROUP DISCUSSION

XIX

GROUP
DISCUSSION

One of the basic characteristics of democracy is that it conducts its business through a free and open discussion of ideas, in speech and in print. Thomas Babington Macaulay called this kind of government "government through speaking." And whether it operates through a Parliament as does Macaulay's England, or through a Congress, a state legislature, a county board of supervisors, a city council, or a town meeting—whatever the instrumentality, a democratic government, indeed any democratic society, is carried on by discussion.

The need for some systematic verbal exploration of ideas is clear. There are many items of business to get done and many decisions to be made at every level of social interaction. The family has to decide how to spend its vacation, and how to finance the education of the children. The community must determine the best method of getting street lights and of eliminating juvenile crime. The nation must choose the best man for its president. The United Nations must articulate a policy for preventing or punishing aggression in specific parts of the world.

Experience shows, however, that no two persons will necessarily agree completely on the specific action that will best meet a given problem. Conflicts of opinion are inevitable. Such conflicts are not in themselves undesirable. It is the concentration-camp, thought-police method of resolving the conflicts which is wholly bad. What intelligent man is willing to exist in an atmosphere wherein decisions are made by fiat and by force, unless perhaps he is the one who makes the decisions? There is little doubt that establishing policy with talk is better than establishing it with guns.

This chapter is addressed to one of the methods for establishing policy with talk, namely, group discussion. The speaker in group discussion has occasion to employ all that he may have learned about speaking to inform, to persuade, even to entertain. In a group discussion he will rarely make a specifically prepared speech; he will make himself generally prepared to speak and will make several speeches when specific occasion calls for them. He will need to form them without rehearsal but with proper attention to purpose, audience, subject, issues, attention, rational and nonrational elements of proof, language, style, and delivery.—the entire range of the chapter headings in this book. He will make these speeches within a context of reflective thinking, a systematic procedure applied to a group rather than an individual. This chapter concentrates on what this context is and on some of the special problems of leadership and participation in group discussion. The details of what a speaker does within this context are covered in the other chapters.

EXPLORING PROBLEMS THROUGH GROUP DISCUSSION

Inherent in the idea of free, open consideration of conflicting opinions is the concept of group participation. Cooperative exploration of subjects is often more productive of good than an examination of the same subject by a lone individual. In seeking the answers to problems of fact, value, and policy, two (or more) heads are usually better than one. Such explorations are called group discussion.

Group discussion can and should and does occur when problems of policy must be solved and when problems of fact and value are examined. When two roommates in college consider mutual vacation possibilities, they are engaged in group discussion. The familiar college "bull session" on matters of religion, politics, and sex is a group discussion. Such discussions often jump from one subject to another without a predetermined pattern and without particular connection, but they are group discussions nonetheless. Group discussion may be found, then, whenever two or more people meet and explore a problem. Not all group discussions, of course, are as vagrant and as formless as the preceding instances are likely to be. Legislative committee hearings and business conferences, for example, are conducted in a much more formal manner.

A group enters into the exploration of a subject to achieve one or the other of two primary ends: (1) to formulate a course of action or establish a policy; or (2) to increase in the group (or in an audience) its knowledge of the subject under discussion.

The most obvious kind of group discussion is the policy discussion involved in the committee meetings of community agencies, business and educational institutions, and governmental organizations. However, discussions to increase knowledge are not unusual. Perhaps in some of your classes in social science or literature you will participate in group discussions that have the purpose of increasing your knowledge without attempting to solve any problem of policy.

Not only may discussion be turned to ends other than the formulation of policy, but policy discussions themselves may be a useful experience even when they explore problems that do not directly affect the group. The decisions of a group, in other words, need not lead to immediate, observable action. Whether overt physical action can be expected as a result of a discussion depends upon the power of the group to act. For example, the Executive Council of the Student Body at North Atlantic University decides that the student body will honor the graduating seniors by hosting them at a breakfast in the Student Union. The Council has the authority to act for the student body at large and is also empowered to disburse student-body funds. This decision can lead to specific, observable action.

These same students may be taking a course in Sociology. Their class asks itself how to improve race relations in the city of Parkland. It is doubtful that any conclusion they come to will have an immediate bearing on policy in that city. Nevertheless, the discussion is valuable. A problem has been posed and a reasonable solution has perhaps been proposed. The knowledge and understanding of the students have been increased. Thus, immediate, direct action is not required to make the group discussion a success.

The subjects of group discussions grow out of the personal, political, religious, and social problems that touch the lives of nearly everyone. They are problems of policy, fact, and value like those described in Chapter III.

The principal concern of this chapter will be with exploratory speaking in its policy-forming role. It is more than likely that the great majority of discussions which engage you in the future will be aimed at the solution of some problem of policy. This emphasis does not mean that the informative aspects of group discussion are being ignored, or that in your class discussions you should not explore questions of fact and value. On the contrary, all three kinds of questions are valuable and interesting subjects for discussion. Keep in mind, however, that in order to resolve a problem of policy satisfactorily, it is necessary also to solve inherent subproblems of fact and value. Thus skill in solving all three kinds of problems is necessary for successful policy discussion.

REFLECTIVE THINKING IN ANALYZING PROBLEMS

Various ways are used to analyze problems. Not all ways are desirable. Some involve a rough associational method of thinking, like that of students you may know: they choose to attend one college rather than another because it has a good football team, or because they know someone who goes there. They select their school without investigating such basic aspects of college quality as finances, curriculum, or the philosophy of the institution. National leaders, too, use associational reasoning when they approve an action (or reject it) without respect to its own merits as fulfilling the needs of their nation but rather because some other nation which they like or dislike is for or against it. Moreover, choices are frequently justified by providing what sound like good reasons after the choice has been made. This latter kind of thinking, called rationalization, is another common flaw in policy making.

The better way to approach a problem of policy is a method called reflective thinking. In reflective thinking, an individual or a group develops a clear understanding of a problem and analyzes it thoroughly to find the best solution. On occasion, however, a group may not be able to find a course of action agreeable to all its members. In such a case, they can at least develop a common understanding of the issues involved. The function of group discussion, then, is to find a solution to a problem through cooperative application of the principles of reflective thinking and, failing that, to discover, through the same procedure, the real issues of disagreement.

THE PATTERN OF REFLECTIVE THINKING

Reflective thinking as a pattern of systematic thought was described a half century ago by John Dewey. He enumerated a series of five steps in the process:

1. *A felt difficulty.* When we become aware of a set of conditions that disturbs us and sets us to wondering about how to improve the situation, reflective thinking can begin.
2. *Location and definition of the difficulty.* The next step in finding a solution to any problem of policy is to raise our awareness of the problem from the level of feeling to that of thinking. We become as fully informed about the problem as we can.
3. *Suggestion of possible solutions.* In the third step, we set up a series of possibilities for solution. These are proposals which, if put into operation, might solve the problems.

4. *Development by reasoning of the merits of the solutions.* Each of the possible solutions that suggests itself is tested and evaluated in order to determine which is probably the best. On the basis of the evaluation, a tentative choice is made.
5. *Further observation and experiment leading to acceptance or rejection of the selected solution.* No amount of reflective thought will bring a problem to an end. Only putting a policy into action can really solve the felt difficulty. This is the final test of whether the conclusion arrived at through reflective thinking is a good one.

The pattern of reflective thinking outlined in the following pages is only slightly modified from Dewey's original description of how people think about problems. We will consider the group-discussion process as developing through the following five steps: (1) location and definition of the problem, (2) analysis of the problem, (3) establishing goals, (4) determining the best solution, and (5) putting the solution into operation.

Locating and Defining the Problem

One's thinking about his problems is conditioned by his needs and desires. The universal motivation to remove the stresses which arise from a felt difficulty makes it easy to seize upon the most obvious answer to a problem rather than to engage oneself in a rational evaluation of possible solutions. Subjectivity is, therefore, a danger; emotionalism, a peril. But to engage in the discussion of a subject with which one has no identification is dull. To pretend complete objectivity on a subject of great concern is foolish. The desirable approach to problems is on some middle ground; not to dehumanize a discussion, only to introduce order and direction into it.

"Feeling" a difficulty, in most instances, means becoming irritated by something in the environment. The very irritation obstructs rational thinking and thus may hinder the finding of a sound solution unless the irritant is first located and defined.

Imagine a suburban bus station where wives in family cars meet husbands as they return from the city. The streets are always congested; in time, the congestion develops into traffic jams. Then, some rainy night, the buses can't even reach the station through the jam of parked and waiting cars. The commuters in the bus feel the difficulty; so do their wives.

In what different ways may they react? In all likelihood, with some degree of annoyance. Despite this, they may meekly begin to seek ways to suffer along with the bad situation: change the dinner hour, take a later bus, take an earlier bus, meet the bus at another station. On the other hand, they may move from annoyance to fury, blame the traffic jam on the town police (perhaps the mayor is among the delayed passengers), and fire the police chief. Neither alternative is the result of a conscious effort to approach the problem reflectively. In each case the problem will have been met without adequate thought —in the one by submission and in the other by blind rage—the people making no effort to understand the situation they faced. The course of action might be much better decided on the basis of an objective look at the parking situation in the light of the town's growing commuter population.

The inadequacy of language creates the second difficulty which makes location and definition of problems necessary. Different people use the same words to mean different things. Joe, in the delayed bus, may remark to Fred, "Well, I guess this traffic is too much for our cops to handle." Joe intends to express compassion for a police force faced with an insoluble problem; Fred hears the remark as a too-temperate complaint against inexcusable inefficiency. Even among homogeneous groups, a problem never presents itself with such clarity that there is immediate and common understanding of its nature. A group of people talking on any subject will think about the topic from differing points of view. When a man talks with others about a set of circumstances, communication often suffers for lack of common ground. Failure to clear away at the outset as many of the obstacles to communication as possible will do much to destroy a potentially good discussion. Consequently, locating the problem is necessary.

The various methods of definition are discussed in Chapter VI. The method to use is the one that will best specify, through clarification of words and phrases, the nature of the problem under consideration. It is important that the participants in a discussion recognize that they are searching for agreement on the problem and, therefore, that a series of dictionary definitions of words in the statement of the problem may be useless, even misleading. The problem is defined to bring about a mutual understanding among a group of what the problem is. It is through the meeting of minds that the subject will be limited and defined. Since the members of the group have the "felt difficulty," only they can appraise or agree on the statement of the problem. And at the conclusion of this step of location and definition, the group should be in agreement about the specific subject under discussion and be prepared to analyze it with a minimum of confusion.

Analyzing the Problem

Analysis is the second step in the problem-solving process. Its function is to find the cause of the difficulty. The thoroughness with which this essential step is conducted determines as much as any other factor the effectiveness of the group in establishing desirable policy.

The first step in analysis is a review of existing conditions. When a doctor sees a patient for the first time, he needs to make a thorough examination. He takes the patient's history. Then he examines and questions the patient for symptoms, the patient's "felt difficulty." From history and symptoms, he endeavors to determine causes. This determination of causes is the important step in the process. The group discussing a policy question can be compared to a group of doctors in consultation. Both analyses require a thorough investigation of facts, a familiarity with conditions past and present, in order that the consultants may penetrate to the causes of the problem.

The causes determined must be sufficient; that is, they must account for all the symptoms and all the history. It is a common mistake to stop looking for causes while some significant symptoms remain unexplained. This mistake can arise from overlooking the symptom or from ignoring it when proposing the possible cause. It is a type of mistake easily made when considering research material from various sources. One member of a group might have studied material, for example, in a Department of Health, Education and Welfare report on urban blight. This report would note and list various symptoms and perhaps submit several surmises or propose a single opinion as to their cause. Another might have studied an article on urban blight from *Harper's* magazine, likewise mentioning symptoms and submitting surmises or opinions about causes. If the two sources were in only partial agreement and if the group accepted symptoms from one and causes from another, the analysis would be foolish. The group must be sure the causes account for the symptoms.

Establishing Goals

Before determining what solution will best meet a problem situation, a person or a group must have some standard for judging or testing a proposed solution. For example, when you go to the store to buy a pair of socks, you may be thinking, "I want them to go with my blue suit, and I want the cheapest all-wool pair I can find." By these standards you evaluate the many different pairs of socks from which you can choose. That is, you determine the goals you want your specific choice to help you attain: three goals—socks to match the blue suit, socks to be inexpensive, socks to be made of wool. Your solution is to buy a specific pair of socks. At another time, you might want a pair of socks that would be long-wearing. This would be a new goal and might, therefore, cause you to select a different pair, that is, arrive at a different solution.

A more complicated set of goals would guide you in exploring serious social questions and the need for determining them would be more apparent. Your decision about the socks is based on an analysis, perhaps almost unconscious, of an existing need and its causes. Decisions about a social problem are similarly based on analysis.

In the same sense that the basis for determining the causes of a problem is an examination of symptoms, the goals of a discussion group are based on what analysis shows the nature of the problem to be. Once established, the goals serve as standards of judgment for evaluating potential solutions. Indeed, this is the reason the symptoms and the causes are explored in the first place—to know better what kind of solution to look for. Through analysis of the problem, the group distills the principles which will tell what a good solution must be.

Determining goals is frequently a difficult step in discussion because goals are not always made explicit outside of discussion. When you are asked why you bought a certain pair of socks, aren't you likely to say, "Because I liked them"? Likewise you may support a certain political party, believe in stricter law enforcement, or want more government intervention to help our older citizens without clearly spelling out why. But there is a why—a goal or set of goals— and if someone insists, you can usually explain. However, if you are to be rational in your personal and group decisions, you must identify goals *before* you propose solutions.

To determine goals, then, is to develop a yardstick to measure the many possible courses of action which will be recognized. If the analysis of the problem has been thorough, the goals will be more easily determined. The more thorough and realistic the goals of a group are, the better are the chances of its choosing the most desirable solution to a problem.

Finding the Best Solution

Determining the best policy requires an examination of the advantages and disadvantages of each possible course of action. Each is compared with the others to see which will best solve the problem, that is, achieve most satisfyingly the goals that have been established. If these are realistic, the best solution, thus found, is the one that most closely fits the specifications inherent in them; it is the one which most effectively cures the causes of the problem, and thus eliminates its bad effects.

All reasonable possibilities should be considered. That is to say, it is quite possible that the policy in force at the time the group meets (the *status quo*) might prove to be the most desirable. It is quite possible, in other words, that any proposed change would be for the worse. At any rate, the *status quo* should always be evaluated in comparison with the alleged advantages of any proposed change in policy.

Putting the New Policy into Operation

The final step in the pattern of group discussion is implementation of any new policy. In this part of the discussion, the group examines the newly concluded policy to see what must be done in such areas as legislation, financing, public education, and the like, in order to put it into action. The problem-solving group must find the most practical way, in the light of our criteria, to implement the solution.

In summary, then, the pattern of group discussion develops through the following steps:

I. Location and Definition of the Problem
   (Clarify the limits of the problem and define all vague, ambiguous, or unfamiliar terms to the satisfaction of all the members of the group.)
II. Analysis of the Problem
   A. Symptoms
      (Examine the specific details and the *status quo* and the pertinent history leading to it, to find evidence of the nature of the problem and its severity.)

      B. Causes
         (Examine the symptoms and history to determine
         what cause or causes produced the undesirable
         elements of the situation.)

III. Goals
    (Develop standards of judgment for the group. That
    is, phrase the specifications which enumerate the
    requirements for a good solution.)

IV. Appraisal of Possible Solutions
    A. List the reasonable courses of action.
    B. Evaluate each to see how well it attains the stated
       goals of the group.
    C. Select the course of action which most closely
       achieves the goals.

V. Procedure for Putting the Solution into Operation

GROUP DISCUSSION IN PROGRESS

The final topic for consideration in this chapter is the discussion in progress. There is much speculation about the nature of group discussion activity. Some attempts have been made to examine this subject scientifically to learn more about the successful operation of group thinking. However, extensive discussion of that subject is beyond the scope of this chapter and the intent of this book. Two areas of immediate practical importance must be discussed: leadership and participation.

Leadership—Procedural and Substantive

Discussions in democratic society invite two kinds of leadership: *Procedural* leadership determines the conduct of the deliberation (procedure); *substantive* leadership exercises control over the ideas (substance). The government of the United States offers an example. The Vice President, as President of the Senate, is the procedural leader of that body. He recognizes who will speak and decides actual questions of policy (substance) only when there is a tie vote. The President of the United States is a substantive leader. He and his administration initiate proposals, develop evidence, and try to lead others to accept their conclusions on matters of substance. The Speaker of the House of Representatives is a combination of the two: As leader of the majority party he exercises a great measure of control over the nature of the substance considered; at the same time he is the procedural leader in the operation of the House.

This distinction between procedural and substantive leadership may help to present clearly the role the leader plays in group activity.

Leadership and Chairmanship

It is usual to think of a chairman, the person in charge of the procedure, as *the* leader of the group. In fact, however, he may not be the leader at all. That is, he may be assigned to control the group but actually be a mere figurehead, not leading the group but following the procedural and substantive suggestions of another member of the group. This other member is the real leader. In short, unless the appointed chairman guides the discussion procedure or the substance of discussion, or both, he is not the leader.

Leadership is a function of the group; that is, the members decide who will direct their thought. Leadership may change hands as the attitudes of the group or the area of discussion changes. The members of a deliberative body may accept the leadership of one person on one topic or on one phase of a problem and at another time turn for leadership to another member. The group decides not only whom they will follow, but also how much authority they will give him and how long they will accept him as their leader. The nature of leadership is one of those complex problems which we will not consider in depth but by examining the techniques of chairmanship we can perhaps gain some insight into leadership.

CHAIRMANSHIP—EMERGENT AND ASSIGNED. Your instructor may assign a chairman for your discussion group or let you elect one. He may also do what seems to invite chaos—have your group discuss without a chairman. Assigning a chairman, or electing one, tends to institutionalize the functions of the chair in a single person. Ordinarily a chairman is expected to concern himself primarily with matters of procedure, as does the President of the Senate. This restriction allows him to maintain an unbiased position in the group. He becomes an objective arbiter to whom the participants in discussion can turn in a time of disagreement about procedure.

Should your group, however, launch into discussion without a designated procedural leader, every member of the group must be prepared to assume the responsibilities of the chair. If you note, for example, that the group should move on to another phase of the discussion, you do not wait more than briefly for someone else to make the suggestion; you make it yourself. Perhaps someone else will emerge as leader, and thus you will not need to take upon yourself the procedural initiative. But every member must be prepared to act if the need for procedural leadership arises.

There are acknowledged and obvious disadvantages to a system of leaderless discussion. A struggle for power may develop among those who want to assume leadership. Power struggles can develop even when a leader has been assigned, but people in discussion are generally less likely to challenge a properly constituted authority than they are to challenge a leader who has no mandate from the group. However, there are also advantages to unassigned leadership. Chief among these is the fact that *emerging* chairmanship is more likely to produce the *real* leaders of the group—the leaders of procedure and substance that the members acknowledge. When it does so, profitable discussion is more likely to result.

Think of situations within your own experience. When you sit with a group of friends in the college cafeteria and discuss some campus problem, you do not elect a leader or call upon the student-body president to appoint one. Despite the lack of a formally appointed chairman, someone will emerge as leader of the discussion. Discussions do not fail because no leader is assigned. They may fail because the participants have insufficient knowledge, or because they don't think reflectively about the subject, or because they don't really want to engage in serious exploration of a problem. The success or failure of a group is not determined by whether the leader is appointed or allowed to emerge.

THE TECHNIQUES OF CHAIRMANSHIP. In a group discussion, the chairman is more a moderator than a parliamentarian. As such, he must do three basic things: (1) he must get the discussion started, (2) he must keep the discussion moving along efficiently, and (3) he must bring the discussion to a successful conclusion.

Getting the discussion started. The first of the chairman's three responsibilities, getting the discussion off to a good start, is probably the most difficult. Once it has been started and the group is functioning, the discussion tends to move along. In class discussions there will be a panel of participants, together with listeners who, for the most part, will be less informed on the topic than the participants. Whenever there is an audience, the chairman should introduce both the panel and the topic. His introduction of the question should be clear, brief, and interesting. He may give a short résumé of the history and background of the problem, or he may show briefly the nature and importance of the question. He will want to say enough in his introduction to make the problem meaningful to the audience, but he must remember that it is not his responsibility to analyze the problem. He should introduce the members of the discussion group to the audience by name and even if there is no audience, the group members should know each other by name. If they do not, it is the responsibility of the chair to introduce each one. This much is easy. It is a set of functions that must be performed, but is not the vital problem in getting started.

Any serious fumbling by a chairman tends to occur in beginning the analysis of the problem. Visualize a situation in which the inexperienced chairman, having finished his introductions, assumes that the discussion will proceed spontaneously. He will be sharply forced to the realization that it will not; the members of the group are still waiting for some kind of starting gun. Hence the chairman may try to push the discussion off with the question, "Well, who wants to begin?" This will almost inevitably fail to get the discussion started efficiently.

It is true that some groups are eager to rush on; these may need to be held back. Most groups, however, have to be led into useful and worthwhile discussion. There are several ways of helping these less vocal groups to get under way.

A question, carefully designed to elicit an intelligent response, can be a useful device for getting started. This opening question should ordinarily be directed to the group rather than to an individual. It would probably be unwise to put any particular person "on the spot" this early in the discussion. Moreover, the question should be general rather than specific. It may well be that a specific piece of information is an item no one has at his fingertips. If they are asked for one, the whole group may freeze up beyond the point of easy thawing.

A useful maneuver for the chairman is to quote some statement referring to the problem at hand and ask the group for comment. He can cite some specific instance or illustration of the problem and ask for comment on this. If the topic is a broad one, he may want to ask for some specification or limitation. In each of these cases, any member of the panel should be able to give a reasonable comment.

Keeping the discussion going. Once started, a well-informed group will usually move along quite briskly with a minimum of prodding from the chairman. His major functions, once he gets the discussion started, are to encourage general participation, to keep the discussion on the track, and to guide the group away from hasty, unrealistic action.

One of the main problems the chairman faces is that of keeping at least a reasonable balance in the amount of participation from each member of the group. There is, more often than not among student groups, at least one person who is too talkative and at least one who is too reticent. It is the job of the chairman to see that everyone participates, and that no one monopolizes the time of the group. If several speakers try to get the floor at the same time, the one who has, up to that point, spoken less frequently, should be given the opportunity to speak first. Sometimes real diplomacy is necessary to keep the discussion from becoming one-sided. Because the chairman is not a dictator, and should not be, his qualities of tact, geniality, and good humor come into play.

There are two dangers to be avoided. In curbing the overly talkative speaker, the chairman must be very careful not to offend. If he does, he stands a good chance of losing all effective contribution from a potentially valuable member of the group. On the other hand, in the effort to get some contribution from a timid person, the chairman is often tempted to ask a direct question requiring specific information. As we said earlier, this tactic is dangerous; should the person asked lack the necessary data, he will, in all probability, be even less inclined to speak thereafter. It is usually safe to ask for a comment or an opinion regarding an idea, a contribution, or data already advanced by another member of the group.

It is a great temptation in group discussion, because of the informality of the situation, and because of the group's easy familiarity with the detailed information it involves, to wander around the topic, digressing at length. Such digressions are often valuable in bringing out ideas and interpretations of data. Here again, the chair must determine when the digression is worthwhile and when it is a waste of time. The safest, and perhaps most efficient, way to avoid wasting time in interesting but unnecessary and fruitless digressions is to guide the group tactfully and courteously, but firmly, through the five steps of the discussion pattern.

One of the chairman's most useful devices is frequent brief summary of what the group has accomplished up to the point of summary. Then, to help keep the group on the track between summaries, it is advisable to make very short paraphrases of significant contributions as they are made. Such paraphrases are especially helpful if a speaker has held the floor for a comparatively lengthy statement. Brief summaries and even briefer paraphrases of individual remarks serve a triple purpose. They help to avoid needless repetition. They help to keep the discussion on the track. They point out areas of agreement and disagreement, and thus indicate the precise status of the discussion at any given moment.

Probably the most important function of the chairman in group discussion is to see to it, as best he can, that the group makes a thorough, impartial, and rational investigation of the problem at hand. More than this, it is important that there be a clear understanding of the areas of agreement and disagreement. To accomplish these functions, the chairman must see to it that all important points are heard.

Not only must these points be heard; they must also be examined critically and clearly. Both evidence and reasoning must be submitted to rigorous test. It is the responsibility of the chairman to see that the testing is done. Since he does not want to involve himself directly in argument, he can best accomplish this through the use of guiding questions. By means of such questions, he can accomplish several ends. First, he can make sure that all important facets of the problem are viewed. Second, he can require the members of the group to consider and comment on the evidence and reasoning of others. Thus he will avoid using questions that can be answered *yes* or *no*. Instead, he will raise the all-important questions of fact and value that must be clearly thrashed out before any group conclusion can be of real worth.

Ideally, the goal of any policy discussion is consensus, general agreement among the members of the group on what the best course of action will probably be. As we have pointed out, consensus is not always possible. Remember, a policy discussion comes about in the first place because there is conflict, an honest difference of opinion as to what policy should be adopted. There is nothing in the nature of discussion that inherently assures success in the effort to eliminate these areas of disagreement. No matter how conscientious a group is, no matter how impartially and reasonably its members investigate available data, they may still retain honest differences of opinion at the end of the discussion. No outcome of group exploration is more useless than a contrived or forced consensus. Differences of opinion are not to be strangled. The moderator will want to point out and stress the areas of agreement that do exist, but it is also important that the differences be brought out; otherwise, they can never be eliminated. Consensus is valuable only when it results from a realistic and rational adjustment of honest differences.

Bringing the discussion to a close. The time will come for deliberation to end, especially in class discussions where the bell rings at the end of fifty minutes. The type of conclusion the chairman will use is determined largely by the results achieved in the discussion. If the group has reached an agreement on policy, he can summarize the action recommended. When no conclusion is reached because still existing issues need further discussion, the chairman can put his conclusion into the form of a progress report.

The Participant in Discussion

A group discussion can be conducted without a chairman but not without participants. The panel of participants is thus of far greater importance than the chairman in the success or failure of any group discussion.

In large measure, the success or failure of a group discussion is determined before the group meets. The degree of thoroughness with which each member of the panel prepares for the discussion is the determining factor. Let us assume, however, that all the participants in the discussion are well informed, and have followed the procedures for preparation outlined in earlier sections of this chapter. We may then ask, "What principles should guide the participant in speaking to explore?" If you conduct yourself in accordance with the following suggestions, you will be an effective member of a panel.

Be open-minded. You have heard of the man who says, "My mind is made up. Don't try to confuse me with facts." This sort of person comes to a discussion prepared to force his own opinions on the rest of the group. He knows what is "right" and is prepared to advocate it to his last gasp.

Impartiality and freedom from prejudgment should mark the thinking and speaking of the participant in group discussion. He does much to destroy the whole function of the group if he comes to the meeting prepared to defend his own point of view against all comers.

Be responsible. Each member of the group shares the responsibility of the entire group for concluding a policy. Being responsible, the individual participant will want to make the part he plays worthy of himself. The discussion speaker who accepts his share of the responsibility of the group will be eager to contribute to its effectiveness because he knows that he shares in any failure as well as in any success. There is no place in good discussion for the grandstander, nor for the speaker who hangs back and who is reticent or unwilling to contribute. Each member of the group must give what he has to offer, but, because he is responsible, he will think before he speaks and he will have adequate basis for what he says. He will both give and expect serious consideration of the problem.

Be objective. Objectivity shows itself both in the attitudes and in the language of a discussion speaker. In attitude he is impersonal and impartial. Many of the problems he will attack in discussion will touch his life directly. His own emotional involvement may then become a threat to his objective consideration of the problem. Issues are almost certain to arise. When they do, each member of the group must avoid the attitude that disagreement with his ideas constitutes a personal attack on him. Conversely, each must put his questions and criticisms on a basis that is impersonal, fact centered, and idea centered.

The language the speakers use can contribute significantly to the objectivity of a discussion. Avoid ambiguity, vagueness, and generalities. Define terms carefully. Even when a panel member feels strongly about a point, he can use language of moderation and avoid adding emotional conflicts to what may already be a complex set of rational disagreements. Try to make language as objective as possible.

Objectivity in discussion is by no means to be confused with apathy and lack of interest. Speaking to explore requires as much vigor, animation, and enthusiasm as any other speaking occasion. But objectivity in language and attitude helps to avoid much of the ill will that can easily spring up when there are issues to resolve.

Be cooperative. Group discussion is by necessity cooperative. It requires the cooperation of all members of the group for maximum success.

Cooperativeness demands that the individual member of a panel be ready and willing to compromise when necessary and to retract when it is reasonable to believe he might be wrong. Ideally, he is firm in defending a position rationally held, but not blind to the possibility of his own error; he is willing to compromise in the sense of adjusting his own position to that of others but he will not abandon a well-supported position just to become "one of the gang."

Be a good listener. The participant should be an attentive, courteous, but critical listener. A good discussion speaker does not monopolize the group's time, nor does he seek to dominate the conversation. Being a good listener not only imposes responsibility but also brings benefit. It enables him to keep his contributions responsible, meaningful, reasonable, and relevant. One obvious mark of an inattentive, uncritical member of a group is an irrelevant comment. Contributions to the discussion are meaningful only when they are put into the context of what has gone before. Every statement should relate to the ideas then under discussion and not simply be dumped into the conversation.

SUMMARY

The freedom that characterizes democratic society comprises the freedom to disagree. Conflicts arise over solutions to questions of policy, fact, and value. These conflicts are explored through group discussion—a process that assembles in a cooperative effort several informed persons who together search for solutions to problems.

Reflective thinking is the basis of problem-solving and takes place in five steps:

1. A "felt difficulty" is identified and defined as a problem.
2. The problem is analyzed to discover the symptoms that manifest it and the conditions that cause it.
3. The goals of the group exploring the problem are established as criteria for evaluating possible courses of action.
4. Alternative proposals for solution are weighed in the light of their comparative advantages and disadvantages.
5. Steps are outlined for implementing the proposal which appears to offer the greatest relative advantage and the fewest relative disadvantages.

Substantive leadership in discussion, control over the ideas, is usually emergent and shifting; it grows out of the group and tends to move from person to person. Procedural leadership, guidance in the conduct and progress of the group, is the responsibility of the chairman when a chairman is elected or assigned. When no chairman is specifically appointed, procedural leadership must emerge from the group. The responsibilities of the chair are primarily three in number:

1. To get the discussion started.
2. To keep the discussion moving along.
3. To bring the discussion to a close.

In group discussion, as in any other form of public speaking, it is a primary responsibility of the speaker to be well prepared. Once he comes to the meeting, he will contribute to the effectiveness of the discussion to the extent that he is open-minded, responsible, objective, cooperative, and a good listener.

QUESTIONS

1. What is a group discussion?
2. What is a learning group? How does it differ from a problem-solving group?
3. What is associational thinking?
4. What are the steps in reflective thinking?
5. Why must symptoms be considered in determining causes?
6. Why is the establishment of goals so difficult?
7. Why must the *status quo* be examined as a possible solution?
8. Differentiate between procedural and substantive leadership.
9. Distinguish leadership from chairmanship.
10. How should a chairman go about getting a discussion started?
11. How does the chairman put a stop to a discussion when no definite conclusion has been reached?
12. How does the chairman use the summary?
13. What attitude should a participant bring to a group discussion?

EXERCISES

1. Make an analysis of some personal problem, using reflective thinking. How worthwhile do you find this method? What alternate possibilities can you think of as effective means of analyzing a problem?
2. With four or five other members of your class form a discussion group. Select a problem to discuss. Word it. Come to some basic understanding about what the terms of the question mean. Let each member of the group gather material and make an outline for himself. Present the group discussion in class a week after you have chosen the topic.
3. Observe the chairman of some group to which you belong. Is he

the leader of the group? If so, in what way does he lead? If not, who is the leader and how does he take control? Write a short paper explaining what happened on the occasion of your observation.

4. The following is a student's outline for a group discussion on a problem of policy: "What program of sex education in secondary schools should be adopted in the State of California?" As you examine it, consider these questions:

    (a) Are the definitions of "California," "sex education," and "secondary schools" adequate?

    (b) Have other terms inherent in the problem been left undefined?

    (c) Does the analysis of the problem recognize all of the principal symptoms and causes?

    (d) Is the evidence persuasive?

    (e) Are the criteria reasonable? If they are met, are they likely to eliminate (or at least mitigate) the causes of the problem?

    (f) To what extent are the advantages and disadvantages of the proposed policy related to the criteria?

    (g) Do you see additional strengths or weaknesses in the proposed plan?

I. DEFINITION OF THE PROBLEM.

A. The State of California would by defintion include the State Legislature, the Superintendent of Public Instruction, and the local districts which must decide what the policies on sex education will be in their respective communities. (*American Education*, II, November 1960, p. 19)

B. Sex education is taken to denote more than the biology of reproduction.

    1. A student can learn about reproduction without gaining an understanding of sex. (*Saturday Review*, XLVIII, December 18, 1966, p. 55)

        a. According to Helen Manley, the main purpose of sex education is to help young people understand what masculinity is to boys and men, femininity to girls and women, and the relationship of each to the other. (*PTA Magazine*, LXI, May 1967, p. 5)

            (1) It is not properly concerned with the facts of reproduction as much as with the development of proper attitudes toward sexuality. (*Ibid.*)

            (2) It does not dwell on the health concerns of venereal disease. (*Ibid.*)

(3) It is certainly more than information about the mechanics of the sex act. (*Ibid.*)

   b. Sex education distinguished from sex information can perhaps best be described as character education. (*Ibid.*)

  2. Sex education as defined by Dr. Mary Calderone, executive director of Sex Information and Education Council of the United States (SIECUS), is an emotional and mental development continuing from the moment of birth until the end of life, through which the individual develops his sexuality as part of his total personality. (*Changing Times*, XX, June 1966, p. 8)

C. The term secondary schools includes grades seven through twelve.

II. ANALYSIS OF THE PROBLEM.

A. Symptoms of the problem.

  1. Reported cases of syphilis among teen-agers have more than tripled since 1956. (*Look*, XXX, March 8, 1966, p. 20)

   a. Two hundred thousand to three hundred thousand teen-agers are affected yearly with venereal disease. (*PTA Magazine*, LXI, May 1967, p. 5)

   b. Young people under twenty account for more than one in five cases of venereal disease. (*Look*, XXX, March 8, 1966, p. 21)

  2. Rising suicide rates among teen-agers give cause for speculation whether there is a relationship between anxiety about unsolved sexual problems and rising suicide rates. (*Today's Health*, XLIV, February 1966, p. 16)

  3. There is a prevalence of delinquency and sex problems among teen-agers.

   a. In 1962 there were 478,000 juveniles before United States courts and 10 percent of the charges against the girls were sex offenses. (*Library Journal*, XCI, January 15, 1966, p. 320)

   b. Girls seventeen and under account for 22 percent of illegitimate births and almost 17 percent of all brides are pregnant when they are married. (*Look*, XXX, March 8, 1966, p. 20)

   c. In Chicago Public Schools, 1,100 pregnancies among unmarried girls were reported in 1964 among a population of 270,000 girls; only half of that population was past puberty. (*Today's Health*, XLIV, February 1966, p. 20)

   d. In 1964, girls of high-school age aborted 180,000 pregnancies. (*Look*, XXX, March 8, 1966, p. 20)

B. Causes of these conditions.

  1. Few people are adequately equipped to deal with the problem of effective sex education.

   a. Physicians can discuss the biological aspects but are not equipped for the psychological or moral issues. (*Saturday Review*, XLVIII, December 18, 1965, p. 55)

b. Ministers are unsuccessful because they can reach only a minority of their congregation. (*Ibid.*)

c. Many parents are unsuccessful because of the barrier between the generations. (*Ibid.*)

    (1) Behind each ignorant teen-ager there is usually a shy or ignorant parent. (*Look*, XXX, March 8, 1966, p. 20)

    (2) Parents belong to a generation that by and large regards public discussion of sex from a Puritan background. (*New York Times Magazine*, June 11, 1967, p. 24)

    (3) 82 percent of the nation's children get their knowledge of sex outside of the home. (*Ibid.*)

    (4) Parents are too often beset by their own sexual problems or guilt feelings to be good teachers. (*Time*, LXXXIX, June 9, 1967, p. 36)

    (5) In the teen years communication breaks down and parents have great difficulty in discussing these highly sensitive and personal matters. (*PTA Magazine*, LXI, May 1967, p. 5)

d. Schools rarely provide a unified, comprehensive, sequential pattern of instruction starting in the elementary grades and continuing through high school. (*American Education*, II, November 1966, p. 17)

    (1) Sex-education courses have existed for years in the United States but have been few in number because of a lack of trained personnel, who in turn suffer from a lack of courage, insight, and realism. (*Look*, XXX, March 8, 1966, p. 21)

    (2) The instruction of the scientist, sociologist, and biologist leaves the student ethically neutral. (*Saturday Review*, XLVIII, December 18, 1966, p. 21)

    (3) Sex education for boys may be little more than a discussion of health by the athletic coach. (*Time*, LXXXIX, June 9, 1967, p. 37)

    (4) Sex-education courses are often mere extensions of animal biology and fail to deal with meaningful issues that trouble teen-agers. (*Newsweek*, LXVIII, July 11, 1966, p. 83)

    (5) For the most part, children receive an indoctrination about sex rather than an education. (*Today's Health*, XLIV, February, 1966, p. 16)

2. While we educate our children concerning the world in which they live, preparation for the responsibilities of motherhood, parenthood, and family life is left largely to chance. (*Ibid.*)
3. There are uniquely urban factors which can influence sex education adversely.
   a. When the child is young, he is often quite effectively cut off from the kind of experiences of the natural world that will both prompt questions and help to answer them. (*Library Journal*, XCI, January 15, 1966, p. 319)
   b. Children are deprived of what used to be learned through simple observation of farm life. (*Time*, LXXXIX, June 9, 1967, p. 36)
4. Adults have taken down all protective barriers, done away with chaperons, supervision, rules and close family ties; thus children are left totally vulnerable to the onslaught of sexual exploitation. (*Ibid*, p. 37)

III. GOALS—CRITERIA BY WHICH TO JUDGE PROPOSALS.

A. The proposal should be carried out efficiently and uniformly throughout all secondary-school districts in the state of California.
B. The proposal should be widely accepted and supported by the populace of California.
C. A form of sex education should be built into the school curriculum and taught in an educationally normal manner. (*American Education*, II, November 1966, p. 18)
D. Every facet of sex should be dealt with: emotional and sociological as well as biological. (*Time*, LXXXIX, June 9, 1967, p. 36)
E. This education must be begun and carried out before the college level. (*Look*, XXX, March 3, 1966, p. 2)
F. This education should enable every individual to make use of his sexual faculties in mature, creative, and responsible ways in all his relationships, not just the sexual ones. (This is the goal of SIECUS.) (*PTA Magazine*, LXI, May 1967, p. 5)

IV. POSSIBLE SOLUTIONS.

A. The program of sex education can be carried on as it has been for years in the secondary-school system of California. (This is the *status quo*.)
B. The state of California should develop through the State Department of Education a uniform program of sex education in the schools with adequate provisions for adaptation to meet individual and local mores and should support such a program financially.

V. APPRAISAL OF THE POSSIBLE SOLUTIONS.

A. Carry out the program of education as has been done in the past in California.

  1. Advantages.

     a. This course of action will not stir up any real controversy nor will it call for creative thinking, which can be bothersome.

     b. The *status quo* would cancel the need for funds for a widened sex-education program.

  2. Disadvantages.

     a. The program of sex education as it is now being carried out is inefficient and has not accomplished any real level of sophistication in the majority of California schools.

     b. The program as it now stands lays the burden of sex education on the home, and studies have shown that the home very seldom carries through with its responsibilities in this area.

B. A redevelopment of the sex-education program of California should be initiated by the state immediately.

  1. Advantages.

     a. This plan would be acceptable to teachers, as has been shown in a study in which eight out of every ten teachers in the National Education Association in 1965 recommended that sex education become a part of the secondary-school curriculum. (*Look*, XXX, March 8, 1966, p. 20)

     b. Independent studies have shown that 95 percent of parents questioned on sex education felt that it should be offered in the schools. (*Today's Health*, XLIV, February 1966, p. 16)

     c. The American Medical Association is in full support of sex education in the schools because they feel that it is sound preventive medicine. (*Ibid.*, p. 17)

     d. Education at school leads to meaningful discussions at home. (*American Education*, II, November 1966, p. 17)

     e. The Office of Education will support family-life education, and many programs are eligible for grants. (*Ibid.*)

     f. Studies show that a school in Washington, D.C. with a sex-education program had its illegitimate birth rate halved. (*Look*, XXX, March 8, 1966, p. 21)

  2. Disadvantages.

     a. One must consider what code of ethics children are to be taught, how, and with what aim.

     b. There is a shortage of qualified teachers. (*Time*, LXXXIX, June 9, 1967, p. 37)

     c. Many parents have moral fears of their children being exposed to sex in school. (*New York Times Magazine*, June 11, 1967, p. 24)

d. Too much may be expected of a sex-education program; the programs are often asked to provide solutions to problems that are really problems of society. (*Time*, LXXXIV, June 9, 1967, p. 36)

e. Education is limited in its ability to influence behavior and sex education is no exception. (*Today's Health*, XLIV, February 1966, p. 17)

f. Individual teachers if improperly trained or informed can do irreparable harm. (*PTA Magazine*, LXI, May 1967, p. 5)

(Therefore, it seems to follow that the plan for a redevelopment of the sex-education program in the state of California is the one which should be adopted. It appears that this plan would most nearly meet all of the criteria set out in Section II, B of this outline.)

VI. SUGGESTIONS FOR PUTTING THE SOLUTION INTO OPERATION.

A. California's sex-education program could be modeled after those systems which have been successful, as in Evanston, Illinois, and University City, Missouri. (*Look*, XXX, March 8, 1966, p. 23)

B. California has a prominent sex-education program in Anaheim which could be studied and expanded throughout the state. (*Time*, LXXXIX, June 9, 1967, p. 37)

C. Teachers should be given in-service training to adequately equip them for teaching sex education.

D. The home, church, school, and community should support each other jointly in this effort or they will fail independently. (*Today's Health*, XLIV, February 1966, p. 17)

CRITICIZING SPEECHES

I. Why speeches are criticized
II. The steps in rhetorical criticism
   A. Analysis
      1. Rational proof
      2. Motivation
      3. *Ethos*
      4. Structure
      5. Language and style
      6. Delivery
   B. Synthesis
   C. Evaluation
      1. Of effects
      2. Of artistic merit
      3. Of historical truth
      4. Of ethical worth
III. Preparing the criticism
   A. Begin the criticism with evaluation
   B. Point up the relationship of evaluation to synthesis
   C. Use the analysis to support both synthesis and evaluation
IV. Questions and exercises

XX

CRITICIZING SPEECHES

The primary concern of this book has been to outline the principles which a speaker applies to make messages more effective with audiences. An understanding of such principles is important not only for speakers but for listeners as well. Each of us spends more time as a receiver of communication than as a sender. Consequently, each of us must lend a critical ear to the communication of others. In a speech class a student is called upon to evaluate his colleagues' speeches. The lectures of college professors are continuing objects of critical evaluation by students. Community leaders and public officials are subjects of continued evaluation as they try to affect opinion, attitude and belief in situations ranging from small group meetings to nationwide television broadcasts. This evaluation is called rhetorical criticism.

The principles of rhetorical criticism are applicable to *all* verbal communication: essays, novels, plays, motion pictures, and television, among others; but because of the nature of this book we will emphasize the criticism of speeches. The object of rhetorical criticism, a speech, may be presented to the critic through many different media and in a variety of places but essentially the same principles of criticism are applied in all cases. Sometimes the only source of speeches is the printed text. This is particularly true of speeches delivered before recordings and motion pictures were available.

Regardless of how the speech comes to a rhetorical critic, the primary dimension of his evaluation will be an examination of that speech in light of the interaction between the speech and its audience. In examining a speech of Daniel Webster, Thomas Jefferson, or Abraham Lincoln, the rhetorical critic will make a judgment of the extent to which the speaker, in the words of Aristotle, discovered "the available means of persuasion" to influence the beliefs and actions of his audience.

373

WHY SPEECHES ARE CRITICIZED

The criticism of speeches is useful for several reasons. Perhaps the most obvious is the improvement of one's own speaking. By examining the techniques used effectively by other speakers, one can better see what techniques he himself might use. The criticism one does in class lets him see in action the methods which he has read about in this book. What may be effective at one time with one audience will not necessarily be effective in other circumstances; nonetheless, by seeing how an audience responds to techniques a speaker gains insights into the kinds of situations wherein certain techniques are most useful.

Criticizing speeches will also improve listening skills. Frequently, one hears a speech and judges it to be good or poor without testing his conclusion by asking what, specifically, makes it good or poor. By asking this question a listener helps himself to see the specifics of what the speaker says and thus gets more out of what he listens to.

The criticism of a speech also gives insight into the total meaning of the communication. It helps one to see the interrelation of speaker, speech and audience. When Franklin D. Roosevelt said in his first inaugural address, "We have nothing to fear but fear itself," it had great meaning for the depression-ridden people of the 1930's. To read that speech and analyze it against the background of the times will bring more sharply into focus the problems of the era and the attitudes of the people who lived in America at that time.

The criticism of speeches not only offers an understanding of some particular point in history but, more broadly, it gives insights into the nature of mankind in general. The critic who studies speeches from a number of eras soon becomes aware that, although issues change and techniques change, many attitudes and feelings remain constant. The arguments advanced during the late 1960's by opponents of the war in Viet Nam are essentially the same as those advanced in the 1840's by opponents of the Mexican War, such as Senator Tom Corwin. The effective public speaker, whether purposely or not, reflects the prevailing ideas of the times; he reflects in addition his own insights into all mankind. The rhetorical greatness of William Shakespeare is that he so thoroughly understood the Elizabethan audience that he provided insight into all men in every age.

THE STEPS IN RHETORICAL CRITICISM

A volume could be written on each of the three major steps of rhetorical criticism. This chapter will provide only a broad outline of these three steps: analysis, synthesis, and judgment. A speech is first analyzed, that is, taken apart so that the various elements of the speech can be seen individually: rational proof, motivation, *ethos*, structure, language, and delivery: This analysis is then *synthesized* around the most important critical points and the less important points are viewed in relation to them. Finally there must be *evaluation*, not merely a statement that a speech is "good" or "bad," but an indication of strengths and weaknesses, and of why the speech is worth study or emulation. If evaluations are made on the basis of judicial analysis and synthesis, they will be worth the attention of others. No one expects a student in a beginning speech class to be an accomplished rhetorical critic but he should begin early to develop critical ability.

Analysis

The analysis of a speech begins with the speaker's ideas and the support he gives them. From classical times the rhetorical critic has recognized three elements in proof. The rational (frequently called "logical") proof, motivation, and *ethos*. Although all three are viewed as equally important and involve the interrelation of audience, speaker, and speech, the rational function is more directly related than the others are to the message, motivation bears most upon the audience, and *ethos* is concerned most with the speaker himself.

RATIONAL PROOF. The analysis of the message itself emphasizes the speaker's ideas and the support he gives them. Reference to Chapter IV will help the critic to identify the issues in the controversy and to discover what are (or might conceivably be) the most effective arguments in support of a particular proposition. Here are some questions to consider in analyzing the elements of rational proof:

1. Is the speaker aware of the issues which divide opinion?
2. What ways of looking at the issues does he propose?
3. Does he meet opposition arguments?
4. What reasoning does he use in developing his arguments?
5. What supporting materials does he provide?

MOTIVATION. The motivational appeals a speaker makes to his audience must be identified. The critic must examine the specific value system which the speaker reveals and the motive appeals which he develops from that value system.

Identifying value systems is not easy. But one can begin by looking carefully at those words which carry value judgments. The critic will first, then, establish the nature of the positive and negative terms used from which he will seek to discover what the speaker regards as good or bad.

In his first Inaugural Address, President Woodrow Wilson called for reform of the nation's economy in the interest of a "New Freedom." In the following passage from that speech terms labeling notions Wilson considers *good* are in italics and those he considers **bad** are in bold face.

But the **evil** has come with the *good*, and much *fine gold* has been **corroded.** With *riches* has come **inexcusable waste.** We have **squandered** a great part of what we might have *used*, and have not stopped to *conserve* the exceeding *bounty* of *nature*, without which our *genius for enterprise* would have been **worthless** and **impotent, scorning** to careful, **shamefully prodigal** as well as *admirably efficient.* We have been *proud* of our industrial achievement, but we have not hitherto stopped *thoughtfully*, enough to count the **human cost,** the **cost** of *lives* **snuffed out,** of *energies* **over-taxed** and **broken,** the **fearful** *physical* and *spiritual* **cost** to the men and women and children upon whom the **dead weight** and **burden** of it all has fallen **pitilessly** the years through.

From an examination of the value words which carry Wilson's argument we can see the value system underlying what he says. To paraphrase him, we must with candid and fearless eyes conserve our riches (the bounty of nature) through careful, efficient use of our genius for enterprise with due pride in our industrial achievements. We must reject the corrosion of fine gold through waste, squandering, overtaxing, the snuffing out of lives, and the great spiritual and physical costs. Further, we must discontinue our attention to worthless things. We must stop being impotent, prodigal, and selfish.

Wilson appeals to the Puritan values so basic to American society: a respect for nature and enterprise, a rejection of selfishness, waste, and false pride. These values form the basis of his motivation. Further examination will show that the emphasis of this passage is negative; that is, President Wilson uses the words of his value system to reject what he considers bad more than to identify what he supports.

This illustration identifies the basis for some of the analytical questions the critic will ask:

1. To what value systems does the speaker appeal?

2. What motive appeals does he emphasize at the most critical points in the speech?
3. Is the motivation justified by the subject?
4. Does the motivation remain consistent throughout the speech?

Other questions will be brought to mind by the discussion of motivation in Chapter XI.

ETHOS. *Ethos* is built through the speaker's projection of his trust-worthiness, competence, and goodwill. The critic may characterize the speaker's ethos by identifying two images the speaker projects: his image of himself and his image of his opponent. The critic asks, which qualities does he identify with himself and which does he use for his opponent? In the election of 1952 the Republicans pictured their candidate (General Eisenhower) as tough and hard-thinking, a man of action with the experience needed to solve the problems of the Korean war. They characterized their opponent (Adlai Stevenson) as a dreamer, an idealist who had been taken in by the "Truman gang."

The speech to be criticized may not have an opponent in the form of a specific person. The antagonist may be an idea, a party, a way of life. Martin Luther King, Jr.'s, speech "I Have a Dream" has an opponent in certain existing ideas in the society. True, there are people who hold these views but the speaker does not identify them directly. Who could deny that there is an opponent with whom Dr. King had to deal? When, for instance, the audience agrees with the speaker but is apathetic, one could say that apathy is his opponent. Much patriotic ceremonial oratory is of this nature, as is a reasonable proportion of all preaching.

A further distinction in the classification of ethos is direct and indirect ethos. In direct *ethos* the speaker refers directly to himself, his attributes, and his accomplishments, and he does the same for his opponent. Indirect *ethos* is developed more subtly. Although not directly referring to himself, the speaker identifies himself with certain attributes by the position he takes.

In October 1952, President Richard Nixon, then a Senator and a candidate for the Vice Presidency, appeared on television to defend a fund which had been raised for him by wealthy Californians. In that speech, Mr. Nixon made heavy use of direct *ethos*.

I worked my way through college and, to a great extent, through law school. And then in 1940, probably the best thing that ever happened to me happened; I married Pat—sitting over here. We had a rather difficult time after we were married, like so many of the young couples who may be listening to us. I practiced law; she continued to teach school. I went into the service.

Let me say that my service record was not a particularly unusual one. I went to the South Pacific. I guess I'm entitled to a couple of battle stars. I got a couple of letters of commendation but I was just there when the bombs were falling and then I returned. I returned to the United States and in 1946 I ran for Congress.

When he delivered the Commencement Address at the University of Rochester on June 5, 1966, Mr. Nixon built his *ethos* in a very different, very indirect way by identifying himself with ideas which would bring him respect. Although he never mentions himself, this passage reveals something of the image he has of himself.

A generation ago, "Four Freedoms" became a rally cry for the forces of democracy: Freedom of speech and of worship, freedom from fear and from want. Today let us discuss the *Four Academic Freedoms*.

There is the academic freedom of the student to investigate any theory, to challenge any premise, to refuse to accept old shibboleths and myths.

There is a second academic freedom of the student to espouse any cause, to engage in the cut and thrust of partisan political or social debate, both on and off campus, without jeopardy to his academic career.

The third academic freedom is for the teacher—freedom from fear of reprisal while speaking or publishing the truth as he sees it, governed by the dictates of his own intellect and of the disciplines of scholarship.

Finally, there is a fourth academic freedom—this one within the academic community—that is the freedom of the student from tyranny of the faculty, and conversely, freedom of the faculty from student tyranny.

STRUCTURE. The structure of the speech helps the critic to see how well the speaker gives his message *unity*, *order*, and *coherence*.

The primary constituent of unity is singleness of theme. The critic asks whether all the ideas, arguments, and motivations of the speech are relevant to one main theme. Suppose there seem to be several themes. Are they related to one another and developed in such a way as to give a sense of unity?

Similarly *scope* is a function of unity, for the impression of unity is created not solely by the singleness of the speaker's theme but is influenced by the listener's perception as well. Is the speech limited to what the listener can attend to and yet broad enough to continually engage his interests?

Order is the sequence of ideas in a speech. It is found in what can be called *thematic emergence*, the manner in which the main idea (the theme) of the speech emerges. Is the cat let out of the bag one whisker at a time? Does this main theme become clear somewhere around the middle of the speech? Does the theme emerge at the beginning, full blown and stated unequivocally to the audience? In addition, the critic asks how the speech is organized: chronologically? geographically? by cause and effect? from problem to solution? Finally, he wants to judge whether the order the speaker uses is the one best calculated to achieve his purpose.

Coherence is directly related to both unity and order. It can be thought of in terms of the transitions a speaker uses to link one thought with another and to what extent these transitions will help a listener develop a clear and correct understanding of what the speaker says. Thus the critic analyzes a speech to discover how its theme emerges, what order is used to organize the material and what means are used to link one idea with another.

LANGUAGE AND STYLE. Language is the fundamental "hardware" of a speech; it is the vehicle which carries the other objects of critical study (idea and support, motivation, *ethos*, and structure). In a very real sense, therefore, whatever the critic learns about these must come to him through his analysis of the speaker's language. But in addition to making this kind of analysis, the rhetorical critic examines the language of a speech in order to evaluate how well the speaker's language exemplifies the primary constituents of style: clarity and interest.

Clarity. In judging whether a speaker's language will be clearly understood by a listener, the critic asks questions about the levels of language used. No speaker wants to use a vocabulary which is insulting because of its simplicity or confusing because of its complexity. Imagine addressing an adult audience in the language of the first-level reader. "See Puff. See Puff run. Run, Puff, run. Run, run, run." Or imagine the response of an audience addressed in the complex jargon of a field which it does not understand. The critic must, therefore, determine something about the level of vocabulary within the audience's understanding.

Syntax is potentially as serious a problem as vocabulary. Given words it understands, an audience can often do a reasonably good job of straightening out unclear sentences but, to the extent that syntax is awkward and unsure, the communication of both denotative and connotative meaning will be impaired. The problems syntax may generate, however, do not necessarily mean that simple sentences are to be preferred. A well-developed complex sentence may be just as clear as a series of short ones, perhaps even more so. Indeed, subtle ideas or shades of meaning may be lost in simple sentences.

The critic of the printed speech text must learn to listen with his eyes. From what he has heard about the speaker's delivery, he must imagine pauses and other factors of delivery which help to clarify meaning. The critic who actually hears a speech will, of course, trust his ears in judging the clarity of syntax. Clarity, however, does not necessarily mean correctness. The acceptability or unacceptability of formal language, slang, and even bad grammar depends on the audience addressed.

Interest. In judging the interest values of language, the critic gives his attention to embellishment, the stylistic devices which the speaker uses. First, he must consider the *level* of embellishment used. To a degree, the critic can determine how embellished a speaker's style is by comparing his language with that of others speaking in similar situations. The critic will consider next what *kinds* of figures this speaker tends to use. The late President John F. Kennedy became well known for his use of antithesis. Some speakers make extensive use of metaphor, others do not. These stylistic characteristics should be noted.

Having considered such factors as vocabulary, syntax, and embellishment, the critic should be able to characterize the language of the speech. Is it plain, given to short direct sentences, simple vocabulary, and few figures of speech? or is it highly embellished with complex sentence structure, vocabulary, and many figures of speech? Perhaps the language is somewhere between these two extremes, characterized, for example, by a simple vocabulary but an extensive use of figures of speech. From his examination of these factors, the critic makes his judgment about the merits of the speaker's style.

DELIVERY. The facial expressions, gestures, vocal quality, and vocal emphasis of a speaker are all agents of speech which tell the listener what the speaker wants to say. The policeman holds up his hand to say "Stop." When the Indian of the Western movie holds up his hand, he means "Peace." Whether a speaker smiles or frowns, speaks loudly or softly, emphasizes one word or another, he says something to the audience.

The critic of delivery will ask such questions as these: Do the gestures, vocal quality, and other elements of delivery add meaning? Do they draw attention to themselves? In short, is the delivery an aid or a hindrance in eliciting the meaning the speaker wants his listeners to have? The critic must judge whether gesture, facial expression, vocal quality, and loudness are coordinated with the ideas of the speech. He must judge whether they add emphasis or merely exhibition.

The first step in rhetorical criticism, then, is analysis, that is, the examination of rational proof, motivation, *ethos*, structure, language, and delivery to discover what the speaker does in the speech. In his examination and the conclusions he draws about the interrelationship of speaker technique and audience response, the critic will attempt to find the basis for a synthesis of these independent points of analysis.

Synthesis

The purpose of synthesis is to reconstruct the speaking situation for the reader or listener in order to emphasize the important factors of the critic's analysis. Thus, the critic says, "Given this audience with its opinions, attitudes, and beliefs, what strategy did this speaker use?" His answer to the question is not a catalog of appeals but an identification of the emphasis the speaker has given them.

For one speaker, an argumentative development may be central. For him the basic appeal is to reason; he builds *ethos* by presenting himself as a "reasonable" man. Another strategy will emphasize the trustworthiness and the good will of the speaker. In such a case other rhetorical elements will be subservient to *ethos*. Still another speaker may center his rhetorical strategy in the deeply felt needs of his listeners. This strategy reveals itself through the emphasis given to a particular appeal throughout the speech and especially at critical junctures.

Although the term strategy, used here to characterize the emphasis of a speech, usually implies design, it is not necessary to know the speaker's design. It is useful to know what the speaker intended to do, but it is not essential to an understanding of what happened on a particular occasion. More important is to discover what actually happened between speaker and listener, irrespective of the speaker's intent.

The Presidential election campaign of 1952 has been synthesized in the following way: The major attack of the Republican campaign was calculated to dramatize the difficulties which were obvious to everyone. Eisenhower emphasized the seemingly endless stalemate in Korea, the corruption in government, the problem of inflation, and the inability of America to do more than contain communism. He attacked an Administration which seemed unable to handle these problems. Eisenhower, therefore, shifted the emphasis from issues to frustrations. He gave "Leadership" as a battle cry consonant with the voter's dilemma of favoring a policy and objecting to its results. In short, Eisenhower asked no one to give up a single view on policy, but only to trust Eisenhower. This approach was most evident in the dramatic "I shall go to Korea" statement in his October 24 speech at Detroit. But, more than dramatic, this statement was symbolic of the campaign. Eisenhower submitted himself on every issue. His only real promise was that he would be "fair" to the American people and would, through his fairness, bring an end to national and international conflicts, frustrations, and fears. The problem was frustration, and the solution was an esteemed national leader.

Stevenson, on the other hand, was a speaker in the tradition of classical rhetoric. Perhaps this is part of the reason for the impression he made on the intellectuals in 1952. He examined the primary issues which political thinkers have argued throughout the history of the western world. Such concepts as the nature of man, of the state, and of society, and the methodology of political action were of far greater concern to Stevenson than to Eisenhower. In all probability these problems were of greater concern to Stevenson than to any major American politician since Woodrow Wilson.

His argument was more thorough than that of most contemporary political speakers. His motive appeals were restrained and linked to the ideas which he wished to develop. Stevenson called on the American people to rise to the tremendous problems facing them. He emphasized the ego-expansion of the people through their capacities of patience, struggle, and intelligence. He did not, as Eisenhower did, relieve the people of responsibility. Stevenson's ethical proof, while bold, was not flaunted. He spoke of his wide variety of administrative experience. He linked his cause with names of intellectual and political stature from Aristotle to Roosevelt. Always he was careful to point out that he was human and therefore fallible. An examination of post-election studies supports the contention that those who voted for Stevenson were not particularly impressed with his personality, but were solidified on issues and favored him because of his position on the issues.

Evaluation

Because there is considerable discussion about the varieties of evaluation, we cannot now go into that complicated argument, but we can note that most writers generally identify four varieties of criticism. Many maintain that a critic should make only pragmatic judgments about the immediate and long-range *effects* of a speech on a listener and on society. Only the naivest evaluation of effects considers the merit of speech to depend solely upon whether the speaker succeeded in getting the audience to do what the speaker wanted them to do. One speech, standing alone, may have little discernible effect but the results of a series of speeches may be cumulative. A speaker, moreover, may produce results he did not even intend but which, nonetheless, introduce noticeable changes into his society. It may very well be that in a particular case no adequate means of persuasion are available to *any* speaker. Nor does counting votes after an election determine the more effective speaker of a pair of candidates. Others say that the critic must consider the *artistic merit* of the speech. This variety of criticism aims at evaluating the techniques to determine the literary beauty and grace of the product. Some critics look for the *historical truth* of the ideas. They ask whether or not history bears out the truth of what the speaker said. They evaluate the extent to which the speaker reflects, leads, or trails behind the society in what he believes and says. Judgments are made by some critics as to the *ethical worth* of what the speaker says. In making an evaluation of this kind, a critic determines the merits of a speech by weighing the speaker's ideas in the balance of his own ethical norms.

Regardless of whether a critic emphasizes one or all of these standards of evaluation he must, nevertheless, make his judgments in terms of the audience and in terms of the times in which the speaker lived. Certainly, most would agree that it is generally unethical to be untruthful but for the rhetorical critic it is more important to know why a speaker is successful when he is untruthful than it is to know that he is untruthful. To evaluate the historical truth of a speech without being aware of the knowledge which was available to the speaker and his audience in his time is foolish. John C. Calhoun argued that slavery was a positive good, yet he is regarded as a genius and one of America's great orators. The same arguments today are deemed nonsense. We judge Calhoun by his times and the contemporary racist by ours. The long periodic sentence, the parallel structure, the classical and Biblical allusions, and the involved metaphor so prized in the style of earlier oratory seem overdone today, but yesterday is not judged by today.

The critic, therefore, renders an evaluation of the speech based not upon how the world ought to be, or ought to have been, but upon how well the speaker discovered and used the means of persuasion available to him. While Dwight D. Eisenhower might capitalize on his credibility as a military hero by saying "I shall go to Korea," it would have been ludicrous for Adlai E. Stevenson, his political opponent, a man without a military reputation, to have used the same phrase in 1952. That was simply not a means of persuasion available to Stevenson. "Don't change horses in midstream" represents an argument which only an incumbent officeholder can use. The opinions, attitudes, and beliefs of the audience about the speaker, about the issues, and about the times constitute the bases for criticizing the speaker's efforts.

PREPARING THE CRITICISM

Obviously, the form and depth of critical analysis will differ as situations differ. As the critic of a classmate's speech, a student will have far less time to consider, study, and prepare than when he has several weeks in which to pore over a text, check items in the library, and write a paper with care. However, the basic approach and attitude will be the same.

Variety in critical approach is unlimited but a few general principles will be helpful to the beginning critic in expressing his evaluative judgments.

Begin the Criticism with Evaluation

Evaluations are what your listeners or readers are most interested in. Avoid at all cost the "laundry-list" analysis ("He said this, ... then this, ... then this ...."). Center on the two or three important evaluative statements about what you regard as good or poor in the speech.

Point up the Relationship of Evaluation to Synthesis

Reveal in your evaluation that you see the strategy of the speech. Reconstruct, if necessary, the situation which led you to your evaluation. Show how individual judgments join to provide an over-all impression of the speech.

Use the Analysis to Support Both Synthesis and Evaluation

To say merely that something was good or bad, or that it was central to the persuasive effort is not enough. The critic must show how arguments, motive appeals, ethical appeals, style, delivery or structure illustrate the strategy of the speech and the evaluation. Of course, not everything discovered through analysis will be used but only what is necessary to support the critic's evaluations.

Analysis, synthesis, and evaluation—the three elements of criticism—are closely comparable to the elements of communication discussed in earlier chapters. The judgments of a critic are like the specific purpose of a speech. They identify what the critic wants his audience to know or to believe. Synthesis provides a basis for identifying major critical points and for giving order to the criticism. Analysis provides the critic with specific supporting materials necessary for an understanding of the critical points made. It is equally incumbent on the speaker and the critic to have something to say and to say it well. These are the objects of criticism and the end of speech: content and communication.

QUESTIONS

1. In what sense can rhetorical criticism be said to apply to all forms of communication?

2. Why are speeches criticized?

3. Name and explain the major steps in rhetorical criticism.

4. What effect would it have on the criticism to omit any one of the three major steps?

5. Can one adequately criticize a speech he has only read?

6. What kind of questions does a critic ask about a speaker's rational proof? About his motivation?

7. What is the difference between direct and indirect *ethos?*

8. How are unity, order, and coherence related?

9. What kind of judgments does the critic make about a speaker's style?

10. What are the varieties of criticism?

11. Compare the method of preparing a criticism with that of preparing a speech.

EXERCISES

1. Act as a critic for one of your classmate's speeches. In your oral criticism, explain what you believe to be the two greatest strengths and the two greatest weaknesses of the speech. Give specific examples to support your judgment.

2. Hear a speech by some local person (your minister for instance) and write an evaluation of his speech.

3. With a group of classmates prepare and hold a group discussion evaluating a speech by some nationally known person delivered on television.

4. Write an evaluation of a speech of historical importance such as Abraham Lincoln's "Second Inaugural Address," Booker T. Washington's "Atlanta Exposition Address," or Woodrow Wilson's "Speech at Des Moines on the League of Nations." Emphasize the ways in which the same speech delivered today might be differently received.

5. Hear a speech by a person appearing on campus and write a paper on some phase of analysis assigned by your instructor.